Hardly more than a decade old, the twenty-first century has already been dubbed the Asian Century in recognition of China and India's increasing importance in world affairs. Yet discussions of Asia seem fixated on economic indicators—gross national product, per capita income, share of global trade. *Makers of Modern Asia* reorients our understanding of contemporary Asia by highlighting the political leaders, not billionaire businessmen, who helped launch the Asian Century.

The nationalists who crafted modern Asia were as much thinkers as activists, men and women who theorized and organized anticolonial movements, strategized and directed military campaigns, and designed and implemented political systems. The eleven thinker-politicians whose portraits are presented here were a mix of communists, capitalists, liberals, authoritarians, and proto-theocrats—a group as diverse as the countries they represent.

From China, the world's most populous country, come four: Mao Zedong, leader of the Communist Revolution; Zhou Enlai, his close confidant; Deng Xiaoping, purged by Mao but rehabilitated to play a critical role in Chinese politics in later years; and Chiang Kai-shek, whose Kuomintang party formed the basis of modern Taiwan. From India, the world's largest democracy, come three: Mohandas Gandhi, Jawaharlal Nehru, and Indira Gandhi, all of whom played crucial roles in guiding India toward independence and prosperity. Other exemplary nationalists include Vietnam's Ho Chi Minh, Indonesia's Sukarno, Singapore's Lee Kuan Yew, and Pakistan's Zulfiqar Ali Bhutto. With contributions from leading scholars, *Makers of Modern Asia* illuminates the intellectual and ideological foundations of Asia's spectacular rise to global prominence.

MAKERS OF MODERN ASIA

MAKERS

OF

MODERN

ASIA

EDITED BY

RAMACHANDRA GUHA

The Belknap Press of Harvard University Press

Cambridge, Massachusetts

London, England

2014

Library of Congress Cataloging-in-Publication Data

Makers of modern Asia / edited by Ramachandra Guha.
pages cm
Includes bibliographical references and index.
ISBN 978-0-674-36541-4 (alk. paper)
1. Asia—Politics and government—1945–   2. Politicians—Asia—
Biography.   3. Asia—Foreign relations—1945–   I. Guha,
Ramachandra.
DS35.2.M36 2014
950.4'20922—dc23
2014006043

CONTENTS

MAKERS OF MODERN ASIA

INTRODUCTION

The Politics behind the Economics of Asia's Rise

RAMACHANDRA GUHA

I

IN JULY 1920, the philosopher Bertrand Russell moved to Beijing with his wife, Dora Black. Russell was that rare animal—an English internationalist. He had already traveled through the Soviet Union and was curious to know more about countries and civilizations farther to the east. He spent several months in China, lecturing on technical subjects—symbolic logic, idealism, the theory of relativity, etc.—while, on the side, studying the country's history, culture, geography, and politics. He interacted extensively with students, both on philosophical matters (his Chinese admirers had begun producing a monthly journal devoted to his work) and on their hopes for the future of their country.[1]

Following the end of World War I, nationalist and democratic sentiments were on the rise across Asia. Russell's own time in China coincided with the so-called "May Fourth Movement." A great intellectual and political ferment was abroad. Long suppressed by foreigners and emperors, the Chinese people were seeking to finally take charge of their destiny.

What Russell saw, studied, and heard was contained in *The Problem of China*, a short book that he published in 1922 on his return to England. This presented a wide-ranging survey of China past, present, and future, written in the philosopher's crisp, economical style, and with a characteristic boldness of generalization. The first paragraph set the tone, declaring that "all the world will be vitally affected by the development of Chinese affairs, which may well prove a decisive factor, for good or evil, during the next two centuries."[2]

Russell's book began with a discussion of China's ancient and medieval history. It then investigated China's encounters with (and humiliation at the hands of) European powers, as well as its equally tortuous and conflict-ridden relations with Japan. The family-oriented traits of Chinese culture were elaborated, and contrasted with the individualist tendencies of the West. The book ended with chapters on education and industrialization in contemporary China.

Russell was critical of state corruption and the lack of a tradition of philanthropy in China. He noted, and worried about, the political disunity and division, which needed to be overcome if China was to emerge as a self-reliant, self-confident nation in an increasingly competitive world. The main instrument of national renewal, he thought, would be Chinese intellectuals. He distinguished between two generations of modern-minded thinkers: older men who "had fought their way out of the traditional Confucian prejudices," followed by "a vigorous movement of young reformers, who, if they are allowed a little time, will revivify China and produce something immeasurably better than the worn-out grinding mechanism that we call civilization."[3]

In his final chapter, "The Outlook for China," this sympathetic Englishman sought to put himself in the shoes of "a progressive and public-spirited Chinese and consider what reforms, in what order, I should advocate in that case." He outlined three main aims: "(1) The establishment of an orderly Government; (2) industrial development under Chinese control; (3) the spread of education." These aims had of course "to be pursued concurrently, but on the whole their urgency seems to come in the above order."

The establishment of a stable government, Russell further noted, required the cultivation of a sense of cultural as well as political independence. The philosopher was clear that the great powers of the day—America, England, Russia, Japan—all had "interests which are incompatible, in the long run, with China's welfare. Therefore the Chinese must seek salvation in their own energy, not in the benevolence of any outside Power."

"I think a spirit of patriotism is absolutely necessary to the regeneration of China," insisted Russell. However, this did not mean a retreat to the "bigoted anti-foreign spirit of the Boxers," but a move toward a more enlightened, open-minded, patriotism "which is willing to learn from other countries while not willing to allow them to dominate."[4]

Bertrand Russell was one of the most prolific writers of his time (or any other). Not all of his several dozen books or thousands of essays have stood the test of time. To the scholar or expert *The Problem of China* may seem superficial and impressionistic. Yet in one key respect—the placing of politics before economics—it speaks directly to the concerns of this book. For what Russell said about China could equally be said of India, Vietnam, or Indonesia in 1922. These were all likewise subject to humiliation by the West—arguably greater humiliation, since unlike China, each of their territories was entirely controlled by a colonial power. These countries had likewise to gain—or regain—their political and cultural independence before they could embark on economic modernization.

The rise of the nations of Asia is now a commonplace of academic and media discussion. A decade ago, the focus was on the so-called East Asian Tigers—Japan, South Korea, Singapore, Taiwan—whereas now much attention is being paid to the emergence as global players of the world's two most populous countries, China and India, whose economic and technological surge has caused a great deal of admiration—and perhaps an equal amount of alarm—in the West. Just as the nineteenth century belonged to Europe, and the twentieth century belonged to America, we are told that the century we now live in will be dominated by Asia, whose rise is said to be "irresistible."[5]

Recent debates on the so-called Asian Century have been largely—if not exclusively—oriented toward the economic realm. They focus on rising national incomes in Asia, on the rising share of world trade of its countries, on the growing numbers of billionaires in the countries of the region. Western commentators and politicians praise—and sometimes fear—the achievements of Korean car manufacturers, Chinese consumer goods producers, and Indian software engineers. They speak of how Singapore and Shanghai might come to match London and New York as global financial centers. The praise (but not the fear) is welcomed by Asian leaders, gratified that nations long condescended to are at last being taken seriously.

Back in the nineteenth century, when their countries were under the colonial yoke, some Asian thinkers sought solace in the depth of the philosophical traditions to which they were heir. The West might dominate materially and militarily, but in moral and spiritual matters the East was said to be superior. This argument appealed to some

Western thinkers as well, including German Idealists and American Transcendentalists who invoked Hindu and Buddhist texts while seeking to temper their own society's obsession with material production and material possessions.[6]

That the Asian continent was the cradle of ancient civilizations, that it had produced great thinkers, musicians, and artists was easy to acknowledge. Yet Asia was not supposed to catch up with (still less surpass) Europe or the United States in economic or technological terms. That societies so long identified with poverty, pestilence, and disease, with back-breaking labor in the field using primitive agricultural techniques, and with conservative social traditions and high levels of illiteracy could come to pose a serious economic (and even political) challenge to the powerful, modern, industrial West ran somewhat counter to the logic of history. Hence the sentiments of surprise, wonder, and alarm that have in recent years been so manifest in articles and books on this striking shift of global economic power toward the east.

The debates on Asia's rise have been dominated by politicians, journalists, businessmen, and economists, who all tend to look at the present and the immediate future. To them, the "problem" of China—and of India, Indonesia, Vietnam, too—that Bertrand Russell identified in his book is no longer urgent or current. That is to say, for these commentators the political independence and autonomy of these Asian countries is assumed, taken for granted. They thus present a partial, slanted picture of the Asian resurgence, for the economic achievements they speak of could scarcely have been possible without the creation (often by disorderly means) of an "orderly government" in these once poor, once divided, once colonized nations.

The economic successes of some (not all) Asian countries are certainly noteworthy. And yet, behind this rise lies a now somewhat obscured history of agitation and consolidation that created unified, stable (or more or less stable) nation-states out of fragmented territories and fractious social groups. It is this history that the still-proliferating literature on the (mythical or real) "Asian Century" has so conspicuously ignored. And it is this history that the present book seeks to bring to center stage, in the belief that in understanding where Asia is today, and where it might be headed tomorrow, the politics matters just as much as the economics. For the nationalist revolutions in China, India, and Vietnam—among other places—were the essential precondition to their economic rise. These revolutions each nurtured a spirit of national unity and laid the foundations of a modern state that—among other things—created a consolidated national market without which the impressive growth rates that these countries have recently experienced would have been inconceivable.

The depth, variety, and robustness of the Asian nationalisms explored in this book have been somewhat underplayed in global debates. There are several reasons for this. From the late nineteenth century until World War II, nationalist sentiments in Asia (and Africa) were generally dismissed by the colonial powers as the handiwork of a few disgruntled elites. After the end of the war, dozens of new nations were nevertheless born. This fact and its significance were certainly noted in the Western historical profession. Scholars such as George Kahin (for Indonesia), John K. Fairbank (for China), and Stanley Wolpert (for India) produced fine specialist studies on the ideological and political foundations of the nations that they had been trained to study.[7]

Yet, in the wider public consciousness, there was little appreciation of the process by which India, Indonesia, China et al. came to be constituted. Meanwhile, the onset of the Cold War preempted the need for a reflective look backward. What mattered now was which bloc a particular Asian country supported, not what it stood for independently of any alliance with the United States or the Soviet Union. By the time the Cold War ended, the emergence of these new nations had receded even farther in popular memory. With the attention now focused on the economic domain, the history and politics behind Asia's rise were rendered largely invisible in public debates.

III

The political history of modern Asia brings together several interlinked themes. The first is that of anticolonial revolution. In 1911, the capital of British India moved from Calcutta to Delhi. A magnificent new city came up on what was previously farmland and shrub forest. The city was designed by two British architects but built by thousands of Indian masons and laborers. The scale and splendor of New Delhi was a sign of how sure the British were of their rule—if not a Thousand Year Raj, this would (in the eyes of those who ran it) surely last for several centuries at least. The French in Indo-China and the Dutch in Indonesia were likewise quite certain that their political (and military) hold on their Asian possessions would endure well into the future.

In the event, the British left New Delhi a mere thirty-six years after they moved there. (And half this time was spent living in temporary structures, waiting for the edifices of the imperial capital to be ready for habitation.) The Dutch departed Indonesia a year later, while the French left Indo-China—extremely reluctantly—in the 1950s. These retreats were hastened by popular movements against foreign rule that took different forms, depending on the nature of their leaderships and the character of the colonists they were opposing. But all were genuinely mass movements, bringing in a wide swathe of the population.

Unlike India, Indonesia, or Vietnam, what is now China was never wholly or formally controlled by a single European power. This was a "semi-colony," subject to treaties of dependence, rather than a full-fledged occupation. The experience was humiliating nonetheless, and made more so by the fact that China and its resources were coveted not merely by the West. In the 1890s, and again in the 1930s, China was savaged by Japanese aggression. Both Western and Japanese colonialists were resisted by middle-class political activists, who were able to draw workers, peasants, intellectuals, and businessmen into their struggle.

The second theme is that of nationalist consolidation. Each of these colonies was extremely heterogeneous, with populations divided along lines of caste, class, religion, language, ethnicity, and gender. Nationalist leaders sought to build alliances among these groups, sometimes in the name of anticolonial solidarity, at other times invoking precolonial states and empires that (in fact or in fiction) represented the ancient past of the Vietnamese or Chinese or Indian "nation." For all this, national unity was still elusive and imperfect at independence. And the departure of a common enemy made it more elusive still. With the foreign ruler having departed, personal and political rivalries emerged starkly into the open. Parties and factions battled over what constituted the essence of the nation.

In every major Asian country, the struggle for national unity was an arduous process. Each nation faced problems peculiar to it. China was torn apart by a ferocious civil war, which lasted for the better part of two decades and was fought between two well-armed and extremely motivated political parties. What became Indonesia was a conglomeration of thousands of islands, many of which had little previous connection with one another. India, at independence, was confronted with bringing on board some five hundred chiefdoms, which never formally formed part of British India. Pakistan, the other nation created by the British when they relinquished their raj in August 1947, had two distinct wings, separated by a thousand miles of Indian territory. In these (and other) Asian nations, territorial integration was therefore a massive challenge, as serious and as problematic as emotional integration. As with the French and the British and the Germans in the eighteenth and nineteenth centuries, here too the process of building a shared sense of citizenship was an enormously complicated process, shot through with suspicion, conflict, and disorder.

A third theme of modern Asian history relates to the choice of political system adopted after independence. This was sometimes determined in the course of the anticolonial struggle. In India, for example, the leading nationalist party, the Congress, had, as early as 1928, committed itself to multi-party democracy based on universal adult franchise. In China and Vietnam, where a Communist Party emerged as the leading player, a multi-party system was foreclosed; here, following the Leninist model, one party would be in command, controlling the state, forbidding opposition parties, and forcing writers and thinkers to conform to the party line.

Notably, while classical Marxist theory disparaged nationalist sentiments, Communist regimes in Asia were deeply nationalist. In both China and Vietnam, the ruling Communists partook of a deep sense of national and even civilizational pride. The interests of one's country were usually placed above that of socialist (or proletarian) internationalism.

Multiparty democracy on the Anglo-Saxon model and communist dictatorships in the image of Soviet Russia did not exhaust the alternatives on display. In Indonesia and Pakistan, for example, the military was a key player, extremely influential in political matters even when a civilian leader was formally president or prime minister. And there were other varieties of authoritarianism—such as in Singapore—that did not depend either on military support or on communist ideology.

A fourth theme is that of economic strategy. Most Asian nationalists were clear that their country's subordination was largely a consequence of the industrial and technological superiority that the Western nations enjoyed. On independence, therefore, they resolved to modernize in the manner of their erstwhile masters, shifting people from villages to cities and from the farm to the factory. Gandhi, in India, was an exception; he thought, or hoped, that with the departure of the British, the village would once more be placed at the center of social and economic life in India. But he was outvoted by his own colleagues, who—despite their admiration for Gandhi as a mobilizer of people and movements—thought him an antediluvian reactionary in economic and technological matters.

To end both mass poverty and political uncertainty, these new nations required economic development. Rapid economic growth was required not only to raise living standards, but also to sustain a spirit of national solidarity. Such was the broadly accepted consensus, which, however, admitted of variations in particular policies adopted (or rejected) by postcolonial governments. Where Communists were in charge, there was a push to nationalize industries and eliminate private-sector production units. In agriculture, family farms were discouraged, and collective farms encouraged. Yet even in non-Communist countries the state assumed a predominant role in industrial production, although agriculture remained in private hands. Some countries left feudal systems of landholding intact; others gave ownership rights to tenants or sharecroppers. There were also variations on the question of international trade and capital flows. Some countries rigorously protected their own industries from external competition, erecting high tariff barriers; others adopted a more flexible trade regime, selectively permitting foreign goods and capital into their territory.

A fifth core theme in the history of modern Asian nations is that of foreign policy. Countries governed by Communist parties were allied with the Soviet Union in the Cold War—although they were not as completely servile to the Soviets as was sometimes claimed. Other Asian countries allied with the United States—partly because their rulers faced challenges from indigenous Communists, partly because of the appeal of Western financial and technical aid. Yet other countries chose to strike out on a path of "non-alignment," choosing not to closely identify with either the Russians or the Americans.

There were also other transnational alliances that had become feasible. In nations that were formerly British colonies, the question arose as to whether they would join the Commonwealth and, even if they did, whether they would play an active role. Countries with a dominantly Muslim or dominantly Buddhist population sometimes sought to ally themselves with countries with broadly the same religious configuration.

Relations with one's neighbors were often a key area of concern. As each of these new nations sought to settle their boundaries, their claims clashed. A shared history or a common ruling ideology was not always conducive to boundary agreements. China and Vietnam, China and India, India and Pakistan—in all these cases, the definition of what was one's land and what was the other nation's varied enormously from one side of the border to the other.

The sixth theme that this book foregrounds is the attitude of the postcolonial state and its leaders to traditional beliefs and customary practices. Where a majority of the population was identified with one religion, must this be formally recognized as the religion of the nation? Or should respect be equally accorded to all faiths? Or, finally, should the state impose a thoroughgoing secularism, forcing matters of faith and religious belief into the private domain?

These questions were actively debated, as were the questions of the state's attitude to social customs. Patriarchy, the idea that men were inherently superior to women, was very nearly ubiquitous across Asia. It was encoded in scripture and in social practice. On the achievement of independence, most nations accepted that women and men would henceforth be equal citizens of the nation. However, the extent to which gender equality was promoted (by political practice or legislative fiat) varied greatly across the region.

Then there was the sometimes very urgent question of language policy. This was a linguistically fecund region, home to many languages and many scripts. Most (though not all) Asian countries decided that to cement their unity, they had to make one language the official language of the nation. Even so, they had to decide whether to treat other languages with sympathy, allowing them to flourish in particular social or territorial contexts, or to refuse to accord them any official recognition whatsoever. There were also tough choices to be made in the domain of education policy. Should the medium of instruction in schools be in the national language alone? Or should a second language also be taught? If so, what might this be? Was the language of the erstwhile colonial power (English, Dutch, French, etc.) to be encouraged in a postcolonial context? The choices were complex, and sometimes very confusing indeed.

IV

The course of the anticolonial movement in each country; the varying processes of nationalist consolidation; the adoption of a particular form of government; the specific choices made with regard to economic, foreign, and social policy, respectively—these are the six master themes of modern Asian history. These themes are explored in this book through the means of portraits of major political leaders.

For many years, the biographical method was disparaged by academic historians, in large part because of the influence of sociological and structural perspectives (among them, Marxism). Historians are now rediscovering the potential of using an individual life to explore wider social and political processes. Much depends, of course, on the methods of the historian, his or her zest for primary research, his or her analytical and literary skills, his or her commitment to scholarly depth, his or her willingness to eschew mere sensationalism. Much also depends on the nature of the subject, his or her importance and impact. Yet if scholar and subject are properly matched, biography can be a productive and often very illuminating window into history.

Biography is a study of an individual in his or her context. The life illuminates the times, and vice versa. Another, and perhaps less appreciated aspect of biography is that it is a study of a life in relation to *other* lives. An individual's credo and career are most effectively re-created when he or she is seen as the center of a constellation of forces and persons. The life of a great military general must necessarily involve studying the generals on the other side, as well as his own fellow officers and his political masters. The life of a great writer must pay attention to the writers who influenced her, the writers with whom she was in a competitive relation, the writers whom she inspired, and the publishers, editors, and critics with whom she had to deal. Likewise, political biography, even when ostensibly focused on a single individual, must showcase a larger cast of characters who were in relations of friendship, contention, superiority, or subservience to the main subject.

A renewed interest in political biography is most evident in Europe and North America. There have, in recent years, been fine studies of the careers of the American presidents John F. Kennedy, Lyndon Johnson, Richard Nixon, and Ronald Reagan; of the British prime ministers Harold Macmillan and Margaret Thatcher; of the French presidents Charles De Gaulle and François Mitterrand. And of course studies of the major leaders of World War II, such as Roosevelt, Churchill, Stalin, and Hitler, are numerous enough to fill an entire library.

Makers of Modern Asia takes this new interest to a domain where it has not yet been extensively or carefully applied. Twentieth-century Asia is a superb showcase for the potential of biography as history.

Countries such as China, India, Indonesia, and Vietnam have all had rich, diverse, complicated, and deeply contentious histories. Their premier nationalists and state-makers led influential and controversial lives. They were both actors *and* thinkers who organized popular movements against colonial rule, directed military campaigns (and on occasion opposed them), founded new nation-states, and subsequently shaped their political systems as well as their economic and social policies.

There are eleven individuals featured in this book. As many as four come from China, for the reasons that it is the world's most populous country and the Asian nation whose economic and political advance has attracted most attention across the globe. Three were lifelong members of the Communist Party of China: the acknowledged leader of the Chinese Revolution, Mao Zedong; his close ally and confidant, Zhou Enlai; and Deng Xiaoping, a man purged by Mao who nevertheless lived long enough to be resurrected and then to reshape Chinese (not to say global) economic history by his revisionist policies. The fourth Chinese leader profiled here is Chiang Kai-shek, who fled to the island of Taiwan after his Kuomintang party lost to the Communists in the civil war. Chiang was thereafter airbrushed out of official Chinese history. Recent scholarship, however, has rescued him somewhat from the condescension of posterity, recognizing his key role in the war against Japan and in anticipating some of the future economic policies of the Communists themselves.

Three other portraits come from India, the second most populous nation in the world, as well as its largest democracy. India merits attention because of its size, its diversity, and the peculiarities of both its anticolonial struggle and its postcolonial political history. This book explores modern Indian history through the lives of Mohandas Karamchand Gandhi, Jawaharlal Nehru, and Indira Gandhi. The first led the freedom movement against the British and also thought deeply about viable future paths for India and the world. Nehru and Indira Gandhi were the country's two most long-serving prime ministers, together serving as head of government for thirty-three years, roughly half of India's history as an independent nation. Their legacies are vigorously debated, yet even those who dislike (not to say detest) Nehru and Indira accept that they had a colossal impact on the course of the nation.

The four remaining individuals profiled in this book come from four different countries. There is the Vietnamese nationalist Ho Chi

Minh, a figure around whom many myths have accrued, in part because of his peripatetic journeys across the world and in larger part because he became the symbol of popular resistance to the French and then to the mighty Americans. There is the Indonesian nationalist Sukarno, whom we might perhaps see as playing the same role in his country that Nehru played in his. He was the first foundational head of government, in a position from which he could design the economic, foreign, and social policies that would determine his nation's future.

Finally, we have a leader apiece from Singapore and Pakistan. In the former case there could be only one choice: Lee Kuan Yew. Lee was—is—a man of forceful views, who came to more fully embody his (admittedly far smaller) nation than perhaps any of the other figures in this book. The power of his personality mandates his inclusion here—as does his articulation of a system of "Asian values" distinct from, and in some crucial ways opposed to, Western ideas of political practice and state-making.

For Pakistan, a safe or conventional choice would have been Muhammad Ali Jinnah. A successful lawyer, and a focused and tactically brilliant politician, Jinnah played a—perhaps one should say *the*—critical role in the founding of Pakistan. However, there is little visible impact of his legacy in his country today. So we chose instead to profile Zulfikar Ali Bhutto, another charismatic and highly intelligent individual. From a family of feudal landowners, Bhutto was educated at Stanford and Oxford, yet had an uncommon appeal among the poor. His relations with Pakistan's powerful military were extremely complicated—first he worked under them, then he broke free of them, then he was deposed and hanged by them.

These are the eleven leaders profiled here. We had also considered including some others, such as Mahathir Mohammed of Malaysia, Aung San Suu Kyi of Myanmar, and Park Chung Hee of South Korea. Mahathir was a colorful character, much given to chastising the West while in office, yet his long-term impact on Malaysian history is unclear. The story of Suu Kyi is a heroic one, and her courage in the face of oppression has attracted an almost universal admiration. However, her political life is still unfolding; we don't know whether she will become the first president of a post-junta Myanmar or will always be in opposition. So we finally decided not to have an essay on either. As for Park of Korea, his political orientation is not entirely unrepresented in the book, for as an authoritarian modernizer he distinctly resembled both Lee Kuan Yew and Deng Xiaoping.

The omission of a Japanese leader should perhaps be explained. This is because of the radical break in Japan's history constituted by its defeat in World War II. We did not of course wish to include a prewar figure identified with a militarist, imperialist past. In the postwar period, Japan's dependence—at once economic, political, ideological, and military—on the United States was massive. The role of the prime minister is highly circumscribed by the political culture; besides, most incumbents do not last more than a couple of years in office. As a consequence, it is hard, if not impossible, to name even one major Japanese politician who has provided an autonomously developed idea of his country's place in the world. There has, it appears, been no modern Japanese Mao, Nehru, Lee, or Sukarno. Their original thinkers have tended to be artists, such as the novelist Kenzaburo Oe or the filmmaker Akira Kurosawa.

In spatial terms, this book also excludes that liminal region lying between Europe and Asia known variously as "the Middle East" or "West Asia." There are no essays on Ayatollah Khomeini or Gamal Abdel Nasser here. This is not a commentary on their political importance— which was considerable—but on the fact that the contemporary histories of Iran and Egypt are defined through a somewhat different set of relations with the West—those constituted by Cold War rivalries, terrorism, and the so-called Clash of Civilizations.

For all that it omits, this book does contain a reasonably representative cast of characters whose lives, taken together, present a fairly comprehensive portrait of modern Asia's political history. The ideologies these leaders articulated were as diverse as their countries themselves. The individuals profiled include communists, left-wing populists, authoritarian capitalists, liberals, communitarians, and social democrats, of, variously, Buddhist, Hindu, Islamic, Christian, Confucian, and atheist backgrounds, operating against a canvas that contains a staggering diversity of social forms, technologies, ecological regimes, economic production systems, and—not least—national histories.

Of the eleven leaders featured in this book, only one—Lee Kuan Yew—is still alive. Yet all their legacies continue to have an enduring impact. The politics of China and India are still shaped by the legacy of Mao and Nehru, respectively. The economies of China and India still bear the impress of the ideas of Deng Xiaoping and Indira Gandhi.

And while Zhou and Chiang do not loom as large in contemporary China as Mao or Deng, their legacies are still widely discussed. Bhutto gave Pakistan a democratic constitution and founded a political party and dynasty that were until recently in power. Sukarno and Ho are regarded in more senses than one as the fathers of their nations.

By foregrounding politics and political lives, this book hopes to provide a richer, more nuanced context for the contemporary understanding of the economic rise of Asia. Yet our aim is not merely to expand Western appreciation of the fascinating modern history of the world's most populous continent. We hope also to facilitate cross-national understanding across Asia itself.

Indians and Pakistanis and Chinese and Vietnamese all know something—and often a great deal—about such Western leaders as Churchill and Kennedy. Yet they typically know very little about the histories of Asian countries other than their own. Or of their leading political figures. Even educated Indians are unfamiliar with the life or legacy of Ho and Sukarno. What they know (or think they know) of Bhutto or Mao is distorted by the memory of armed conflicts between India on the one side and Pakistan and China on the other. This ignorance and/or distortion is reproduced across the continent. What does an average Indonesian businessman know about Bhutto or his politics? Or the typical Chinese professional about Gandhi and his ideas? Often nothing at all.

v

Each of the contributors to this book has devoted many years to the study of his or her subject. I shall not therefore attempt to summarize or synthesize the depth of their research and the subtlety of their analyses. The reader is invited to read the individual essays by themselves. And so, in this concluding section of my introduction, I wish merely to flag a few themes of more general interest.

Let me note, first, that while there is no portrait of a specific Japanese leader, Japan as a nation is not entirely absent from this book. It figures most obviously in the chapters on Chinese leaders because of the bitter wars that the two nations fought from the late nineteenth century onward. As the first industrial nation in Asia, and the first one to win a war against a European power, Japan commanded a considerable interest among anticolonial leaders in other parts of Asia as well.

Second, this interest in Japan was characteristic of a wider curiosity in the political paths and choices of Asian nations other than their own. In Asia today, citizens, scholars, and even politicians tend to work and think in nationalist silos. This was not always the case. Chiang was fascinated by Japan; Ho and Nehru deeply interested in China; Bhutto obsessed with India. Sukarno closely followed developments in both India and China. These leaders looked to other Asian countries for clues to run their administrations more effectively or end poverty more quickly.

Finally, the essays in this book each deal, albeit in different ways and with varying emphases, with the understanding (and sometimes misunderstanding) of European history that these nationalist and postcolonial elites possessed or articulated. Several among these leaders had been educated in Europe or North America; others had worked or traveled overseas in their youth. For Zhou, Deng, Ho, Bhutto, Nehru, and Lee, the years they spent abroad were absolutely fundamental to their political and intellectual orientation. But even those Asian leaders entirely educated and always based at home were intensely fascinated by the Western experience. For the Western countries had been the first to create modern nation-states and to build modern economies based on industrial production and city living rather than on agriculture and the village.

Even when they hated the French, British, or Dutch for colonizing their societies, even when they suspected the Americans of having hegemonic aspirations in the postwar world, nationalist leaders recognized that this political domination was a consequence of an overwhelming technological superiority. To best the West in political terms, and to equal or exceed them in economic terms, involved a certain understanding of Western political forms, Western economic theories, Western social and cultural practices. Whether this understanding involved *emulation,* and if so, to what extent and in what particular ways, were matters of intense debate all across the continent in the nineteenth and twentieth centuries, when Asia was as much possessed with the West as the West is now obsessed with Asia.

ONE

GANDHI, INDIA, AND THE WORLD

RAMACHANDRA GUHA

I

BORN IN THE WESTERN INDIAN PORT TOWN of Porbandar in 1869, educated in Rajkot and London, Mohandas Gandhi came to South Africa in May 1893 to help settle a dispute between two merchants. He spent much of the next two decades there, shuttling between Natal and the Transvaal. It was in South Africa that he developed the techniques of political protest for which he remains best known and to which he gave the name *satyagraha*, or truth-force.

The idea of what became known as *satyagraha* was first enunciated in Johannesburg's Empire Theatre on September 11, 1906. Some three thousand Indians had assembled there on that day. Merchants, hawkers, waiters, and workers, they had come to protest a new ordinance of the government of the Transvaal that sought to end Asian immigration and place sharp restrictions on Asians already in the colony. They were to produce fingerprints, carry an identity card at all times, and be confined to specific locations so that they would not, so to say, "contaminate" the ruling whites. The resistance to the ordinance was led by Gandhi, a lawyer from Gujarat who had become a figure of considerable authority in the immigrant community.[1]

On September 11, the Indian residents of Johannesburg stopped work at 10 a.m. The meeting was to begin at three in the afternoon; however, the doors were opened at noon to accommodate the people coming in from the suburbs and the countryside. By one thirty, the theater was packed to overflowing. The scene inside was described by a correspondent of the *Rand Daily Mail*:

Even in its palmiest days, the old variety theatre could never have boasted of a larger audience than that which assembled yesterday. From the back row of the gallery to the front row of the stalls there was not a vacant seat, the boxes were crowded as surely they had never been crowded before, and even the stage was invaded. Wherever the eye lighted was fez and turban, and it needed but little stretch of the imagination to fancy that one was thousands of miles from Johannesburg and in the heart of India's teeming millions.

Five resolutions were presented to and passed by the meeting. One outlined what in the ordinance was repugnant; a second asked the Transvaal government to withdraw it. Two others conveyed the sentiments of those present to the imperial authorities in London. The crucial resolution was the one that enjoined the audience to court arrest if their demands were not met. It said that

> In the event of the Legislative Council, the local Government, and the Imperial Authorities rejecting the humble prayer of the British Indian community of the Transvaal in connection with the Draft Asiatic Law Amendment Ordinance, this mass meeting of British Indians here assembled solemnly and regretfully resolves that, rather than submit to the galling, tyrannous, and un-British requirements laid down in the above Draft Ordinance, every British Indian in the Transvaal shall submit himself to imprisonment and shall continue to do so until it shall please His Gracious Majesty the King-Emperor to grant relief.

Speaking to the audience, Gandhi said that the responsibility for advising them to go to prison was his. "The step was grave, but unavoidable," he remarked. "In doing so, they did not hold a threat, but showed that the time for action—over and above making speeches and submitting petitions—had arrived." Gandhi added that he had "full confidence in his countrymen." He "knew he could trust them, and he knew also that, when occasion required an heroic step to be taken, he knew that every man among them would take it."

Gandhi warned his compatriots of the hardships along the way. "It is quite possible," he remarked, "that some of those who pledge themselves may weaken at the very first trial." For "we may have to remain hungry and suffer from extreme heat and cold. Hard labour is likely to be imposed upon us in prison. We may even be flogged by the warders." The leader was clear that the "struggle will be prolonged." But "provided the entire community manfully stands the test," he foresaw that "there can only be one end to the struggle, and that is victory."[2]

Thus far, the movement to get the Indians a fair deal in South Africa had followed a strictly legalistic route. Letters, petitions, court cases, delegations—these were the means by which Gandhi and his fellow reformers had attempted to challenge policies that bore down unfairly on them. Now, however, they were threatening to defy this new law and go to jail.

Shortly after the meeting at the Empire Theatre, Gandhi left for London to give the methods of petitioning and appeal one last chance. He met members of parliament, influential editors, and powerful ministers, among them the secretary of the colonies and the secretary of the India office. His hope was that the imperial government would lean on the government of the Transvaal and make them withdraw the Asiatic Ordinance.

In a leading article on Gandhi's visit to London, the *Times* explained why it was foredoomed to failure. South Africa was a land of opportunity for ambitious and energetic Europeans. Sugar in Natal and gold in the Transvaal were creating a massive economic boom, attracting migrants from all parts of England and from the Continent as well. In the late nineteenth century, the Afrikaners who controlled the Transvaal had come into conflict with English investors and prospectors. The two sides had gone to war but had since forged a truce, after which they chose to come together in a white alliance against the colored races. And so the *Times* commented:

> No young democratic community of white men can be expected to deal out even-handed justice to formidable rivals in their trade and business who come from another race, with other traditions, other creeds, and other complexions than their own. The fact that the interlopers are subjects of the same Sovereign, and can claim to be treated as members of the same Empire, will probably never, in our time, outweigh these considerations with them. The lapse of years, and perhaps of generations, may be needed to create, if indeed it can ever be created, such a spirit of common Imperial citizenship as will greatly mitigate the combined force of race prejudice and of self-interest.[3]

When the Transvaal government refused to yield, Gandhi and his colleagues courted arrest. They declined to carry passes—or burned them—defied nighttime curfews, and hawked without licenses. Between 1907 and 1910, several thousand Indians were put in prison by the Transvaal authorities. Gandhi himself served three terms in jail.

Later, in 1913, Gandhi led another protest movement in defense of Indian rights. This originated in Natal, the province where the majority of the community was based. This struggle had three aims: (1) the elimination of a punitive annual tax imposed by the state on indentured laborers who stayed on after the expiry of their contract; (2) the recognition of Indian marriages conducted under traditional religious rites (a recent judgment had rendered these marriages invalid); (3) a more general relaxation of the harsh laws that impinged on Indian rights of residence, travel, and work in South Africa.

The movement of 1913 was even more intense than the one preceding it. Coal miners and plantation workers went on strike across Natal. Indian merchants closed shops, Indian waiters refused to serve customers, and Indian railway staff stayed at home. Women joined the struggle, including Gandhi's wife, Kasturba. Gandhi led a march of several thousand Indians across the border into Transvaal, in a spectacular collective defiance of a law that restricted colored people to the province where they normally resided. Once more, thousands of Indians served prison sentences ranging from a few weeks to a few months.

The struggle in South Africa attracted great attention in India. Meetings of solidarity were held all across the subcontinent. The interest was particularly keen in South India, the region from where the majority of the protesters came. A Tamil paper published out of Madras praised the "wonderful determination" of "Mr Gandhi and his followers"; they had "glorif[ied] the good name of India by means of their noble and courageous conduct, risking even their lives." A Kannada paper printed in Bangalore saluted "the leadership of that zealous servant of India, that generous and heroic personage, Mr. Gandhi." A Telugu weekly in Guntur reached for mythic parallels—Gandhi, the leader of the resistance, was like the hero of the Mahabharata, Arjuna, brave and fearless.[4]

Back in 1906, the imperial government had declined to intervene in South Africa. Now, however, it worried about the impact on the growing nationalist movement in India, where the viceroy himself recognized that the passive resisters led by Gandhi had "the deep and burning sympathy" of their compatriots. He went on to say that "if the South African Government desires to justify itself in the eyes of India and the world, the only course open to it is to appoint a strong impartial committee, whereon Indian interests will be represented, to conduct the most searching enquiry" into the causes of the troubles in Natal and the Transvaal.[5]

Leaned on by London, the South African government did this time constitute an inquiry committee. This repealed the punitive annual tax, legalized Indian marriages, and agreed to issue identification certificates for three years at a time (rather than for one year, the existing practice).[6] Eight years of sustained struggle had resulted in some gains. The whites still would not recognize Indians (or indeed Africans) as equal citizens, but now they were at least allowed to practice their trade and live with their families without undue harassment by the authorities.

II

The *satyagrahas* led by Gandhi in South Africa rejected the cautious incrementalism of petition-writers. To defend one's rights, one had sometimes to defy discriminatory laws and court arrest. But *satyagraha* also emphatically rejected the violent methods then fashionable among nationalists and revolutionaries. In Europe, anarchists sought to bring about political change by assassinating kings and prime ministers; socialists, by organizing the working class in violent insurrections. These methods were emulated in India, where young radicals sought likewise to kill colonial administrators in a bid to frighten the British into leaving the country.[7]

From where did Gandhi get the idea of nonviolent collective resistance? In his native Kathiawar, he had seen or heard of sit-down strikes by peasants protesting high taxes, and hunger-fasts by creditors at a debtor's door. In South Africa, he had Baptist friends who told him of their "passive resistance" against Anglican orthodoxy. But a deeper influence than either was that of Leo Tolstoy, whose idea of "non-resistance to evil" powerfully spoke to him.

Like many of the other leaders profiled in this book, Gandhi's political philosophy—and practice—was shaped in part by Western ideas and thinkers. But where Mao and Ho admired Marx and Lenin, and Nehru the British Fabians, Gandhi's main mentor was the greatest Russian novelist of his age. So far as we can tell, Gandhi had not read *Anna Karenina* or *War and Peace*. Yet he had read—and reread—Tolstoy's philosophical tracts. One of his favorite books was *The Kingdom of God Is within You*, which argued that in matters of faith an individual must follow his own inclinations and his own conscience, rejecting creeds and credos imposed by ancient scriptures or authorized clerics.

Gandhi also admired Tolstoy's pacifism and the movement of conscientious objectors in Tsarist Russia he had helped spawn. He was further impressed by the fact that as a man of aristocratic birth, Tolstoy had deliberately declassed himself, seeking to live simply and work with his hands. After more than a decade of reading Tolstoy, Gandhi wrote to him in 1909, outlining how the Russian's life had "left a deep impression on his mind." He told Tolstoy of the *satyagrahas* led by him in South Africa and of how they drew on his own example and writings. The writer, flattered to find this new disciple in the East, praised the struggle of "our dear brothers and co-workers in the Transvaal," which had—as in Russia—opposed "meekness and love against pride and violence."[8]

III

In South Africa, Gandhi was in essence a *community* leader. He spoke for the 150,000 Indians who lived in Natal, Transvaal, and the Cape Colony. His role was limited; so were his aims. Recognizing the force of white prejudice in South Africa, Gandhi never fought for full citizenship for his fellow Indians. When he first became politically active in Natal, he wrote a pamphlet demanding that educated Indians be given the franchise. He dropped this demand in later years, asking only that their rights of residence and livelihood be protected and their family and community customs not be threatened or dishonored.

Some astute observers recognized that behind these apparently modest demands was a larger cultural and social force. The racial laws in the Transvaal were implemented by the Boer War hero General J. C. Smuts, who served as secretary of the interior. When Gandhi and his mates began to troop into prison, an old Cambridge friend of Smuts's, H. J. Wolstenholme, wrote to him that those he had jailed "belong to a race, or complex of races, with an ancient civilization behind them, and a mental capacity not inferior to that of the highest Western people, who are developing rapidly a feeling of nationality and a capacity for the more active and practical life of the more materialized West."

The Cambridge scholar saw an "epoch-making" change taking place in relations between East and West, whereby the Japanese, the Chinese, and the Indians would no longer accept exclusion and disability on grounds of race. It was increasingly clear that those whom Europeans had dismissed as "inferior peoples" were not inferior in capacity; they claimed, demanded, and deserved equal rights. Wolstenholme told Smuts that "it would surely be wise statesmanship, as well as good human fellowship, to concede in time and with a good grace what is sure eventually to be won by struggle."[9]

Notably, despite his modest following and limited aims, Gandhi himself saw the struggle in South Africa as having a far wider relevance. The leading political organization in his homeland was the Indian National Congress, which was dominated at this time by liberals who believed in moderation and dialogue, in polite appeals to the king-emperor, and in British traditions of fair play. In October 1909, Gandhi wrote to an influential Indian editor that the Congress should concentrate its attention on the South African struggle, for it might then "perchance find out that for the many ills we suffer from in India it is an infallible panacea." He was "sure it will be found" that nonviolent resistance, or *satyagraha,* was "the only weapon suited to the genius of our people and our land."[10]

IV

The India that Gandhi came back to in 1915 was rather different from the one that he had left in 1893. Although still a colony of the British, it was far more active in a political sense. The Indian National Congress now had branches in most major cities and towns, and had greatly broadened its appeal among the middle classes.

On the advice of his mentor, the Puné liberal Gopal Krishna Gokhale, Gandhi spent a year traveling around India, getting to know the land and its peoples. His first major public appearance was at the opening of the Banaras Hindu University (BHU) in February 1916. Among the invitees to this event were the princes and philanthropists whose donations had enabled the creation of the new university. Also present were important leaders of the Congress. Compared to these dignitaries, Gandhi was relatively unknown. He had been invited on account of his work in South Africa, rather than his status within India.

When his turn came to speak, Gandhi charged the elite with a lack of concern for the laboring poor. The opening of the BHU, he said, was "certainly a most gorgeous show." But he worried about the contrast between the "richly bedecked noblemen" present and "millions of the poor" Indians who were absent. Gandhi told the privileged invitees that "there is no salvation for India unless you strip yourself of this jewelry and hold it in trust for your countrymen in India." "There can be no spirit of self-government about us," he went on, "if we take away or allow others to take away from the peasants almost the whole of the results of their labour. Our salvation can only come through the farmer. Neither the lawyers, nor the doctors, nor the rich landlords are going to secure it."[11]

Gandhi's speech at Banaras in February 1916 was, at one level, merely a statement of fact—namely, that Indian nationalism was an elite phenomenon, a creation of lawyers and doctors and landlords. But, at another level, it was also a statement of intent—the first public announcement of the returning expatriate's own desire to make Indian nationalism more properly representative of the Indian people. In the last month of that year, Gandhi was presented with an opportunity to put his precepts into practice. At the annual Congress meeting, held in Lucknow in December 1916, he was approached by a peasant from Champaran in Bihar, who told him about the harsh treatment of peasants by British indigo planters. Gandhi was to spend much of 1917 in Champaran, seeking to obtain for the peasants security of tenure as well as the freedom to cultivate the crops of their choice. The following year, 1918, Gandhi was involved in two campaigns in his home state of Gujarat. First, he intervened in a labor dispute in Ahmedabad, demanding better working conditions for the textile mill workers. Then, he joined peasants in Kheda in asking the state for the remission of taxes following the failure of their harvest.[12]

These initiatives in Champaran, Ahmedabad, and Kheda marked Gandhi as a nationalist with a deep sympathy for the poor. Yet these were all local struggles. Then, in 1919, the colonial rulers delivered into Gandhi's lap an issue from which he could construct a much wider movement. During World War I, the British had instituted censorship of the press and permitted detention without trial. Now, on the recommendation of a committee chaired by Sir Sidney Rowlatt, these tough measures were continued. In response, Gandhi called for a countrywide campaign against the so-called Rowlatt Act. In towns across north and west India, life came to a standstill, as shops shut down and schools closed in response to the *bandh* call. The protests were particularly intense in the Punjab, where many men had served on the British side in the war. Expecting to be rewarded for their service, they were instead given the Rowlatt Act.[13]

Gandhi was detained while proceeding to the Punjab, and prominent local congressmen were arrested. The situation in the province grew progressively more tense, reaching a bloody climax in Amritsar in April 1919, when a British brigadier ordered his troops to open fire on a nationalist meeting. More than four hundred people were killed in what became known as the Jallianwala Bagh massacre.

It was the Rowlatt *satyagraha* that made Gandhi a truly *national* leader. Emboldened by its success, he called for a campaign of "non-co-operation" with British rule. Indians opposed to colonial rule were asked to stop attending schools, colleges, and law courts, and to not pay taxes. They were asked to adhere to a "renunciation of [all] voluntary association with the [British] Government." If noncooperation was effectively carried out, said Gandhi, India could win freedom within a year.

To further broaden his movement, Gandhi had joined hands with Muslim leaders who sought to restore the Caliphate, a symbol of Pan-Islamism that had recently been abolished in Turkey by Kemal Attaturk. Gandhi hoped that by coupling noncooperation with the "Khilafat" movement, India's two major religious communities, Hindus and Muslims, could collectively bring about an end to colonial rule.[14]

Noncooperation and Khilafat together unleashed a surge of popular action that was altogether unprecedented in British India. Students stopped going to colleges run by the government. Lawyers refused to attend court. The working class went on strike in many towns and cities: according to official figures, there were 396 strikes in 1921, involving 600,000 workers and a loss of seven million workdays. Meanwhile, the countryside was seething with discontent. Hill tribes in northern Andhra violated the forest laws. Farmers in Awadh did not pay taxes. Peasants in Kumaun refused to carry loads for colonial officials.[15]

As a consequence of the noncooperation movement, the British raj was shaken to its foundations for the first time since the Great Revolt of 1857. Then, in February 1922, a group of peasants attacked and torched a police station in the hamlet of Chauri Chaura, in the United Provinces. Several constables perished in the conflagration. This act of violence prompted Gandhi to call off the movement of noncooperation. "No provocation," he insisted, "can possibly justify [the] brutal murder of men who had been rendered defenceless and who had virtually thrown themselves on the mercy of the mob."[16]

By 1922, Gandhi had transformed Indian nationalism, thereby redeeming the promise made in his BHU speech of February 1916. It was no longer a movement of professionals and intellectuals; now, hundreds of thousands of peasants, workers, and artisans also participated in it. Many of them venerated Gandhi, referring to him as their "Mahatma." They appreciated the fact that he dressed like them, lived like them, and spoke their language.

This identification with the common folk was strikingly reflected in his dress: while other nationalist leaders dressed formally, wearing a Western suit or an Indian *bandgala,* Gandhi went among the people in a simple *dhoti,* or loincloth. Meanwhile, he spent part of each day working on the *charkha* (spinning wheel), encouraging other nationalists to do likewise. The act of spinning allowed Gandhi to break the boundaries that prevailed within the traditional caste system between mental and manual labor.

Wherever Gandhi traveled in India, rumors spread of his miraculous powers. In some places it was said that he had been sent by the king to redress the grievances of the farmers and that he had the power to overrule all local officials. Rumors spread of how villagers who criticized Gandhi found their houses mysteriously falling apart or their crops failing.[17]

While Gandhi's mass appeal was undoubtedly genuine—and in the context of Indian politics, without precedent—his success in broadening the basis of nationalism was also based on careful organization. New branches of the Congress were set up in various parts of India. Gandhi encouraged the communication of the nationalist message in the mother tongue, rather than in the language of the rulers, English. Thus, the provincial committees of the Congress were now based on linguistic regions, rather than on the artificial boundaries of British India.

For several years after the noncooperation movement ended, Gandhi focused on social reform. In 1928, however, he began to think of reentering politics. That year there was a countrywide campaign in opposition to the all-white Simon Commission, sent from England to inquire into conditions in the colony. Gandhi did not himself participate in this movement, although he gave it his blessings, as he also did with a peasant *satyagraha* in Bardoli in western India in the same year.

In the last days of 1929, the Congress held its annual session in the city of Lahore. The meeting was significant for two things: the election of Jawaharlal Nehru as president, signifying the passing of the baton of leadership to the younger generation; and the proclamation of a commitment to "Purna Swaraj," or complete independence. Now the pace of politics picked up once more. On January 26, 1930, an "Independence Day" was observed, with the national flag being hoisted in different venues and patriotic songs being sung. Gandhi himself issued precise instructions as to how the day should be observed. "It would be good," he said, "if the declaration [of independence] is made by whole villages, whole cities even. . . . It would be well if all the meetings were held at the identical minute in all the places."[18]

Soon after the observance of this "Independence Day," Gandhi announced that he would lead a march to break one of the most widely disliked laws in British India, which gave the state a monopoly in the manufacture and sale of salt. In every Indian household, salt was indispensable; yet people were forbidden from making salt even for domestic use, compelling them to buy it from shops at a high price. The state monopoly over salt was deeply unpopular; by making it his target, Gandhi hoped to catalyze a wider movement against British rule.

Although Gandhi had given advance notice of his so-called Salt March to Lord Irwin (the viceroy), he failed to grasp its significance. On March 12, 1930, Gandhi began walking from his ashram at Sabarmati toward the ocean. He reached his destination three weeks later, making a fistful of salt as he did and thereby making himself a criminal in the eyes of the law. Meanwhile, parallel salt marches were being conducted in other parts of the country.

As with noncooperation, apart from the officially sanctioned nationalist campaign, there were numerous other streams of protest. Across large parts of India, peasants breached the hated colonial forest laws that kept them and their cattle out of woods in which they had once roamed freely. In the towns, factory workers went on strike, lawyers boycotted courts, and students refused to attend government-run educational institutions. As in 1920–1922, Gandhi's call had again encouraged Indians of all classes to make manifest their discontent with colonial rule. The rulers responded by detaining the dissenters. In the wake of the Salt March, nearly sixty thousand Indians were arrested, among them, of course, Gandhi himself.[19]

The progress of Gandhi's march to the sea can be traced through the secret reports filed by the police officials deputed to monitor his movements. These reproduce the speeches he gave at the villages en route, in which he called upon local officials to renounce government employment and join the freedom struggle. In one village, Wasna, Gandhi told the upper castes that "if you are out for Swaraj you must serve untouchables. You won't get Swaraj merely by the repeal of the salt taxes or other taxes. For Swaraj you must make amends for the wrongs which you did to the untouchables. For Swaraj, Hindus, Muslims, Parsis and Sikhs will have to unite. These are the steps towards Swaraj." The police spies reported that Gandhi's meetings were well attended by villagers of all castes and by women as well as men. Thousands of volunteers were flocking to the nationalist cause. A senior police official noted that "Mr Gandhi appeared calm and collected. He is gathering more strength as he proceeds."[20]

The progress of the Salt March can also be traced from another source: the American newsmagazine *Time*. This, to begin with, wrote with disdain of Gandhi's "spindly frame" and his "spidery loins." In its first report, *Time* was deeply skeptical of the marchers reaching their destination. It claimed that Gandhi "sank to the ground" at the end of the second day's walking; the magazine did not believe that "the emaciated saint would be physically able to go much further."

Within a week it had changed its mind. The massive popular following that the march had garnered, wrote *Time*, had made the British rulers "desperately anxious." Gandhi himself they now saluted as a "Saint" and a "Statesman," who was using "Christian acts as a weapon against men with Christian beliefs."[21]

The Salt March was notable for at least three reasons. First, it brought Gandhi to world attention, with the march being widely covered by the European and American press. Second, it was the first nationalist activity in which women participated in large numbers. The socialist Kamaladevi Chattopadhyay had persuaded Gandhi not to restrict the protests to men alone. Kamaladevi was herself one of numerous women who courted arrest by breaking the salt or liquor laws. Third, and perhaps most significant, it was the Salt March that forced upon the British the realization that their raj may not last forever and that they would have to devolve some powers to Indians.

To that end, a series of "Round Table Conferences" were convened in London. These resulted in a new Government of India Act promising greater representation to Indians in government. In 1937, in an election held on the basis of a restricted franchise, the Congress won a comprehensive victory. Now eight out of eleven provinces had a Congress "prime minister," working under the supervision of a British governor.

In September 1939, two years after the Congress ministries assumed office, World War II broke out. Gandhi and Nehru promised Congress support to the war effort if the British, in return, promised to grant India independence once hostilities ended. The offer was refused. In protest, the Congress ministries resigned in October 1939. Through 1940 and 1941, the Congress organized a series of individual *satyagrahas* to pressure the rulers to promise freedom once the war ended.

In the spring of 1942, the British prime minister, Winston Churchill, was persuaded to send one of his ministers, Sir Stafford Cripps, to try and forge a compromise with Gandhi and the Congress. Talks broke down after the Congress insisted that if it was to help the British defend India from the Axis powers, the viceroy had first to appoint an Indian as the defense member of his executive council.[22]

After the failure of the Cripps mission, Gandhi launched his third major movement against British rule. This was the "Quit India" campaign, which began in August 1942. Although Gandhi was jailed at once, younger activists directed strikes and acts of sabotage all over the country. In several districts, such as Satara in the west and Medinipur in the east, "independent" governments were proclaimed. The British responded with much force, yet it took more than a year to suppress the rebellion.[23]

v

Between 1917, when he went to Champaran, and 1942, when he was arrested for starting the "Quit India" movement, Gandhi was undoubtedly the most powerful force in Indian politics. His name was recognized all across the country. Hundreds of thousands of ordinary Indians had courted arrest at his command. Under his leadership and guidance, the Congress had become a genuinely all-India party, reaching beyond the middle class to embrace large sections of the peasantry and the working class as well.

Gandhi was not universally admired, however. Among his critics were three Indians who each commanded considerable intellectual powers as well as political influence. They each represented a social base different from, and an ideological tendency opposed to, Gandhi's. They each led parties of their own, which rejected the claim of Gandhi's Congress that it was the main or even sole representative body of the Indian nation-in-the-making.

The first of these rivals of Gandhi was the revolutionary-turned-reactionary Vinayak Damodar Savarkar. Gandhi and he had met in London in 1909, where they had intense arguments about the relative merits of violence and nonviolence. Savarkar himself was arrested in 1910 and spent a decade in the infamously harsh and horrible Cellular Jail in the Andamans. Released on a promise of good behavior, he then wrote a series of tracts and plays in his native Marathi. In 1937, he was elected president of the Hindu Mahasabha, a party that criticized the Congress for being unduly respectful of the rights of religious minorities. Once a proponent of Hindu-Muslim cooperation, Savarkar had now come round to the belief that independent India should be run as a Hindu state.[24]

The Hindu Mahasabha was a political party. Its ideological presuppositions were largely shared by a social organization called the Rashtriya Swayamsewak Sangh (or RSS), which had been founded in 1925 and was also dominated by Maharashtrians. The RSS (whose name would translate as "National Volunteer Corps") admired Mussolini for having—as they saw it—brought discipline and order to his unruly and divided nation. RSS workers suspected Muslims and Christians of harboring divided loyalties, of owing allegiance to creeds and holy places foreign to India. They wished, like the Mahasabha, to re-create India as a Hindu nation, from which vantage point Gandhi and his Congress were naturally viewed as adversaries.[25]

Savarkar and the RSS chastised Gandhi for being too sympathetic to Muslims. On the other hand, a growing number of Muslim leaders had come to feel that Gandhi and the Congress did not adequately represent the interests of their community. Muslims had energetically participated in the noncooperation movement. However, except in Gandhi's native Gujarat, they did not come forward to take part in the Salt March. Muslim intellectuals resented Gandhi's references to classical Hindu texts such as the Gita and the Ramayana. Muslim businessmen and professionals feared competition from Hindus, who were generally better educated and had access to greater economic (and social) capital.

In 1906, a group of Muslim aristocrats formed a political party to advance their interests. Called the Muslim League, it often cooperated with the Congress in the early decades of its existence. But by the 1930s, the two parties had drifted apart. The elections of 1937 deepened the rift, with the Muslim League charging Congress ministries with promoting policies that disregarded the rights and interests of religious minorities.[26]

The leader of the Muslim League at the time was Muhammad Ali Jinnah. Born two years after Gandhi, and like him a Gujarati lawyer educated in London, Jinnah had been active in politics since the first decade of the century. In the 1910s and 1920s he was a liberal constitutionalist who saw street protests in the Gandhian mode as dangerously akin to anarchy.

At this time, Jinnah still believed that Hindus and Muslims could strike a *modus vivendi*. By the 1930s, however, he had concluded that if the British left India and handed over power to the Congress Party, this would lead to the subordination of his fellow Muslims. The 1940 annual meeting of the League, held in Lahore, committed itself to an independent Muslim homeland, to be named Pakistan. Jinnah's speech on this occasion outlined why he thought Hindus and Muslims could not live together in a shared polity. "It is a dream," he said, that

> the Hindus and Muslims can ever evolve a common nationality, and this misconception of one Indian nation has gone far beyond the limits and is the cause of our present troubles and will lead India to destruction if we fail to revise our notions in time. The Hindus and Muslims belong to two different religious philosophies, social customs, literatures. They neither intermarry nor interdine together, and, indeed, they belong to two different civilizations which are based mainly on conflicting ideas and conceptions. Their aspects on life and of life are different. . . . They have different epics, different heroes, and different episodes. Very often the hero of one is a foe of the other. . . . To yoke together two such nations under a single state, one as a numerical minority and the other as a majority, must lead to growing discontent and final destruction of any fabric that may be built up for the government of such a state.[27]

Jinnah believed that Gandhi and the Congress essentially represented the Hindu interest. A third London-educated lawyer, B. R. Ambedkar, argued that in fact they spoke largely for Hindu upper castes. Born in a home of untouchables, Ambedkar was a brilliant scholar who had taken degrees at Columbia University and the London School of Economics before becoming active in Indian politics.

Gandhi was more than twenty years older than Ambedkar. From the early 1920s he had actively campaigned against untouchability himself. When the two men first met, in August 1931, Gandhi stressed the length of his own service, and Ambedkar felt patronized. There was a larger political difference regarding how untouchables could find adequate and effective political representation. The British had already granted separate electorates for Muslims. Ambedkar wished for the same privilege to be extended to untouchables, so that they could find their own leaders regardless of the wishes of the caste Hindus. Gandhi disagreed. His view was that untouchables were part—albeit a grievously disadvantaged part—of the larger Hindu fold. He argued instead for quotas for untouchable legislators within a larger category of all Hindus.

In 1932, the British rulers awarded separate electorates for untouchables. Gandhi went on a fast-unto-death in opposition. With widespread fears of Gandhi losing his life, Ambedkar yielded to joint electorates. But he felt coerced. He was confirmed in the view that his people needed to mobilize for their own rights rather than depend on upper-caste benefactors, however well-meaning and sweet-talking they appeared to be.[28]

Among the issues that divided Ambedkar and Gandhi was that of economic policy. Gandhi argued for a village-centered economic order, based on local production for local use. He asked for a revival of village industries and for the strengthening of community systems of natural resource management. Ambedkar, on the other hand, believed that in urbanization and industrialization lay both the future of India in general and the emancipation of the untouchables in particular. In this, Ambedkar was not alone. Within Gandhi's own Congress Party, the dominant view was that when India became free, it should adopt a model of heavy industrialization, showcasing steel mills, large dams, highways, etc.[29]

A last group of critics of Gandhi were the Communists. The Communist Party of India was established in 1921 and attracted to its fold some intelligent and very motivated young men. At that time, the Bolshevik Revolution still had a romantic aura around it. The facts about the purges and the famines were not widely known. Indian Communists hoped to do what they presumed their comrades to have done in Russia—forcibly pull a backward, hierarchical society into the modern age. Here Gandhi was an impediment, partly for his economic views and more so for his political method. Themselves believers in the liberating power of violence, Communists saw Gandhian *satyagraha* as effeminate and supine, if not a deliberate device to wean the masses away from the revolutionary path.[30]

While the Congress leaders languished in jail following the "Quit India" movement, Jinnah and the Muslim League worked patiently at expanding their influence. It was in these years that the League began to make a mark in Punjab and Sindh, provinces where it had previously had scarcely any presence.

In June 1944, with the end of World War II in sight, Gandhi was released from prison. Later that year, he held a series of meetings with Jinnah, seeking to bridge the gap between the Congress and the League. In 1945, a Labour government came to power in Britain and committed itself to granting independence to India. Meanwhile, back in India, the viceroy, Lord Wavell, brought the Congress and the League together for a series of talks.

Early in 1946, fresh elections were held to the provincial legislatures. The Congress swept the "general" category, but in the seats specifically reserved for Muslims, the League won an overwhelming majority. The political polarization was complete. A cabinet mission sent in the summer of 1946 failed to get the Congress and the League to agree on a federal system that would keep India together while allowing the provinces a degree of autonomy. After the talks broke down, Jinnah called for a "Direct Action Day" to press the League's demand for Pakistan. On the designated day, August 16, 1946, bloody riots broke out in Calcutta. The violence spread to rural Bengal, then to Bihar, and then across the country to the United Provinces and the Punjab. In some places, Muslims were the main sufferers, in other places, Hindus.

In February 1947, Wavell was replaced as viceroy by Lord Mountbatten. Mountbatten called one last round of talks, but when these too proved inconclusive, he announced that British India would be freed, but also divided.[31]

The formal transfer of power was fixed for August 15. When that day came, Gandhi was not present at the festivities in New Delhi. He was in Calcutta, but he did not attend any celebratory function or hoist a flag there either. Gandhi marked the day with a twenty-four-hour fast. The freedom he had struggled so long for had come at an unacceptable price, with a nation divided and Hindus and Muslims at each other's throats.

Through September and October 1947, writes his biographer D. G. Tendulkar, Gandhi "went round hospitals and refugee camps giving consolation to distressed people." He "appealed to the Sikhs, the Hindus and the Muslims to forget the past and not to dwell on their sufferings but to extend the right hand of fellowship to each other, and to determine to live in peace."[32]

After fasting to bring peace to Calcutta, Gandhi had shifted to Delhi, from where he hoped to move on to the riot-torn districts of Punjab. While in the capital, his meetings were disrupted by refugees who objected to readings from the Koran or shouted slogans asking why he did not speak of the sufferings of those Hindus and Sikhs still living in Pakistan.

There was an attempt on Gandhi's life on January 20, 1948, but he carried on undaunted. On January 26, he spoke at his prayer meeting of how that day had been celebrated in the past as Independence Day. Now freedom had come, but its first few months had been deeply disillusioning. However, he trusted that "the worst is over" and that Indians would henceforth work collectively for the "equality of all classes and creeds, never the domination and superiority of the major community over a minor, however insignificant it may be in numbers or influence." He also permitted himself the hope "that though geographically and politically India is divided into two, at heart we shall ever be friends and brothers helping and respecting one another and be one for the outside world."[33]

Other Indians were less forgiving. At his daily prayer meeting on the evening of January 30, Gandhi was shot dead by a young man. The assassin, who surrendered afterward, was a Brahmin from Pune named Nathuram Godse. The editor of an extremist Hindu newspaper (and former protégé of Savarkar's), Godse denounced Gandhi as an appeaser of Muslims.

VII

In India today, Gandhi is an extremely controversial figure. Presidents and prime ministers visit his memorial in Delhi on the days of his birth and death. On other days of the year, these dignitaries do not appear to remember Gandhi, for the governments they preside over are marked by rampant nepotism and shockingly high levels of corruption. More constructive and plausible followers of Gandhi's views are activists in the environmental and civil liberties movement, as well as workers for rural development, community health, and girls' education.[34]

Gandhi today has some enthusiastic Indian admirers and some hostile and aggressive critics. While the two men were alive, many more Hindus followed Gandhi than Savarkar. In the 1930s and beyond, many more erstwhile untouchables voted for Gandhi's Congress than for parties led by Ambedkar. However, the posthumous battles have swung somewhat in the other direction. Both the right-wing Hindu radicals and the left-wing anti-Hindu radicals have a strong following in India today. Political parties with influence and power presume to speak in their names and against Gandhi's. Meanwhile, there is also a Maoist insurgency active in parts of central and eastern India, whose leaders and cadres sometimes decapitate statues of Gandhi to show their contempt for the "Father of the Nation."

Outside India, on the other hand, Gandhi has few critics, and a huge (and apparently still growing) number of admirers. His techniques of nonviolent protest have had a colossal impact across the world. The civil rights movement in the United States owes a great deal to the influence of Gandhi. Long before Martin Luther King Jr. arrived on the scene, Gandhi's name and doings were widely written about in the African American press. In the 1930s, the leading black preacher Howard Thurman came to India to seek his counsel. Another important black activist, Bayard Rustin, had closely studied Gandhi's political campaigns.

King himself heard of Gandhi through his teacher Mordecai Johnson and the (white) American Gandhian thinker Richard B. Gregg. In 1959, he came on a visit to India, meeting with people who had worked with Gandhi. He also acquired a reasonable acquaintance with Gandhi's own writings.

Gandhi himself never visited America, yet he was to have a decisive posthumous impact on the politics and culture of that land. Through the late 1950s and 1960s, the methods of protest used by Dr. King and his colleagues were powerfully shaped by Gandhi's example. Marches to state and national capitals; breaches of racially biased laws by blacks and whites traveling together; the willingness to spend time in jail; the rhetoric of forgiveness and reconciliation—in all these respects King appeared (and was happy to be seen) as the American Gandhi. The persistence and sheer heroism of the protests he led forced major changes in the law. A hundred years after the Civil War, African Americans were finally equal citizens in their own land.[35]

In Africa, a continent Gandhi lived in for more than two decades, he has likewise been an absent presence. The nationalist leaders who brought down British and French colonialism were often inspired by what he had done in India. In South Africa, the early opposition to apartheid was led by committed Gandhians. Chief Albert Luthuli, leader of the African National Congress (ANC) in the crucial decade of the 1950s, had read Gandhi, visited India, and exalted the power of nonviolence. The first major transracial challenge to apartheid, the Defiance Campaign of 1952, followed Gandhi, and anticipated Dr. King, in its nonviolent breaches of discriminatory laws.[36]

After the Sharpeville massacre of 1960, the ANC abandoned non-violence. Even so, leaders like Oliver Tambo and Nelson Mandela often cited Gandhi appreciatively, as having been the first to show the power of collective resistance to the arbitrary exercise of state power. After the ending of apartheid, Mandela in particular reached out to his opponents in an affectingly Gandhi-like manner. South Africans remain proud that it was on their land that Gandhi achieved political and moral maturity. They like to tell visiting Indians that "you gave us a lawyer, we gave you back a Mahatma."[37]

In his own continent, Asia, Gandhi inspired nationalist struggles in several countries. And he continues to provide a reference point for activists struggling against communist regimes and military dicta-torships. The Tibetan leader, the Dalai Lama, is visibly influenced by Gandhi. So is his fellow Nobel Peace laureate, the Burmese activist Aung San Suu Kyi. Apart from her commitment to nonviolence, Suu Kyi also finds Gandhi's reconciliation of modernity and tradition ap-pealing. "In spite of his deeply ingrained Hinduism," she once remarked, "Gandhi's intellectual flexibility made him accept those elements of western thought which fitted into the ethical and social scheme he con-sidered desirable."[38]

VIII

Gandhi was born in 1869, a decade after the publication of Charles Darwin's *On the Origin of Species*. This was a time of widespread skepticism among the educated classes in Europe, a sentiment cap-tured in the title of Thomas Hardy's poem "God's Funeral." Outside the Continent, this was also a time of heightened missionary activity. In their new colonies in Africa and Asia, European priests sought to claim the heathen for Christianity.

For his part, Gandhi rejected both the atheism of the intellectuals as well as the arrogance of the missionaries. He did not think science had all the answers to the mysteries of the universe. Faith answered to a deep human need. Yet Gandhi did not think that there was one privileged path to God either. He believed that every religious tradition was an unstable mixture of truth and error. From these three beliefs followed a fourth, which was that Gandhi rejected conversion and missionary work. He encouraged interreligious dialogue, so that individuals could see their faith in the critical reflections of another.

Gandhi invented the interfaith prayer meeting, where texts of different religions were read and sung to a mixed audience. At an International Fellowship of Religions, held at his *ashram* in Sabarmati in January 1928, he said that "We can only pray, if we are Hindus, not that a Christian should become a Hindu, or if we are Mussalmans, not that a Hindu or a Christian should become a Mussalman, nor should we even secretly pray that anyone should be converted [to our faith], but our inmost prayer should be that a Hindu should be a better Hindu, a Muslim a better Muslim and a Christian a better Christian. That is the fundamental truth of fellowship."[39]

What does it mean to be a better Hindu or Muslim or Christian? The sacred texts of all religions have contradictory trends and impulses, sanctioning one thing, but sometimes also its opposite. Gandhi asked that we affirm those trends that oppose violence and discrimination or which promote nonviolence and justice. The high priests of Hinduism claimed that the practice of untouchability was sanctioned by the scriptures; Gandhi answered that in that case the scriptures did not represent the true traditions of the faith. Islamic texts might speak of women in condescending or disparaging terms in one place and in terms of reverence and respect in another; surely a Muslim committed to justice would value the second above the first? Likewise, a Christian must privilege the pacifism of Jesus's life above passages in the Bible calling for retribution against people of other faiths.

Besides his religious pluralism, Gandhi is also becoming known for his early anticipation of the environmental predicament. Take this remarkable passage from his journal, *Young India*, of December 20, 1928: "God forbid that India should ever take to industrialization after the manner of the West. The economic imperialism of a single tiny island kingdom (England) is today keeping the world in chains. If an entire nation of 300 million took to similar economic exploitation, it would strip the world bare like locusts."[40]

Two years earlier, Gandhi had claimed that to "make India like England and America is to find some other races and places of the earth for exploitation." As it appeared that the Western nations had already "divided all the known races outside Europe for exploitation and there are no new worlds to discover," he pointedly asked: "What can be the fate of India trying to ape the West?"[41]

From this diagnosis of the ills of industrialism flowed Gandhi's proffered solution, wherein economic development would be centered on the village. He wished, above all, to see that "the blood that is today inflating the arteries of the cities run once again in the blood vessels of the villages." When he was accused of turning his back on the great scientific inventions, including electricity, Gandhi remarked: "If we could have electricity in every village home, I should not mind villagers plying their implements and tools with the help of electricity. But then the village communities or the State would own power houses, just as they have their grazing pastures."[42]

In 1973—twenty-five years after the Mahatma's death—a group of Gandhian activists mobilized peasants in the Himalaya against commercial logging. This movement, known as the Chipko Andolan, sparked a series of struggles across India, which defended community rights in nature and natural resources against the encroachments of industry. The environmental movement has since been deeply shaped by Gandhi's legacy. His moral call for restraints in consumption, his political techniques of *satyagraha*, his emphasis on constructive work in the villages—all have been taken forward by those working in the realms of community forestry, water management, sustainable energy, and organic agriculture. Outside India, too, Gandhi has been something of an icon for modern environmentalists. Influential thinkers such as E. F. Schumacher, Wolfgang Sachs, and Rudolph Bahro have acknowledged a debt to Gandhi's writings, as has the German Green Party itself.[43]

IX

September 11, 2001, or 9/11 for short, is a date commemorated with great sentiment and feeling in the city of New York. It is also remembered and marked all over the world as a day, and date, that was the outcome of the politics of violence, hatred, and intolerance. In these respects it is the "Other" of an earlier 9/11, that which took place at the Empire Theatre in Johannesburg in 1906 and which gave birth to the politics of nonviolence in South Africa, India, and the world.

Among Gandhians and Gandhi scholars, the significance of that original 9/11 is well known. I want to end this essay by focusing on one aspect that is now forgotten—the fact that in that crowd in the Empire Theatre were some Chinese migrants to South Africa. For the Asiatic Act of the Transvaal Government discriminated against them, too.

Numbering about eleven hundred in all, the Chinese in the Transvaal worked as merchants, gardeners, and laundrymen. Their leader, a Cantonese named Leung Quinn who sold bottled water for a living, decided to make common cause with Gandhi. As the *satyagraha* unfolded, the Chinese went in large numbers to jail, burnt certificates, made speeches, and threw parties for resisters.

The significance of the Indian/Chinese partnership in the Transvaal was recognized by two of Gandhi's closest friends in South Africa. In January 1908, just after Gandhi had been sentenced to jail for the first time, the Baptist priest Joseph Doke called his campaign "a heroic struggle for conscience's sake." He marveled that "a little handful of Indians and Chinese should have so imbibed the teaching of Christ in regard to the inherent nobility of man that they should become teachers of a mercenary age, while Christians stand by and smile or are silent as they suffer." Two days later, the Jewish radical Henry Polak told a "crowded and enthusiastic meeting of the Chinese residents" of Johannesburg that "the 15,000 Asiatics in the Transvaal were fighting a race fight which was of the utmost importance for the whole world, and that struggle was whether the Asiatic peoples were eternally to be kept in subjection or treated on terms of equality, regarded as fellow-men, as fellow human beings, to be treated as men to men, and not as men to slaves."[44]

Seeking to suppress the protests, the Transvaal government deported some activists to India, one of whom was the Chinese leader Leung Quinn. In a speech in Madras, he explained why he and his compatriots had joined Gandhi's struggle. The laws in the Transvaal, "erected by reason of racial antipathies and jealousies," were such that even Chinese ambassadors welcomed in the courts of Europe would not be allowed into the colony. It was, said Quinn, "not possible for us, who belong to an ancient and dignified civilisation to sit silent under such a flagrant insult." Judging that the "honour of Asia was at stake," the Chinese joined the Indian resisters. Quinn told his Indian audience that "the Transvaal colonists have foolishly thrown down the gauntlet to the whole of Asia. Neither they nor other Europeans should be surprised if Asiatics, as a body, take it up."[45]

Between 1906 and 1910, Indians and Chinese in the Transvaal jointly gave birth to the idea of *satyagraha*. Thirty years later, the American journalist Edgar Snow went to meet Mao Zedong at the end of the latter's Long March. Snow was coming from India, where he had met and come to admire Gandhi. After the Salt March, Gandhi had become a figure of great world appeal. Snow told Mao about Gandhian techniques of nonviolent resistance. Mao was dismissive, since, unlike the Chinese Communists, Gandhi had not undertaken an agrarian revolution by forcibly dispossessing large landlords.[46]

In the 1930s and 1940s, there were few takers for Gandhian methods in China. However, in China today there is an increasing interest in Gandhi and what he stood for. A prominent Chinese blogger has a portrait of Gandhi on his profile. Another admirer of Gandhi is the Nobel Laureate Liu Xiabao. A recent collection of his essays has many references to Mao, all critical, and several references to Gandhi, all appreciative. In January 2000, Liu Xiabao wrote:

> Compared to people in other nations that have lived under the dreary pall of communism, we resisters in China have not measured up very well. Even after so many years of tremendous tragedies, we still don't have a moral leader like Vaclav Havel. It seems ironic that in order to win the right of ordinary people to pursue self-interest, a society needs a moral giant to make a selfless sacrifice. In order to secure "passive freedom"—freedom from state oppression—there needs to be a will to do active resistance. History is not fated. The appearance of a single martyr can fundamentally turn the spirit of a nation and strengthen its moral fibre. Gandhi was such a figure.[47]

What Liu Xiabao did not know—but we may hope one day shall know—is that the "moral giant" and "martyr" who was Gandhi was supported, at an early and crucial stage of his political career, by Chinese activists such as Leung Quinn.

TWO

CHIANG KAI-SHEK
AND CHINESE MODERNIZATION

JAY TAYLOR

THERE IS or was something called "Mao Zedong Thought," but no one has heard of the "Thoughts of Chiang Kai-shek." Yet, there is a striking historical irony. Chiang was devastatingly defeated in China in 1949 and his relevance to China's future was seemingly thrown into the dustbin of history. However, Chiang's pragmatic but authoritarian Confucian vision of modernization is much more closely and immediately relevant to China today than the Chairman's grand view of governance. It was not and is not uniquely Chiang's vision. Wide variations of hard and soft authoritarianism as distinct from totalitarianism are of course still commonplace. Over time, Chiang led both versions. But despite the brutality of his early reign on Taiwan, he fostered the stability and profound social changes that created the conditions for a future economic takeoff and—unconsciously—a dynamic democracy.

When Chiang was born in 1887, China had been in a state of decline and national humiliation for more than forty years. In the second half of the nineteenth century, unlike Japan, China's Manchu dynasty and much of China reacted to the obviously superior power of the intruding West with obscurantism and desultory resistance. This fraught situation, however, was little felt in the small hamlet of Xikou in the mountainous Zhejiang province where Chiang was born. His father ran a small store selling salt and wines—a store the boy inherited when he was nine. He probably spent little time clerking as his mother wanted him to be a scholar. After private tutoring, she sent him off to boarding schools that taught the new modern curriculum, but also Confucian ethics and principles.

By the time Chiang was eighteen, he was already a revolutionary republican and modern Confucianist—and so, he cut off his pigtail, worn as a symbol of submission to the ruling Manchus.[1] He was influenced by the new generation of neo-Confucian teachers who supported dramatic reform and modernization but within China's cultural context (as had been done in Japan). The teachers understood that the trait of Confucian culture that is most relevant to the subject of modernization is its obvious compatibility with modern commerce, science, technology, and engineering, as well as with administration of large-scale organizations and projects. Education and knowledge were this culture's highest values next to a deep obligation to one's elders and ancestors as well as to future generations. Thus, there was a strong commitment to the future as well as to the past.

Chiang's Worldview

The worldviews of Chiang's generation were shaped fundamentally by China's near-absolute helplessness before foreign powers. The country's glaring backwardness and self-degradation were manifest in the horrors of the Boxer Rebellion. Japan's sinking of the Imperial Russian fleet in 1905, however, proved to these young Chinese that an Asian nation following the Western model of modernization could in two generations match the power of a major European country. Like many revolutionary-minded young Chinese, Chiang spent almost six years off and on in Japan and learned to speak and read Japanese.

About thirty-four thousand Chinese studied in Japan from 1900 to 1937. Many would occupy important positions during Chiang's career, including his most senior army general during the Great War with Japan, He Yingqin.[2] Chiang saw the Imperial Army and Navy's *bushido* code of honor unto death as the principal reason for Japan's stunning military successes. But he also understood the brutality and thirst for power that lay in the heart of the Samurai. Chiang foresaw that China was the ultimate target of Japan's increasingly powerful ultra-nationalists. But this did not change his love of Japanese culture nor his admiration for its heavily state-directed industrialization.

Japan was by no means his only foreign experience. In his twenties Chiang read widely, including translations of John Stuart Mill and

Jean-Jacques Rousseau. Beginning in 1917, he read a good deal about the Russian Revolution and for a while studied Russian. In 1923, sent to the Soviet Union by Sun Yat-sen, he spent three months there seeking Soviet military aid for the coming campaign against the northern warlords and also learning about post-revolutionary Russia. Thereafter, for three years (1924–1927), he dealt closely with Soviet advisers to the Kuomintang military forces, then with the Germans, who, after his purge of the Chinese Communist Party (CCP), replaced them.

Foreign diplomats usually found Chiang informed and articulate. Shortly after Pearl Harbor, he traveled to India and won Gandhi and Nehru's pledge that they would not try to weaken the Allied war effort in Asia.[3] His numerous foreign technical advisers were virtually all Westerners. While General Joseph Stilwell proved a constant enemy, General Claire Chennault was an ardent admirer. He established a mutually respectful and important correspondence with President Franklin Roosevelt, although both would at times be highly disappointed in the other. In Taiwan, his cabinet would contain more American PhD holders than the presidential cabinet in Washington. Chiang's American-educated wife, Soong Meiling, and her Western-educated family were of course key influences. And, as he promised his future mother-in-law, he became a devout Christian. Notably, Chiang's broad exposure to people and things not Chinese was quite in contrast to Mao's limited experience in this regard.

THE KUOMINTANG

A key influence on Chiang's concept of modernization in all its forms was, of course, that of the early Kuomintang (KMT), or Nationalist Party, and its leader, Sun Yat-sen, along with several of Sun's key followers, like Chen Qimei and Dai Litao. Chiang quickly adopted Dr. Sun's Three Doctrines of the People[4] as the blueprint for a modern China. The model included a constitutional, parliamentary government, a democratic-socialist political economy, and extensive redistribution of land. After the Xinhai Revolution in 1911, a Sun-led democratic government replaced the Qing dynasty. But once the ancien régime was overthrown, within a year the old military forces soon imposed a dictatorship dominated by various warlords. Sun and his followers, including Chiang Kai-shek, once again became revolutionaries and took up arms, battling on through another sixteen years of combat and intrigue. This long struggle and the debacle of the first Chinese experience with democracy stoked in Chiang's mind a deep skepticism that the new order could succeed without a powerful army that could defeat those of the old order and also without much more knowledge and experience of democracy among the general population. Sun also felt this skepticism and in 1918 formally declared that after the victory of the revolutionary forces would come an indefinite period of tutelage or military rule, which would dismantle the earlier regime while spreading knowledge and—at the lower levels—the practice of a controlled, representative democracy.

CHARACTER DEVELOPMENT

Chiang was recognized early on as a dedicated and brave officer. But even one of his few close companions told him he was "self-willed . . . to an almost incorrigible extent." Sun Yat-sen also warned the young officer about his "fiery temper" and "excessive hatred" of mediocrity. But he praised Chiang's "courage and sincerity" as well as his "knowledge of war."[5] Sun, no doubt, also admired the young officer's persistent loyalty—particularly on one difficult occasion when many others had deserted the leader—as well as his apparent honesty and lack of a military force or political faction of his own.

In 1921, when Chiang was a thirty-four-year-old veteran revolutionary, his mother died, and he went through a neo-Confucian reconversion. He drew up a new life plan, promising to adhere in practice and not just in theory to the ideals of neo-Confucianism—sincerity, rectitude, serenity, constancy, fidelity, and self-directed, determined action. It was now "evident" to him that he would be one of China's great men of destiny, devoting his life to the restoration of national unity, prosperity, and its unexcelled if not preeminent place in the world.[6] Chiang, however, also saw himself as a Confucian leader of virtue who espoused a culture of harmony, love, and humanity. But in keeping with another Confucian tradition and the universal reality of power as he saw it, he could be ruthless when he thought it necessary to assure stability and protect the nation and the people and, by "benign" extension, his own leading role. After Sun's death in 1925, the Nationalist government promulgated the "Provisional Constitution of the Political Tutelage Period," which, in 1931, authorized a "temporary" one-party system with supreme power vested indefinitely in the Central Executive Committee of the KMT. This turn to authoritarianism suited Chiang, who by nature possessed a command personality, not a democratic one.

CAREER DEVELOPMENT

Chiang became military leader of the KMT's revolutionary army in 1926. When, in 1927, the left wing of the Kuomintang, including the Communist Party, put out a secret order for his arrest or assassination, Chiang ordered the bloody purge of the Communists—carried out in Shanghai by the Green Gang. This action was the first demonstration of his willingness to use brutal means if necessary to attain what he saw as critical goals of the revolution—namely, protecting it from foreign control and the rise of an extremist party that was pledged to dismantling much of Chinese culture in the pursuit of a radical model of modernization. In 1917, Chiang wrote that Japan posed an increasing threat to China, and during a trip to Tokyo in 1927, Japanese Premier Tanaka Giichi warned him that the Revolutionary Army should not cross the Yangtze into North China and Japan's sphere. From that point on Chiang saw Japan as the gravest threat to China's sovereignty and even its civilization. A threat that surpassed that of the Chinese Communists.

In 1928, Chiang captured Beijing, and the Manchurian warlord Zhang Xueliang joined the KMT. For the first time since the fall of the Qing dynasty, 95 percent of traditional China at its peak was formally united under one flag. But in fact Chiang's full authority extended only to the Chinese-administered part of Shanghai, the city of Nanjing, and several neighboring provinces. Warlords also flying the KMT flag, a few Communist enclaves, the small foreign concessions, and the Japanese occupiers in Taiwan controlled all the rest.[7] In 1932, Chiang flirted with a domestic fascist approach but two years later abandoned it. Nevertheless, a book he wrote in the 1940s made clear his authoritarian outlook.[8] During the coming war with Japan, however, he would continue to have to cater carefully to powerful groups within the KMT, including its various military factions. Chiang was an earnest, cultural chauvinist who believed that for over five thousand years China's "wars with its neighbors" had "been only righteous war" waged in self-defense, and that the minorities in China were originally all members of the same race as the Han—the 92 percent ethnic core of the country. On the other hand, he strongly rejected the idea of "a superior civilization and superior race."[9]

The Nanjing Decade (1927–1937)

Chiang hoped to have a decade—or if possible, two—to try to close the huge gap with Japan in military and industrial power. Thus, his first step in 1927 was to arrange the German-led—largely Chinese-funded—program to modernize the country's army. But he knew that a modern army first of all required an ordinance industry, which in turn required a broad industrial base. In 1928, the KMT National Congress issued plans promoting the state role in developing basic industries.[10] Chiang also promised to achieve a strong, effective, and honest central government. Such a government was in his as well as China's interest. One promising factor was the role played by his Harvard-educated brother-in-law, T. V. Soong (Song Ziwen), who served from 1928 to 1933 as minister of finance and later also as governor of the new Central Bank of China. Soong was a fiscal conservative who advocated strict control of government credit, limitations on military spending, and promotion of a national economy. It was through his influence, as well as intimidation by the pro-Chiang Green Gang in Shanghai, that the bankers in the city bought up the securities of the new government in Nanjing. Chiang's other brother-in-law, H. H. Kung (Kong Xiangxi), who was the husband of Meiling's older sister, Ailing, and an economics graduate of Oberlin and Yale, served as minister of industry and commerce. In 1933, he took over T. V.'s portfolios when the latter resigned over what he saw as excessive military spending. Soong and Kung were premier examples of the dominant influence that Western-educated young Chinese would have by 1930 on the modernization process under Chiang Kai-shek. The two Chiang brothers-in-law were highly qualified, but also reflected the prominent role of nepotism in Chinese regimes, past and present.

Shortly after his call for a focus on development and reform, powerful diversions appeared in the form of new fierce fighting with both the Soviet-supported Communists and a coalition of warlords; a rebellion in Xinjiang; horrific flooding of the Yangtze; drought elsewhere; related famine; and of course the great world depression. Chinese exports declined by half. During this Nanjing Decade, Chiang also faced strong opposition not just from the Communists and the warlords, but also from several old KMT political figures, including his longtime political rival Wang Jingwei.[11] In 1931, Japan captured economically vital Manchuria, which accounted for four-fifths of

China's iron production, and soon followed up with a bloody attack on Shanghai. Then, over the next five years, the Imperial Army proceeded on a piecemeal occupation of much of North China.

During this time, Chiang hired several dozen Western experts on the economy. The American Arthur N. Young would become his leading financial adviser. Germany also played a special role, not only in modernization of the Chinese Army but also in the embryonic industrialization program, all in return for Chinese raw material.[12] During the Decade, foreigners were advising on national budgets, taxation, finance, central bank matters, and a range of other issues.[13] Because of the introduction of a modern, Western-oriented educational system early in the century, a large number of young Chinese-educated graduates were also available to the government and the civilian sector to serve as economists, administrators, and accountants, as well as engineers and other specialists. Under Chiang, the government undertook new measures to orient Chinese university education toward science and engineering.[14] Of those listed in China's *Who's Who* in 1939, 71 percent still had received their post-high school education abroad—36 percent in the United States and, by then, down to 15 percent in Japan.[15] An important British graduate was Qian Changzhao, a Cambridge-educated scholar of Fabian socialism, who developed a close personal relationship with Chiang. It was Qian who suggested the creation of a national defense-planning agency—later named the National Resources Commission—reporting directly to Chiang and coordinating every aspect of government activity related to industrial development.[16]

In the Nanjing Decade, the economy was largely run on free-market principles but with increasing government ownership of some important enterprises and even entire sectors. Reflecting Chiang's commitment to central planning, an ambitious three-year blueprint emerged in June 1936 with the help of German "experts."[17] Industrialization was the new government's primary goal, but this segment was a remarkably small element of the economy. With regard to the strength of their respective industrial bases, and thus their militaries, China and Japan differed dramatically. In 1937, not counting government arsenals, the number of factories in China with more than thirty workers was fewer than four thousand and they employed fewer than half a million workers.[18] In a population of about five hundred million, this was a tiny industrial sector. Before and after 1937, the Republic of China, despite some attempts, could produce no war planes that merited the name. By comparison, Japan's heavy industry would produce over seventy thousand highly competitive military aircraft from 1937 to 1945.[19]

Nevertheless, while in 1928 the state-owned ordinance industry could only manufacture "enough cartridges for one year's target practice and weaponry for one division," between 1932 and 1936, production accelerated to 325,942 rifles, 5,451,533 hand grenades, and 105,480 "bombs."[20] Much of this success was due to Chiang's appointment of a fellow Zhejiangese, the Harvard PhD Yu Dawei, as deputy director and then—after two years studying ordinance production in Germany—director of the Chinese Army's ordinance department. German advisers and technicians also cooperated in this successful effort, and new German arsenal machinery played an important role.[21] Equally important, German investment led to the procurement of equipment for construction of a critical iron and steel works.

In 1929, Chiang's government successfully pressed the relevant foreign powers to return the right to set its own tariff. It subsequently raised the rates, greatly increasing customs revenue. Also on the income side, the Nanjing Decade saw the consolidation of various tax offices and made central government taxes the same in every locality.[22] These moves further increased collection of taxes on tobacco, cotton yarn, and other products. The central administration, however, also ended the "liken" tax on cross-province trade and reduced taxes and levies on farmers by fifty million Chinese *fabi* (the Chinese currency).[23] By surrendering the land tax to the provinces, Nanjing relinquished its right to tax a segment of the economy that produced 65 percent of the national budget.[24] But the farmers' increased net income heightened the incentive to produce more—which they did—and this in turn spurred the economy in general. Recovering from the aforementioned wretched weather early in the 1930s, China produced the best grain crop in twenty years.[25] Among noneconomic advances during the Decade—but one that promised a more predictable economic environment—scholars and bureaucrats wrote new law codes and regulations that were increasingly applied across the country.[26]

For the first time in the history of China, the government issued "fairly complete and accurate" financial statements and developed an "effective system" of budgets and accounts. Despite the continuing world depression, by 1936, exports were growing, and the country's foreign exchange assets expanded to 67 percent of its note issue. A major reform led by H. H. Kung in which China abandoned the silver standard also succeeded, leading to the fundamental achievement of a standard, nationwide currency—a serious advance toward true unification.[27]

FINANCIAL CONTROLS

The Communists declared that Chiang's regime was a tool of the Shanghai bankers, but the KMT leader soon controlled the banks rather than the other way around.[28] During the world financial crisis of the early 1930s, he exploited the difficulties to achieve an effective government takeover of the major banks.[29] Issuing new government bonds, Kung purchased government majority control of these institutions and also of several other commercial enterprises. The Ministry of Industry also got into the investment business, specializing in joint enterprises involving two levels of government but selling half the stock to private citizens. For example, in May 1937, the ministry incorporated a new China Tea Corporation capitalized with half the investments coming from the ministry and six provincial governments and the other half sold to the public.[30]

An example of the scope of the government's growing involvement in and control of the private sector was the activity of T. V. Soong—by then director of the government-controlled Bank of China group (different from the government's Central Bank of China). Led by Soong, this bank in effect acted like a US Wall Street investment bank in the twenty-first century. In the late 1930s, the group was "making its own investments, managing projects for the National Resources Commission, organizing joint public-private ventures with other bankers, provincial governments, and national agencies, purchasing control of private enterprises, establishing marketing firms, and cooperating with foreign investors."[31]

In the last two years of the Nanjing Decade, exports were up, leading to a favorable balance of trade, a steady growth of government holdings in gold, silver, and foreign exchange, and an increase in local and even foreign investment. The budget was not balanced, but the printing presses did not finance the deficit. Bond sales to the public and Chinese banks served the purpose. There was no personal income or corporate taxes at the time, although big businesses and banks were still pressured—sometimes again by the Green Gang—to buy government bonds.

By 1937, the interest rate on Chinese government bonds was down to 8 percent. Impressively, despite staggering strains on the budget, the regime had settled about 80 percent of the principal amount due on outstanding foreign loans to previous Chinese governments— namely, the dynasty and the warlord regimes that followed.[32] By July 1937 "stabilization of the [government's] finances was within reach." A balanced budget was expected that year—a striking turn of events in a time of many troubles.[33] In its first year, the Three Year Plan's ten major projects had shown encouraging results, but then on July 7, 1937, Chinese and Japanese soldiers exchanged lethal fire at the Marco Polo Bridge not far from Beijing.[34] The Resistance War had begun. Most of the planned industrial projects were only partially completed, but still, as William Kirby wrote, "the achievements were dramatic."[35] Although a great deal of key equipment for the steel mill was seized by the Japanese before it could be delivered, the NRC was able to build eight smaller mills in Sichuan and Yunnan provinces.[36]

Chiang came away from Nanjing with the belief that the threat of inflation could be delayed much longer than the experts believed. For one thing, he concluded, money did not mean much in most rural Chinese households and therefore the question of inflationary spending operated in a quite different framework than in developed countries in terms of its national impact.[37] In any event, he thought, he had no choice but to pay for arguably critical military expenditures to save the nation from Communists, warlords, and Japanese. In his writings, Chiang emphasized the need for a peaceful and fair but extensive program of land reform, which "occupies a central place in the economic problems of China."[38] He even suggested that a "collective farm system might easily be adopted." But in the Nanjing Decade, the war years 1937–1945, and the post–World War II civil war period, he failed to address the issue. From 1936 on, however, he probably had sufficient popularity and authority in important areas of the country to have begun a peaceful and limited reform program. Such models of land reform could have been highly popular, although they might have been opposed by warlords and the rural gentry as well as by military officers and party officials who were often sons of the gentry. Consequently, Chiang thought that to act decisively on the land problem under the circumstances was inadvisable, as it was with regard to the problem of inflation and the bane of corruption. Instead, the government sought to improve rural conditions by expanding agricultural production through mechanization, pest control, better transport, and water conservation.[39]

Chiang's handling of dishonesty in the government and the military were similar to his non-action on the issue of land tenure. Before the 1926 Northern Expedition against the warlords began, he tried hard to persuade the corps commanders in the Revolutionary Army to agree to one central finance office for the armed forces. Such a central office would have handled all payroll and other money matters in the military. But the commanders refused even to think about it. As a result, payrolls padded with ghost soldiers and other forms of official thievery continued to plague the armed forces. Chiang chose not to resign over this issue but hoped to deal with it in the future. He finally did implement this fundamental and effective procedure on Taiwan.

As with the banks, during the Nanjing Decade, the government took over a good number of other business firms or established new ones that soon proceeded to grab the market from existing enterprises. All this probably reflected in good part the activity of persons with *guanxi,* or connections to Chiang's regime or one of the provincial leaders. In the hurly-burly of the times, some or even much commercial and financial activity probably involved minor or major bribery and influence peddling. Chiang, however, thought the problem was not serious. It was one of the three evils—inflation, corruption, and land tenure—that could be dealt with when control and stability had been assured.

The War Years

As soon as the long War of Resistance against Japan began, the Chinese, amid the chaos, showed their "Great Wall" organizational skills—and patriotism. Six hundred factories, over one hundred thousand tons of industrial equipment, tens of thousands of finished products and machine parts, and ten thousand skilled workers were moved from the seaboard to the interior.[40] Put in overall charge of this massive undertaking was an obscure official in the Ministry of Economic Affairs. But the ordnance chief with a Harvard doctorate in mathematics, Yu Dawei, directed the exodus of the most strategic segment—the ordnance industry, which included the unfinished steel mill and other related factories. Left behind, however, was probably a substantial majority of the rest of the country's small industrial base.

With remarkable speed, new sites were found in the free areas, and many of the factories called for in the Three Year Plan were built in whole or in part or reassembled, most especially those producing arms, ammunition, and input products. Most universities in the coastal provinces and thirty million refugees also decamped to the west and southwest. Incredibly, nineteen thousand crates of precious art from the Palace Museum, stored earlier in Nanjing for this contingency, were dragged on barges through the gorges of the Yangtze to Szechuan.[41] Meanwhile, the government reserves in gold, silver, and foreign currencies were also shipped hurriedly out of Shanghai just ahead of the Japanese.

After a year of fighting, Chiang's government still held three-quarters of the country and two-thirds of the population. But the expense of just holding the line militarily could threaten financial collapse. The only seaports open for trade to and from free China were foreign ones in Indochina, which were eventually closed. There was no road linking China to Lashio, the nearest Burmese railhead to the port of Rangoon in Burma. In 1938, Chiang duly ordered a mammoth and exceedingly difficult road project over the mountains from Kunming to Lashio, which—with little or no machinery—was completed in early 1939 by two hundred thousand Chinese workers and engineers.

As the battles raged up the Yangtze Valley, government spending exploded. With the loss of revenue sources and most forms of borrowing, the deficits had to be covered mostly by cranking up the printing presses that had also been drug through the gorges to Chongqing, the new provisional capital. Chiang Kai-shek's first non-military task was to manage a relatively slow decline in the value of the *fabi* so that the general population and the new producer economy—a combination of existing local businesses and exiled government and private enterprises—might have time to modify their respective finances, procurement, and other matters to somehow cope with inevitable high inflation.

The Neutrality Act, passed by an isolationist US Congress, forbade the American government from giving direct aid, loans, or credits to belligerents. But in the first year and a half of the fighting, the United States helped Chongqing achieve its immediate objective with purchases of Chinese government silver—of which there was a good supply—made at favorable prices for the Chinese side. These sales kept up the foreign reserves of the Central Bank of China, which on the market bought Chinese *fabi* with US dollars to sop up the excess currency generated by the heavy flood of unfinanced government spending.[42] This action purchased up to four hundred million Chinese *fabi* and resulted in holding the rise of consumer prices in the first eight months of the war to a mere 28 percent. By comparison, in Great Britain, during the first nine months of World War II, consumer prices would rise about the same—29 percent.

For the first four years of the Sino-Japanese War, prices increased about twenty times.[43] While considered runaway inflation in normal conditions, such a rate at this stage was far from hyperinflation and again it was probably not out of keeping with sharp price rises in some European countries during both world wars. Prices rose sharply again in 1942, by 235 percent, but then surprisingly leveled off for the next three years.[44] But a basic problem for the economy in general was a shrinking ability to import and export. The Japanese captured Rangoon in early 1942, and after that the only way consumer and producer goods could enter China was via the long haul through the deserts of Xinjiang and Central Asia. This route would be blocked when the June 1941 German juggernaut invaded the Soviet Union. After the United States entered the war, the US Air Transport Command occasionally flew strategic ores and other ordnance-production material into China over the Himalayan foothills or the "Hump."

Wartime Modernization, 1937–1945

An eminent scholar on the subject, Morris L. Bian, concludes that Chiang Kai-shek was "the driving force" in the broad institutional and bureaucratic rationalization that took place in the Nationalist government during the Nanjing Decade and the Sino-Japanese War.[45] Chiang, most scholars agree, "dominated the political scene . . . [and] sought to recruit the most gifted intellectuals, scientists, and technicians."[46] The development system and strategy emerged within the context of Chiang's development philosophy, which was compatible with a besieged, wartime environment in stressing state ownership, ordnance-related heavy industry, other aspects of national defense, and a central planned economy.[47] A new feature in this model was the strong emergence of the *danwei*, or "work unit" system in state enterprises. This practice provided housing, canteens, basic and preventive medical care, and schools for children of employees. Later, in the People's Republic of China, the *danwei* system would become universal and virtually a comprehensive cradle-to-grave arrangement.[48]

Chiang insisted that new infrastructure and industrial projects would continue along with the war effort. During the entire conflict, development projects would in fact consume about 10 percent of the budget. The National Resources Commission from Nanjing days continued to plan construction of new factories and, after completion of the projects, to manage them as well.[49] Chiang also created and chaired a Party and Government Work Evaluation Commission, which audited and evaluated government bodies.[50]

Between 1939 and 1941, a new Three Year Plan for Heavy Industrial Reconstruction resulted in a total cost of about fifty-eight million *yuan*, which came from government-owned banks as well as from profits from the export via Rangoon (until 1942) of mineral resources that the commission controlled.[51] This was a small capital investment for a land the size of "free China" but was key in providing power and inputs to the vital arms industry. For example, generation of electric power increased by almost seventy times from 1937 to 1945.[52] This was one key reason, as Morris Bian reveals, that during the Sino-Japanese War the Chinese arsenals were able to meet between 63 and 99 percent of the Army's need for bullets, rifles, light machine guns, mortars, grenade launchers, and grenades.[53] Meanwhile, Chiang made sure the government continued to exercise a dominant position in banking and in 1940 assumed the chairmanship of the administrative agency that controlled the four big government banks.[54]

THE PACIFIC WAR

Chiang and Stalin had been bitter enemies since 1927 when Chiang purged the CCP. But with the rise of Hitler, the Soviet leader had a vital interest in diverting Japanese expansionism into the vastness of China and, once the war began, in keeping Japan from overrunning China. Thus, when the war began the Soviet Union was the only source of foreign military aid for China. This aid arguably made the critical difference in the Chinese Army's ability to fight the Japanese to a stalemate in the first two years of the conflict. Thus, in June 1941, when Germany invaded the Soviet Union, Chiang, like Roosevelt and Churchill, saw a vital interest in Russia eventually defeating Japan's powerful European ally. But again, like Washington and London, he wanted the attack to go ahead thus ending the hyper-threatening Nazi-Soviet Pact. So, he waited until a day or so before the invasion to pass a warning to Stalin of Chinese intelligence predicting Barbarossa—the German invasion of the Soviet Union—was imminent.[55] But Chiang had long thought of the Christian, anticommunist United States as the most trustworthy as well as the most powerful of possible allies. His wife and in-laws no doubt encouraged this pro-American sentiment. Together with Winston Churchill, Chiang pressed Roosevelt to maintain the highly tough position on Japan's occupation of China that the president adopted in the summer of 1941. All this led to Pearl Harbor and the Sino-American alliance in the Pacific War.

Because of the Anglo-American "Europe-First" policy, however—until Germany's surrender in April 1945—China would receive less than 2 percent of America's total lend lease deliveries of $50 billion to all its allies. A US credit of $500 million given to China at the start of the war could not play any significant role in construction and development projects or purchase of weapons during the war. With virtually no imports, there were few new producer or consumer goods to absorb all the *fabi* being printed to pay for the war. Spending in this currency by US military units inside China during the Pacific War totaled about $400 million and increased the Chinese government's dollar holdings but again did little or nothing to help the economy during the war.[56] Instead, this spending further aggravated the fall of the *fabi*.[57] It was not until the last year of the war that US military aid began to provide significant material support to the Chinese land forces inside China itself. Up to that point, except for the vital role played by the US Army Fourteenth Air Force (formerly the Flying Tigers), American military involvement in and support for the war against Japan within China itself had been almost entirely indirect, dedicated largely to the campaigns in Burma.

During the Sino-US alliance, Chiang made in late 1944 one impressive new move on the anticorruption front. At his request, the US Army nominated one of its best logistics officers to become commanding general of the enormous and chaotic Chinese Army Supply Corps. Soon, the logistics of the Chinese Army were "beginning to work fairly well"—meaning with less leakage.[58] But overall, the American presence had a debilitating effect inside China. After the presumed Allied saviors arrived, probity among senior Chinese officials and officers began to unwind. Meanwhile, Chiang also continued to put off any sort of serious reform of land tenure in the countryside. Notably Mao did the same—probably in part to keep up the image of moderation.

Chiang's performance in the postwar period (1945–1949) on economic and financial/fiscal matters was an absolute failure. The root cause was his overwhelming concentration on defeating the Communists. Before V-J Day, Chiang had been pessimistic about the prospects of achieving a military victory over a Soviet-backed CCP army. With Soviet cooperation and the reception of Japanese surrendered weapons, the CCP quickly established a powerful and extensive presence in Manchuria. Chiang initially was undecided whether or not to fight for that economically important region. Washington at first encouraged him to make the effort. But by the spring of 1946, General George C. Marshall (on a mission to broker a Nationalist/Communist democratic government headed by Chiang) came to believe that the National Army ultimately could not defeat the Communists anywhere. The United States abruptly ended military aid and sales to the Republic—even for items paid for. But despite this virtual abandonment by the Americans, Chiang—after a string of military victories in 1946—believed he could win the war in eight to ten months.[59] The implication was that he could then right the ship of state and deal decisively with the three evils, two of which—inflation and corruption—were spiraling out of control. Given what is now known to have been extensive Soviet assistance in military arms and supplies to the CCP's Peoples Liberation Army, it was highly unlikely that Chiang could have prevailed militarily even if US military aid and sales had continued.[60] The unwinding of the regime's moral authority by rampant corruption and inflation accelerated this outcome.

Taiwan

Arriving on Taiwan in May 1949, Chiang believed that after two decades of constant turmoil and war on the mainland, his years on the island would be undisturbed by either internal or external conflict. He could then show the world—especially the mainland—how a Chinese society could "achieve true progress."[61] Chiang's rule on the mainland had been a quasi-soft to a semi-hard authoritarian one. On Taiwan, it was on the political front simply a hard brand of dictatorship.

Politically, the authoritarian Confucian model sought first of all to create "harmony" in the kingdom—meaning, when necessary, employing strong coercive measures to create peace, stability, and control so that the "benevolent" ruler could create a humane and productive life for the people. Back in February 1947, Chiang's infamous suppression of an unexpected uprising on Taiwan slew some twenty-eight thousand native Taiwanese. Not content with the intimidation wrought by this bloody event, after his 1949 retreat to the island, which had remained perfectly pacified, Chiang launched a new white terror "to kill the chicken to scare the monkey."[62] About four thousand more persons were slain—mostly native Taiwanese.

Chiang then replaced most of his vaunted "Whampoa clique" of loyal senior officers—whose ties to him went back to the 1920s—with younger officers. One hundred generals were told to resign. The Green Gang and certain civilian foes, including some one-time allies within the KMT, were kept or driven off the island. Thus, for the first time, Chiang would have not only peace and stability at home but also firm, dictatorial control of his government, party, and army.[63] In the 1960s, Chiang had police drag long-haired youth into the station for haircuts, but social life was essentially uncontrolled. Anti-regime views could be uttered privately to friends and family—or foreign diplomats. Political expression, dissent, and openness to outside opinion and events were far more advanced than on the mainland.

Economically, Chiang's "way" to modernization would continue to reflect his social/economic philosophy as it had further evolved during the war with Japan. Again, it would emphasize a state monopoly of basic infrastructure and state ownership of a wide range of enterprises but also included in some sectors an opening for competing private firms. Central planning in theory aimed at a socialist economy dominated by heavy industry. But in practice, during Chiang's first decade on Taiwan, the economy would be dominated by the effects of land reform, the creation of new light industries in the private sector, and the policy of import substitution. The plan would still give high priority to military needs but this time equal or even greater weight to control of inflation. The paternalistic *danwei* (unit or enterprise) system—suitable for the evacuated workers, staff, and families sent to Chongqing—was not, however, duplicated on Taiwan.

In late 1949, the PLA began massing thousands of junks and barges for a grand invasion of the island. Mainlander refugees and Chiang's armies had increased Taiwan's population by about 18 percent. The CIA and the US consulate in Taipei were predicting financial, economic, and political chaos. In early 1950, the CIA predicted that Taiwan would fall to the Communists in a matter of months. Washington continued its "hands off" policy toward the civil war. But as he had on the mainland, Chiang continued to believe events would somehow again turn the United States into an ally.

This time he had one of the two major conditions he had long thought he needed to address the three demons of corruption, inflation, and land tenure, and thus make it difficult for the United States not to send help. He had firm political control and as described below the beginning of serious land reform, but he also needed a growing, predictable economy. He quickly appointed more American-educated Chinese specialists to high positions on economic and financial matters as well as in foreign affairs and the military. He also drew upon the large numbers of China-educated economists and specialists in finance, management, engineering, and other professions who had fled to the island rather than risk their futures under the Communists. The huge haul of gold and foreign currency taken from the vaults in Shanghai provided another important resource, as did the unknown but no doubt significant amount of gold and US dollars that the mainlander refugees had brought with them.

The technocrats put together a tight budget, and Chiang ordered the military to adhere to spending limits. He even approved temporarily pegging the new Taiwan dollar to gold.[64] Despite the looming invasion threat, business began to pick up. *Deus* suspended above the stage in his *machina* now intervened on Taiwan's side. Mao agreed that Kim Il-sung could invade South Korea while the PLA would wait a year to "liberate" Taiwan. The Korean War began and the US Seventh Fleet moved into the Taiwan Strait to protect the island. Confidence soared. From 1953 to 1959, the national budget deficit on the island averaged only 6 to 7 percent of GDP.[65]

LAND REFORM

The third evil—the land tenure problem—was even more rapidly and successfully addressed than that of inflation. Before arriving on the island, Chiang gave the go-ahead to the first stage of a sweeping reform proposed by the Joint (that is, Sino-American) Commission on Rural Reconstruction (JCRR).[66] This phase was a reduction of land rent paid in kind by tenant farmers to a maximum of 37.5 percent. This was followed by government sale on credit at bargain prices of previously Japanese-owned arable land to poor or landless farmers. Demonstrating the extraordinary extent to which Japanization had taken place on the island, these sales involved an amazing 21 percent of all cultivable land.

The JCRR also provided fertilizer on credit to low-income farmers. The record harvest the next year (1950) was one immediate result of these steps, and the price of rice fell by 40 percent. Moreover, while Chiang remained a mostly reviled figure in the cities of Taiwan, in the countryside he found significant approval because of this program.[67] In January 1953, the government decreed that no landlord could own more than 7.2 acres of medium-grade rice land. As compensation, the landlords received government bonds as well as stocks in four government corporations, formerly belonging to the Japanese.[68] The biggest landlords bought up most of the stocks of other owners. The values escalated, and these former big landlords and their descendants became the first new business magnates on the island, playing a major role not only in expanding the old industrial sector but also in financing and managing the hundreds of new light industries that with government subsidies sprouted up in the 1950s.[69] The JCRR also funded hundreds of provincial medical centers that reduced diseases like tuberculosis, malaria, and trachoma by 80 percent.

A comprehensive land reform program was made easier on Taiwan than on the mainland for many reasons, including especially the enormous amount of land taken over from Japanese owners without compensation and the ability to compensate landlords with stocks in large, profitable, formerly Japanese corporations. Almost everyone affected was happy except the Japanese. In addition, the redistribution of land and corporate ownership did not affect KMT mainlander officers and officials or their relatives. Neither did they lose anything in the process.

CORRUPTION

To fight corruption, Chiang required banks to provide the tax authorities copies of all monthly account statements. Soon after arriving on the island, he closed the most important hangar door that on the mainland had let out a constant stream of phantom soldiers and other forms of corruption in the military. A new military staff would henceforth handle all payroll and other military expenditures. Moreover, after some hesitancy, Chiang approved and later praised strict audits by American government auditors of all military and government accounts, a measure that was perhaps unprecedented in international relations and that had a major effect.[70] The revived Political

Warfare Department in the military was another check on corruption in the services. Civilian internal security people also were watching for possible corruption. Even senior, longtime loyal supporters were secretly monitored. In other words, Chiang could afford politically to clamp down hard on graft, and he did. American journalists soon reported that foreigners, Taiwanese, and mainlanders all spoke of the comparative absence of "kleptocracy" on the island. Seven years later (1958), the *New York Times* reported that "corruption had been largely stamped out."[71] But Chiang did not punish General Zhou Zhirou when he discovered large-scale skimming of money by the armed forces chief of staff. In his diary, Chiang simply wrote that he would have "to help [the General] come to his senses and improve." For Chiang, the higher the level, the more loyalty gained in importance.[72]

Planning and Poverty

Central Planning was soon officially reborn. In the early 1950s, a new Stabilization Board prepared the first Four Year Plan for Attainment of Economic Independence. One of the board's early goals was to reverse the trade deficit by an import substitution strategy that involved tax subsidies and high tariffs. This led in some cases to unproductive investments, but as a result, over the next few years, hundreds of viable new factories appeared producing light manufactures, and new jobs were thus available for the surplus rural workforce.

On the mainland, poverty had seemed an endemic problem that might be redressed over several generations. On Taiwan, however, the process of land reform, combined with the pronounced and rapid shifting of the economy and population from rural to urban areas, fulfilled another goal—or dream—of modernization: namely, significantly reducing disparities of income. Taiwan inherited to some degree Japan's Confucian-influenced culture of corporate paternalism, a culture that presumably could endorse higher wages and benefits than simple supply and demand for labor would dictate. Moreover, under Chiang Kai-shek, all good-sized enterprises on Taiwan were required to have KMT party cells with worker representation, and this practice also probably contributed to the phenomenon.[73] In addition, the party conducted polls that sought to learn the needs and opinions of the people in order to develop "the mass line." This goal and its language reflected Chiang's intention to duplicate some of the popular mobilization strategies of the Communists.[74] Whatever the reasons,

Taiwan moved from an income inequality about equal to that of Mexico in 1953 to the lowest in the non-Communist world.[75]

A Basic Shift in Modernization Strategy

While some of the biggest former Japanese corporations on the island went to the landlords, infrastructure and an extraordinary number of industries and other corporate enterprises remained in government hands: telephone and telegraph, radio, railways, cigarettes, electric power, petroleum, coal mining, steel, and several others. These companies provided key revenue to the government and also executive-type jobs vacated by repatriated Japanese—jobs that went mostly to mainlander refugees. The Kuomintang received some enterprises as revenue earners for the party. Chiang's socialist instincts were hereby assuaged.

But despite his attachment to a state-dominated economy, Chiang was not opposed to private sector or foreign investment. During the Nanjing Decade the government had been open to the possibility of foreign investment, but the prospects for capitalization in this form disappeared during the twelve years of war with the Japanese and then the Communists. Likewise, in the first decade after Chiang set up his island regime, foreign investors were few. But once US support seemed assured, some overseas Chinese in Hong Kong and Southeast Asia began to make direct investments in light manufacturing on the island.

In the first fifteen years of Chiang's rule from Taiwan, US economic aid to the island was by far the largest foreign contributor to capitalization, accounting for 40 percent of all capital formation. Between 1951 and 1964, American aid to Taiwan would total $1.6 billion—the largest such program in the world on a per-capita basis. Infrastructure and education were key parts of this program. US military aid of approximately $1 billion also contributed indirectly to the economy, precluding additional spending out of the national budget for defense.

In 1958, the United States urged a more rapid economic expansion that would allow the aid program to end by 1965.[76] Chiang's technocrats drew up a nineteen-point plan that aimed to increase production, liberalize trade, encourage both savings and private investment, and hold military expenditures to the real 1960 level.[77] The effect was to move distinctly away from Chiang's old strategy of import substitution and the goal of self-reliance.

With his approval, the government passed a statute that offered foreign investors complete remittance of profits, a five-year tax holiday, 100 percent foreign ownership, and other concessions. An export-oriented economy was on the way. But Chiang also approved government manufacture and wide distribution of IUDs (intrauterine devices) for birth control. As often in the past, his pragmatism had overcome his and the KMT's ideological vision. A major part of the new strategy was the opening in 1965 of several Export Processing Zones—a development tactic Deng Xiaoping would enthusiastically embrace some thirty-five years later. This shift to a more modern Confucian modernization process was the beginning of Taiwan's true economic takeoff and the private sector's larger and larger share of the expanding GDP pie.

In the 1960s, education as a percentage of the government budget rose to about 13 percent, and compulsory schooling increased to nine years. Meanwhile, returning students who had gone to the United States in the tens of thousands for graduate degrees (the highest figure in the world) began to provide an increasing new pool of specialists in management, engineering, and scientific fields. Thus, by 1970, Taiwan presented a microcosm of a state-of-the-art Confucian economy-in-waiting—one that was ready to supply the entrepreneurial and engineering talent as well as the semi-skilled, skilled, and literate workforce for medium- to high-tech enterprises. In expanding numbers, Japanese and American investors flooded into the export zones. US aid had ended as scheduled, but Taiwan's annual growth rate continued to climb. Under Chiang Ching-kuo, it would be the fastest in the world—over 12 percent. The political consequence of rapid economic growth was an educated, informed, well-off urban population that increasingly demanded a rule-of-law open democracy.

As one gesture toward eventual representative democracy, the elder Chiang early on authorized the holding of direct local elections at the county, city, and provincial (that is, Taiwan) level. As a party, only the KMT was allowed to take part in these contests, but independents could and did run, and a number of spirited elections resulted. The independents, including some who became popular mayors and magistrates, eventually formed a quasi-party—known unofficially as the "non-party," which in 1988 finally became the legal Democratic Progressive Party. In 2000, it won the presidency of Taiwan, and then in 2008 returned the presidency to the KMT in another free election.

After the end of the Truman administration, Chiang would frighten Washington off any thought of détente with China by threats of Taiwan's collapse, a military coup against himself, or even—through planted leaks—his own possible defection to Mao Zedong. But secretly informed by Zhou Enlai in 1969 of Richard Nixon's intention eventually to recognize Beijing and break ties with Taiwan, Chiang realized he could not stop a boulder pushed off the cliff by both Nixon and the American Democratic Party.[78] Instead, he adopted a calm posture focused on retaining confidence in the stability of the island among the Taiwan people as well as foreign investors and importers. In addition, he sought to retain as much support as possible for Taiwan among the American people, especially military, media, and political leaders.

Finally, part of Chiang's reaction to the threat or likelihood of being cast into international limbo was further to accelerate the advance of Taiwan's economy into more capital-intensive sectors, while again raising the level of compulsory education and taking new steps to promote the rise of personal income among average Taiwanese households. Overall, this response to Nixon's "treachery" was a dramatic example of Chiang's willingness when dealing with a weak hand and facing seemingly inevitable defeat to reverse course, accept losses and humiliation, and take the least damaging approach possible while strongly adhering verbally to key principles. Still, as insurance against the seemingly inevitable loss of Taiwan's American security blanket, some years earlier he had ordered a speed-up in his secret effort to build a nuclear weapon.[79]

Commentary

Criticism has rightly been strongest regarding Chiang's acts of moral blindness or turpitude in his twenty-three years of leadership on the mainland. These acts include his bloody purge of the Communists in 1927; his blowing up the dikes of the Yellow River in 1938 to stop the Japanese advance across central China; his sacrifice of tens of thousands of Nationalist soldiers in North China in late 1948 and early 1949 so that he might have time to prepare his retreat to Taiwan; and the February 1947 massacre on Taiwan. On the island, this sort of ruthlessness was repeated in the 1950s "white terror." Some of these acts could be considered crimes against humanity. As suggested earlier, Chiang's rationale would be that in these cases, he acted to save the nation from the Communists, the Soviet Union, the Japanese, and—in the case of Taiwan—internal division.

On economic matters, valid censure focused on his failure on the mainland to deal satisfactorily with any of the "three evils." But the fact that once on Taiwan and enjoying stability and peace, his government was able to deal satisfactorily with all three suggests that the awful conditions—including the constant "dogs of war" that tormented all his years on the mainland—contributed importantly to these failures. On lesser matters, Arthur Young and others have blamed Chiang for not exhausting the possibilities of raising more revenue from the well-to-do during the Chongqing years. Again, on Taiwan, expansive state ownership of enterprises, the initial import-substitution strategy, and an antiforeign investment mind-set in the KMT conceivably held back the economy in the 1950s, but did succeed in achieving a relatively low inflation rate and respectable economic growth during those years.

If, as many believe, democratization is an important part of modernization, then Chiang certainly failed badly in this area. On the mainland, he ruled as an authoritarian leader, playing off against each other many powerful internal forces, but as emphasized during all his years on the island, he was a full dictator. Still, he always claimed that this "military tutelage" was temporary, which at least sometimes put his regime on the defensive and certainly did during his son's reign. He did establish the framework of a highly controlled and limited democracy at the local and provincial level, which in fact eventually lived up to its capability of evolution to higher forms.

Except for this extended postponement of democracy, Chiang believed China had to modernize in most ways—even promoting the IUD—and most of his specific economic goals and objectives were those of the more moderate, nationalist, often authoritarian Third World modernizers of the twentieth century. But on Taiwan, he not only succeeded more than most contemporaries in dealing with the three evils, he also led a stirring economic takeoff that brought about profound changes in the lives of one rural and economically backward Asian population. Urbanization, a civil, more cosmopolitan society, growing affluence and education, and spreading contact with the outside world set the stage for much more of the same under Chiang's son. The latter's achievements would transform Taiwan into one of the "miracle" East Asian economies of the 1980s but also provoke an ever-growing demand for full democratic reform. The result was the peaceful emergence of one of Asia's most vibrant, free democracies. Chiang would have thought this democracy too raucous, but he would no doubt be pleased that, as he had envisioned, the island has become a tantalizing example for the people of China.

THREE

HO CHI MINH

Nationalist Icon

SOPHIE QUINN-JUDGE

HO CHI MINH BECAME A SYMBOL of anticolonialism in the 1940s and 1950s. An object of fascination to his French and American enemies, who still argue about his bedrock political beliefs, he has suffered from his use as a national icon in Vietnam. His reputation as an austere and unpretentious patriot has been a source of the legitimacy enjoyed by the Vietnamese Communists after their 1975 victory. His embalmed body still lies in its tomb in Hanoi's Ba Dinh Square, despite his own wish to be cremated. But as the party itself grows more tarnished by corruption and abuse of power, Ho's saintly persona appears increasingly doubtful or irrelevant to young Vietnamese.

Both within and beyond Vietnam, there is still a widespread assumption that during his lifetime Ho Chi Minh maintained a Stalin-like grip on his Communist Party and the political life of the Democratic Republic of Vietnam (DRV). The use of Ho's name to represent the Vietnamese Communist leadership became common in the 1950s and has never really disappeared. The *Times* (London) employed this usage, for example, when they reported on December 7, 1950, that the Vietminh were preparing an attack on Hanoi to coincide with "the anniversary of Ho Chi Minh's original attack against the French forces in Indo-china." The documented ups-and-downs in his political fortunes, however, show that his more public symbolic role as a nationalist leader has been far more stable than his real political power turned out to be.

The strength of Ho's reputation is surprising, when one considers how little exposure he had on the international stage. Other than his travels around the Communist bloc and a 1958 visit to India, he had relatively little chance to be feted as a world leader. He did not attend the Geneva Conference or the Bandung Conference of Asian and African leaders in 1955; he never made it to New York for the UN General Assembly. His one chance to return to France as a head of state in the summer of 1946 was marred by the failure of the Fontainebleau negotiations. Yet even before Vietnam's victory at Dien Bien Phu in 1954, he was known around the world. A check of the *New York Times* archive, for example, reveals that from 1945 to 1954 he was mentioned in 742 articles. Perhaps what has cemented Ho's place in history is the fact that his battles with the French and the Americans epitomize the David and Goliath struggle for decolonization. His apparent weakness is part of his charisma, and it is also, perhaps, what provoked some of his Western opponents to see him as a fake or a cheat.

This essay focuses on the intense period of Asia's struggle to create independent nations, when Ho Chi Minh's transition from leader of Vietnam's post–World War II governing coalition to iconic figurehead occurred. The process begins with his first attempts to gain recognition for his new government and continues as this coalition is eclipsed by Vietnam's Communist Party. Communist influence would increase within Vietnam as the Viet Minh front grew more isolated from the West; within the DRV they consolidated their position once Communists came to power in China in 1949. The little-known irony is that this process weakened Ho's grip on power, as it strengthened his more hardline rivals within his own party.

For this essay, I rely on the year-by-year chronology of Ho's career published in Hanoi; memoirs, especially the two-volume journal of Le Van Hien, minister of finance of the Vietminh government from 1946 to 1951; and of course on the work of other historians who have covered this period. These are years full of controversy, so I should emphasize that at some future time I hope it will also be possible to consult the files of the Vietnamese Communist Party (under its various names: the Indochina Communist Party from 1930 to 1951, the Lao Dong or Workers' Party from 1951 to 1976, and the VCP thereafter). Until then, the published highly selective collections of party documents *(Van Kien Dang)* are available as a guide to party thinking, but by no means do these constitute a fully open window onto the party's activities or debates.[1]

Ho's Pre-Power Career

Ho Chi Minh grew up in a milieu of elite anticolonial activism, less privileged than someone like Nehru perhaps, yet with a wealth of overseas experience and social capital that he could call on when he came to power. He was the third child of a scholar from the north-central province of Nghe An, in the region that the French designated Annam, still under the nominal control of the emperors at Hue. In 1901 his father passed the highly competitive national exams to become a civil servant and initially work as a teacher in the Ministry of Rites. French reforms of the Vietnamese bureaucracy at the turn of the century had led to the emasculation of the emperor and his mandarins, however. By 1904, one member of his father's examination class, Phan Chau Trinh, had left his official post and started a campaign to reject the traditional examination system and to modernize education. Another traditional scholar, Phan Boi Chau, from the home district of Ho's family, started a movement (known as the "Eastern Travel" movement) to send young men to Japan to study in military schools. He selected a young member of the royal family to depart with him, to serve as the figurehead of an anti-French government in exile. These movements for change were referred to loosely as the "Modernization Movement." When a popular revolt against the head tax and the French-imposed corvée arose in 1908, the French blamed both the nonviolent advocacy of Phan Chau Trinh and the violent plots of Phan Boi Chau as the sources of the unrest. A roundup of modernizing scholars followed, with many sentenced to hard labor on the prison island of Poulo Condore (Con Son). Not long afterward, Ho's father lost his post in the bureaucracy, after being accused of causing the death of a prisoner in his custody. Although he disputed the charge, he was demoted several ranks and left the mandarinate to spend his remaining years in Cochinchina. His son lost his place in the elite National Studies Academy (Quoc Hoc) and by 1911 was on his way to France, having to work for his passage as a cabin boy.

The political views of his father are not certain, but we do know that by the time Ho left Saigon, he was already part of an anti-French network that coalesced in Paris before World War I. The leaders were the lawyer Phan Van Truong and the scholar Phan Chau Trinh, amnestied from hard labor thanks to the intervention of French Socialists. Thwarted in his attempt to enroll in a French training school for colonial administrators, Ho moved on to London, where he took odd jobs and studied English. He stayed in touch with Phan Chau Trinh in those years, writing the occasional postcard to keep him informed of his activities. Both Phans were imprisoned in Paris at the start of World War I, on suspicion of receiving aid for anti-French plots from the Germans. At the end of the war, Ho joined the "Group of Patriots" in Paris, where they lobbied the statesmen gathered for the Paris Peace Conference to grant more freedom to Vietnam, without success. The Vietnamese were not the only ones who failed to gain a hearing. The failure of Woodrow Wilson and other Western leaders to heed the demands for freedom of colonial nations is well known: it led to major protests in Korea and China and set many Asian patriots on their path to communism.

At this moment, Lenin entered the anti-imperialist fray with his "Theses on National and Colonial Questions," published in the French Socialist newspaper *l'Humanité* in the summer of 1920. With the establishment of the Communist International in 1919, Lenin had created an organization to support his call for Western workers to aid the anticolonial movements of the East. For Ho Chi Minh, the timing of Lenin's appeal sealed his fate. Having failed to gain support from the western democracies, he joined the French Socialist radicals who elected to join the Comintern at their Tours Congress in 1920. Ho soon became active in the colonial section of this faction. By the summer of 1923, increasingly pressured by the French police, he made his way to Moscow in the hope that he would receive support for his return to Asia, to establish a Vietnamese Communist movement. One of his missions in Moscow was to goad the Comintern's Western European members to pay more attention to the plight of the colonized.

Ho Chi Minh went to Moscow as a neophyte Communist, eager to share his new discovery with his Vietnamese compatriots; he left Moscow late in 1924 as a trainee and low-level worker for the Comintern. He had already experienced the contest for power following Lenin's death and Trotsky's fall from grace by the time he departed for Canton. In China he worked as a translator for the Russian news service, established along with the aid mission to support Sun Yat-sen's republic. As a rule, Ho stayed out of doctrinal squabbles in order to concentrate on his objective of obtaining aid for Vietnam's independence movement. He had laid the groundwork for a Vietnamese revolutionary youth movement and recruited an inner corps of Communist members among the expatriates, when he had to flee China in 1927, following Chiang Kai-shek's coup against the Communists within the United Front.

Although the Comintern would develop a more radical line by 1928, Ho Chi Minh always remained attached to the United Front policies of his first years in the Soviet orbit. He stuck to the traditional Marxist view that undeveloped colonial countries were not ripe for communism; he adopted Lenin's plan that they should carry out a two-stage revolution, first nationalist and antifeudal, then Socialist. He envisioned the Communists as acting within a larger nationalist coalition, without a precise timetable for the implementation of Socialist policies such as the confiscation of large landholdings.

On his return to Moscow in 1927, Ho received new instructions on forming a Communist party for Vietnam, as part of a broader nationalist movement. He was becalmed in Berlin for several months, where he waited for funding to arrive from Moscow. Finally, in April 1928, he received enough money for his return to Southeast Asia and his first six months of organizing. After that, he would have to rely on his own resources, he was informed. The Comintern's somewhat distant attitude seems to have arisen from the power struggle that was taking place, both within the Soviet Communist Party and the Comintern, over agricultural policy and the party leadership. Ho managed to remove himself from these debates of 1928–1929, while he traveled in northeast Siam to create more revolutionary groups among Vietnamese émigrés. He was called back to Hong Kong by his old comrades in the overseas leadership to settle a dispute among rival groups of Communists, each of whom wanted to take charge of party formation in Vietnam. Thus, in February 1930, Ho Chi Minh presided over a meeting in Hong Kong that has been designated the founding of the Vietnamese Communist Party, with a few representatives of the rival factions from inside Vietnam present to accept Ho's fiat.

Subsequent events show that Ho's party program was not accepted by all groups within Vietnam; nor was it endorsed by the Comintern of 1930, which was now following a policy known as the "New Course," advocating radical class struggle on the part of the worldwide proletariat. Ho Chi Minh and his contemporaries were criticized as too "petty bourgeois" and nationalist, without a proper understanding of the role of class struggle.[2] Younger trainees fresh from Moscow replaced him at the head of the renamed Indochina

Communist Party in October 1930, while he remained in Hong Kong with an unclear mandate, acting as a "post box" as he later complained.[3] In the meantime, those young Communists influenced by the Chinese Communist Party had begun to organize a movement of strikes and demonstrations, both in factories and among the overtaxed peasants, with the goal of creating autonomous local governments known as "soviets."[4] These actions led to the creation of the "Red Soviets of Nghe Tinh" during a roughly six-month period when the French-backed mandarins were driven out of several districts in Ho's home province and the province to the south, Ha Tinh. Although cruelly put down by the French in the summer of 1931, this revolt came to be a rallying cry for the Vietnamese revolutionaries, who had demonstrated their "proletarian" mettle and earned themselves full membership as a party of the Comintern. It ended with the imprisonment of most party leaders, including Ho himself, who was held by the British in Hong Kong until the winter of 1933. Ho had written reports of the uprisings to rally support overseas, but given his critiques of the uprising as "putchism," it is almost certain that he was not the originator or main architect of these events.

After Ho Chi Minh was released by the British in January 1933, thanks to the work of a legal team supplied by the "Red Help" branch of the Comintern, he made his way back to Moscow again. His Hong Kong arrest led to his exclusion from a political role in the Comintern. After a stint at the Lenin School, where cadres returned from overseas were put through an early form of thought reform, he became a low-level instructor within the Comintern and worked on the early stages of a thesis on agricultural policy. He was not given an audience by the Comintern leadership until he was finally assigned to return to southern China, to become once again a trainer of Vietnamese expatriates eager to fight the French. Soviet policies and advice to fraternal Communist parties were evolving, as the threat of German and Japanese Fascism became more immediate. Once again, United Front tactics gained acceptance, as Socialists and Communists became more aware of the dangers they faced from the Right. This meant that when Ho finally established contact with his party's central committee, he could re-create the sort of nationalist front that he had started to build in the 1920s. Although rival Vietnamese leaders in southern China did not always accept the Communists' offers of cooperation, the alliance that became known as the Vietminh was born out of this policy change.

The Vietminh took shape first in meetings on the Chinese side of the border, in 1941–1943. By the final years of the Pacific War, they were drawing in Socialists, nonparty students, and some members of the Vietnam Nationalist Party, the Viet Nam Quoc Dan Dang (VNQDD or Vietnamese Kuomintang) within Vietnam. The inner group of leaders was Communist, but it should be noted that some of the most radical Communists declined to join the Vietminh. This was the case in Cochinchina, where the urban Communists disapproved of the demotion of class struggle in favor of nationalist goals.[5] But it was the Vietminh Communists, especially Ho Chi Minh, Vo Nguyen Giap, and Pham Van Dong, who built up relations with allied intelligence figures in southern China and finally welcomed a team from the Office of Strategic Services (OSS, precursor of the CIA) in the summer of 1945 in their guerilla zone. The few weeks of training that the OSS Deer Team imparted to Ho's small force was not the only military training received by the Vietminh troops—some volunteers had joined military courses led by the Kuomintang on the Chinese side of the border. A few had been enrolled in the Huangpu (Whampoa) Military Academy in the 1920s. But the link with the Americans in 1945 gave Ho Chi Minh a special standing as part of the Allied team. At an August meeting in the highland village of Tan Trao, north of Hanoi, Ho was recognized as chairman of the provisional government.

Post–World War II

In the early years of the DRV, the new state's chances of survival seemed slim. Ho had inherited a famine in Tonkin, the northern part of Vietnam, and an economy disrupted by war and government instability. A Japanese coup against the French Vichy administration in March 1945 set the stage for a new phase of political activity by competing political groups, including those who had collaborated with the Japanese. Moreover, the Communist Party was rife with localized factions; some Communists, mainly in the southern "Vanguard" faction, did not recognize the Vietminh as their representatives. The August dropping of the atomic bombs on Hiroshima and Nagasaki brought the Japanese to surrender more quickly than Ho and his allies had been expecting, and the members of his provisional government were still in their guerilla base miles from Hanoi when the war ended. Taking control of various local Communist groups in Tonkin, not to mention Cochinchina, took several months after the official declaration of independence on September 2. In some districts the local people had already begun to confiscate the land of French landowners, even before the Japanese surrender. The new government would have to call a halt to spontaneous violence against Vietnamese landlords, too, before the Vietminh could establish the broad-based national coalition they envisioned.[6]

As we now know, when Ho Chi Minh declared independence before an enthusiastic crowd in Ba Dinh Square on September 2, 1945, he was in the vanguard of a momentous shift of power in Southeast Asia and the entire colonial world. But at the moment, the only sign of international support for his new government was the team of Americans from the OSS who had parachuted into the Viet-Bac resistance zone in June. They had moved into Hanoi, following Ho and the other Vietminh leaders from the highland village of Tan Trao, where they had been planning the future government. The brief declaration of independence that Ho read out borrowed its opening lines from the United States' Declaration and was a concise indictment of French misrule. If ever a people deserved support from the West, the Vietnamese seemed to be ideal candidates. Some of Ho's accusations were familiar from his earlier writings such as *The Trial of French Colonialism*—the inhumane laws, the artificial division of the country into three separate regions, the building of more prisons than schools, the monopoly on and forced use of alcohol and opium, the unjustifiable taxes, the robbing of rice fields, mines, forests, and other resources.[7] But since the start of the Japanese occupation in the autumn of 1940, the French had proven themselves doubly unworthy to rule over Vietnam: they had twice sold the country to the Japanese, the second time when they yielded to the Japanese coup in March 1945. The "double yoke" of French and Japanese rule did not ease the suffering of the peasants, and the famine that began at the end of 1944 caused two million deaths, in Ho's estimation. (Other sources claim one million.) "The truth is," he concluded, "that we have wrested our independence from the Japanese and not from the French."[8]

From the moment of the DRV's birth until the breakdown of the shaky French-Vietminh relationship in December 1946, Ho Chi Minh maneuvered to maintain broad support for his government. He was too realistic to believe that his small guerilla force could carry out a revolution by force of arms without international support. He announced the dissolution of the Communist Party in November 1945 to avoid the appearance that the DRV was dominated by the

Communists—and possibly to curb the power of rival groups who were less committed to the Vietminh United Front program than his own inner circle. Throughout 1946 and into 1947, this inner group within the DRV included Vo Nguyen Giap, Pham Van Dong, Pham Ngoc Thach, a French-trained medical doctor, and Hoang Huu Nam, whose real name was Phan Boi. (All of these men were from the central provinces of Vietnam, like Ho himself. Most, including Ho, had attended the prestigious Quoc Hoc School in Hue.) Hoang Huu Nam, a party veteran, had received a year of training as an intelligence specialist from MI6 in India, after he was freed from French imprisonment on the island of Réunion. In 1944 he and two other ex-prisoners had parachuted into the Viet Bac guerilla base near Cao Bang to join the Vietminh.

With the arrival of Chinese Kuomintang troops to take the Japanese surrender north of the 16th parallel, Ho was persuaded to make further concessions to their favored political party, the Vietnam Quoc Dan Dang (VNQDD). During the December preparations for a national election, he agreed to reserve 70 seats out of a total of 350 in the National Assembly for the opposition; 50 of these were promised to the VNQDD.[9] In the national unity government formed in March following the elections, in which most Vietminh candidates won large majorities, the foreign affairs portfolio went to VNQDD leader Nguyen Tuong Tam, while another pro-Chinese nationalist, Nguyen Hai Than, became the vice president. Another VNQDD leader, Vu Hong Khanh, was appointed deputy chairman of the Committee of Resistance headed by Vo Nguyen Giap.[10]

These concessions to the Chinese did not stop the French from pressing ahead with their own demands—demands that gradually eroded Vietnam's independence. The March "Preliminary Agreement" that Ho negotiated with Jean Sainteny followed a French-Chinese agreement on the withdrawal of the Chinese occupation forces. The French would now return to replace the Chinese as the guarantors of the Japanese surrender; at the same time they recognized the Republic of Vietnam as a free state with its own government, parliament, army, and finances within the French Union. The fifteen thousand French troops due to occupy the DRV were scheduled to depart in 1951. Regarding the Vietminh demand for the reunification of the three French-created territories of Vietnam (Tonkin, Annam, and Cochinchina), France agreed to abide by the results of a popular referendum.[11] This agreement, signed by Ho and Vu Hong Khanh in the presence of British, Chinese, and US observers, coincided with the return of the French navy to the waters off Haiphong.

The return of French forces to the north was a blow to all the nationalists but had the advantage of removing Chiang Kai-shek's rapacious army from Vietnamese territory by the end of September. Yet the actions of both of these parties as well as the VNQDD would gradually narrow the options remaining to Ho and his government. For one thing, the French high commissioner, Admiral Georges Thierry d'Argenlieu, less sympathetic to the Vietminh than many in the French government in 1946, pushed ahead with his own unilateral plans to establish an independent entity in the former colony of Cochinchina. He turned the May Dalat Conference, intended as a preliminary to negotiations planned for Paris in the summer, into an endorsement of a renewed Indochina Federation, with no clarity on the future referendum in Cochinchina. Ho Chi Minh was already well into his journey to France when he received this news. More ominously, d'Argenlieu also sent French forces into the central highlands to occupy the ethnic minority territory around Banmethuot, breaking the cease-fire agreed on in March.

On arrival in France, Ho Chi Minh had to wait in Biarritz while the French cobbled together a new government, following their June 2 elections. He was eventually received in Paris as a state guest, once the new government was formed on June 24. He left the negotiations at Fontainebleau to Pham Van Dong, while he concentrated on a campaign of public relations and diplomacy, in an effort to win sympathy for Vietnam's independence quest. Just as he had charmed the Americans in the OSS, he made a mainly positive impression on his interlocutors in France, from the wealthy Saigon student Truong Nhu Tang, to the director of protocol of the Ministry of Foreign Affairs, Jacques Dumaine. After lunching with Ho, the latter wrote, "One had to admire the mastery of this self-taught man, his language skills, his ability to make his views accessible, to make his intentions seem moderate, and his politeness."[12] One of the clearest accounts of his views at the time comes from the deposition of a Malagasy freedom fighter, Jacques Rabemananjara, at his own trial in Madagascar in 1947. Jacques and his brother Raymond had come to pay their respects to Ho at the Hotel Monceau. Ho advised them that

> There is salvation for all of us in the French Union, and you are lucky because it is an organization based upon the voluntary

participation of its members, so you will be spared a war. However, we must clearly define what the term French Union means. . . . The key is to rid the French Union of all imperialist ideas, and above all to bestow upon it this character of free consent, which makes it both new and original.[13]

The Fontainebleau negotiations in the end produced no breakthroughs, and the Vietnamese delegation returned home empty-handed. Ho remained in Paris a few days after their departure, preparing to sail home on the same French naval escort vessel that had brought the emperor Bao Dai to France in 1932. He agreed to sign a modus vivendi to keep channels for dialogue open. This document made more concessions to France on economic issues—for example, by accepting a customs and monetary union within Indochina; it agreed that conditions applying to French businesses would be the same as those fixed for Vietnamese enterprises. Most of the big questions, such as the promised referendum to decide the future of Cochinchina, were left open, to be worked out in negotiations due to continue in January 1947.[14] However, a clause agreeing to a cease-fire throughout Vietnam, to begin on October 30, could have been interpreted as a French recognition of Vietnamese rights and institutions south of the 16th parallel.[15]

Ho's voyage home lasted one month; he was returning to turmoil in domestic politics, as complaints about his concessions to France rose from a challenging array of forces: from the VNQDD and the formerly pro-Japanese Dai Viet party; and on the left from Trotskyists and the radicals in his own party. "The campaign of the extremists was essentially directed against Ho Chi Minh," writes Philippe Devillers, one of the earliest chroniclers of these events.[16]

The months that Ho had spent in France were marked by a rapidly shifting political and military reality that Ho's surrogate Vo Nguyen Giap had to confront. The government had carried out a reorganization of the police, even putting members of the VNQDD in nominal charge for a few months. But by June 1946, as the Chinese troops began to withdraw, Communist-controlled police units trained to investigate counterrevolutionaries were in place.[17] The threat appears to have been real: the Dai Viet were running a military training camp staffed by Japanese officers near the northern border in Lao Kai, while their underground leader remained in Hanoi;[18] members of the VNQDD had joined them in an anticommunist alliance, known as the Dai Viet Quoc Dan Dang. This group was planning terrorist actions against the French for July, which they hoped would incite the French to attack the Vietminh.[19] Giap oversaw the raid on VNQDD headquarters that led to a sustained campaign against their political infrastructure and military outposts.

Be that as it may, the VNQDD maintained enough force to threaten disruption on Ho's return from France. Yet Devillers reports that on his train journey from Haiphong to Hanoi, Ho Chi Minh was welcomed by throngs of peasants and youth. As Devillers sums up the situation, "For those who still doubted the popularity of Uncle Ho, the population's attachment to him and the effects of skilful propaganda, the spectacle of his return removed all illusions. The President was truly the symbol of the nation."[20]

In order to consolidate support for Ho's policy of accommodation with France, a new session of the National Assembly was called. But before the assembly met, the Vietminh carried out a second round-up of the opposition; in police raids between October 23 and 27, more than two hundred people were arrested and an unknown number assassinated, including the editorialist of the VNQDD newspaper, *Viet Nam*.[21] This was not a nonviolent or loyal opposition, however, and given the pro-Chinese parties' armed efforts to halt the return of French troops to the northern border, one can understand General Giap's predicament. His government was committed to implementing the French-Vietnamese peace agreement, which stipulated that these troops would remain for five years, on allied orders. If the Vietminh could not guarantee the peace, their governing authority would be seriously undermined.

On October 31, the National Assembly met and charged Ho with forming a new government. He took for himself the double role of president and minister of foreign affairs, with Hoang Minh Giam, one of the Fontainebleau negotiators, as secretary of state for foreign affairs. Vo Nguyen Giap took the Ministry of National Defense, while the old scholar Huynh Thuc Khang, a non-party cabinet member, remained minister of the interior, with Hoang Huu Nam as his under-secretary. Le Van Hien, a native of Danang, became the minister of the national economy, with Pham Van Dong as his under-secretary.[22] There were no more VNQDD leaders in this cabinet, as they had now fled to China. The other leaders of the Indochina Communist Party (ICP), whose power base had been the Northern Regional Committee (Truong Chinh, Tran Huy Lieu, Hoang Quoc Viet, Le Duc Tho, and

Nguyen Luong Bang), all remained in the shadows, with at this point no defined or open role in the life of the nation.

While Ho Chi Minh may have hoped that by temporizing he could maintain the peace until a more compatible French government came to power, the presence of the strong-willed Thierry d'Argenlieu as high commissioner in Indochina made this difficult. D'Argenlieu's interpretation of the modus vivendi of September denied the Vietminh role in Cochinchina and demanded that they be disarmed; those fighters from Tonkin would be sent back to the north.[23] The September agreement's stipulation regarding a customs union was also a point of discord, and control of customs would cause the November conflict in Haiphong that ended any pretense that a ceasefire was in effect. Ho Chi Minh had led the DRV down a path of conciliation with France that was destroying the nationalist coalition he had worked so hard to nurture during the first months of 1946. The collapse of French-Vietminh relations had clearly not been his wish, but the Vietminh had run out of options by December 1946. There was no longer a middle ground between surrender and all-out resistance. They had been readying their base in Tuyen Quang province, where they had prepared their takeover of power in August 1945, and by early 1947, Ho Chi Minh had returned to the maquis.

During the chaotic first days of the Resistance, in Ha Dong province west of Hanoi, Ho continued to send out peace feelers to the French. A January 10 broadcast from Vietminh radio, picked up in Saigon, listed Ho's peace terms: (1) immediate cessation of hostilities in Cochinchina, Annam and Tonkin; (2) immediate meetings of committees provided for in the September modus vivendi; (3) immediate resumption of the Fontainebleau negotiations for a definite settlement between France and Viet Nam.[24] In the January rains that made roads nearly impassable, the DRV government organized the withdrawal from Hanoi and methods of financing a resistance war. At the same time, Ho Chi Minh kept foreign relations in the forefront of his policy. In an open "Letter to the Leaders and People of All Nations" he underlined the effects that the "French-provoked war" in Viet Nam would have for "the great Asian family," as well as for world peace and the fate of the French Union.[25] On January 15 he prepared a letter to wish the Burmese people well on the occasion of their national day; in the same letter he thanked all of the Asian leaders who had expressed their sympathy with the people of Viet Nam.[26] Following what was then Indian Independence Day, January 26, Ho sent a cable of congratulations to Nehru, at that point still the deputy chairman of a provisional government. Ho asked to "share the joy of the Indian people" and expressed his confidence in the "victory of the Asian peoples in their struggle for freedom and progress."[27]

The French were not forgotten, as Ho fulfilled the protocol duties of a head of state. On January 18 he cabled congratulations to Vincent Auriol, who had just been elected French president. Once again Ho stated the DRV's goals, namely, independence within the French Union; he also suggested that the two leaders immediately reestablish peace.[28] Auriol, as a Socialist politician with Communists in his governing coalition, may have still inspired some hope that there would be a French change of heart.

Unfortunately for the Vietminh, in 1947 the Cold War in Asia began to develop more quickly than their own efforts to reopen talks with France. The political divide in Europe would begin to harden policies within the Communist bloc, while within the world of Southeast Asian Communism a quiet crisis erupted that increased fears of infiltrators and spies. This was the result of the unmasking of Loi Tek, the leader of the Malayan Communist Party and a British double agent, who disappeared on March 3 before a special party meeting to examine his case. He took with him the party's funds and detailed knowledge of its structures. After Loi Tek's departure, his successor, Chin Peng, shifted the moderate policies he had been implementing in cooperation with the British Military Administration in Malaya toward a phase of violent militancy.

Loi Tek's career almost certainly had larger repercussions in Southeast Asia. This was because he had come to Malaya around 1934 as a former member of the Indochinese CP, who let it be known that he had worked with Ho Chi Minh, studied in the Soviet Union (probably not true), and carried out delicate work for the international Communist movement in Shanghai. He was thought to be a Sino-Vietnamese or pure Vietnamese.[29] Moreover, as Singapore had served since the 1920s as the central communications point of what the Chinese referred to as the "Nanyang," or South Seas Committee of the Chinese CP, other Communists in the region may well have been in contact with Loi Tek. He probably possessed information about Communist affairs that went well beyond the confines of Malaya. His disappearance came at an awkward time for Ho Chi Minh. Ho's moderate policies and attempts to negotiate an internationally recognized role for the Vietminh might now be construed by his own party as traitorous, or influenced by the policies followed by Loi Tek. One of these policies was the official dissolution of the Indochinese Communist Party in 1945. Already by the autumn of 1946, the ICP general secretary, Truong Chinh, had openly criticized what he considered the overly conciliatory attitude taken toward enemies of the revolution, following the August 1945 seizure of power.[30] And by the spring of 1947 the Vietminh and its underground party had suffered a crushing reversal of fortune—they were on the run in both north and south, searching for allies in the international arena. Yet another potential embarrassment for Ho was the fact that one of his right-hand men, Hoang Huu Nam, had spent a year being trained in intelligence work by the British.[31]

A freak accident in late April deprived Ho Chi Minh of this valued member of his inner circle. In 1946 the chief Vietminh representative to the French-Vietnamese commission overseeing the cease-fire was Hoang Huu Nam. Nam was also running the Interior Ministry. As many of Ho's letters to Nam have been preserved, one can follow the record of Ho's communications with him in early 1947 almost on a daily basis. He was tasked with everything from investigating policemen charged with stealing from the people, to making a list of cadres who needed financial support, to organizing the camouflage for vchicles on the Tuyen Quang road. On April 25 Nam fell and drowned while bathing in the Tuyen Quang River. When Le Van Hien, a fellow minister, described the accident in his journal, he could not help but express scepticism as to its cause. "It was extraordinary," he wrote, as from the first day of his arrival in Tuyen Quang, Nam had not gone near the riverbank. He advised his colleagues to avoid bathing in the cold water of the river, for health reasons, while he washed only in warm water. Nam also knew how to swim and had taught his friends when they were in Madagascar. There was nothing particularly dangerous about the place where he was said to have fallen and been dragged down by the current. "Considering all these points, it was beyond imagining that Nam could drown," Hien wrote.[32]

Ho led a meeting of the government council at the end of April that selected two new leaders for the Ministry of the Interior: the old southern revolutionary and labor organizer, Ton Duc Thang, was made the minister, replacing the recently deceased Huynh Thuc Khang. The thirty-five-year-old Hanoi doctor, Tran Duy Hung, became his deputy to replace Hoang Huu Nam. Whether or not Nam's drowning was the result of foul play, this death was a severe loss for Ho Chi Minh. It removed someone with extensive revolutionary experience and links to the British, still a key power in Southeast Asia. In late April the government had been preparing for Ho Chi Minh's meeting with Paul Mus, the personal emissary of the new high commisioner, Emile Bollaert. (D'Argenlieu had at last been sent home to Paris.) At the planning meeting on April 30, Ho Chi Minh opened with a eulogy for his two dead compatriots, after which the remaining members proceeded to plan their strategy for the coming talks with Mus.

The Vietminh seemed to have little hope of sustaining their government. However, they understood the weakness of their opponent and had faith in the solidarity of their Asian neighbors, who at this moment were also negotiating and fighting to define their future status. In fact, Ho had just received a cable from the Indonesian prime minister, Sutan Sjahrir, congratulating him on the fighting spirit of the Vietnamese nation and expressing the hope that the two countries could exchange official representatives. The council approved this idea at their April 30 meeting and selected Pham Ngoc Thach as their emissary.[33] The Vietminh kept abreast of the problems France was facing in its colonies and knew that the French economy was in crisis. As Le Van Hien noted in his diary on May 13, almost all of the French colonies were rising up to demand their independence. After Vietnam had come Madagascar, then Algeria, Morocco, and Tahiti.

The meeting between Ho and Paul Mus on May 15 produced nothing but renewed determination on the part of the Vietminh. Mus was carrying the demand that the Vietminh disarm their soldiers and permit free circulation of the French troops throughout the country. Ho, in turn, told him that in the French Union there was no place for cowards; "if I accept these conditions I would be one."[34]

Paul Mus would be the last French diplomat to meet Ho until 1954. At this point in 1947, having been driven out of Hanoi and Saigon, without official diplomatic recognition from any Western power or the Soviet Union, the Vietminh had one main window to the outside world: the kingdom of Thailand, easily accessible via Laos or Cambodia, or by sea. They used Thailand as a logistics base and the capital, Bangkok, as a diplomatic contact point to meet US representatives and supportive members of the Thai elite. There, Ho's envoy Pham Ngoc Thach had several meetings with the US representative Abbot Low Moffat in the spring of 1947, but this produced no effort on the US part to intervene with the French or to extend the talks.[35] In September a Vietminh representative in Bangkok attended the founding meeting of a Southeast Asian League. This was a grouping that hoped to strengthen struggles for independence by giving them greater international legitimacy (and might be seen as a precursor of ASEAN). The meeting was attended by representatives from the three Indochinese countries, as well as Indonesia, Malaya, and the host Thailand. This grouping had a short life. A military coup in November returned the Japanese collaborator Phibun Songkhram to power, forcing Pridi Banomyang, a leader of the Free Thai who had worked with the British during the war, to flee to Singapore. For the Vietminh representative Tran Van Giau, who made no attempt to hide his Communist connections, Thailand was no longer a hospitable environment. By 1948 the Vietminh relied on secretive trips to Hong Kong via southern China for their contacts with the outside world. Their representative in Paris, Tran Ngoc Danh, remained there until late in 1948, but without official recognition.

As Ho Chi Minh's government became more isolated, a Vietnamese emissary made a secret visit to Switzerland in September 1947, where he turned up unannounced at the Soviet consulate in Bern. He had come to Switzerland disguised as a Chinese businessman, on the pretext of treating his tuberculosis. He is thought to have been Pham Ngoc Thach, extending his diplomatic mission from Asia to Europe. A doctor and specialist in treating tuberculosis, he was another revolutionary who enjoyed a high degree of trust with Ho, perhaps due to old family connections. The Russian summary of this meeting says that the envoy had been sent by the secretariat of the president of the DRV Council of Ministers, who was Ho Chi Minh.[36] The comments of this special envoy lead one to believe that the Vietnamese leader was expecting or already experiencing criticism for his decision to disband the ICP in November 1945. With the changing political climate in Europe and the Soviet Union, this action could be seen as dangerously reformist. The envoy explained to his Russian interlocutor that, although the Vietnamese CP was illegal, it was still the strongest party in the country. Of the Vietnamese government's eighteen members, the envoy said, twelve were Communists, although only three had announced their membership in the party. The ICP had been dissolved in 1945 to avoid arousing US opposition, he explained. The envoy also reported on the state of the Communist parties in Southeast Asia, a region with which he knew the Soviets had little recent contact. This report does not mention any discussion of the Malayan Communist leader, but one imagines that some references were made to his damage to the regional Communist networks. The envoy finally asked for permission to travel to Moscow, to report personally on the situation in Southeast Asia. This was apparently refused.

All of Ho's efforts in 1947 to break out of diplomatic isolation had failed to win outside support for the Vietminh. In January 1948, in the secure zone of Tuyen Quang province, a rugged landscape of limestone outcrops that made the DRV base relatively inaccessible to the French ground forces, a new round of meetings began. Le Van Hien describes being summoned to an expanded Central Committee meeting at short notice on January 13; he had to cover twenty-five kilometers on horseback to get to his destination in the dense jungle, meeting comrades such as Vo Nguyen Giap at different gathering points along the way. Bonfires kept the attendees warm at night. When the meeting opened, Ho proposed that they elect three honorary chairmen: Stalin, Mao, and Maurice Thorez, the French party leader. Then "a Central Committee member" unnamed in Hien's account, gave a report on the world situation, followed by an account of the Vietminh's situation versus the French.[37]

Le Van Hien does not describe the content of the Central Committee discussions, apparently due to regulations on party secrecy. In keeping with what would become the unbreakable pattern of DRV political life, the party meeting was followed by a meeting of the Government Council (Council of Ministers) at another location. Then, on January 28, Hien chaired a meeting of his own ministry, which around twenty cadres attended. His account of this gathering, in outline form, provides an idea of what the Central Committee must have discussed. It opened with a report on the world situation, titled "The Competition between the US and Russian Blocs, Growing Deeper by the Day." This analysis presented a stark division between the forces of reaction and progress, with the United States described as helping the German, Italian, and Japanese Fascists to reestablish themselves; aiding the reactionaries in China, Greece, the Netherlands, and France; and "pulling the Vatican into their camp."[38]

The Russian bloc included the Eastern European nations, the "struggling workers of Western Europe," and the "struggle movement" in Asia and Africa, as well as "the democratic movement in Greece." This was not a world of peaceful coexistence or neutralists, a world whose outlines would only become visible after Stalin's death and the end of the Korean War in 1953. Moreover, this was not a world where Ho Chi Minh's friends in the West could be of use. In his outline of "Common Tasks," Hien lists the need to eliminate any tendency to be "pro-American" or to fear America.[39] There would have been no need to make this point if such tendencies had not existed.

By February 1948 the question of class struggle was taking on new importance in the secure zone. General Giap, recently promoted to the top military rank of Dai Tuong, stopped for lunch at Le Van Hien's encampment on February 24, and afterward Hien and his subordinates sat talking until the early morning. The main topic of conversation was the "wrong understanding" that many people had of the intellectuals (of whom Giap was one), which was starting to alarm the more educated resistance fighters and had caused some to depart for the city. Hien felt that it was important to stress that a large number of intellectuals "had become conscious of the rights of the proletariat" and that many had accepted Communism.[40] Their loss would be a severe blow, as they had essential skills to offer the Resistance.

At the "Central Cadres" meeting in August 1948, the party revealed itself as an elite organization, with the highest level of secrecy and resources within the Resistance. The final approach to the meeting place required a strict inspection of letters of invitation, even for government ministers. This checkpoint was the prelude to a twelve-kilometer march along a slippery path, where the mud reached shin level in places. When the cadres finally arrived at their destination, they were surprised to find a group of "sumptuous" bamboo buildings, with a large meeting hall, dining space, a press room, separate sleeping quarters, and houses for relaxing and refreshment. The halls were illuminated by electric light at night. Le Van Hien praised the architecture and logistical skill that this undertaking demonstrated but criticized its excess and "showiness." "It was not appropriate for the times"; it "was not in line with our policy of shared thrift," he judged.[41] He must have been thinking of the tiny huts the local minority people lived in, where the cadres often slept during their travels.

Ho Chi Minh showed up on the second day of discussions, disrupting all the small group meetings of the morning session when he walked into the courtyard and was mobbed by the delegates. Where had he come from and why was he late? These facts remain unexplained. He had missed the report by Hoang Quoc Viet on popular mobilization and front work, as well as Le Duc Tho's account of the state of the Communist Party. David Marr tells us that at this meeting Tho suggested that the party assume authority over the National Guard and the civil administration, in other words, that it take over supreme governing power. Yet the final conference statement does not mention this change; it would not be until the 1951 Second Party Congress that the party would acquire this explicit leading role in national life.[42] Ho Chi Minh devoted his afternoon talk to a general criticism of the Resistance and to an explanation of "patriotic emulation" as a method of mobilization. Georges Boudarel claims that Ho was able to delay a campaign to start a party "study" or "rectification" movement in 1948; this too would begin in earnest after 1951.[43]

Following the Central Cadres meeting, Le Van Hien and Ho participated in a meeting of the Government Council, as well of the National Defense and General Staff Council, the latter body having been formed early in July 1948 by the merger of the Ministry of Defense and the General Staff, with General Giap taking the combined role of minister of defense and chief of general staff.[44] Ho Chi Minh had initiated this merger to improve the coordination between the two bodies and had at the same time created a "Supreme Council" to oversee the new structure. The Supreme Council consisted of well-known personalities and some of Ho's close associates: Phan Ke Toai, Phan Anh, Vo Nguyen Giap, Ta Quang Buu, and Le Van Hien. Ho became the chairman and assigned Hien to be his deputy, in charge of the council's daily affairs. Le Van Hien was already shouldering very heavy duties as the minister of finance, but he could not refuse this extra charge, as there was as of yet no one else to take it on. But it is notable that there were no members of the ICP's non-government leaders, not even Truong Chinh, on the Supreme Council.

This reorganization appears to reflect Ho's determination to retain control of the Resistance within the Vietminh government, at a time when the Communist Party was building its strength and beginning to assert its right to lead the government. By the end of 1947, the party had grown to over 70,000 members; by the Second Party Congress in February 1951, this number had reached 766,349. It was also creating a new political front known as the Lien Viet, ostensibly with a broader reach than the Vietminh. The Lien Viet would officially replace the Vietminh in March 1951, although the old name continued to be used for the members of the Resistance until 1954. At the Defense Council meeting held in August 1948, the members worked to define its governing regulations and to make explicit the limits of its power and duties. The entire Government Council also concentrated on this issue, deciding that the Defense Council would establish the national defense plan and implement it by taking direct control of the Resistance administrative committees. This could be seen as an effort to assert discipline and curtail random terrorism, perhaps a reaction to the assassinations being carried out in the South. Cadres from the South had informed Hien that there was continuing discord among the various groups in the southern Vietminh front.[45]

The National Defense and General Staff Council met as the second anniversary of the August Revolution was being celebrated in the free zone. But "the old man" could not participate in the celebrations. Ho had to disguise himself as he traveled to avoid random meetings with the local population, which might lead to his location being given away. He left the meeting on his own (with a few guards, presumably) and had to stick to deserted roads through the jungle.[46] This secrecy surrounding Ho seems to have magnified the effect of his appearances at political meetings.

The Aftermath of the Communist Victory in China

After the Chinese Communists' victory in October 1949, the Vietnamese Resistance moved into a new phase. In early 1950, Ho Chi Minh traveled to China and Moscow, where he was finally able to get a hearing from the Soviet leadership. While Stalin was guarded in his relations with Ho, the Chinese leadership vouched for him and defended his unorthodox step of dissolving the Indochinese Communist Party in 1945.[47] Still, Ho's position within the Communist world remained uncertain, in part because criticism from within his own party was making its way to Moscow.

One of his critics was the former DRV Paris representative, Tran Ngoc Danh, a veteran who had studied in Moscow and been arrested in the 1930s. In a January 1950 letter to Stalin's top ideologist, "Comrade Iudin," he complained that the ICP was dominated by its "nationalist, petty-bourgeois element," which "lacked faith in the revolutionary force of the proletariat. The decisive, divisive element," he wrote, "is the personality of Ho Chi Minh. To have an idea, it is enough to refer to the ICP's policy of 1941, that is to say at the moment when he entered the Indochinese political arena directly."[48] The report of a Hungarian diplomat in Moscow from May 1950 reinforces the idea that Ho's dissolution of the party was a point of contention. He attended a lecture on Vietnam by a Soviet expert, a Comrade Podkopaev, who defended Ho's action against the critics who considered it a serious "deviation." The lecturer also defended the Vietminh's delay of agrarian reform as necessary to garner the support of all social groups for the struggle against France.[49]

The Soviets had agreed to a division of labor with the Chinese party in 1949, which gave the Chinese the oversight of Asian Communist movements.[50] This placed Ho Chi Minh in the position of a poor relation with regard to the Chinese leadership, and over the next two years the views of Chinese advisers would become the guiding force within the Vietnamese revolution. This change may have saved the Resistance from extinction (Ho Chi Minh could hardly have turned down Chinese aid), but it also guaranteed a change in the balance of power between the Communist Party and the Vietminh government council. The change for the Ministry of Finance was an immediate improvement: the Chinese undertook the printing of bank notes, a challenging process for the Viet Minh that had been slowing down the financing of the war. Le Van Hien now received advice on taxation policies and impressed his Chinese counterpart with his knowledge of finance, most of it gained since 1946 by reading books in French.

The Second Party Congress in February 1951, held in Chiem Hoa district of Tuyen Quang province, was the event that made the role of the Communist Party open and official. The congress followed the successful autumn offensive, which had given the Vietminh a safe border with China. Until that point the liberated zone had been shrinking, with a smaller population and resource base than in 1947.[51] The party congress reflected the improving fortunes of the Resistance: before the opening, a Soviet film entitled *The Fall of Berlin* was shown; a band was on hand to play the "International." This time, in addition to the delegates selected by party committees, there were also delegates appointed by the Central Committee, some as full members and others as candidates. The special advisor from the Chinese CP, La Quy Ba, was present. Le Van Luong introduced the congress, reading out the lists of the Politburo, the Secretariat, the various committees, and even the seating arrangements. After a morning of formalities, Ho Chi Minh delivered the political report on the first afternoon, February 11. The changes he announced had been discussed in party meetings for close to a year, so there was little opposition. The chief novelty was that the Communist Party would now become an open organization, named the "Workers' Party of Vietnam." Le Van Hien praised Ho's skill at creating a "friendly, jolly" atmosphere with his joking and gesticulation.[52]

The following day Truong Chinh presented the report on the draft program of the Vietnamese Revolution. His presentation carried over to the following morning, after an afternoon break for small group discussions. During one of the rest breaks Ho went into the courtyard with a group of delegates to try out the latest dance steps "brought back from abroad by some of the comrades." But the light atmosphere turned tense on the second day, with most of the tension focused on the definition of "the three stages of the Vietnamese revolution." The other issue that exercised the delegates was "who does the party belong to?" Le Van Hien might have been expressing Ho's own thinking when he remarked that "there was a lot of theory, with no new contributions regarding the concrete work ahead. We had already wasted a month on this discussion, but the argument was continuing." He saw the debate as an expression of a "liberal" tendency *(tu do chu nghia)* on the part of some comrades.[53] It would be interesting to know how he felt about this five years later, when the "rectification" movement overseen by Le Van Luong was turning into a witch hunt, arresting Resistance veterans and destroying Vietminh committees in many districts of the North.[54]

The surfacing of the Workers' Party in 1951 was the moment when Ho Chi Minh was identified in the new party newspaper *Nhan Dan (The People)* as the "soul of the Vietnamese revolution and the Vietnamese resistance." At the same time, the party's general secretary, Truong Chinh, was now titled the "builder and commander" of the revolution in his *Nhan Dan* biography.[55] This was a bald statement of the rearrangement within the DRV's decision-making hierarchy. Ho's inspirational role is emphasized in Le Van Hien's account of the Second Congress. He describes how Ho rose to speak after General Giap's rousing speech on the successful growth of the Vietnamese army. Ho spoke to praise the people's army, saying that an important factor in their success was the teachings of Marx, Engels, Lenin, Stalin, and the "outstanding leader" Mao Zedong. "Ho spoke eloquently, but raised practical points that could be of concrete use for our work . . . this was the liveliest and most meaningful session at the Congress," Hien wrote. "At moments like this, one could see clearly Chairman Ho's talent for educating the cadres and raising the spirits of the people."[56] What was left unsaid by Le Van Hien is that Ho may have been asserting his party's independence of Mao Zedong and the CCP, by mentioning Mao as only one of the model Communists the Vietnamese would follow and as a political leader rather than a "thinker." An account of the 1951 congress written by a party leader with close ties to China, Hoang Van Hoan, emphasizes that by accepting "Mao Zedong Thought" as part of its guiding ideology, the Workers' Party was cementing a special friendship, creating a relationship as close as "lips and teeth."[57]

After 1951, Ho Chi Minh played his part as the wise elder, as Chinese advisers helped to set up the land reform campaign and gave their advice on training and tactics for the military campaigns ahead. The Americans became the financial backers of the French, as the French-Vietnam War was incorporated into the broader Cold War. Following the Dien Bien Phu victory in May 1954, Ho once again could play the peacemaker. In July 1954, as the outlines of the Geneva settlement were becoming clear, Ho was ready to offer concessions to the former colonial power. In his report to the party, he set out his thinking:

> Before, we confiscated the French imperialists' property; now that we have negotiated, we can follow a policy of equality and each side should receive some benefits; we can preserve the economic benefits and culture of the French in Indochina ... we have to make concessions to each other at an appropriate level ... before we failed to take into account the French Union; now we have accepted to discuss participation in this Union [Lien Hiep Phap] in an equal and voluntary manner. ... Before, we called for the extermination, the wiping out of the puppet forces in order to unify; now we are using the policy of generosity [khoan dai], the method of a nationwide general election, to arrive at national unity.[58]

This policy promising reconciliation with both external and internal foes was elaborated with the support of his Communist allies to counteract the American threat on the horizon. It was stillborn, as the US backing for a separate state in the South and their refusal to recognize the nationwide election set for 1956 meant that the French never had a chance to implement the political provisions agreed upon at Geneva. The preservation of a divided Vietnam, thanks to US power, delayed the advent of peace and reunification for another twenty-one years after Geneva.

The Workers' Party also played a part in the polarization between North and South, launching a land reform campaign that moved into a militant phase in 1955 and escaped the government's efforts to constrain excessive measures such as "struggle meetings."[59] Ho Chi Minh's hopes to create a more open and generous government were undermined by the growing radicalism of the land reform committees and the widening search for enemies among the local Vietminh Resistance leaders. This period of excess is the blackest in Hanoi's history, yet Ho may not have had a long enough reach to stop the persecution of innocent landowners or the execution of approximately seven thousand people, judged by people's tribunals to be cruel landlords or enemies of the people. In October 1956, possibly in reaction to Khrushchev's denunciation of Stalin, the party finally removed the leaders deemed responsible from their posts, including Truong Chinh, who was forced to step down as general secretary of the Workers' Party, to be replaced by Ho Chi Minh. Ho Viet Thang, head of the Central Land Reform Committee, was removed from the Central Committee, and Le Van Luong, who had led the "Rectification" of party organizations, lost his place in the Politburo Secretariat and had to yield his role as chairman of the party's Central Organization Committee. General Vo Nguyen Giap made an open criticism of the errors committed by the land reform committees, in a speech of apology printed in *Nhan Dan* on November 1, 1956. Many cases were reexamined, and a large number of people had their classification as landlords changed and regained their civic rights. Ho apparently gained more political clout at this moment, as in October 1956, both he and General Giap were added to the Central Committee Secretariat, the body that runs the party's daily affairs.[60] But in 1960 both of them would be removed from this body.

De-Stalinization created a political thaw in the DRV, but it was an all too brief moment. By 1958 intellectuals were having to accept the restraint of party control in all their works; cooperativization became the new movement shaping the life of the peasants. Once again war loomed on the horizon, as the southern Communists decided to fight back against the repression of Ngo Dinh Diem. Ho Chi Minh becomes a more cardboard character in these years, although he continued to attend gatherings of world Communist leaders until 1960. In

1957 he toured Eastern Europe and signed a joint communiqué with Tito, calling for peaceful coexistence of all countries, "irrespective of existing differences in their social and political systems."[61] He remained temperamentally committed to a peaceful, political solution of Vietnam's division, in agreement with his Communist patrons. By 1963, however, as the Sino-Soviet split was growing more intense, a Workers' Party plenum at the end of the year demonstrated that his political influence had waned. Ho ended up on the losing side of an argument about Soviet and Chinese policies and on Christmas Day 1963 announced to the Soviet ambassador that he was giving up his day-to-day political responsibilities.[62] Policies of "peaceful co-existence," once promoted by both the Chinese and Russians, were now denounced as part of a Soviet "revisionist" deviation. Among Vietnamese party members, led by Le Duc Tho, there was now talk of "Ho Chi Minh's two mistakes." This theory maintained that Ho's two fatal errors were, first, to have compromised with the French in 1945, and second, to have compromised in 1954 at the Geneva Conference, to permit the partition of the country. As Martin Grossheim explains, "Besides undermining Ho Chi Minh's reputation, this theory also aimed at his closest comrades in arms during the anti-French resistance who now mostly opposed the shift toward Beijing." Above all, this meant Vo Nguyen Giap, who was considered to have a close relationship with the Soviet military.[63]

The overthrow of Nikita Khrushchev in October 1964 heralded an improvement in Soviet-Vietnamese relations, as the Russians began to match the US escalation of their war in Vietnam with shipments of heavy weapons to Hanoi, along with military advisors and trainers. The precise constellation of the leadership in the war years remains murky, with Le Duan, made party first secretary in 1960, sharing power with the leaders who had come to prominence in the early 1950s. Truong Chinh returned to a position of influence as a theoretician quite rapidly, as head of the party's Institute of Marxism-Leninism from 1956 to 1957, and again from 1961 to 1966. He was also the chairman of the National Assembly's Standing Committee. Le Duc Tho is seen by many observers as the most powerful member of the Politburo by the mid-1960s, thanks to his post as the head of the all-important Party Organization Commission and also as a theoretician, serving as director of the Institute of Marxism-Leninism in 1958–1960, and again in 1967–1968, when he led a purge of the Party.[64] By 1967 Ho Chi Minh himself was rarely seen in public.

Ho Chi Minh in these years became a more remote but idealized figure. His power to heal factional divisions in the early days of the Communist movement was reverently described in the party's historical journal in 1964, just as the Communists were trying to close their ranks to confront the American threat.[65] As everyone's Uncle Ho, he had to be a symbol of devotion to the nation, to make an example of his simple life and exhort the people to work harder. If, as some documentary evidence indicates, he had been married once or twice, that became forbidden knowledge. Although no longer the chief party leader, Ho had become the national saint, even before his death and embalming in 1969.

Conclusion

The Cold War forced former Asian colonies to align themselves with the United States or to lean toward one of the Communist powers for protection. The tragedy of Ho Chi Minh was that his efforts to make peace with France came to be viewed by his own party as mistakes. In the end he was forced to seek alliances with China and the Soviet Union that in many ways curtailed Vietnam's independence. But the only other option before him appeared to be national extinction. Ho was no more a denier of universal values than Nehru had been. In his early internationalism, he embraced both French and American values of equality and freedom.[66] Yet because he never had the chance to serve as a peacetime leader, he was deprived of the opportunity to prove his sincerity or provide a model of "open nationalism" for the new century. That he also had faith in the promise of Marxism to create an egalitarian, just society cannot be doubted. But his desire to unify all Vietnamese patriots into one movement was far stronger than his attachment to Communist dogma; he preferred peaceful political transformation to revolutionary violence, in strong contrast to Mao Zedong's outlook.

Since 1992 Ho Chi Minh has been promoted to become Vietnam's leading ideologue, the originator of the latest national ideology: "Ho Chi Minh Thought." While Marxism-Leninism is no longer the guiding ideology of Vietnamese economic life, the VCP, like the Chinese Communist Party, still clings to its identity as a Marxist organization. But at the same time, "Ho Chi Minh Thought" has become a key element in the party's efforts to justify its dominant role. Since the collapse of the Socialist Bloc, Ho's every action and utterance have been scrutinized in order to establish the fundamentals of this new ideology, in spite of the fact that Ho himself never presumed to be an ideologist. Party experts write booklets on Ho's attitude to every aspect of life—from women and children to literature and military strategy. Unfortunately, this approach leads to an amorphous body of ideas, as it does not discriminate between scripted political speeches and Ho's interventions at closed meetings. The Vietnamese Communist Party's claims to legitimacy continue to rely on their Ho Chi Minh lineage. In future the party leadership may realize that in order to restore Ho's relevance for a new generation, they will have to open up a more honest examination of his political career and the battles that he waged.

FOUR

MAO ZEDONG
AND CHARISMATIC MAOISM

RANA MITTER

MAO HAS THE DISTINCTION, along with Gandhi, of being one of the very small number of non-European political leaders to achieve brand-name status in the twentieth century. Mao has been used as an endorsement for a wide variety of movements, from the radical Naxalite movement in India, to the Khmer Rouge genocide in Cambodia, to the anti-establishment protests of Paris students in the 1960s. The grand narrative of Chinese modernization through radicalization of the peasantry and the establishment of a Chinese state that, in Mao's words, "stood up" has been a staple of liberation discourse in the global south for decades, even at a time when the Maoist economy has long since disappeared under a corporatist/capitalist mixture in China itself.

So, does Mao have relevance for China today, and more broadly, for a world in which Asia's rise has a new geopolitical significance? This essay will argue that he does. I explore these issues with an analysis of the continuities, as well as the changes, in Mao's thought, and the use of his thought, at the two extremes of his life—his early years when he was developing as a thinker, and the extremism that marked the Cultural Revolution of the 1960s. Mao had many facets, and it is some of his least well-remembered ideas that explain his continuing influence, both explicit and implicit, within China and outside it. Mao started out as a young man worried about China's fate and became an early advocate of radical and often violent solutions to its problems. Throughout his life, he remained devoted to such solutions, culminating in the Cultural Revolution of 1966–1976.

Yet Mao did not only unleash the massive destruction and suffering with which he has become associated. His obsession with the idea of liberation of the self provides powerful, and sometimes surprising, insights into events as far apart as China's fight against imperialism in the early twentieth century to the creation of a dynamic economy in the neoliberal world of the early twenty-first.

The Early Mao and His Role

When Mao was born in 1893, he appeared in a China whose most basic assumptions had been under assault for decades. For millennia, Chinese society had, broadly speaking, operated on the basis of norms that emphasized certain qualities—social stability, maintenance of hierarchies—that inevitably concentrated power in particular hands (rulers, husbands, men). In the troubled era when the last dynasty fell and the uncertain Republic came into being, political strategies aimed to destroy the system of power relations that a "traditional" Chinese culture had maintained and to replace it with one inflected by what was perceived as "modernity." Surface dazzle and triumphalistic language from the modernizers, particularly the most antitraditional, should not conceal the reality that a premodern set of categories and values continued to reproduce structures of dominance at odds with the modernizing elites. Modernizers in early twentieth-century China were in office, but it is harder to state unequivocally that they were in control.

The cultural moment known as the "May Fourth era," roughly from the mid-1910s to the early 1930s, was a particularly important one for understanding how Mao would be shaped. For Mao was a child of his time, the very late Qing dynasty and the early Republican era. When he was eighteen, the 1911 revolution overthrew the two-thousand-year-old imperial system, ushering in a period of Republican government marked by instability and militarism on the one hand, but a significant flowering of different models of political thought on the other. Politically weak governments allowed the spread of the innovative and often iconoclastic current of thought known as the "May Fourth" or "New Culture" period. The term "May Fourth" comes from the student demonstrations in Beijing on May 4, 1919, protesting against the unjust treatment of China at the Paris Peace Conference; yet the "May Fourth" or "New Culture" period refers to a much wider sense of national crisis linked to cultural opportunity felt among many Chinese from the mid-1910s to the mid- to late 1920s. The idea of "newness" shaped political discussion of the time and involved a rejection of the Confucian norm that age and precedent were preferable tools for dealing with crisis.

In fact, the whole of the late Qing and early Republican period was marked by a political culture where "the new" and "renewal" were an integral part of political discourse. A prominent example was the development by the late Qing political activist Liang Qichao of the idea of the "new citizen." The "new citizen" was contingent on the idea of a "new people" *(xinmin),* and the definitions of the terms showed the debate between ideas of nationalism that were racially or civically defined.[1] From the mid-nineteenth century, Yan Fu and other thinkers brought powerful ideas of evolution and social Darwinism to a troubled Chinese political class. Yet the May Fourth era took these ideas even further. In the interwar era, the internationalist climate, rise of nationalism, and a new global obsession with youth and renewal helped to give wider context to China's attempt at intellectual and political regeneration.[2] "The Chinese Enlightenment" or "Chinese Renaissance," as it was later termed, was influenced by a variety of Western concepts both rational and romanticist, as well as by figures such as Gandhi and Attaturk, who seemed to provide a non-European way forward against imperialism.[3]

What brought the May Fourth movement together, however disparate its elements, was the conviction that Confucian culture needed to be changed as China coped with modernity. For the most iconoclastic of that generation (such as Mao and the writer Lu Xun), this meant the complete destruction of the old Confucian norms, while the more moderate (such as the journalist Zou Taofen) argued for the adaptation of Confucian values in a hybrid modern form. A common thread among them was the conviction that the old ethical core of the Confucian value system had disappeared and that something new had to take its place.

For the moderates, who included Sun Yat-sen, this ethical gap meant that they had to find a way of reconciling Confucian assumptions with modernity. For radicals such as Mao, however, the ending of the old world provided an exhilarating opportunity to recast ethics in a mold completely in opposition to the old norms; shaped by winds from Europe and the West, youth, violence, and dynamism became part of an anti-Confucian message of intoxicating potency. Mao became part of the group that would eventually seek a political solution in Marxism; among his fellow-founders of the Chinese Communist Party (CCP) were Chen Duxiu, Li Dazhao, and Cai Hesen. But no May Fourth experience was felt in isolation: though Mao was a Marxist, he was also a romanticist, and that brush with the exhilaration of irrationality as part of modernity shaped his life from then on, all the way to the Cultural Revolution. Pragmatic Mao (and Maoism) and charismatic Mao (and Maoism) were not at war with one another. They were merely different facets of the May Fourth experience.

The most radical antitraditionalism was fuelled by a reaction against "Confucianism." The term was used as a catch-all device to define a variety of different ideas that angered radical thinkers, notably Chen Duxiu, one of the founder members of the Chinese Communist Party in 1921. For them, the Confucian obsession with reverence for age, precedent, and order in society was the major problem with the old culture that was holding China back; the most radical manifestations of modernity, exemplified by a fixation with youth, dynamism, and a Dionysiac creative destruction, were a necessary corrective to China's crisis. One of the most emblematic texts is Chen Duxiu's 1915 "Call to Youth," in which he declared "Youth is like early spring, like the rising sun. . . . It is the most valuable period of life."[4] This was a distinct departure from the Confucian assumptions of the past. The social Darwinist tone of this work is no accident. The influence of ideas of evolution and zero-sum assumptions about racial struggle had heavily shaped Chinese modernizing discourse from the late nineteenth century onward.[5]

In its opposition to Confucianism, the language of the radicals took several paths. In 1918, Lu Xun published his Gogolesque "Diary of a Madman," appropriately enough in Chen Duxiu's New Youth magazine. The story purports to be the ravings of a man temporarily insane, who claims to have discovered that all the people around him are in fact cannibals. In case the meaning of the metaphor is not made clear enough to the reader, the narrator claims to have looked up the reasons for cannibalism in a history book, only to find that every page is covered in scribblings reading, "Confucian virtue and morality," and that reading between the lines, the words "eat people" appear over and over again.[6]

Mao Zedong's earliest writings show a less metaphorical approach to breaking down Confucian norms that he felt were socialized into the Chinese people. In Confucian norms, physical exercise and military prowess had not traditionally been considered worthy attributes of a "gentleman" or "person of integrity." Mao's earliest writings, which predate his turn to Marxism, follow the social Darwinist assumptions that shaped so much of late Qing and early Republican thinking. His essay "On Physical Exercise" (1917) is one of the clearest examples of how the connection between the individual body and the body politic was made in Mao's mind, as it was for other radicals of the era. He declared:

> The superior man's [i.e., the gentleman's] deportment is cultivated and agreeable, but one cannot say this about exercise. Exercise should be savage and rude. To charge on horseback, amid the clash of arms, and to be ever victorious; to shake the mountains by one's cries, and the colors of the sky by one's roars of anger . . . all this is savage and rude and has nothing to do with delicacy.[7]

Mao ended the essay by giving a practical schema for implementation of this bodily (and thereby political) transformation:

> I have . . . put together a system of my own, from which I have derived considerable benefit. . . . Make fists, alternately extend the arms to the front and retract them. Left and right, successively, three times. . . . Unclench the fists. Alternately raise the whole body to a standing position, and return to a squatting position. While squatting, the heels should more or less touch the buttocks. Three times.[8]

This early essay shows some of the hidden problems in creating a language of resistance to tradition. The replacement of an essentially ethical and ordered Confucian norm which disdained exercise with an amoral social Darwinism that equated physical prowess with dynamic progress seems, on the surface, to be a clear change in norms. But one of the reasons that social Darwinism seemed to fit so well in the late nineteenth-century Chinese search for change was that it reflected a much more longstanding Confucian technique of *xiushen*, or "bodily cultivation," that also made a link between individual self-reflection and improvement and the health of the body politic. Chinese society did *not* remain in some way essentially "Confucian" throughout the twentieth century. Rather, the ostensible and real shift to modern practice was carried out in ways that reflected the assumptions of Confucian behavior, whether consciously or unconsciously.

For the radicals of the May Fourth era, however, the construction of a monolithic "man-eating" monster named Confucianism was an essential part of the new language of politics. Unfortunately, the unwillingness of these radicals to allow almost any part of the premodern Chinese past to be useful in their new construction of society meant that that they had to look instead to a thought system that was both alien and imperialist.

The version of "Confucianism" that the radicals put forward was something of a caricature. For the representation of Confucianism simply as a "man-eating" system meant that the whole ethical system on which it was built was dismissed out of hand.[9] However, the wider population did not share the radical elite's enthusiasm for anti-Confucianism, and since its manifestations involved violent rhetoric and action (smashing of temples to set up new schools, for instance), the emergence of a radical agenda of antitraditionalism merely set up one elite discourse in opposition to a previous one.[10]

Ironically, because of the complete rejection of a supposed Confucian hegemony, Chinese radicals had to choose an alternative political vocabulary that derived almost entirely from the imperialist project that emergent Chinese nationalism rejected. The hybrid anticolonial nationalism of a Gandhi or a Tagore was not for them—so much so that Tagore was verbally attacked and vilified on his visit to China in 1924.[11]

Subversion or Attack? Dealing with Patriarchy

Mao's radicalism was visible in his earliest years, even before he became a Marxist. In 1919, Mao assumed the editorship of the *Xin Hunan* (New Hunan) magazine. In November of that year, he wrote no fewer than ten articles dealing with a notorious case, the suicide of Zhao Wuzhen, a young woman who killed herself in protest against an arranged marriage. Mao's initial commentary, published on November 16, 1919, is well known. Mao argued that three "iron nets," Miss Zhao's family, her future in-laws, and "Chinese society" as a whole, had trapped her with no hope of escape.[12] His follow-up articles are less well known, but they illustrate the way in which Mao's anti-Confucian discourse resorts to caricature, as in his piece, "The Question of Miss Zhao's Personality." Mao said he had been asked whether Miss Zhao had had a personality or not. Until the moment of her death, Mao said, she had not had one:

What did I mean by saying that Miss Zhao did not have a personality? . . . Having a personality requires respect from those one deals with. Its prerequisite is freedom of the will. Was Miss Zhao's will free? No, it was not free. Why wasn't it free? Because Miss Zhao had parents. In the West, the free will of children is not affected by the parents. . . . Not so in China. The commands of the parent and the will of the child are not at all on an equal footing. The parents of Miss Zhao very clearly forced her to love someone she did not want to love. . . . If you do not want to love me, but I force my love on you, that is a form of rape. This is called "direct rape." Their daughter did not want to love that person, but they forced their daughter to love that person. This, too, is a kind of rape, which is called "indirect rape." Chinese parents all indirectly rape their sons and daughters.[13]

This short extract shows us, in a very early pre-Marxist phase of his writings, how many of the themes that would underpin Mao's desire to break down the "iron nets" that shaped China were tied up with a whole variety of assumptions that came from the wider impact of modernity on China.

For example, the argument about whether or not Miss Zhao had a "personality" was really part of a wider discussion in the era about the modern self. Mao was contrasting the collective values of Confucianism with the autonomous ideas of the self that modernity had introduced. There is a considerable debate about how "modern" the individuated self is in Chinese culture and whether it exists even now.[14] Most observers, however, would acknowledge that there is a certain level of difference between the Confucian and the modern self; the former tended not to be extinguished, but rather, downplayed. This is very different from what Mao and the most radical of the May Fourth generation argued. For them, patriarchal Confucianism was the man-eating monster of Lu Xun's parody, and no compromise was possible.

However, Mao's rejection of one hegemony, Confucianism, in effect put him in thrall to ideas drawn from a Western model that he accepted in some ways rather uncritically. More importantly, it alienated him from the society that he chose to confront. For Mao, the rejection of Chinese society was the rejection of a monster. Yet for the wider population that he attacked, that supposed monster also consisted of cherished ceremonies, familiar temples, a settled way of life. May Fourth radicalism chose to cut itself off from the society it purported to engage with and liberate, and this tendency continued into Mao's Marxist phase. The desire to break up traditional social bonds and substitute new ones led to the Great Leap Forward and Cultural Revolution, where the breakup of extended families into new structures was recommended by the collective, along with denunciations of parents for crimes against the state. It was even more visible in the brief reign of Mao's most enthusiastic pupil, Pol Pot, in Cambodia in 1975–1978, when a murderous regime effectively abolished all family bonds.

Mao's piece comes over as shrill and unsubtle. In its concentration on the self, it reduces the society that it opposes to a caricature and as such, reduces its own subversive power.

Yet the historical record shows that it was Mao who ultimately rose to paramount power in China. Mao recognized that the simplistic declaration that the old values were dead and gone, however convincing they might seem to May Fourth radicals in the cities, bore little resemblance to the persistent culture based on ritual norms, hierarchies, and premodern ideas about the relationship of the individual to society and the state. The continuing twentieth-century crisis of the modernizing project, whether under the Nationalists or the Communists, is largely due to the modernizers' failure to engage with a system of power relations that is perhaps more vulnerable to constant attrition than all-out assault.

Mao's Turbulent Journey

Mao lived through turbulent times. By the late 1910s, he had moved from Changsha to the excitement of the capital, Beijing. While there, his natural intellectual curiosity led him to Peking University (then, as now, the institution's preferred translation of its title), where he worked as an assistant librarian. While there, he began to attend meetings of the study societies that would eventually, in 1921, become the Chinese Communist Party (CCP).

In its early years, the party was not the machine to rule China that it would later become. But from 1923, it took advantage of a great opportunity to join up with the much larger Nationalist (Kuomintang) Party of Sun Yat-sen with Soviet tutelage. Sun died in 1925, and his place at the top of the party was taken by the younger Nationalist Chiang Kai-shek, who was rather less keen on the alliance with the CCP than Sun had been. Mao became an enthusiastic participant in the United Front between the two parties, which resulted in the Northern Expedition of 1926–1927, a combination of political and military campaigns that defeated or coerced the militarist leaders who had dominated much of China since the 1911 revolution. But the Nationalists had a horrific surprise for their partners. Chiang had grown increasingly suspicious of the intentions of his Communist allies, and in 1927, turned his secret society and security force allies against them, killing thousands in Shanghai and Guangzhou (Canton). The Communists fled to the countryside to regroup and recover.

Chiang Kai-shek's action strengthened the position of those, like Mao, who argued that the Chinese revolution would be nurtured in the countryside and not the cities. Yet this insight did not immediately help Mao. Infighting and over-radicalization of policy alienated the locals in the central Chinese province of Jiangxi, where many in the Party had retreated. As Chiang's campaigns of "extermination" began to take their toll on the CCP, the party made its famous decision to leave for the northwest—a journey that would become known as the Long March.

During the hair-raising months of the March in 1934–1935, Mao's position in the party began to rise yet further. However, there were still rivals to his leadership, including the Moscow-trained Wang Ming, who was able to claim the prestige of having spent time in the world capital of Communism. The making of Mao's leadership was an event he could not have engineered himself, but the outbreak of the Sino-Japanese War in 1937 gave him a superb opportunity.

During the war, the Nationalists and Communists formed another uneasy united front.[15] Yet as the Nationalists found themselves battered and under siege, the position of the Communists in turn became stronger, and Mao's position along with it. In the major base area of ShaanGanNing, with its capital at Yan'an (Yenan), the Communists implemented major policies of agrarian revolution. In addition, through the process of Rectification *(zhengfeng)*, tactics of political indoctrination along with terror were used to create a new cult of personality with Mao at its heart; of some twenty-two texts that initiates into the Party were meant to read, as many as eighteen were by Mao. By the end of the war, Mao was undoubtedly the most prominent figure in the party, and his vision of revolution the one that would shape China.

During the Civil War of 1946–1949, the broken and corrupt Nationalist government was swept away by the better-trained and motivated troops of the CCP. Mao's government put "politics in command," in a phrase used to describe the campaign-driven and political nature of life in China at that time. Of all the campaigns, the most thorough but also most devastating was the Great Leap Forward of 1958–1961. In this attempt to completely remold China's society and economy, mass mobilization of the peasantry turned into a disaster as famine devastated the country and some twenty million or more people died of starvation and related diseases. Following the failure of the Leap, Mao's position in the leadership became more vulnerable, as more pragmatic leaders including Liu Shaoqi and Deng Xiaoping sought to reintroduce elements of private markets into the economy. But by 1966, Mao had found a new strategy to restore his primacy, as well as reinject what he saw as much-needed vigour to Chinese politics: the Cultural Revolution.[16]

In four decades, from the early 1920s to the mid-1960s, Mao had created the body of thought that would become known as Maoism (or "Mao Zedong thought"). What, then, was that body of thought that underpinned Mao's turbulent journey through China's violent twentieth century?

Of course, Maoism is, and must be, considered as a mode of Marxist thought. However, it was a Marxism shaped by a grassroots understanding of China's nature as an agricultural society that could not be changed by a Bolshevik-style urban-based revolution.[17] The Mao who started to develop along these lines was not the paramount leader of later years. Although he was a founder member of the party, and present at its first congress in 1921, Mao's position waxed and waned. A crucial moment came in 1930, when Mao compiled a report on conditions in Xunwu county, in mountainous Jiangxi province, giving an immensely complex and sophisticated account of class divisions among the farmers and elites of the township.[18] Throughout his career, even at the moments of seemingly irrational ideological zeal, Mao continued to stress the importance of grassroots investigation and pragmatic application of theory rather than "bookism" (benbenzhuyi). In particular, the reality that China was a predominantly rural society with great poverty and inequality led to a concentration on rural revolution as the transformative approach favored by the party.

Additionally, Maoism was a strategic approach. Between the late 1920s, when the alliance with the Nationalists (Kuomintang) was abruptly ended, and victory in 1949, guerrilla techniques and strategic withdrawals became a necessary part of survival during the conflicts with the Nationalists, the Japanese, and then the Nationalists again during the Civil War. The corollary of guerrilla tactics was a need, enforced both by ideology and practicality, to become "close to the people."

These aspects of Maoism were the ones most in evidence during much of the Western academic debate on China through the 1970s, much of which looked at Mao's rise to power and rule post-1949 as a question of political science or development studies. These approaches, while immensely fruitful, also tended to stress positivistic and rational models as the most appropriate ones to analyze Mao's rule, as well as to equate the governance of the People's Republic of China (PRC) with Mao's personal rule.[19] This meant that the Cultural Revolution of the 1960s came as a seemingly inexplicable break from the CCP's trajectory up to that point. However, for those who cared to look at the less concrete and pragmatic aspects of Maoism, and at the importance of charismatic leadership to Mao's project, the Cultural Revolution seemed more like a logical, if by no means inevitable, end point. Yet these other aspects of Maoism have only more recently come under scrutiny in a concentrated way.[20]

From the 1930s onward, Maoism became a project based very largely on charismatic leadership. Although the importance of the charismatic element within the wider framework of CCP governance varied, with high points including the Rectification movement of 1941–1944, the Great Leap Forward of 1958–1962, and the Cultural Revolution (particularly in its earliest phase, 1966–1969), there was no stage at which charismatic Maoism was irrelevant after the consolidation of his position in the late 1930s.

The Turn to the Cult of Personality

The cult of personality surrounding Mao Zedong peaked during the initial phase of the Great Proletarian Cultural Revolution (GPCR, 1966–1969). China's youth was mobilized behind the Chairman's call to "bombard the headquarters," and eagerly took part in Mao's revolt against his own party. The role of the young Red Guards caught not only China's but the world's attention. It seemed that they followed Mao not as a political leader, but rather as a god, "the reddest of red suns in all our hearts."

What, in essence, was charismatic Maoism? First of all, it was dependent on a cult of personality. Mao himself became the center of ideological correctness and his work, codified as "Marx-Leninist-Mao Zedong thought," positioned him in a line of succession to the canonical Marxist thinkers. Rather than having to boost his own image, Mao was supported by allies; in the 1940s, in Yan'an, his security chief Kang Sheng was instrumental, and during the 1950s and into the 1960s, Lin Biao and Chen Boda were responsible for propagating Mao's thought through the media and the army.

Mao was not a new emperor, reverting to "traditional" styles of leadership. This interpretation was encouraged by Mao's own comparison of himself to the first unifying emperor of China, Qin Shihuangdi, in the last years of his life, but risks confusing form with substance. Mao's cult of personality, even when it drew on premodern forms, was an essentially modern enterprise. It was based on an idea of the individuated self, a rejection of Confucian values of "moderation" and "order" as well as respect for age. It revered dynamism over stasis and was propagated through the media as an expression of collective, supposedly nonhierarchical mass values. It was profoundly different from, for example, the brief attempt in 1915 by the Republican president Yuan Shikai to ascend the imperial throne and restore Confucianism as the official political doctrine, a genuinely conservative and reactionary move.

The other trap to avoid is what one might consider the reverse of the "emperor" model—that is, the idea that the Mao cult was purely and simply based on Soviet models, and Stalin's in particular. This view was more popular during the height of the Cold War, but is not unheard even now. Soviet models were indeed deeply important for shaping Mao's thought, and the half-admiring, half-resentful relationship that Mao had with Stalin indicates how essential the *Vozhd*'s mode of thought was to Mao. But Mao's own experience makes a simple imitative model insufficient. The specifics of the May Fourth movement, and Chinese cultural currents that were based in premodern norms but reshaped by modern practice, were also highly important.

Both of these models are attempts to try and interpret charismatic Maoism purely as variants of preexisting political strategies, those of the premodern empire and Soviet Bolshevism. But Maoism was not just a version of something else. It was highly distinctive in its own right, using forms of premodern and modern identity, and drawing on China's own experience, in particular during the May Fourth era of the early twentieth century (a period not paralleled either in early twentieth-century Russia or in premodern China), as well as on Mao's own individual personality. These premodern precedents were not irrelevant to Mao and Maoism. But they were not the basis on which Mao's authority *primarily* depended, and it does a disservice to the modern project in China to dissociate Maoism too strongly from similar projects of renewal in the twentieth-century world. For a start, although his authority derived from his participation in the leadership of the CCP, it was not in his role as party chairman that his authority lay; indeed, during the Cultural Revolution, in organizational terms, his leadership of the party was balanced by Liu Shaoqi's installation as head of state, a means of dividing power after the disaster of the Great Leap Forward. Instead, the system of thought, Marx-Lenin-Mao Zedong thought, which he developed, reflected his own personal background and preferences, with which the party then came partly or fully into line.[21]

The Road to Charismatic Maoism

Although even at the height of his power, Mao's position of supremacy within the leadership was never as uncontested as was, say, Stalin's after the late 1920s, it is clear that Mao's status as first, and more, among equals, is fundamental to the formation of Chinese Communism. Mao was not the paramount leader of the party until the mid- to late 1930s, and it was the pragmatic Mao who maneuvered past hostile political enemies and murderous internecine party feuds before that time. The periods during which Mao's charismatic leadership seem to have had the greatest impact were, first of all, during the Rectification movements of 1943–1945, while the party's major base was in the northwest of China, and then during the Great Proletarian Cultural Revolution, the most extreme period of which lasted from 1966 to 1969.

David Apter has suggestively analyzed the Rectification period as one in which the party, and Mao in particular, used "revealing" texts to created "discourse communities" that had a "transformational sense of their own difference."[22] The Cultural Revolution reinterpreted these experiences for a new generation that had known nothing but the PRC.

"The Great Proletarian Cultural Revolution now unfolding is a great revolution that touches people to their very souls," began the CCP Central Committee's (CC) "Decision Concerning the Great Proletarian Cultural Revolution" (August 8, 1966).[23] Just because the

CC said this did not, of course, necessarily make it so. However, it turned out to be true; it was grassroots participation that made the Maoist fervor as strong as it was during the Cultural Revolution. In the 1930s, the establishment of ideologies in Germany and Italy that embraced the mystical and irrational provided a state-sponsored framework in which irrationality could be given free rein. This was less feasible in the Maoist China of the 1960s, where Mao, even at the height of his power, was no Führer, and where the state ideology needed simultaneously to balance its rationalist Enlightenment roots while embracing the charismatic romanticism of the Mao cult. We therefore observe a phenomenon by which elite political declarations on the GPCR tried to hew to a relatively more rational discourse, whereas popular mass responses effectively turned Mao Thought into a sacred doctrine and took it beyond the range of the rational.

The original "Decision" stresses that "In the Great Proletarian Cultural Revolution, the only method is for the masses to liberate themselves, and any method of doing things on their behalf must not be used."[24] The literal truth of this statement is not the issue here; although there were attempts at genuine grassroots organization such as the 1967 Shanghai Commune, in many cases they were quickly infiltrated by the party leadership. However, it is notable that even during this most personalized of campaigns, the myth was maintained at the level of elite discourse that the masses' own will was the driving force of the movement, rather than the will of a supreme leader. The initial document also permits the holding of different views and the protection of minority views.[25]

At point 16 of the "Decision," however, the role of Mao Zedong Thought is spelled out clearly. "Mao Zedong's thought should be taken as the guide to action in the Cultural Revolution," it declares, and argues that party committees "at all levels" "must study over and over again Chairman Mao's writings on the Cultural Revolution and on the Party's method of leadership, such as *On New Democracy*, *Talks at the Yan'an Forum on Literature and Art*, *On the Correct Handling of Contradictions among the People* ... and *Methods of Work of Party Committees*." This technique of rereading texts intensively brought back to mind the Rectification campaigns in Yan'an in the 1940s, when immersion in repeated text-reading was made the point of entry for successful induction into the party.

The shift from pragmatic to charismatic explanations of Maoism is visible in an article, originally from *Red Flag* and reprinted in *Peking*

Review, praising the Red Guards in September 1966. The language is simultaneously more orientated toward personalizing the GPCR as Mao's own movement, and to describing its popular manifestations in terms of a natural, uncontrollable phenomenon, with metaphors of "birth" and "upbringing":

> The Red Guards are something new that has emerged in the tempest of the Great Proletarian Cultural Revolution. . . . The Red Guards have been nurtured in their growth by Mao Zedong's thought. . . .
>
> What our Red Guards love most of all is to read Chairman Mao's works and follow his teachings, and their love for Mao Zedong's thought is most ardent. . . .
>
> Revolutionary dialectics tells us that the newborn forces are invincible, that they inevitably grow and develop in struggle, and in the end defeat the decaying forces. Therefore, we shall certainly sing the praises of the new, eulogize it, beat the drums to encourage it, bang the gongs to clear a way for it, and raise our hands high in welcome.[26]

This statement shows how the premodern and modern elements that went to create the Mao cult came together. On the one hand, the repeated reading of texts, and the idea that entrance to salvation was through a familiarity with a master-text, would have been very familiar in various premodern contexts. In orthodox Chinese society, it was familiarity with the classics and one's ability to carry out detailed literary criticism *(kaozheng)* and separate "correct" from "incorrect" interpretations that defined success in the old imperial bureaucracy. The Confucian system had very clear ideas of what was heterodox and what was orthodox. In heterodox society, the emergence of millenarian cults (White Lotus, Taiping), was also in significant part based on texts. The Taiping state, which held sway in much of central China from the mid-1850s to 1864, used texts largely based on a rewriting of Old and New Testament material to create a framework for the new state (the Heavenly Kingdom of Great Peace) that it sought to establish.

Yet the source of legitimacy in the Maoist cult was different in a crucial regard from the premodern sources of legitimacy. Unlike either official imperial cults or millenarian rebellions, where the source of authority was external to the emperor or rebel religious leader himself, Mao's political legitimacy, particularly in the charismatic aspects boosted by Lin Biao, Kang Sheng, and Chen Boda, rested in the person of Mao. Mao Zedong Thought was a self-legitimizing project: Mao Thought was correct because it came from Mao. Yet its cult of man rather than higher authority was in effect a bow to the idea that man was the measure of all things, while encouraging a political style that seemed to demonstrate the opposite.

These cultural assumptions were also very much grounded in the post–May Fourth, modern sensibility. Imperial cults were part of a strategy of control, as was Mao's cult. But the primary purpose of the imperial cult was to encourage order and stability, and like most of the dominant Confucian culture, it was dependent on harking back to a golden age and far-off practice. In contrast, the Cultural Revolution displayed a *reductio ad absurdum* of the most extreme radical anti-Confucian elements of the May Fourth era. The quotation above betrays both Hegelian/Marxist and social Darwinist assumptions by its emphasis on struggle, which had been such a powerful anti-Confucian model when first introduced into China by Yan Fu and others in the late Qing. It also follows the thread started in the very late Qing and strongly developed during the May Fourth period by praising the new, rather than the old and venerable. It was a cult, but one that drew on the assumptions of Chinese modernity.

The Mao cult was dependent on acolytes. Mao himself rarely praised his own role, and one even finds him making statements that ostensibly seem to play down the cult of personality. This seems disingenuous, however, when one sees how his advocates encouraged that cult. Even Prime Minister Zhou Enlai, who has in retrospect been portrayed as one of the voices of moderation within the leadership during the GPCR, wrote to a prominent group of Red Guards in September 1966: "In the course of this Great Proletarian Cultural Revolution of ours there can only be one criterion of truth, and that is to measure everything against Mao Zedong Thought. Whatever accords with Mao Zedong Thought is right, while that which does not accord with Mao Zedong Thought is wrong."[27] The most important figure in this effort was Lin Biao. Lin's public speeches, an important part of the maintenance of the Mao cult during the GPCR, are more enthusiastic about the importance of Mao Thought above all than the CC directives. In a speech at a mass rally on August 18, 1966, celebrating the Cultural Revolution, Lin declared that "Chairman Mao is the most outstanding leader of contemporary times, the greatest talent of contemporary times." He signs off with what would become an obligatory "Long live Chairman Mao! Long live! Long, long live!"[28]

Yet the most obvious and uncontrollable constituency to respond to Mao's calls to rebellion during the GPCR were the young who formed teams of "Red Guards." Since the 1920s, although youth sections remained important in the politics that emerged, particularly for the KMT and CCP, the autonomous role of youth was steadily suppressed in the straitjacket of politics shaped by national crisis. Mao's conscious decision to liberate the power of youth was based on a very modern sensibility, one shaped by the experience of May Fourth. Yet there was a crucial difference. May Fourth youth had experienced the post-Confucian intellectual atmosphere in a society that offered a multitude of choices. As in Weimar Germany, the precarious pluralism of the Republic reflected both weakness and opportunity. No one idea could dominate in politics or culture because there were too many competing forces: nascent Chinese nationalism, foreign imperialism, and internal warlordism, among others. Post-1949 China was very different. It would be wrong to suggest that it was a successfully totalitarian society, in that we know that policies intended to change behavior from within often failed to be reflected at the grassroots.[29] Yet it was a sealed and inward-looking society, with little contact with the outside world, and little if any space for pluralist thought within the society itself. The generation who came of age in 1919, like Mao, had been exhilarated by the wealth of choices and arguments that they could make. By contrast, the generation coming of age in 1966 were exhilarated by what purported to be scientific certainty being placed before them.

The constant theme of interviews and memoirs by those who took part in the GPCR as young women and men was their genuine enthusiasm for the movement and Chairman Mao. This is reflected in the absolutism and devotion of the Red Guards. The Red Guard period ubiquitously used Maoist language and norms as the vehicle for bonding and socialization mechanisms of various types. These bonding mechanisms drew on modern and premodern practice. They included oaths, songs, and confessions, as well as actions that involved struggle, endeavor, and pilgrimage. For example, in June 1966, Red Guards of the high school attached to Qinghua University declared in an oath of loyalty:

> We are Chairman Mao's Red Guard, and Chairman Mao is our highest leader. Here, facing our great leader Chairman Mao,

facing our beloved party, facing the revolutionary peoples of all China and the whole world, we swear, with the revolutionary Red Guards' most flourishing and solemn oath: We shall preserve eternal faith in the proletariat!—eternal faith in Chairman Mao!—eternal faith in the proletarian revolutionary line represented by Chairman Mao! . . . We have unlimited trust in the people! We have the deepest hatred for our enemies! In life, we struggle for the party! In death, we give ourselves up for the benefit of the people! . . . With our blood and our lives, we swear to defend Chairman Mao! Chairman Mao, we have unlimited faith in you![30]

This expression of undying loyalty is typical of the modern mass movement that draws on the irrational. It does not owe much to the form, as opposed to the language, of premodern Chinese cults, nor, unlike the slightly cautious GPCR documents at the leadership level, does it try and anchor itself too much in the rationalist Enlightenment discourse that shaped most CCP discourse. Instead, it draws heavily on the mystical and irrational as a source of bonding. Oaths were always sworn by blood brotherhoods in premodern China, but by definition, these were part of a heterodox part of society that was at odds with the orthodox, state-defined norms, even when they echoed them in part. The phenomenon of public swearing of oaths, even if it was not consciously modeled on European fascist models, was part of a modern culture of political practice that had become globalized by the mid-twentieth century. The emphasis on primordial elements (blood, life, death) also brings to mind the romanticist urge that had dominated the May Fourth movement and that Mao had maintained throughout life. The repeated emphasis on the personal ("we . . . we") was also a legacy of the modern emphasis on the individuated self, heavily encouraged by the New Culture movement; the repeated use of the personal pronoun was very un-Confucian, despite the repeated references to "loyalty" (zhong), which had been a core Confucian ethic. And of course, that loyalty was also modernized: the personalized fealty to Mao reflects the influence of the Stalin cult, and the importance of techniques of mass propaganda, media, and political socialization in a state that was sealed from most outside influences.

The romanticist, irrational devotion to Mao collided with a peculiarly modernist sensibility that violence and chaos were necessary transformative mechanisms for change in society. This is reflected in the repeated references by the Red Guards to "rebellion" (zaofan), the legitimation of chaos and overturning of social norms: "Long live the spirit of revolutionary rebellion!" declared the students of the Torch high school.[31] It was China's anti-Confucian experience during the May Fourth movement that provided the most obvious precedent for this tendency: after all, Confucianism made order a central part of its worldview. Yet the influences that shaped that "rebellion" had come in significant part from the radical Left and Right in Europe. Futurists and Bolsheviks alike adored technology not just for its instrumental and material benefits, but because of the virility and power that it embodied, the ability to go beyond what had been previously possible. Both radical Left and Right also legitimated "going beyond" what were perceived as bourgeois ethical norms of restraint and embraced violence as a transformative mechanism, giving it a sacralized (though hardly Christian) value. A famous example of this was the young Red Guard Song Binbin, whose personal name means "refined." Her excellence in revolutionary destruction was noted by Mao, to whom she was presented, and at his suggestion, her inappropriate name was changed to "Yaowu," meaning "desiring violence."[32]

Leninist ideas of "terror" as a praiseworthy term were adopted by Red Guards enthusiastically, as with the "Red Generation" group in Harbin, who put out a manifesto in September 1966:

> We cry loudly: Long live Red Terror!
> Today we will carry out Red Terror, and tomorrow we will carry out Red Terror. As long as there are things in existence which are not in accordance with Mao Zedong Thought, we must rebel and carry out Red Terror!
> Chairman Mao said: "Revolution is not a dinner party, it is not writing an essay. . . . Revolution is a violent movement; it is the violent overthrow of one class by another."
> Some people have seen our Red Terror [and said] "It's too destructive." What nonsense! The world [*tianxia*] is ours! The rivers and mountains are ours! . . . We oppose ox-demons and snake-spirits. . . .
> We are natural-born rebels, we are critics of the old world. . . .
> It is right to rebel! Rebel to the end!
> Long live Red Terror![33]

Yet terror here, as in the French Revolution as well as the Bolshevik, became a term seemingly detached from the reality of physical attack, death, and destruction. Once again, the New Culture inheritance of the idea of "renewal," a new generation that rejected the failed past, also shaped the justification for "red terror." The corollary of this was the characterization of opponents as enemies, irredeemably evil and beyond humanity. The more moderate note of "reeducation" that marked at least some of the CCP's practice in the immediate post-1949 period was abandoned for a language that suggested primal notions of good and evil from mythology: "snake spirits," "cow demons," "ghosts," and "devils" were all insults hurled at ideological enemies, literally dehumanizing them.

Other modes of Red Guard behavior also reflect the cult of personality, with Mao as the object of veneration. Since the embrace of physical vigor was yet another way in which the New Culture generation, including Mao, had rejected Confucian social norms, it was unsurprising that the Cultural Revolution generation were also keen to use it as a token of devotion, particularly when Mao himself used gestures such as swimming in the Yangtze to signal the start of a campaign of renewal. Physical vigor was used to highlight values of virility, youth, and strength. But it also had a reverse side: effort and even pain and suffering were made to seem like necessary and worthy marks of experience to achieve entry to a politically enlightened state.

A Naval College "Long March Red Guard team" decided to reenact the march as, effectively, a pilgrimage, a mark of respect for the original event. The *People's Daily* reported the team's progress:

> From the first step of the Long March Red Guards' journey, difficulties appeared from start to finish. . . .
>
> Rain soaked their clothes, sweat drenched their bodies, the journey consumed all of their strength.
>
> During that time, they clung to the "Quotations from Chairman Mao," reading as they walked, where it said: "Be determined, don't be afraid of sacrifices. Remove all difficulties, and fight for victory."
>
> After several days of walking, bloody blisters had appeared on their feet . . . every step that they took was painful. . . .
>
> Mao Zedong Thought is their strength! What does rain matter, who cares about pain?[34]

The ultimate possible endpoint of the pilgrimage was, of course, direct contact with Mao himself, or at least a sighting of the "reddest sun in our hearts." The *People's Daily* reported the meeting of the Qinghua University Middle School Red Guards with Mao on August 21, 1966. The dialogue was hardly complex; the Red Guards are reported to have said "Long live Chairman Mao; we want revolution, we want to rebel" to Mao's face, with the Chairman answering, "I support you determinedly."[35] Yet the legitimacy that could be claimed from a personal encounter with Mao was naturally immense. Even a distant sighting was worth a report and could lead to a transformative experience of "rebirth." Schoolteacher Bei Guancheng excitedly wrote home to colleagues in Shanghai in September 1966: "Let me tell you the great news, greater than heaven. . . . I saw our most most most most dearly beloved leader Chairman Mao! . . . I have decided to make today my birthday. Today I started a new life!!!"[36]

Penitence was also an important part of the cult. This had effectively been the case during the Rectification movements of 1943–1945 as well, but the intervening period had seen a loosening of the stranglehold that Mao Thought had at the most radical period. Not so during the GPCR, however. Seven activists were presumably forced to offer a recantation of their political position in January 1967 to a rival Red Guard group. However, the way in which the recantation was phrased was as a "Letter to Chairman Mao requesting punishment." "Respected Chairman Mao," it began, "We request punishment from you. We were wrong, completely wrong." Having then elucidated in detail the errors of approach that they had made by coming to the capital to denounce a rival grouping, the writers say:

> We guarantee you the following:
>
> 1. Determinedly to read Your books, hear Your words, and act according to Your directions, becoming Your good students. . . .
> 2. We were completely wrong to come to the capital with our accusation, and will receive the criticism of the Scarlet Red Guards. . . .
>
> Long live the reddest of red suns in our hearts, Chairman Mao! Long live! Long, long live![37]

The role of Mao as icon in this letter is worth reiterating. There must be some doubt whether Mao himself would ever have seen such a letter. The aim was to underscore ideologically a victory of one "red" group over another, which had probably been won by force.

The appearance in black and white of a "confession" couched in terms of sin against the driving force of the GPCR gave the winning group moral legitimacy that mere violence could not on its own supply. (In Chinese history, there is a long tradition of "official histories" that record defeated leaders humbly asking for punishment for the sin of having rebelled against the legitimate ruler.)

Finally, one other recourse to primordial sources of legitimacy must be mentioned: the kitsch, implicitly gendered division between male and female that defined "duty." In July 1967, the soldier Wu Kejiang wrote a poem supposedly to dismiss the fears of an overprotective mother. "Fearing that I might be killed by 'white bandits' at the school," Wu wrote, "my mama pulled me back. I said—

> Let me go, mama!
> Don't be afraid for your child,
> Our allies in struggle are everywhere,
> What good are the "white bandits'" sword and shield?

The poem continues over four verses, noting in the last stanza:

> Goodbye mama!
> Our highest commander Mao Zedong orders us to set out. . . .
> Until we have obtained thorough victory in the Great Cultural
>   Revolution,
> I swear . . . never to return home![38]

Yet although the Cultural Revolution was in many ways a deeply sexist and indeed prurient period, it is notable that its cult of youth nonetheless had a huge female element. Female Red Guards were central to the movement, in a way that was never true of the Hitler Youth, or of many religious cults that have made single-sex bonding a significant part of their methodology. And for both sexes, the figure of Mao was not just a "Big Brother" who evoked obedience, but also one who engendered an emotional response that proved an enormously powerful part of the Cultural Revolution's appeal. That appeal also lay in Mao's ability to maintain a distinctive—and very rare—political balance, in which he stood as supreme leader but also at the apex of the forces of rebellion. Few if any other leaders could manage this balance; and certainly it has never been achieved by any of his successors in Beijing.

The Influence of Maoism?

Perhaps the most powerful direct imitator of the Maoist radical model of the Cultural Revolution was not in China itself, but in the heavily Maoist-influenced Khmer Rouge regime in Cambodia. Yet the decades since his death in 1976 have seen Mao's potency as a political symbol fade. Although Mao's image remains in the center of Tiananmen Square, the politics of today's China look at times more like a sanitized version of the vision of his old rival Chiang Kai-shek.

Yet a closer look shows that Mao's legacy still has great significance even in the go-go economy of early twenty-first-century China. At a basic level, Mao's legacy, while contested, still provokes respect among many Chinese. At a time when the state's social welfare provision has been heavily reduced from the days of the "iron rice bowl" of birth-to-death work, education, and health provision, Mao's memory is often invoked to promote an alternative vision. In the early 2010s, rising CCP star Bo Xilai sought to introduce an economic model in the city of Chongqing that drew on a slightly more social welfarist ethos than was the case in some of China's more neoliberal provinces. To burnish his attempt, however, he promoted populist policies that brought to mind the Mao era, including mass singing of the songs of the Cultural Revolution era. As it happened, his evocation of the Mao era turned out to be his downfall; the Politburo had no intention of promoting a leader who drew on the charismatic leadership style of the Great Helmsman, and Bo was purged in early 2012. Yet the potency of his message was clear; even months after his fall, there were plenty of semi-anonymous signs of support that once again called to mind the Mao period and its iconography.

Perhaps the most important legacy of Maoism lies somewhere other than the failed leadership campaigns of would-be leaders. For, however perverse and indeed perverted its attempts became, Maoism did sharpen and clarify certain ideas about the nature of Chinese society. Ever since the late nineteenth century, the idea of the individuated self and its dynamism had held sway in the minds of Chinese reformers. But Maoism was the primary vehicle to transmit that dynamism to the wider population. It also, paradoxically, acted strongly against that tendency, for instance in its drive toward collectivism. But even the disastrous Great Leap Forward had been intended to stimulate the release of individual dynamism even if it was as part of a collective enterprise. When the era of Deng Xiaoping came along, the transfer of that psychology to the sphere of economics was at least partly responsible for the enthusiasm for investment and enterprise. Mao might not have wished to see the economic boom and return of capitalism after 1978 as his psychological (if not ideological) legacy, but he has to take at least some of the responsibility, if not as a Marxist, then as a romanticist or even as a social Darwinist. And in an era when global economics in general betrays more than a touch of the social Darwinist, this is a Maoist legacy that may have relevance well beyond China itself.

FIVE

JAWAHARLAL NEHRU

A Romantic in Politics

RAMACHANDRA GUHA

I

ON CHRISTMAS DAY, 1942, Jawaharlal Nehru sat down to write a letter to Madame Chiang Kai-shek. The two had met in India earlier that year and in China some years previously. While it was Chiang who headed China's Nationalist government, his sophisticated, American-educated wife was an increasingly influential figure in political circles. In her husband's negotiations with Western leaders, her elegant manners and flawless English were a valuable aid. (That she was a Christian by faith also helped.) Madame Chiang, wrote the American publisher Henry Luce, was "an even more exciting personality than all the glamorous descriptions of her."[1] As a cosmopolitan, English-speaking Indian himself, Nehru had been charmed by the lady, and the two got along from the time they first met.

The Chiang Kai-sheks were in India in February 1942. They had long talks with Nehru and also met Gandhi. The Chinese leader supported the Indian demand for freedom and urged the American president, Franklin Delano Roosevelt, to make independence for colonized nations part of the charter of the Allied forces in the war against the Axis powers. Roosevelt was moderately sympathetic, but the British prime minister, Winston Churchill, was not. The viceroy at the time, Lord Linlithgow, was likewise insensitive to Indian nationalist aspirations. When war broke out in Europe in September 1939, the Congress Party—to which both Gandhi and Nehru belonged—offered support to the Allies on condition that they commit themselves to independence for India at the end of hostilities. The offer was ignored.[2]

In August 1942, Gandhi demanded that the British "Quit India." Implicit was a call for the people to rise in (nonviolent) revolt. The government preemptively arrested the major leaders of the Congress. Gandhi was kept in a large house in Poona owned by the Aga Khan, while Nehru and some others were sent to a medieval fort in the Deccan country. It was from this fort in Ahmednagar, four and a half months after his arrest, that Nehru wrote Madame Chiang a long handwritten letter.

Nehru began by saying he did not know whether the letter would reach its intended recipient, for his prison conditions forbade communication with all except near relatives and that only on domestic matters. "In spite of this unfavourable outlook," said Nehru, "the urge to write to you is so strong that I cannot resist it, and I am sending this paper bark on the stormy seas that surround us. Perhaps, who knows?, it might survive the perils and dangers and reach you somewhere, some time or other. Even if it fails to do so, the mere act of writing to you brings some comfort and satisfaction."

The "immediate reason" that Nehru was writing was that he had heard that Madame Chiang was in the hospital. He hoped that she was better now and on the road to recovery. Then he continued, in four evocative paragraphs that constitute the heart of the letter:

> Christmas approaches and the New Year, with all its hopes and desires, is almost upon us. To you and the Generalissimo I send all my good wishes and friendly greetings on the eve of this pregnant year. May it be well with you both, and with China, now and always, and may your light of faith and determination and unswerving courage pierce ever more the encircling gloom, till it spreads out over us all, and darkness is no more.
>
> Need I say that during these long and dreary months, my thoughts have been constantly with you and the Generalissimo, and with China, whose flaming and life-giving symbols both of you are? In my quiet and seclusion, I have thought of and earnestly hoped for the crowning success of your great cause, with which, in my own mind, our own cause is so inextricably intertwined. I cannot separate them, for they are one. My great regret is that circumstances should have so conspired that my col-

leagues and countrymen and I cannot play a more vital and active part in furtherance of this great cause.

On August 8th I gave a message to a Chinese journalist in Bombay. I did not know then that within a few hours I would be arrested and that this would be my last message before I had to retire to seclusion. But I was glad of it later that my last words were addressed to the people of China, and more especially to the Generalissimo and you. In this message I repeated that we shall keep faith with China whatever happened. By that pledge we shall remain, and I trust that the opportunity will be given to us to redeem it in full measure.

I hope you are well and keep in good cheer. I may not mention this place where I am kept except to say that I am somewhere in India. But it is a small matter where I am for my mind is untamed and unbound, and it wanders where it will, crossing seas and mountains and visiting far-away countries. And this mind carries always with it the precious treasure of my friendship with you and the Generalissimo.

Nehru put the letter in an envelope addressed to "Madame Chiang Kai-shek, c/o the Chinese Commissioner, New Delhi." But before the envelope could get to the Chinese diplomat, it was intercepted by the censor, who brought it to the attention of the Home Department, who said "there can of course be no question of allowing Nehru's letter to Madame Chiang to go forward." The letter was retained in a file, which now rests in the India Office section of the British Library.[3]

II

This letter that never reached its recipient says much about Jawaharlal Nehru the man—and politician. Of the individuals profiled in this volume, he was perhaps the most instinctively internationalist in his thinking. Nehru was born in 1889, the son of a successful lawyer in the north Indian town of Allahabad. Motilal Nehru doted on his only son and closely supervised his education. From the time he was seven, Jawaharlal was made to take daily rides on a horse, accompanied by a cavalryman. When the boy turned eleven, a resident English tutor was appointed to teach him. At fifteen he was admitted to a great

English public school, and, two years later, to a great and ancient English college.[4]

When Jawaharlal was at Harrow, Motilal wrote to him:

> I think I can without vanity say that I am the founder of the Nehru family. I look upon you, my dear son, as the man who will build upon the foundations I have laid and have the satisfaction of seeing a noble structure of renown rearing up its head to the skies.

Then, when he had finished with school and gained admission into Trinity College, Cambridge, Motilal assured him:

> It would be something for any man to speak about his connections with these great institutions, but in your case it will be the institutions who will own you with pride as one of their brightest jewels.[5]

After taking a second class degree in Natural Sciences, Jawaharlal joined the Inner Temple. He returned to India in 1912, a time of political quiescence, with major nationalist leaders like Bal Gangadhar Tilak in jail. He practiced at the bar in his hometown—without conspicuous success—before becoming involved in nationalist politics. The Indian National Congress was then divided into two camps—moderate and extremist, with Motilal being a member of the former group.

By 1919, Gandhi had become the major leader of the Congress. When he announced a *satyagraha* against the harsh Rowlatt Act, Jawaharlal was "afire with enthusiasm" for courting arrest, while Motilal was "dead against this new idea."[6] However, having seen at first hand how Gandhi's charisma swayed the members of the Congress, Motilal came round to his son's point of view and enlisted for jail-going as well.

In the 1920s, both father and son emerged as important players within the Congress Party. While Motilal confined himself to the cities, Jawaharlal toured the countryside, acquainting himself with peasant life in northern India. Meanwhile, he read widely in politics and history, seeking to place the Indian freedom struggle in comparative perspective. In between jail terms, he traveled across Europe, expressing a cautious admiration for the Soviet experiment. In 1927 he helped organize an "International Congress against Colonial Oppression and Imperialism" in Brussels.

In 1928, Motilal was elected president of the Congress; the next year his son succeeded him. It was Gandhi who pushed for Jawaharlal to succeed his father. The Mahatma was then readying himself for a fresh round of civil disobedience, for which he felt Nehru *fils* would prove to be a more effective president because of his large following among the youth. Jawaharlal was thus placed at the forefront of the next generation of Congress leaders. Meanwhile, he was also acquiring an independent reputation as a writer. Jailed during the Salt March, he used his time in prison to write a series of essays on trends in world history, in the form of letters addressed to his teenage daughter. During a later spell in prison, Nehru began work on his autobiography. Published in 1936, this was a major success in India. It also appeared in separate British and American editions and was translated into several European languages. Already the voice of the young within the Congress, he was now a spokesman for India in the eyes of the world.

III

In intellectual (or ideological) terms, Jawaharlal Nehru was a European social democrat. Yet the greatest personal influence on him was exercised by three Indians. The first was his father, Motilal, whose own success and social status gave Jawaharlal the opportunity to venture into public life. After his death, the son—by now an international statesman himself—wrote that in profile Motilal "had a marked resemblance to the busts of the Roman Emperors in the museums of Italy." There was, remembered Jawaharlal wistfully, "a magnificence about him and a grand manner, which is sadly hard to seek in this world of today."[7]

In a curious coincidence, the poet Rabindranath Tagore was born on the same day of the same month in the same year as Motilal Nehru (May 6, 1861). Jawaharlal first met Tagore in the 1920s, when he went to Santiniketan following a Congress meeting in Calcutta. In later years he closely read his works and was profoundly influenced by his nonsectarian perspective on India and the world. Tagore had often written that India was a mix and mélange of cultures, and rather than seek to highlight one (the Hindu) part of it, one must rather glory in the diversity of ideas, faiths, and ways of living.

This syncretic approach became Nehru's too. He was also inspired by Tagore's travels across Asia, his attempts to build links with the national resurgence in China, and his opposition to jingoism and war. In *The Discovery of India*, written while he was in Ahmednagar Fort in the 1940s, Nehru often quotes Tagore's poems and stories in seeking to make sense of the civilization to which both were heir. "More than any other Indian," wrote Nehru, "he [Tagore] has helped to bring into harmony the ideals of the East and West, and broadened the bases of Indian nationalism. He has been India's internationalist *par excellence*, believing and working for international co-operation, taking India's message to other countries and bringing their messages to his own people." Tagore was what Nehru himself hoped to be, one "who was full of the temper and urges of the modern age and yet was rooted in India's past, and in his own self built up a synthesis of the old and the new."[8]

Nehru adored his father and admired Tagore. But the man he really regarded as his master and mentor was Gandhi. There is a wonderful passage in *The Discovery of India* where, after gloomily describing the "quagmire of poverty and despair" into which the country had descended under colonial rule, he continues, in a sudden shift of register:

> And then Gandhi came. He was like a powerful current of fresh air that made us stretch ourselves and take deep breaths, like a beam of light that pierced the darkness and removed the scales from our eyes, like a whirlwind that upset many things but most of all the working of people's minds. He did not descend from the top; he seemed to emerge from the millions of India, speaking their language and incessantly drawing attention to them and their appalling condition. Get off the backs of these peasants and workers, he told us; all you live by their exploitation; get rid of the system that produces this poverty and misery. . . . The essence of his teaching was fearlessness and truth and action allied to these, always keeping the welfare of the masses in view.[9]

Gandhi's language was suffused with religious imagery. The Bible and the Gita were two texts to which he frequently returned and which he often quoted. This, and the fact that he advocated nonviolent resistance rather than armed struggle, led Marxists to characterize him as a reactionary whose politics coincided with the class interests of the rich and the propertied. To these "parlour Socialists," Nehru responded:

> But the little fact remains that this "reactionary" knows India, understands India, almost is peasant India, and has shaken up India as no so-called revolutionary has done. Even his latest Harijan activities have gently but irresistibly undermined orthodox Hinduism and shaken it to its foundations. . . . Reactionary or revolutionary, he has changed the face of India, given pride and character to a cringing and demoralised people, built up strength and consciousness in the masses, and made the Indian problem a world problem.[10]

Himself given to agonizing reflection on his place in the world, Nehru greatly admired Gandhi's self-control and strength of character. In an interview to a European journalist some years after Gandhi's death, he pointed out that while the Mahatma "used the mildest language," he was nonetheless "made of steel." Gandhi taught Nehru to "stick to basic principles but be compromising on details and always have a friendly approach even to your opponent." The absence of vitriol distinguished Gandhi from the Marxist revolutionary; as did the fact that "his language was one of continuity." In his person and in his politics, Gandhi represented, for Nehru, a "tremendous link between all the past of India and all the future revolutions of India."[11]

Gandhi and Nehru were united by a common political agenda—the freedom of India—and by intimate personal bonds. Gandhi had four sons of his own; but in some respects he was more attached to Nehru than to his own children. Yet their intellectual temperaments were dissimilar. Nehru saw himself as the upholder of the scientific, rational, spirit; Gandhi saw himself as a man of faith, for whom God and Truth were interchangeable. They also disagreed on the economic path for a future free India. Gandhi wanted this to be based on the village; whereas Nehru advocated rapid urbanization and industrialization.

Gandhi's 1910 tract, *Hind Swaraj,* is, among other things, a paean to the virtues of traditional Indian civilization. Its sentimentalism toward the past was not something that resonated with Nehru.[12] While perfectly willing to acknowledge the rich aesthetic and philosophical traditions of ancient India, he wanted to know why the country had fallen prey so easily to European colonialism. He found the answer in the fact that Europe had adopted science and the scientific method.

India, on the other hand, "fell behind in the march of technique." It stagnated while Europe advanced, its decline and subsequent acquisition as an appendage of Britain proving the adage that "a civilization decays much more from inner failure than from an external attack." As he starkly put it: "It seems clear that India became a prey to foreign conquest because of the inadequacy of her own people and because the British represented a higher and advancing social order."[13]

IV

Despite their varying views on economic development, Gandhi was clear that Nehru would be his political heir. This preference became apparent as early as 1929, when Gandhi pushed for him to be named the next Congress president, and was confirmed in the 1930s, when Gandhi saw that Nehru shared his views on interreligious harmony. Then, on the eve of Independence, Gandhi decisively threw his weight in favor of Nehru against his rivals within the Congress Party, preeminent among whom was Vallabhbhai Patel.

Patel was, like Gandhi, from Gujarat. A shared language and culture brought them together. Patel also commanded affection—and admiration—for the enormous work he had done in building up the Congress as a mass organization. In the summer of 1946, with the end of the world war and the Transfer of Power negotiations getting more intense in India, the question arose as to who would succeed the scholar Maulana Abul Kalam Azad as Congress president. A majority of the provincial Congress secretaries, who had worked closely with Patel, were very keen on him. But Gandhi, looking to the future, and sensing that the Congress president in this critical year was also likely to be the country's first prime minister, prevailed upon Patel to withdraw from the race and to support Nehru instead.

Conservative by temperament, Patel had—unlike Gandhi, Tagore, or Nehru—not made the defense of religious and cultural pluralism a core part of his program. Besides, he was a full fourteen years older than Nehru. Gandhi chose the younger man in the belief that "for representing and uniting Indians of all ages, classes and religions, Jawaharlal seemed more suitable than Vallabhbhai."[14]

And so Nehru became independent India's prime minister. Patel served as his home minister. Early in the new government's tenure, the two had disagreements, partly to do with whether the prime minister was merely first among equals or could trespass into a cabinet minister's domain. Patel was on the verge of resigning, but Gandhi talked him out of it. Days after their conversation, Gandhi was assassinated. Nehru now wrote to Patel of how "the old controversies have ceased to have much significance and it seems to me that the urgent need of the hour is for all of us to function as closely and co-operatively as possible." In "the crisis that we have to face now after Bapu's death," he continued, "I think it is my duty and, if I may venture to say, yours also for us to face it together as friends and colleagues."

Patel, in reply, spoke of how the two had "been lifelong comrades in a common cause. The paramount interests of our country and our mutual love and regard, transcending such differences of outlook and temperament as existed, have held us together." Gandhi's death had, he continued, only awakened "a fresh realisation of how much we have achieved together and the need for further joint efforts in our grief-stricken country's interests."[15]

Despite differences in temperament and ideology, Nehru and Patel worked well as a team. There were some things Nehru could do better than Patel—communing with the masses, relating to the world, assuring vulnerable groups (such as Muslims, tribals, and Dalits) that they enjoyed equal rights with Indians from more privileged backgrounds. There were some things Patel could do better than Nehru—integrating the princely states, carrying along dissidents in the Congress party. At the same time, Patel, writes his principal biographer, was "well aware of Nehru's primacy and popularity" among the Indian public at large.[16] What Nehru's principal biographer called "Patel's stoic decency" allowed him to subsume his own ambitions and work selflessly under a man much younger than himself.[17]

v

In January 1950, India adopted a new constitution that committed the country to a federal system based on universal adult franchise. There was widespread skepticism within and outside India about this choice, for some two-thirds of the population were illiterate. In the West, the vote had been granted incrementally, in stages. However, the Congress Party had committed itself to adult franchise as far back as 1928.

In December 1950, Vallabhbhai Patel died. Then, in early 1952, the Congress won a comfortable majority in the first general elections.

Nehru was now in a position of command, free to design policies and programs that would decisively shape the nation.

The Partition of India had created two sovereign states. Pakistan was designed as a homeland for Muslims. On the other hand, and largely on Nehru's insistence, India fashioned itself as a secular state with equal rights for all regardless of their religious affiliation. He boldly pushed this policy against the grain of public opinion, a large section of which wanted retributive violence against the Muslims who had chosen to stay behind in India. In the crucial months after Independence, when the clamor for revenge was at its strongest, Nehru wrote two remarkable letters to the heads of the provincial governments, urging them to stick to the inclusive framework laid down by Gandhi himself:

The first letter is dated October 15, 1947, and reads:

> We have a Muslim minority who are so large in numbers that they cannot, even if they want to, go anywhere else. They have got to live in India. This is a basic fact about which there can be no argument. Whatever the provocation from Pakistan and whatever the indignities and horrors inflicted on non-Muslims there, we have got to deal with this minority in a civilised manner. We must give them security and the rights of citizens in a democratic State. If we fail to do so, we shall have a festering sore which will eventually poison the whole body politic and probably destroy it.

In the next letter, dated October 17, 1948, Nehru wrote:

> We are faced, particularly in East Punjab and Delhi, with the psychological problem created by the events of the last few months. These have created in the minds of people, not merely among the refugees but also among others, a bitterness, a sense of desperation and a desire for retaliation—in short, a serious spiritual malaise. . . . The difficulties have been partly due to our inability effectively to tackle the problem of rehabilitation . . . and partly due to the continuing evidence of hostility and barbaric conduct towards the minorities in Pakistan. The result has been that sections of the Hindu community are not in tune with and do not understand Gandhiji's approach to the Muslim problem in India. They resent his approach and think that it is some-

how or other inimical to their own interests. And yet any person with vision can see that Gandhiji's approach is not only morally correct, it is also essentially practical. Indeed it is the only possible approach if we think in terms of the nation's good, both from the short and long distance points of view. Any other approach means perpetuating conflict and postponing all notions of national consolidation and progress.[18]

In later years, when the specter of religious civil war no longer haunted India, Nehru continued to worry that Muslims were not adequately represented in the public services. In September 1953, he urged chief ministers to "create a sense of partnership in every group and individual in the country, a sense of being a full sharer in the benefits and opportunities that are offered." Six months later, he reminded them that "it is always the duty and obligation of the majority to win the goodwill of the minorities by fair and even generous treatment."[19]

Gandhi himself was as keen on linguistic as on religious pluralism. In the 1920s, he had made a commitment on behalf of the Congress that when independence came, provincial boundaries would be reorganized on linguistic lines. Nehru likewise recognized that India was unique in its number of literary and classical languages, each with a distinct script of its own. Unlike in Europe, where nation-states usually privileged a single language, India would allow the residents of each state to be educated in and administered in their own language.[20]

After Independence, the murder of Gandhi and the rising tide of religious violence made Congress leaders less willing to concede this long promised demand for linguistic states. In the Andhra country, there was a strong movement to create a separate state from the Telugu-speaking districts of the Madras presidency. Nehru and Patel were no longer sympathetic to the idea—they worried that with the country having just been divided on the basis of religion, further fragmentation on the lines of language would undermine an already fragile sense of nationhood. But, on the ground, movements for linguistic states grew stronger. Even with the ruling Congress Party, the dominant view was that each major group should have its own state—a Karnataka for the Kannadigas, a Maharashtra for the Marathi-speakers, a Kerala for the Malayalis, etc.

Nehru now constituted a States Reorganization Commission. Its recommendations, made public in 1955, were in favor of linguistic states. So these were duly created. Meanwhile, Hindi chauvinists wished Nehru's government to abolish English and make their language the lingua franca for all of India. This was resented by the southern states, which saw their own languages as, in a cultural and historical sense, by no means inferior to Hindi. Nehru wisely chose to retain English as a link language as well.[21]

As a modern-minded man, Nehru was also keen that women play their part as equal citizens in the nation. Unlike in the West, women did not have to wait to be granted the franchise—they got it at the same time as men. Nehru was nonetheless distressed to find that there were few women candidates in the first general elections. He reminded the chief ministers: "A nation cannot go far ahead unless it gives full scope to its women."[22] Four years later, he said in a speech in Calcutta that "a basic revolution takes place in a country only when the women change. . . . I think you can test a revolution in a country by looking at the change that might have taken place there in the position of women, in every aspect, that is legal, economic, social and so on."[23]

India's two main religions, Hinduism and Islam, were both deeply patriarchal. Their scriptures and their historical practice relegated women to an inferior status. Women were not allowed to assume positions of power and authority. Women were denied the right to follow the profession of their choice. Men could choose to have several wives at once, but women had to be content with a single husband, this chosen for them by their father or grandfather. Moreover, she was bonded to this man, not of her choosing, for life; regardless of how well or badly he behaved.

In the late 1940s, the law minister B. R. Ambedkar supervised the drafting of new laws to give Hindu women the right to own and inherit property, to choose their spouse (even if he was of another caste or another religion), and to divorce him in case he abused or illtreated her. This reform of personal laws was opposed at every stage by the guardians of Hindu orthodoxy. They did not want their Hindu sisters to be allowed to choose their marriage partners. They thought women incapable of owing or managing property. And they were extremely reluctant to allow them to look for employment outside the home.

Frustrated at the slow pace of change, Ambedkar resigned in 1951. However, when victory in the general elections gave Nehru a firm mandate, he introduced the laws afresh in Parliament. They were eventually passed in 1955 and 1956.[24]

The inauguration of a multiparty democracy based on universal adult franchise, the nurturing of religious and linguistic pluralism, the promotion in law of gender equality—these count as among the successes of Nehru and his government. Among the notable failures were the continuing discontent in two hill regions, Nagaland and Kashmir, where movements for secession from India were active all through Nehru's tenure as prime minister.

The Nagas were a group of tribes inhabiting the Eastern Himalaya, along the border with Burma. In the nineteenth century they fought a series of fierce wars against the British. Their territory passed on to the successor Indian government, whose authority they likewise disputed. Nehru was amenable to creating a distinct Naga state within the Indian Union, which would have autonomy over most matters. This was acceptable to some Naga leaders, but a more hardline faction held out for independence. Through the 1950s, the rebels battled the Indian Army, with many villagers also suffering in the cross-fire.[25]

The other trouble spot was Kashmir, formerly part of a princely state ruled by a Hindu maharaja but with a majority Muslim population. It shared borders with Pakistan and India, and in 1947 had the option of opting to join either. The maharaja chose, however, to consider a third option—that of independence. He saw his state as a sort of Eastern Switzerland. Seeking to force his hand, raiders from Pakistan invaded the valley. The ruler now acceded to India, which sent its army to secure the capital, Srinagar, from the raiders. For over a year, India and Pakistan fought on in the mountains, till a cease-fire supervised by the United Nations called hostilities to a halt. India retained possession of the southern part of the erstwhile princely state and Pakistan of the northern part. Crucially, the Kashmir Valley remained with India.

Both India and Pakistan desperately wanted control of the vale of Kashmir. For Pakistan, since the valley was mostly Muslim, it belonged by right to their nation. For India, which saw itself as a secular state, the fact that the most popular Kashmiri leader, Sheikh Abdullah, was a socialist who admired Nehru provided proof that his people could likewise live with dignity and honor in their country.[26]

It was true that Abdullah liked Nehru. But he was less certain of the sentiments of the ordinary Indian. From 1948 to 1953, he ran the government of Jammu and Kashmir, formally a part of the Indian Union. In this period he vacillated a great deal. As a secular socialist, he was extremely uncomfortable with the idea of Pakistan. But he also worried that, after Nehru went, Indian politics would adopt an increasingly Hindu cast. So he went searching for a third option. In September 1950 he met the American ambassador to India and asked whether the United States would support an independent Kashmir.[27]

To encourage Sheikh and his Kashmiris to join India, Nehru had negotiated a special package, whereby they could fly their own flag, be autonomous of the Indian Supreme Court, and be free to design their own laws. In 1952, an agitation broke out in the Jammu region of the state—which, unlike the valley, was now predominantly Hindu. This asked for an end to the state's special status and full integration with India. The agitation was endorsed by Dr. S. P. Mookerjee, the leader of the Jana Sangh, a new national party committed to promoting the Hindu interest.

In April 1953, the American politician Adlai Stevenson came to the valley and met Sheikh Abdullah, who once more asked whether the United States would support his case for independence. The next month Dr. Mookerjee threatened to enter the valley and launch a popular movement against Abdullah's government. He was imprisoned but died of cardiac arrest while in detention. His death intensified the resentment against the special privileges granted to the Kashmiris by New Delhi.

On the last day of July 1953, Nehru wrote to a colleague that "the internal situation in Kashmir has been progressively deteriorating." Sheikh Abdullah, in theory the head of the government, had now begun "functioning as the leader of the opposition." The "problem of Kashmir," he continued, was "symbolic of many things, including our secular policy in India. Therefore anything that happens there has larger and wider consequences."[28]

In August, the rumor reached Delhi that Abdullah was planning to declare independence on the day of the Id festival. He was dismissed as chief minister and put into prison. He stayed in detention until 1958, when he was released, but was quickly arrested once more when his speeches were deemed too provocative.

The decade-long incarceration of Kashmir's most popular leader damaged Nehru's reputation as well as his country's case. That no formal charges were brought against Abdullah, that there was no trial where he could answer his critics, made the detention appear even less legitimate. To make matters worse, Abdullah's successor as chief minister, Bakshi Ghulam Mohammed, was an unprincipled politician who fixed successive elections and promoted his own kin, to the extent that his administration became known as the "BBC," the Bakshi Brothers Corporation.[29]

VI

In 1944 a group of prominent Indian industrialists—G. D. Birla and J. R. D. Tata among them—issued a manifesto (known as the "Bombay Plan") outlining their hopes for the country's economic future. This frankly admitted the limitations of the private sector in enhancing productivity and ending mass poverty. To build the infrastructure of a modern economy, to ensure "a satisfactory distribution of the national income," it was crucial that "the State should exercise in the interests of the community a considerable measure of intervention and control." India's leading capitalists thus argued that "an enlargement of the positive as well as preventative functions of the State is essential."[30]

The Bombay Plan is all but forgotten. It is important to remind ourselves of it now, when free-market views have much more salience in India and around the world. In their document, Birla, Tata, and their colleagues approvingly quoted the Cambridge economist A. C. Pigou's claim that socialism and capitalism were "converging." In his own enthusiasm for the mixed economy, Jawaharlal Nehru was carried along by—and found endorsement in—this *zeitgeist*, this spirit of the times, where even outside the Communist world the state was expected to occupy the "commanding heights" of the economy. The need for a strong public sector was more acutely felt in newly independent countries, where there was a natural suspicion of foreign capital (India, after all, had first been colonized by a Western multinational corporation), and where businessmen lacked the resources, and often the know-how, to move into such capital-intensive sectors as steel mills, large dams, ports, and the like.[31]

The need for coordinated national planning for economic development was first expressed in India by the technocrat and civil servant M. Visvesvaraya, in a series of books and pamphlets published in the 1920s and 1930s.[32] Then, in 1938, the Congress appointed a National Planning Committee, of which Nehru was chairman. After Independence, a Planning Commission was formed, composed of technocrats and economists who held ministerial rank.

Nehru took a close interest in the planning process. He gave his personal imprimatur to the crucial Second Five-Year Plan, which focused on dams and factories in the public sector to create jobs and build a solid productive base for further growth. Private enterprise was allowed into the consumer goods sector, but here too it was subject to a system of licensing, with the state issuing permits selectively and deciding on production targets and wage rates. Certain sectors were exclusively reserved for small or household units.[33]

In September 1954, G. D. Birla wrote to the prime minister's secretary that "the Nehru Government has full backing of the business community in its foreign and economic policy."[34] This was largely but not wholly true. Most entrepreneurs were happy to be regulated by the state and to operate in sectors where capital was not scarce. A significant exception, however, was J. R. D. Tata, who had now begun to move away from the Bombay Plan toward a more explicit bias in favor of the market.

In January 1955, a session of the Indian National Congress, held at the Madras suburb of Avadi, committed the country to "a socialistic pattern of society." Nehru now suggested a series of consultative meetings between cabinet ministers and top industrialists so that they could understand each other better. Birla took the idea to his fellow businessmen. He himself had "no misgivings about the Avadi resolution" and was happy for the state to play an important role in the economy. So were other leading businessmen such as Kasturbhai Lalbhai and Dharamsey Morarjee. On the other hand, J. R. D. Tata

> is discontented, has deep misgivings, takes a gloomy view of the future of the private sector and does not appreciate the spirit of the Avadi resolution. . . . The Congress, according to him, is drifting to the extreme left; the private sector is being tolerated as long as it serves the purpose; and the conception of cottage industries is based on confusion. He believes in open criticism of Government where we disagree. A strong opposition, according to him, is essential in the interests of the country as also the Congress itself.

Birla did not agree with this bleak diagnosis. He thought it important that government and big business continue to work together. To canvass for a strong and open opposition, he told Tata, would weaken the Congress and open the way for the Communists.[35]

Nehru himself was enchanted with the economic projects that the state had taken charge of. After a visit to the Tungabhadra dam, he wrote: "Whenever I see these great engineering works, I feel excited and exhilarated. They are visible symbols of building up the new India and of providing life and sustenance to our people."[36] A collective commitment to economic growth would help overcome the divisive tendencies within Indian society. As he told his chief ministers in December 1952:

> Behind the Plan lies the conception of India's unity and of a mighty co-operative effort of all the people of India. That should always be stressed and the inter-relation of one part of India with another pointed out. If we adopt this approach, we shall be dealing with the major disease or weakness of India, i.e., the fissiparous tendencies and parochial outlook that often confront us in this country. The more we think of this balanced picture of the whole of India and of its many-sided activities, which are so interrelated with one another, the less we are likely to go astray in the crooked paths of provincialism, communalism, casteism and all other disruptive and disintegrating tendencies.[37]

Nehru was a socialist in economics but a democrat in politics. He pressed the governmental machinery to enlist the "enthusiasm and co-operation of the people," so that ordinary citizens had "the sensation of partnership in a mighty enterprise, of being fellow-travellers towards the next goal that they and we have set before us."[38] As one "bred up in the Gandhian tradition," he could not appreciate the violence generated by the Russian Revolution. The "repeated purges and the like" created, in his mind, "further doubts and distaste" with regard to Communism.

At the same time, Nehru was attracted by the promise of planning, of using science and technology to promote economic growth and end poverty. And so, in the context of India, he yet wondered: "Could the new economic approach, shorn of its violence and coercion and suppression of individual liberty, be helpful in solving our problems or the world's problems? The older methods, evolved by the capitalist world, had failed and offered no solution. Indeed, they had led to great wars and they themselves, whatever their protestations, were based on violence and suppression of countries and peoples, and lack of integrity and moral approach."[39]

Today, Nehru is often criticized for according the state too great a role in economic affairs. The criticism is anachronistic. At the time, most businessmen wanted the state to build infrastructure projects and to protect them from foreign competition. Nehru's approach represented a broader consensus. On the other hand, he could certainly have done far more to promote primary education. As the economist B. V. Krishnamurti wrote in 1955, the sums allotted to education in the Five Year Plans were "absurdly low." He continued:

> A concerted effort . . . to educate the mass of the population, specially in the rural areas, would undoubtedly have far-reaching benefits of a cumulatively expansionist character. This would greatly lighten the task of the Government in bringing about rapid economic development. For in a reasonable time, one could expect that the ignorance and inertia of the people would crumble and an urge to improve one's material conditions by utilising the available opportunities would develop. If this were to happen, the employment problem would take care of itself. The people of the country would begin to move along the lines of those in the advanced democratic countries such as Great Britain and Switzerland.[40]

The advice was disregarded. While Nehru was enchanted by cutting-edge technology, he paid scant attention to the basic task of educating the ordinary citizen. Had he used his enormous prestige to making the promotion of literacy an urgent national priority, the barriers of caste would have been undermined, and a climate of equal opportunity created. For someone who was both a democrat and a socialist, this was a strange blind spot indeed. The lack of emphasis on primary education was the greatest failure of the Nehru years.

VII

Nehru served as prime minister from the time of Indian independence until his death in May 1964. Throughout this period he served concurrently as minister of external affairs.

Nehru's foreign policy was shaped by two central (and interconnected) beliefs: pan-Asianism and nonalignment. In March 1947 he organized an Asian Relations Conference in New Delhi. This had delegates from twenty-eight countries, Afghanistan and Burma and Indonesia and Vietnam among them, but also seven "Asian republics" of the Soviet Union. China and Tibet sent separate delegations. In his inaugural address, Nehru spoke of how "for too long we of Asia have been petitioners in Western courts and chancelleries. That story must now belong to the past. We propose to stand on our own feet and to cooperate with all others who are prepared to cooperate with us. We do not intend to be the playthings of others."[41]

Following Nehru, a representative of each country then spoke of how, in the postwar, imminently postcolonial, context, they saw Asia in the world. The plenary was followed by roundtables on such subjects as "economic development and social services," "status of women and women's movements," and "racial problems and inter-Asian migration."[42]

The Asian country that most interested Nehru was, of course, China. There were, in his view, three reasons why India and China would come closer together. These were their shared civilizational ties, their shared history of resistance to European colonialism, and their similar economic problems. These were both backward, agricultural, massively populated countries seeking to end poverty and destitution.

"A variety of circumstances pull India and China towards each other," wrote Nehru to his chief ministers in June 1952. In spite of differences in their forms of government, they were drawn together by "the long pull of geography and history and, if I may add, of the future."[43] With the defeat of Chiang Kai-shek, Nehru moved quickly to recognize the Communist regime in China. At his invitation, Zhou Enlai came to India in 1954, where he impressed his host, not least because his talk was free of the "slogans and cliches" of "the average Communist."[44]

Later that year, Nehru himself visited China, to a rapturous reception. The talk in his circle was all of brotherhood between the two nations, as captured in the slogan "Hindi-Chini Bhai Bhai." In 1956, Zhou came for another visit, bringing the Dalai Lama with him (India was then celebrating the 2500th year of the Buddha's birth). The Tibetan leader escaped his Chinese minders and told Nehru of the troubles he and his people were facing. He was now tempted to seek asylum in India; Nehru dissuaded him, saying he would talk to the Chinese and ask them to follow a more sympathetic policy toward the Tibetans.[45]

Unlike China, which was strongly allied to the Soviet Union, India sought good relations with both superpowers. Nonalignment was for Nehru a moral as well as practical imperative. For with both the United States and the Soviet Union now in possession of hydrogen bombs, any country drawn into their rivalry risked disaster. So Nehru's, and India's, policy was to ensure that "if again war breaks out, in spite of endeavours to the contrary, then we shall keep out of it and try to keep as many other countries as possible out of it."[46]

In 1949, Nehru spent three weeks in the United States. Six years later, he visited the Soviet Union, where he "was struck repeatedly by certain similarities between the Americans and the Russians who are today so hostile to each other." Both were "very friendly and hospitable people"; both had "made a god of the machine and have developed or are developing a highly technical civilization."[47]

By this time, Nehru had begun to tilt ever so slightly toward the Soviet Union. The proximate cause was the arms pact that the United States signed with Pakistan in February 1954, which Nehru saw as "a clear breach of neutrality." In any future dispute between India and Pakistan, the Americans were now more likely to take the other side.[48]

In May 1954, the industrialist G. D. Birla visited the United States. He asked his prime minister what he should tell his hosts about Indian foreign policy. Nehru's reply presciently anticipated the fate of later American interventions in Asia and the Middle East. Thus, speaking of the recent conflicts in Korea and Indo-China, he remarked:

I do not think that there are many examples in history of such a succession of wrong policies being followed by a country as by the United States in the Far East during the past five or six years. They have taken one wrong step after another, and now all their pride rebels against this stalemate. And so, they think of another wrong step which will make matters worse for them. They think that they can solve any problem with money and arms. They forget the human element. They forget the nationalistic urge of people. They forget the strong resentment of people in Asia against impositions.

Meanwhile, continued Nehru, "France has behaved with extreme folly in Indo-China. They have rejected time and again fairly honourable terms of settlement." The West claimed to be in favor of the worldwide spread of democracy. Nehru was a democrat, too, but as he sharply remarked, "the policy of America in the East and of France in Indo-China has given every help to the non-democratic elements, and indeed to Communism."[49]

Nehru's characterization of Western hypocrisy rang true. However, his own romantic ideas of pan-Asian solidarity were soon put to the test. From 1957, relations between China and India began deteriorating. The Chinese had built a road linking their troublesome territories of Xinjiang and Tibet—this ran through territory claimed by India. The Chinese press released maps claiming some parts of India as theirs. Then, in April 1959, after a failed revolt against the Communist regime, the Dalai Lama fled into India and sought asylum. Later that year, Chinese and Indian troops clashed several times on the border.

On October 1, 1959, Nehru wrote to his chief ministers that while he didn't think a war likely, "the basic fact remains that India and China have fallen out and, even though relative peace may continue at the frontier, it is some kind of armed peace, and the future appears to be one of continuing tension."[50] In April 1960, Zhou Enlai came to Delhi to seek a resolution of the dispute. There was a possible—as well as plausible—compromise. The Chinese transgressions were in the western sector, in the region of Ladakh, where the historical claims of India were robust. On the other hand, in the eastern sector (what is now Arunachal Pradesh) the Chinese had strong claims to territory currently controlled by India.

Zhou recommended that each side negotiate on the basis of actual control rather than ancient claims. Nehru was amenable, but in India's democratic system the matter had to be discussed in Parliament. Opposition MPs were outraged at the idea of a single inch of Indian territory being conceded. Nehru's own cabinet ministers were opposed to any compromise.[51]

Zhou went back without the settlement he (and Nehru) had hoped to arrive at. The situation now became steadily worse. Both sides sent in troops to fill in the high, harsh, unoccupied sections of the Himalaya that constituted a by-now massively disputed border. In July 1962, and again in September, Indian and Chinese troops clashed at several points. Finally, in the third week of October, the Chinese simultaneously launched an invasion in both sectors. They met with some resistance in Ladakh, but in the east they swept through Indian defenses, coming down the Brahmaputra Valley to reach the town of Tezpur. Then the Chinese returned as suddenly as they had come.

Within India, the defeat was seen in intensely personal terms, as the failure not of the military, but of Jawaharlal Nehru's policies. As one wit put it, "Hindi-Chini Bhai-Bhai" had become "Hindi-Chini Bye-Bye." Nehru was blamed for being too trusting of the Chinese, and for placing the wrong man as defense minister. This was V. K.

Krishna Menon, who, in the crucial years leading up to the war, had alienated large sections of the army while—for ideological reasons—refusing to buy arms from the more technologically advanced Western countries.[52]

In his last letter to chief ministers for the year 1962, Nehru sought to understand the reasons for the breakdown of his China policy. "What were the motives that drove the Chinese to attack us in a big way?" he asked. Nehru speculated that they did so to drive India firmly into the American fold, to clear the way for the Chinese to present themselves as the leader of an Afro-Asian bloc opposed to Western imperialism. Russia's "softening of revolutionary ardour," said Nehru, had greatly annoyed the Chinese, who were cross that the Soviets now cultivated non-Communist countries like India in the name of peaceful coexistence. By attacking India, the most prominent of the nonaligned countries, the Chinese hoped to reactivate the Cold War, for—as Nehru reasoned their reasoning to be—the fact that India would be forced to seek American help might make the Soviets come closer to the Chinese.[53]

The war of 1962 put paid to both pan-Asianism and nonalignment. Nehru now sought American assistance for rebuilding India's military capability. He also turned his mind toward a fresh resolution of the Kashmir issue. Thus, in early 1964, Nehru decided to free Sheikh Abdullah from his decade-long confinement. After the humiliating defeat against China, Nehru thought it prudent to mend fences with Pakistan, lest his country face two hostile fronts.

On April 8, 1964, Abdullah walked out of Jammu Jail. He traveled to the valley, from where, after consulting with his advisers and sounding out his constituents, Abdullah proceeded to Delhi. He stayed with Nehru, his now reconciled friend and comrade. They had long conversations, following which the Kashmiri leader left New Delhi to tour the country, seeking advice from senior Indian politicians.

There is no public record of what Nehru and Abdullah talked about in private. But, from notes written by officials, it seems that Nehru was now thinking seriously of a confederation among India, Pakistan, and Kashmir. On May 24, 1964, Abdullah traveled to Pakistan as Nehru's personal emissary. He had hoped to spend two weeks traveling through all parts of the country, speaking to a wide cross-section of leaders and thinkers. He began with two four-hour meetings, one on the 25th and another on the 26th, with the president of Pakistan, Ayub Khan. The next day he proceeded to the part of Kashmir held by Pakistan. It was in the Kashmiri town of Muzzafarabad—

which he had last seen in 1947—that Abdullah heard that Nehru had passed away in Delhi. He flew back at once. When he saw Nehru's body, reported one eyewitness, "he cried like a child." Some hours later, at the cremation, "Sheikh Abdullah leapt on the platform and, weeping unrestrainedly, threw flowers onto the flames."[54] The grief was political as well as personal; with Nehru gone, Abdullah knew that a resolution acceptable to all three parties would now be virtually impossible to secure.

VIII

Through the 1950s, the personality and ideas of Nehru dominated discourse in and about his country. The prime minister "was a great golden disc shining in the middle of Delhi" (to use the words of an Indian[55] growing up in a political family at the time). Western observers saw him likewise as larger than life, as embodying the collective hopes and fears of his nation. The journalist Tibor Mendes—a Hungarian exile then living in France—asked Nehru in 1955, "What will happen when India is deprived of your leadership?" and then outlined his own understanding of Nehru's alleged indispensability to India in these terms:

> Firstly, you are first of all the head of the ruling Party; of that machinery which, as you have said the other day, is indispensable to rule a vast and complicated country. You unite all the different elements within the Party. In fact, you act for it as a kind of universal fireman; wherever flames appear, you dash there, sprinkle your magic words and the flames are put out.
>
> Secondly, a most important function, you provide a link between what might be called middle-class India and village India. To provide this link is by no means an easy task.
>
> Then, thirdly, and I would emphasize this because this seems to me the most important, you represent that extra ounce—I should rather say, that extra ton—which tilts the balance of all the developments in India today in a progressive direction. I mean in internal as well as in external affairs. You give a social colouring to all what is happening and you direct India's attention toward the outside world, thus lessening the chance of India being chauvinistically closed in in her own universe. This third function of yours seems to be the most important.

JAWAHARLAL NEHRU

You might conceivably be replaced as Party head, possibly even in your role as a link between middle-class and village India, but I wonder if India will find the successor who will exert this same influence in the socially-minded, in the progressive direction.

To this widely asked question, "What will happen when India is deprived of your leadership?" Nehru now replied:

There is no answer to that question. But I might tell you that I have no fear about the future. Partly, because, it is no good to have fears. Partly, because one does his best.[56]

The equivocation notwithstanding, what comes through is the self-esteem, the self-regard—for Nehru did seem to think that he was indispensable to India's present, if not its future. He had become accustomed to seeing himself in these terms because of the acclaim he received at home and abroad. He had almost single-handedly led the Congress to victory in three general elections. And as the *Guardian* wrote after Nehru had addressed a press conference in London in the summer of 1957:

A hundred men and women of the West were being given a glimpse of the blazing power that commands the affection and loyalty of several hundred million people in Asia. There is nothing mysterious about it. Mr Nehru's power is purely and simply a matter of personality. It is as intangible as that. Put in its simplest terms, it is the power of a man who is father, teacher and older brother rolled into one. The total impression is of a man who is humorous, tolerant, wise and absolutely honest.[57]

These words are quoted by Sarvepalli Gopal, in whose biography Nehru towers above his colleagues and rivals within India. In truth, the power of his personality and the electoral legitimacy he commanded notwithstanding, Nehru's policies were vigorously contested by other parties and politicians within India.

Among the most unforgiving of Nehru's adversaries were ideologues of the Left and the Right. In 1952, the Jana Sangh was set up. This was a party based on religious identity, which insisted that Hinduism defined the essence of the Indian nation, and therefore Hindu faith and sentiment must guide its programs and policies. Conservative on matters of gender equality, the Jana Sangh was supportive of small business but suspicious of big capital. It also advocated closer political (but not economic) ties with the United States. In the 1950s and beyond, it made slow but steady progress in North India, finding a sympathetic audience among traders, shopkeepers, priests, and refugees.[58]

From the Left, Nehru and the Congress were opposed by the Communist Party of India (CPI). Set up in the 1920s, the CPI had attracted to its ranks some extremely able intellectuals and writers. Whereas the Jana Sangh saw Nehru as too much of a socialist, the Communists saw him as not socialistic enough. They advocated a thoroughgoing nationalization of private property, a closer relationship with the Soviet Union, and active opposition to American policies everywhere. In Nehru's lifetime, the CPI made important strides in West Bengal and in Kerala, where, in 1957, they dramatically defeated the Congress to win power in state elections.[59]

The Hindu Right and the Communist Left had both stayed away from the Congress-led national movement. Nehru and his party had long recognized them as adversaries. More interesting, perhaps, were the criticisms of the prime minister made by four former Congress colleagues of his. All were remarkable men, unjustly given short shrift in scholarly (and popular) studies of Jawaharlal Nehru and his times.

The most distinguished member of this quartet was C. Rajagopalachari, whom Gandhi once called "the keeper of my conscience." The preeminent Congress leader in South India, "Rajaji" was a scholar steeped in Tamil and English literature, and the author of widely acclaimed translations of the Ramayana and the Mahabharata. In his long service in the Congress cause, he had served as chief minister of Madras, home minister in Nehru's cabinet, governor of West Bengal, and governor-general of India. In 1959, at the age of eighty, he started a new party, Swatantra, which promoted free-market economics as well as better relations with the Americans. But it eschewed the conservative idiom of the Jana Sangh, strongly advocating Hindu-Muslim harmony as well as the abolition of untouchability.[60]

Rajaji had once been personally close to Nehru. Even closer was Jayaprakash Narayan, a radical from Bihar educated in the United States and a great hero of the Quit India movement of 1942. After Independence, Narayan (who was popularly known as JP) left the Congress to start the Socialist Party of India. A few years later he turned his back on party politics and became a social worker. JP was a firm believer in political decentralization and, in the Gandhian way, in the revival of the village economy. Also reminiscent of Gandhi were his attempts at mediating between the state and rebels in Kashmir and Nagaland.[61]

Despite their disagreements, Nehru and Narayan were enormously fond of one another. Nehru tried hard to get Narayan to join the Union cabinet. Narayan, even while chastising the prime minister for being neglectful of the village economy, always addressed him as "Bhai," elder brother. Another Socialist originally from the Congress stable was more truculent. This was Rammanohar Lohia. A well-trained social scientist with a PhD from Berlin, Lohia was the one Indian who could match Nehru in his grasp of international politics. He complained that the prime minister was too soft on the Soviets. However, his main criticism was that Nehru represented an alien, English-speaking, upper-caste sensibility and was thus out of touch with the ordinary folk. Lohia took at face value Nehru's jocular, self-deprecatory representation of himself as "the last Englishman to rule India." A true Indian democracy, Lohia believed, would come to pass only when lower castes, tribals, and other oppressed groups acquired effective political power themselves.[62]

The last of these comrades-turned-critics was J. B. Kripalani. Kripalani's nationalist credentials were even older than Nehru's, for he had joined Gandhi during the Mahatma's first *satyagraha* on Indian soil, in Champaran in 1917. Originally from Sind, and a teacher of history by profession, Kripalani stayed within Gandhi's inner circle until Independence, serving several terms as president of the Congress. In 1950 he left and started his own party, which he later merged with the Socialists.

Kripalani was a man of character and intelligence. Yet, unlike Rajaji, JP, or Lohia, his views are hard to pinpoint in ideological terms. His opposition to Nehru was based simply on the democratic right to dissent. He thought no individual should have so much power and authority within party and especially within government. He also accused Nehru of sheltering a coterie of loyalists, singling out the defense minister, V. K. Krishna Menon, the target of some of his most memorable speeches in Parliament.[63]

These men, and their parties, consistently opposed Congress policies in Parliament and in state assemblies. During the China conflict, their criticisms grew more strident. The Jana Sangh, the Swatantra

Party, the Socialists all laid the blame on the military defeat at Nehru's feet. In August 1963, they went so far as to bring a no-confidence motion against the government. The majority that the ruling party commanded meant that the motion was defeated, yet the speeches made by Kripalani and others signaled, in form, length, and content, a considerable decline in the stature of the prime minister. The People's Prince, the great golden disc, the indispensable link between India and the world had now become "an old man, looking frail and fatigued, with a marked stoop in his gait, coming down the gangway [of Parliament] with slow, faltering steps, and clutching the backrests of benches for support as he descended."[64]

IX

After Nehru's death in May 1964, Lal Bahadur Shastri succeeded him as prime minister.[65] A small man with a self-effacing personality, he exceeded all expectations in his new job. Shastri allocated more resources to agriculture and agricultural science, so as to make India self-sufficient in food grains. He asked for a loosening of the state's stranglehold over the industrial sector. When Pakistan sent infiltrators into Kashmir, hoping to provoke an uprising against the Indian state, Shastri opened a front in the Punjab, forcing the aggressor back on the defensive. The war ended in a cease-fire, brokered by the Russians. At a conference to discuss its terms, held in Tashkent in January 1966, Shastri died of cardiac arrest.[66]

Who would now succeed Shastri? The leading candidate was the veteran freedom-fighter and administrator Morarji Desai, who had served both as chief minister of Bombay State and finance minister in the Central Government. Nehru himself had once written that there "were very few people whom I respect so much for their rectitude, ability, efficiency and fairness as Morarji Desai."[67] However, the influential Congress president, K. Kamaraj, threw his weight behind Nehru's daughter, Indira Gandhi. She had served a term as Congress president in the 1950s and had been a junior minister in Shastri's cabinet. Despite her relative lack of experience and stature, Kamaraj felt that around her he could build a wider consensus to pull the nation through the shock of these consecutive deaths of prime ministers.[68]

The political career of Indira Gandhi is the subject of another essay in this volume. Here I must deal with her long tenure as prime minister (from 1966 to 1977, and again from 1980 to 1984) only in terms of how it has impacted Nehru's own posthumous reputation. First, the decades after Nehru's death saw a steady erosion of Congress hegemony. Thus, the general elections of 1967 saw major gains at the provincial level by the Jana Sangh, the Communists, the Swatantra Party, and the Socialists. This anticipated the historic defeat of the Congress in the general elections of 1977, when it was routed by a new party called Janata, composed of four fragments—the Jana Sangh, the Swatantra Party, the Socialists, and old-style Congressmen (including Morarji Desai) who had fallen foul of Indira Gandhi.

Second, while Nehru himself had no desire that his daughter would succeed him as prime minister, in 1975 Mrs. Gandhi brought her son Sanjay into politics, making it clear that he would henceforth be the second most important person in the party and the government. Sanjay died in an air crash in June 1980, whereupon the prime minister directed her other son, Rajiv, to leave his job as a commercial pilot and work with her in the Congress instead.

In June 1975, Mrs. Gandhi imposed a state of emergency, abrogating democratic processes and jailing major opposition leaders. These included Jayaprakash Narayan, Jana Sangh and Communist politicians, as well as Swatantra and Socialist MPs. (Rajaji and Lohia were no longer alive; otherwise, they could well have been put behind bars too.) Meanwhile, cabinet ministers took their orders from Sanjay Gandhi. Sanjay was also principally responsible for the major human rights violations of the emergency, among them the demolition of parts of Old Delhi and forcible sterilizations across northern India.[69]

Mrs. Gandhi's regime thus saw a sharpening of the conflict between the ruling Congress and its critics. This now had an intense personal edge, due to the persecution of opposition leaders during the Emergency and the conversion of the Congress itself into a family firm. Nehru's own scrupulous respect for democratic procedure was now forgotten. In the popular imagination, his daughter's policies and preferences were said to be his, too.

In October 1984, Indira Gandhi was assassinated. Her son, Rajiv, succeeded her as prime minister. His five-year term saw, on the positive side, a push toward technological modernization, but, on the negative side, the pandering to religious bigots (both Hindu and Muslim), as well as a spate of corruption scandals in government. The grandson's errors and misdeeds helped further erode the public standing of the grandfather.

Rajiv Gandhi was assassinated in May 1991. Later in the same year, I published a short essay in the *Indian Express* calling attention to the fact that while Mahatma Gandhi's standing among the intelligentsia had rapidly risen in recent years, Jawaharlal Nehru's had precipitously fallen. (The newspaper gave it the title "Nehru Is Out, Gandhi Is In"). While Nehru commanded colossal respect in his lifetime, I wrote that "today few other than the career chamchas [sycophants] are willing to defend him, and fewer still to understand him." Yet I had "no doubt that in time Nehru's reputation will slowly climb upwards, without ever reaching the high point of the 1950s."[70]

When I wrote this in 1991, it seemed that the dynasty, such as it was, had come to an end. I expected that the death of Rajiv Gandhi would lead to a more rounded assessment of India's first prime minister. Some of Nehru's ideas had run their course; thus, for example, both political devolution and market-friendly economics were now widely recognized as more suitable to India's present needs than the earlier emphasis on central planning. It was also now evident that Nehru's relative neglect of health care and primary education was partly responsible for the country's poor record in human development.

Yet it seemed to me in 1991 that other aspects of Nehru's legacy were relevant and needed to be reaffirmed: his commitment to Parliament and parliamentary procedures, his attempts to insulate public institutions from political interference; his vigorous defense of religious pluralism and of gender equality; his nurturing of centers of scientific research and teaching that had helped create India's software boom. Younger Indians also would, I thought, come to recognize the enormity of the challenges Nehru and his colleagues had to face in the first critical years of Independence.

However, I was mistaken in thinking that Nehru was being finally freed of the burden of his descendants. In 1998, Sonia Gandhi was asked to take charge of the Congress Party. At the time of writing, she has been Congress president for a staggering fifteen terms in succession, a record that even Indira Gandhi could not match. Meanwhile, her son Rahul has been explicitly anointed as her successor. The younger Mrs. Gandhi has promoted dynastic politics in other ways, by, for example, making a cult of her dead husband and mother-in-law, naming hundreds of new government programs after one or the other.

As the sociologist André Béteille has remarked,[71] the posthumous career of Jawaharlal Nehru has come increasingly to reverse a famous biblical injunction. In the Bible, it is said that the sins of the father will visit seven successive generations. In Nehru's case, the sins of daughter, grandsons, granddaughter-in-law, and great-grandson have been retrospectively visited on him.

And so the Hero of his age has become the Outcast of ours. The object of perhaps excessive adulation while he was alive, Nehru's achievements have been progressively undervalued after his death. The demonization of the man is now ubiquitous in popular and political discourse, and especially so in cyberspace. So long as Sonia and Rahul Gandhi retain their profile and prominence, this state of affairs shall prevail. Only after the last member of his family has exited the stage of Indian politics might a judicious and credible appreciation of Jawaharlal Nehru's life and legacy finally become possible.

SIX

ZHOU ENLAI

AND CHINA'S "PROLONGED RISE"

CHEN JIAN

I

ON APRIL 19, 1955, Zhou Enlai, premier and foreign minister of the People's Republic of China (PRC), delivered a speech at the conference of Afro-Asian leaders in Bandung, Indonesia. "The Chinese delegation," he said, "has come here to seek common grounds, not to create division." Despite their differences, the Asian and African countries had all suffered from "the calamities caused by colonialism" and were linked together by their "continuing struggle for complete independence." Zhou acknowledged that he believed in communism as the preferred path toward modernizing China and transforming the world. But he emphasized that this did not block him in endorsing "the Five Principles as the basis for establishing friendship, cooperation and good-neighbor relations among us."[1]

Comparing Zhou's speech with the revolutionary international discourse that the PRC had adopted in its first five years, its basic tone sounded rather conciliatory. It also seemed that the Chinese premier was in favor of crossing such Cold War dividing lines as differences in ideologies, and political programs and agendas, while championing a vision of Afro-Asian unity on the basis of shared experience. In its essence, however, Zhou's message was profoundly revolutionary on the *normative* level. Indeed, Zhou sought to introduce a whole set of new principles, thus posing a fundamental challenge to the norms and codes of the existing international system dominated by the United

States and other Western powers. Potentially, the message also challenged the international Communist movement's existing structure with Moscow as the center.

Furthermore, although Zhou highlighted equality and cooperation among Asian and African countries, one may detect that underpinning his message was the Chinese Communists' profound consciousness that it was they who occupied the moral high ground from which to define equality and other similar terms/norms in international relations. Such consciousness was with deep historical and cultural origins as well as complex domestic connections. When Zhou was making his presentation in Bandung, he was addressing not merely those who sat in front of him, but hundreds of millions of his compatriots in China. Indeed, when he spoke to that gathering of Asian and African leaders, Zhou seems to have had in mind Mao's famous statement: "The Chinese people have stood up."

For Zhou, his performance at Bandung, together with his widely acclaimed contributions to the Geneva Conference held a year earlier, represented the arrival of a brilliant diplomat on the international scene. So this was the moment of his rising star in world affairs. Less known was that behind Zhou's "glorious moment" stood what I must call the darker aspects of the Chinese Communist revolution. Zhou's diplomatic gesture might have earned him international acclaim, but for Mao the premier was at times too conciliatory. Not long after Bandung, Zhou encountered a furious Mao when the chairman found that he was opposing "rash advance" in China's economic policies (as Zhou believed that this would throw the country's development out of balance), and the premier was forced to make endless "self-criticism." This happened at the time that two of the most disastrous events of Mao's China—the Anti-Rightist movement and the Great Leap Forward—were sweeping across its cities and countryside.

Thus, if indeed Zhou's speech at Bandung was a moment that witnessed China's rise, it should also be understood in ways that the dilemmas and complex meanings of China's "age of revolutions" should be taken into serious consideration. In fact, this is not only true about Zhou's Bandung experience; this is also true when we try to evaluate Zhou's dilemma-ridden career as a Communist revolutionary, a statesman, and a person. Zhou's experience probably should be treated as a "test case," one that epitomized not only the constructive results of China's "age of revolutions" but also its paradoxes and complex legacies.

Zhou Enlai was born on March 5, 1898, into a declining mandarin's family in Huai'an, Jiangsu province. As a child, Zhou read classic Chinese literature and was cultivated in Confucian ethics. As he grew up, in his conceptual realm there was always a place reserved for the teachings of the ancient sages that he had learned in his childhood, even when he seemed to have wholeheartedly embraced Communist ideologies. In 1910, he left Huan'an to live under the patronage of his uncle, first in Shenyang and then in Tianjin, a major treaty port. While receiving modern education, he was exposed to the larger world, in which a backward China was sinking into an ever-deepening national crisis. He diligently studied Chinese classics and absorbed new knowledge. He also developed great interest in politics, increasingly longing for ways to make "China rise high again in the world."[2]

In September 1917, after graduating from Tianjin's Nankai School, Zhou left China to study in Japan, largely because he wanted to know how a country with cultural traditions and a modern experience similar to China's could rise to become a recognized power in a few short decades. Constrained by his inability to command Japanese, however, he repeatedly failed Japan's college entrance examinations. Yet his setbacks in academic study gave him more time to participate in political activities. Despite his strong opposition to Japan's imperialist policy toward China, he was impressed by the effectiveness of Japan's modernization drive. But when he saw the deep divisions in Japanese society, he became increasingly interested in the ideas of socialism, vaguely feeling that this could solve China's problems.[3]

In March 1919, on the eve of the May Fourth movement, Zhou returned to China. Two months later, when the Versailles Conference imposed on China the deal of allowing Japan to take over the prewar German sphere of influence in Shandong, the long-accumulated nationalist sentiment among the intellectuals and students broke into a series of mass protests.

Zhou, then in Tianjin, immediately participated in the protests. He and fellow students organized an "Awakening Society." In January 1920, as the commander of a student protest against the authorities' "surrenderist attitudes toward Japan," Zhou was arrested. During the six months he was in prison, he read widely, touching upon "all kinds of new thoughts." He was now further pushed toward embracing Marxism, in the belief that "the goal of the future is to bring about fundamental transformation of society."[4] After his release from prison, he decided to go to Europe for the purpose of identifying the ways "to solve the problems facing our own nation."[5]

From December 1920 to August 1924, Zhou was in Europe, mostly in France. When he arrived in Europe, he was not yet a Communist. Four years later, he was firmly committed to Communism as the lodestar for China's salvation and liberation. In the many letters and essays that he wrote in Europe, a path of intellectual growth with three outstanding yet interrelated features can be identified. First, on the most urgent level, Zhou was genuinely ashamed of China's backwardness. A persistent theme in his thinking was how to promote China's development and salvation.

Second, Zhou was enthusiastically attracted by the concept of national liberation. It was here that he found in Communism the intellectual and political instrument for realizing his ideals and goals. Thus, after comparing England's reformist changes with Russia's radical revolutionary transformations, he concluded that unless China followed Russia's example, "the goal of transformation is unlikely to be realized."[6]

In a deeper sense, though, Zhou did not take the transformation of China as his ultimate goal. For him, this would not make sense unless it also touched upon the hearts of the people and led to their "rebirth" or "new birth." It is here that one finds the ultimate reason of Zhou's turning to communism in his intellectual journey. He saw a Communist revolution as the only way to lead to a "new China" and a "new world." For this, any sacrifice was justified and any price was worth paying.[7]

With his mind increasingly penetrated by communist ideas, Zhou resolutely turned to action. In May 1921, he joined a group of Communists and Communist sympathizers in Paris. After the establishment of the Communist Party of China in July 1921, Zhou became a founding member of its European branch and served as its director of propaganda. In a few short years, Zhou's name became widely known among members of the CCP circle in Europe.

At the moment, China itself was on the eve of the "Great Revolution," which was carried out by the CCP-Kuomintang (KMT) United Front and took the various warlords as its target. In July 1924, following the Comintern's instructions, the CCP's European branch decided to send its members back to China to participate in the Great Revolution. Zhou was selected and boarded a ship for China in late July.

Zhou arrived in Guangzhou, the center of the Great Revolution, in September 1924, and quickly emerged as one of the main figures in the CCP. In the ensuing quarter century, as the CCP took a tortuous path toward seizing political power, Zhou had his bright times and dark moments, yet all through would remain a main figure of the Chinese revolution.

In November 1924, Zhou assumed the directorship of the Political Department at the Whampoa Military Academy, which was established by Sun Yat-sen for training revolutionary officers and cadres. He immediately demonstrated an extraordinary ability in matters of organization and propaganda, instilling a new "revolutionary spirit" into Whampoa's curriculum. In Guangzhou, Zhou met Mao for the first time, which opened the half-century-long bond that would later be characterized by Zhou living and working in the shadow of Mao's authority, ideas, and programs.

The CCP-KMT United Front was short lived. A critical turning point came in April 1927, when the KMT leader, Chiang Kai-shek, launched a bloody anticommunist coup in Shanghai. Then the Comintern ordered the CCP to carry out uprisings in major cities. Mao and a group of his comrades, however, moved to the countryside in southern China, where they organized the Red Army and, by mobilizing the peasants, waged a violent "Land Revolution." Mao found it necessary to create a rural-centered pattern of Communist revolution, as he sensed that China's social conditions precluded an urban-centered uprising. He also perceived that China's backwardness in development made it easier for a revolution by the peasants to succeed.[8]

Like Mao, Zhou also believed that "political power comes from the barrel of a gun." Among CCP leaders, he was one of the first to put this maxim into practice. In August 1927, Zhou organized the Nanchang Uprising, which began the CCP's military challenge to Chiang. But, unlike Mao, Zhou's thoughts remained urban-centered, so he and his comrades led their troops to march toward Guangzhou, hoping to establish a base that would allow them to receive aid from the Soviet Union by sea. Encountering a much stronger enemy force, however, the march failed.

From late 1927 to late 1931, Zhou was based in Shanghai, the location of the CCP center. During this period, the CCP's top leader's position was occupied by several different individuals. Zhou never claimed that post, although he obviously had the opportunity to do so as he actually controlled the party's organizational links and intelligence network. Several times he was even criticized for his tendency of paying too much attention to operational details and not enough attention to "big issues."[9] However, all top leaders and the Comintern's representatives had to depend on him for keeping the party's operations going.

Under the Comintern's direction, the CCP leadership's attitudes toward Mao's "Land Revolution" was skeptical. While Mao's efforts in organizing the Red Army and establishing the Red Zone were appreciated, he was repeatedly instructed to attack big cities. When Mao acted on his own, tensions emerged between him and the CCP center. On several occasions, Zhou also criticized Mao. But the continuous existence and development of the Red Army under Mao also left Zhou with the impression that the future chairman was a military and strategic genius.

By late 1931, when Chiang tightened encirclement of the underground CCP center, Zhou moved into the Red Zone in Jiangxi. He arrived at a time that the long-existing friction between Mao and the party center had worsened, and Mao's suppression of the "hidden reactionaries" had resulted in huge tensions in the Red Zone. This led to Mao's dismissal from his position as the Red Army's political commissar at the Ningdu Conference in October 1932. Zhou, who chaired the conference, criticized Mao's mistakes while acknowledging his contributions. Had it not been for Zhou, Mao could have been more severely punished. However, as Zhou became the person to take over Mao's position in the Red Army, the future chairman would always remember this as one of Zhou's "crimes" against him and his "correct political line."[10]

At the time, Zhou controlled huge political and military power and thus could have striven for the party's top leadership role, but he did not do so. When the CCP center moved into the Red Zone in late 1932, Zhou yielded power to Bo Gu, a returnee from Moscow in his mid-twenties. Zhou concentrated his efforts on managing the Red Army and the Red Zone.

In late 1934, facing the overwhelming pressure of Chiang Kai-shek's troops, the Red Army was forced to evacuate from the Red Zone, a move that would later be named the "Long March." On the verge of being eliminated by the enemy, the CCP leadership held an important conference in Zunyi in January 1935, at which Mao was elected to a three-person "military commanding group" headed by Zhou. As it turned out, this change opened the path for Mao to emerge as the CCP's top leader. Zhou played a pivotal role in the process. Believing that Mao was probably the only person who could get the Red Army out of the military abyss, he carefully prepared for the conference to change the party's leadership. At the conference, he persuaded Bo Gu to give up his resistance. Later, although officially head of the three-person group at the helm, he let Mao play the leadership role. If the Zunyi Conference indeed witnessed the beginning of Mao's re-rise, Zhou was the person who opened the door for Mao.[11]

During the later phase of the Long March and beyond, the sheer need for survival combined with the Comintern's adoption of a new "anti-Fascist international united front" strategy form the context in which the CCP turned toward pursuing an anti-Japanese united front with the KMT. Thus, the CCP was engaged in negotiations with both Chiang and General Zhang Xueliang, whose forces were stationed in areas next to the Red Army's new bases. From the beginning, Zhou was the central CCP figure to handle these negotiations. His persuasiveness and charisma won Zhang's trust. On December 12, 1936, Zhang waged a coup and kidnapped Chiang in Xi'an. Zhou immediately was called upon to help settle the incident. Chiang agreed to stop the war with the Communists, so that the country could unite to fight against Japan. When the Sino-Japanese War erupted in July 1937, the CCP and the KMT entered another united front.

The ensuing eight years of China's war against Japan witnessed the CCP's substantial growth in military strength and political influence. Holding high the banner of nationalism, the CCP and its military forces carried out Mao's strategy of placing the expansion of themselves as the top priority mission. In the meantime, with Moscow having to concentrate on its own war efforts and the Comintern dissolved in 1943, the CCP won the independence that it had not enjoyed since its birth.

Zhou spent most of the war years in Chongqing, China's wartime capital. His task was to carry out "united front work" with the KMT and other political forces, as well as to develop the CCP's international connections. He and his associates strived to characterize Chiang's reign as totalitarian and corrupt. They also presented the CCP as both nationalistic and democratic, creating an image that China's future belonged to it. Judging from reactions from China's third parties and foreigners (including many Americans), Zhou was quite successful, and he also earned a reputation as a capable politician and diplomat.

But Zhou also had his dark moment. In late 1943, Mao called Zhou back to Yanan to participate in the Rectification movement, an event central in the rise of Maoism. When Zhou arrived in Yanan, he immediately sensed Mao's growing authority and power. So in his first public speech, he extolled Mao as "the banner of the Chinese revolution." Still the treatment that he received was a surprise to him. At a lengthy Politburo meeting in late November–early December, he tried his best to put blame on himself. Yet he could not pass the test. Zhou's comrades even went so far as to accuse him of being a "collaborator" with Chiang and betraying the revolution. Not until the intervention of Georgi Dimitrov, the Comintern's former general secretary, did Zhou's ordeal finally end.

When the Soviet Union entered the war against Japan in August 1945, Mao thought that the CCP's moment was coming. However, what Mao and the CCP did not know was that, in the Soviet-US Yalta accord, Stalin had agreed to support Chiang Kai-shek's position as China's national leader in exchange for his acceptance of a Soviet sphere of influence, as well as Mongolia's independence.[12] Under Stalin's pressure, Mao had no choice but to go to Chongqing to negotiate with Chiang. Zhou, accompanying Mao, managed all the details for the chairman.

In mid-1946, a full-scale civil war broke out between the CCP and the KMT. Zhou was with Mao and served as the chairman's chief of staff. With the CCP gradually winning an upper hand on the battlefield, Mao introduced the "Intermediate Zone" thesis, according to which there existed a vast unaffiliated zone between the United States and the Soviet Union, and the US imperialists could not attack the Soviet Union until they had controlled the zone. Although the postwar world order was characterized by US-Soviet confrontation, the "principal contradiction" in the world rested with the struggles between peoples in the intermediate zone—especially China—and the reactionary US ruling class.[13] What was revealed here was the CCP's determination to challenge the United States as a dominant imperialist power and to stand on the side of the Soviet Union. Meanwhile, it also highlighted the Maoist perception of the central role that China was to play in bridging the world revolution and decolonization.

On October 1, 1949, the People's Republic of China was established. Mao, now chairman of the PRC, announced that "we the Chinese people have stood up." Zhou was appointed premier and foreign minister. A few months earlier, Mao had stated that China would lean to the side of the Soviet Union in the Cold War.[14] On February 14, 1950, Beijing and Moscow entered a treaty of strategic alliance, which concluded Mao's two-month visit to the Soviet Union. Zhou was summoned by Mao to Moscow during the later stage of the visit and signed the treaty.

If indeed the new China's rise meant that "the Chinese people have stood up," how could this be reconciled with Mao's "leaning to one side" approach? How exactly would China's position in the world be defined? Zhou knew that these were the questions that the Chinese people would ask. He had his answers. "Leaning to one side" actually was one of the three legs of the PRC's foreign policy structure. Along with it, as Zhou summarized, were "making a fresh start" and "cleaning the house before entertaining guests," which meant that the new China would discard all of the "old China's" diplomatic legacies and pursue a "new international diplomacy."[15]

Thus Mao personally started a nationwide anti-imperialist propaganda campaign, labeling the United States as China's worst enemy in modern history.[16] Zhou faithfully carried out this policy, and his central message to the Americans was that "Asia's matters must be handled by Asians themselves."[17] In the ensuring two decades, anti-Americanism would dominate China's political and cultural discourse and even everyday life.

The outbreak of the Korean War in June 1950 presented a major challenge to the PRC. Almost immediately, Beijing prepared to enter it. Zhou was in charge of planning and coordination. In discussions between Mao, Zhou, and other CCP leaders, they concluded that unless "China's strength is added to the side of the Korean comrades, . . . the U.S. imperialists would become rampant" in Asia, and the "world people's cause of anti-imperialism" would be jeopardized.[18]

Beijing's final decision to enter the war was made in the first three weeks of October. In face of the prospect that this could result in a total war with the United States, many CCP leaders had serious reservations about whether China should send troops to Korea. And Stalin was reluctant to provide Chinese troops with air cover. Still, with Mao's persistent push, the CCP leadership made the decision to enter the war. Zhou was a crucial figure here, as he supported Mao despite some reservations. He also traveled to the Soviet Union to negotiate with Stalin, making the Soviet leader agree to offer military support, including defense of China's air space and, in two months, air support to Chinese troops fighting in Korea.[19]

In addition to defending China's borders with Korea, Mao, Zhou, and their comrades also had an Asian or Eastern vision, which was associated with their aspiration of turning the war into a powerful source of extensive domestic mobilization by holding high the banner of internationalism and revolutionary nationalism. Mao emphasized that China's entry into the war was "very important to the interests of China, Korea, and the East."[20] Zhou elaborated that "we should strive for victory in fighting against the United States in Korea, and should give U.S. imperialists . . . a heavy blow and beat their arrogance. Only by achieving such a victory will . . . the national liberation movements in the East inspired by the victory of the Chinese people not be suppressed."[21]

China's intervention in Korea caused the loss of hundreds of thousands of Chinese lives, forced hundreds of millions of dollars for war purposes at the expense of the country's reconstruction, and resulted in its prolonged confrontation with the United States. Yet, for Mao, Zhou, and the CCP, China's gains were considerable. During the war years, the CCP found itself in a position to penetrate into almost every area of Chinese society through intensive mass mobilization, dramatically promoting its authority and legitimacy in the minds of the population. Internationally, Beijing had occupied a powerful position from which to claim that friends and foes alike had to accept China's status as a great power.[22]

After the Korean War, Mao, Zhou, and the CCP leadership turned their attention to China's domestic reconstruction, focusing on "creating the foundation of a socialist society." They understood that if they were able to present a strong case of advancement in the PRC's international status, they could more effectively promote the party's mass mobilization plans at home.

It was against this background that Zhou attended the Geneva Conference of 1954 and the Bandung Conference of 1955. This turned out to be Zhou's moment. Central to Geneva's agenda was how to make peace in Korea and Vietnam. Zhou worked closely with the Soviet delegation to persuade or even pressure their Vietminh comrades to accept a solution that would leave Vietnam divided. While doing so, Zhou emphasized that such a settlement in Indochina would promote the interests of the peace camp throughout the Asian-Pacific region.[23] Zhou also seized the opportunity to build working relationships with leaders from Britain and France who were in Geneva.

These activities were crucial for the Geneva conference to reach a breakthrough on the Indochina issue; they also widened Beijing's international visions and activities. In late June, during an interval of the conference, Zhou visited India and Burma. Together with India's Prime Minister Jawaharlal Nehru and Burma's Prime Minister U Nu, Zhou introduced the "Five Principles of Peaceful Coexistence."

Despite the widespread impression about Zhou's success at Geneva, Mao's attitude toward him was not always positive. One week after the conclusion of the Geneva Conference, Mao dispatched a telegram to Zhou, who was then still traveling in East Europe, sternly criticizing the premier's "mistake of failing to raise the Taiwan issue."[24] In the ensuing months, a major international crisis emerged in the Taiwan Strait. On September 3, the People's Liberation Army shelled the KMT-controlled Jinmen (Quemoy) islands. In early 1955, the PLA further attacked and occupied two strings of KMT-controlled islands off Zhejiang province. In response, Washington signed a treaty of mutual defense with Chiang's regime in December 1954. Washington even considered using nuclear weapons if the crisis escalated.

Such was the complicated background to the Bandung Conference. For Zhou and Beijing's leaders, Bandung was an occasion crucially relevant to the PRC's claim to a central role in international affairs. The basic Chinese tone at Bandung had been set in advance, but Zhou's charisma and diplomatic skills refined the tone. Zhou cautiously avoided ideological language in describing China's domestic and international policies. At private meetings, he repeatedly stressed that Beijing favored peace and that China would not export revolution to other countries. In public presentations, he carefully avoided running into any direct conflict with dissenting voices. Thus, he made the speech described in the opening paragraph of this essay. Toward the end of the conference, Zhou announced that Beijing was willing to negotiate with Washington for reducing "tensions in the Far East" and solving bilateral problems between the two countries.[25]

After Bandung, Beijing tried to apply the Five Principles to the relations between Communist countries while, at the same time, opposing

Moscow's pursuing "peaceful coexistence" with the United States. In February 1956, the Soviet leader, Nikita Khrushchev, launched the de-Stalinization campaign. Mao criticized Khrushchev by claiming that he, albeit having "exposed the problems," had "made a mess."[26]

Khrushchev's initiative led to great turmoil within the international Communist movement, and, in October, the Polish and Hungarian crises erupted. Believing that the Polish crisis was primarily "anti-Soviet," the Chinese leaders pushed Moscow to adopt a declaration accepting that all Communist countries were equal and should follow the Five Principles in managing their relations. Viewing the Hungarian event as in essence "anti-Communist," they strongly urged Moscow to use force to settle the crisis.[27]

The fact that Moscow indeed used force in Hungary enhanced the sense of moral superiority on the part of Mao and his comrades. In January 1957, Zhou visited the Soviet Union, Poland, and Hungary. In his report summarizing the visit, he discussed how the Soviet leadership lacked sophistication in managing the complicated situation both within the Soviet Union and in Eastern Europe. The report unmistakably conveyed the self-image of Beijing as the most qualified candidate in claiming leadership in the Communist world.[28]

In the wake of 1956, Mao was more determined to promote China's continuous revolution, especially in politics and ideology. In early 1957, he initiated the Hundred Flowers campaign, in which intellectuals were encouraged to help the CCP to "correct its mistakes." But when some intellectuals indeed voiced their criticism of the party, a movement began to sweep across China that branded hundreds of thousands as "rightists," a label that would shut their mouths and ruin their careers.

During the Anti-Rightist campaign, Zhou also became the target of Mao's criticism. As early as in 1955–1956, potential tensions began to emerge between Mao and some of his prominent colleagues, and Zhou in particular. On the one hand, the advancement of collectivization in the countryside and the transformation of industry in the cities convinced Mao that his revolution should be elevated to a higher stage, one that would accelerate China's economic development and its growth into a socialist society.[29] On the other hand, Zhou believed it essential to maintain balanced social and economic development and that "rash advance" should be avoided.[30]

Beginning in 1957, Mao claimed that Zhou had been seriously mistaken in emphasizing the importance of keeping balance in China's development. In 1958 Mao continued his attack, identifying Zhou's as "a mistake concerning principles, which has damaged the revolutionary vigor of 600 million [Chinese] people." He even said that Zhou was "only fifty meters from becoming a rightist."[31] Zhou acknowledged that he should take "the main responsibility" for committing the "opposing 'rash advance' mistake."[32] In addition, Zhou also criticized his own "rightist-leaning tendency" in handling China's foreign relations.[33]

Against this background, Zhou resigned as China's foreign minister in early 1958. He also intended to resign his premier's position, but in the end desisted, because other Politburo members believed that he should stay on.

The chairman's assault should not have come as a total surprise to the premier. After all, Mao's fierce attack on him during the Rectification movement had occurred only a decade previously. Still, Zhou seemed shocked by the tone and persistence of Mao's criticism, which would further transform their relationship into one characterized by his total obedience to the chairman's ideas and actions.

Emerging from Mao's "victory" in the "rash advance" debate was the prevalence of the "development at any price" model, which provided the foundation for the Great Leap Forward to sweep across China. In summer 1958, the CCP leadership announced that "the realization of a Communist society in China is not far away." For the purpose of rapidly increasing China's industrial production, millions of ordinary Chinese were mobilized to make steel in "backyard furnaces." What excited Mao most was that tens of thousands of "people's communes" were founded throughout the country. In Mao's vision, they had opened the door for China to quickly emerge as a Communist society.

As China's premier, Zhou had access to data indicating that the country's economic growth was totally out of balance. However, he kept silent. Beginning in late 1958, the Great Leap's negative impact gradually surfaced. In summer 1959, when top CCP leaders met at Lushan, Marshall Peng Dehuai, the defense minister, wrote to Mao to criticize the Great Leap and suggested policy changes. Zhou initially was in favor of Peng's opinions. However, when Mao angrily labeled Peng's action as "anti-Party" and "anti-socialism," Zhou immediately stood on Mao's side.[34] The outcome of the Lushan Conference removed the last hope of avoiding the Great Famine that would follow, the biggest peacetime tragedy in twentieth-century history.

Internationally, the Great Leap caused another crisis between the PRC and the United States. At the same time, Beijing's relations with Moscow rapidly deteriorated. In summer 1958, Mao ordered the PLA to shell the KMT-controlled Jinmen Islands. When Washington came to the defense of the Nationalists, the Taiwan Strait crisis of 1958 erupted. Although the Soviet Union was China's ally, Beijing did not inform Moscow about the shelling in advance. Mao also claimed that Khrushchev wanted to make China a Soviet satellite.[35] The Sino-Soviet alliance began to collapse. As China's premier, Zhou did not raise any questions about Mao's international policies. He merely carried out what Mao told him to do.

The Great Leap also accelerated the "socialist transformations" in many Tibetan-inhabited areas, causing widespread resistance. The accumulated tensions finally caused a major rebellion to break out in Lhasa on March 10, 1959. When Beijing used force to suppress the revolt, the Dalai Lama, Tibet's religious and political leader, took refuge in India. This, in turn, led to serious tensions in Sino-Indian relations, and Beijing's and New Delhi's disputes over the borders between the two countries were suddenly highlighted.[36] In fall 1959, two border clashes occurred between Chinese and Indian garrisons, further shattering the trust between Chinese and Indian leaders.

Early in the 1960s, in the wake of the Great Leap's disastrous failure, Beijing's leaders had no choice but to put the "development at any price" model on hold. Liu Shaoqi and Deng Xiaoping now adopted a series of more moderate and flexible policies designed for economic recovery and social stability. They also advocated a less strident foreign policy. Efforts were made to repair the damage in China's alliance with the Soviet Union. Beijing also tried to improve relations with other countries, and its non-Communist neighbors in particular.

Zhou's sympathies lay with Liu and Deng. In line with the adjustment of China's domestic and foreign policies under them, Zhou hoped to improve Beijing's relations with New Delhi. In April 1960, he visited India to seek a solution to the border dispute. After much deliberation, he presented to Nehru a proposal, by which China would give up its territorial claims over the eastern sections of the borders in exchange for India's acceptance of Chinese sovereignty over the border's disputed western sections. Despite Zhou's efforts, however, the Indian side was unyielding. In a deeper sense, the difficulty involved in the Zhou-Nehru negotiation also revealed the potential conflict between

Beijing and New Delhi concerning which country—China or India—should claim the leadership role in Asia in the postcolonial age.[37]

The flexible policies by Liu and Deng did not last long. Mao was unwilling to give up either his revolutionary programs or his position as China's paramount leader. When the economy showed signs of recovery in 1962, Mao began returning to the "first line" of China's decision-making structure. In September 1962, Mao called upon the whole party "never to forget class struggle," placing "the fight against revisionism" at home and abroad as the party's top priority.[38] This symbolized the beginning of a rapid radicalization of China's domestic and international policies. Mao now initiated a series of new campaigns in China's politics, society and culture, opening the path that would eventually lead to the "Great Proletarian Cultural Revolution."

This turn occurred at a time of acute tension between China and India. Given India's crucial position among non-Western countries, Mao and Zhou did not want to get into a direct military showdown with New Delhi. Since the failure of Zhou's April 1960 trip, Beijing maintained a nonconfrontational approach until late 1962. This policy of restraint was abandoned when, on October 20, 1962, China started a large-scale "war of self-defense" along its borders with India. By November 20, it was evident that the Chinese had already won the war. At this moment, Beijing suddenly announced a unilateral cease-fire, and Chinese troops were ordered to retreat to areas twenty kilometers behind the actual control line between the two sides.[39]

Mao was the central figure behind the decision to use force against India. When the situation on the Chinese-Indian borders deteriorated in the second half of 1962, Mao was the first among top CCP leaders to argue for the need for the Chinese troops "absolutely not to yield to the pressure of the invading Indian troops."[40] Early in October 1962, Mao further pointed out that it was necessary for the Chinese troops to give the Indians a "bitter lesson." Zhou supported Mao. CCP leaders particularly emphasized that the Chinese military operation concerned the "reputation and prestige of our country and our army," and, therefore, China must achieve a glorious victory.[41]

In the war against India, Mao reclaimed his central decision-making role. In a deeper sense, when Mao was striving to galvanize strength and momentum for the Cultural Revolution, he attached more importance to international issues with the hope that international tension would serve as a source of domestic mobilization, thus maintaining and enhancing the legitimacy of the PRC, which had been severely challenged by the Great Leap's failure.

Therefore, with Mao reclaiming his role as China's supreme leader, he repeatedly stressed that the country was facing a crisis-ridden international environment, where reactionary forces headed by the US imperialists were preparing to wage a war against China. Mao openly criticized the Kremlin's strategy of "peaceful coexistence," claiming that it obscured the fundamental distinction between revolution and counterrevolution. Further, Mao asserted that socialism in the Soviet Union had been gradually eroded by an emerging "bureaucratic capitalist class." Mao warned that China also faced the danger of the "restoration of capitalism." He also contended that Moscow had long carried out a policy of "great power chauvinism" toward China. The Soviet Union, he argued, was a threat to Chinese sovereignty and independence. Mao thus effectively linked his challenge to Moscow's leading position in international Communism to the safeguarding of China's national security interests, making it impossible for his colleagues, Zhou included, to disagree with him.

Mao now argued that between the United States and the Soviet Union there existed two "intermediate zones." The first was composed of "the vast economically backward countries in Asia, Africa and Latin America," and the second included "imperialist and advanced capitalist countries in Europe."[42] After 1962–1963, Beijing's international discourse increasingly highlighted the central role that China had played in promoting revolutionary movements in the first intermediate zone, challenging both the United States and the Soviet Union. Zhou himself proclaimed that "the center of the world revolution indeed had moved from Moscow to Beijing."[43]

At the center of Beijing's international policy design was Southeast Asia, where Mao believed conditions for revolutions were most mature. Zhou was a central carrier of this policy. In summer 1963, Zhou chaired a "strategic planning" meeting, attended by leaders of the Communist parties from Vietnam, Laos, and Indonesia, for preparing and waging revolutions in Southeast Asia. In July 1964, he chaired another meeting of Chinese, Vietnamese, and Laotian Communist leaders. In his keynote speeches, Zhou emphasized that Southeast Asia had become the focus of confrontation between revolutionary and reactionary forces. He encouraged Communist parties in the region to promote an anti-imperialist, anti-feudal, and anti-"compradore capitalist" revolution by mobilizing the masses and conducting armed struggles. He promised that China would serve as the "great rear" of "Southeast Asian revolutions" and provide them with material support.[44]

China also endeavored to expand its influence in Africa. In late 1963–early 1964, Zhou visited ten African countries. During this trip, he repeatedly emphasized that China was a true friend and natural ally of these newly independent nations. China began to provide economic and technological support to the African countries most friendly to China. Largely because of the endorsement by these countries, the PRC claimed a major diplomatic victory in 1965, when the UN Assembly for the first time voted in a draw on recognizing the PRC as China's sole legal representative at the United Nations.

China was then already on the eve of the Cultural Revolution. And, running counter to the efforts Zhou had made for pursuing China's centrality in the non-Western world, the PRC's aggressive foreign policies in the mid-1960s backfired. Beginning in late 1965, Beijing suffered a series of diplomatic setbacks in Asia, Africa, and Latin America. In 1966, the motion to place the PRC on China's UN seat was defeated by a large margin. For Zhou, these were huge losses in the PRC's international relations. But in Mao's mind this was not necessarily a bad thing, as it further justified the need of having the Cultural Revolution for bringing about "thorough transformations" in China and the world.

v

By the time that the Cultural Revolution began in June 1966, Zhou had sensed that a big political storm was gathering. Mao now pointed his spear at Liu and Deng, claiming that "Khrushchev-style revisionists" had crept into the Chinese leadership. Zhou was deeply uneasy about this. Yet he was determined to stand on Mao's side. In May 1966, Zhou made an unusual presentation at a politburo meeting, pledging complete loyalty to Mao and emphasizing that "no matter how one's achievement in the past has been, if he ruins his loyalty in his old age, all of his achievement will be nullified."[45]

For Mao, Zhou's statement was extremely important. Since Mao returned to the "first line" of his leadership role, he had worked on Zhou and given him the respect that the premier had not had since the period when he opposed the "rash advance" line. After all, Zhou virtually controlled China's administration. Mao knew that both for winning support for his revolutionary programs and for maintaining the state's everyday operations, he needed Zhou on his side.

The mass movements of the Cultural Revolution years resulted in extraordinary upheavals throughout the country. When the revolution reached its peak in 1967–1968, even China's state apparatus and party organization became paralyzed. In the meantime, Beijing's international behavior seemed out of control, making enemies everywhere in the world. The PRC's political influences in Asia and the world had hit a historic low.

Zhou was caught in the center of the storm. He tried his best to follow Mao's orders and to support the Cultural Revolution. Meanwhile, he used his administrative power to maintain the functioning of China's state machine. He also cited the Maoist slogan of "making revolution and promoting production" to make sure that the core parts of Chinese economy and national security, such as transportation, communication, and the nuclear facility, would not be sacrificed to the mass frenzy. Consequently, largely due to Zhou's efforts, in seven of the ten years of the Cultural Revolution era, China still registered significant GNP increases.

In China's foreign affairs, Zhou attempted to combine radical rhetoric with relatively reasonable actions. He publicly described the Cultural Revolution as having profound transformative power, which would further glorify the significance of the Chinese revolution and create a "new Asia" and a "new world." Yet Zhou also used his authority to remedy the diplomatic losses that radicalism in Chinese foreign policy had caused. Thus after the Red Guards set fire to the British consulate in Beijing, Zhou offered an apology.[46] When Prince Sihanouk of Cambodia, who had been friendly to China since the mid-1950s, was scared by the implications of Beijing's radical rhetoric toward his country, Zhou sent him a comforting personal message promising that he could continuously enjoy Beijing's "support and genuine friendship." After the Sino-Soviet border clash in March 1969, Zhou met with Soviet prime minister Kosygin in Beijing to help place an escalating crisis under control.[47]

Mao had initiated the Cultural Revolution for two interrelated purposes. First, he hoped that it would allow him to find new means of promoting the transformation of China in accordance with his ideals, so as to instill a new social order in the hearts and minds of the Chinese people. Second, he sought to use it instrumentally to enhance his much weakened authority and reputation. For Mao, these two purposes were interwoven, as he believed that his preeminent leadership would best guarantee the success of his revolution. By 1968–1969, it had become evident that he easily realized the second objective but failed to reach the first. However, by now Mao was ready to halt the revolution. In July 1968, when he dispatched the "Workers' Mao Thought Propaganda Team" to various Beijing universities to reestablish the party-control system, the Red Guards opened fire on the team. Mao responded with the decision to dismantle the Red Guards movement.[48] For two decades, "mobilizing the masses" had been the key for Mao to maintain the momentum of his "revolution after revolution." At the moment that he openly stood in opposition to the "revolutionary masses" in order to reestablish the Communist state's control over society, the Cultural Revolution had virtually failed.

Internationally, by the late 1960s, China had become one of the most isolated countries in the world. America's war in Vietnam brought China and the United States to the verge of a direct military confrontation. The hostility between China and the Soviet Union culminated in March 1969, when two bloody clashes erupted between Chinese and Soviet border garrisons.[49] China also faced hostile enemies from the east (Taiwan, Japan, and South Korea), and from the west (India).

The fading status of Mao's "continuous revolution" programs combined with the grave security situation facing the PRC created the context in which the Sino-American rapprochement occurred.[50] And this would become another of Zhou's moments, one with an impact even larger than Geneva and Bandung.

As early as 1969, even before the Chinese-Soviet border clash, Zhou had, with Mao's approval, already asked four PLA marshals to "study international politics." While doing so, Zhou added his personal touch by emphasizing that they should be "bold, candid, and visionary." The marshals obviously got the message. In their reports, they described the difficult international situation that China was then facing, proposing that Beijing should consider the possibility and utility of "playing the American card."[51]

Zhou seemed quite willing to listen to the marshals' suggestions, and he had Mao's support. Beginning in late 1969, when Mao and Zhou received the signal that US president Richard Nixon was interested in improving relations with China, Zhou quickly turned his attention to exploring the possibility of reaching a rapprochement with

Washington. Through Pakistani president Yahya Khan, Zhou communicated with the White House. This paved the way for the "Ping Pong diplomacy" to occur in April 1971, when a US table tennis team visited China. In late May 1971, Zhou followed Mao's orders by convening a Politburo meeting where he said that improving relations with the United States would "be beneficial for the struggle against imperialist expansionism and hegemonism, beneficial for maintaining peace in Asia as well as in the world, and beneficial for maintaining our country's security and pursuing the unification of the motherland and Taiwan in peaceful ways."[52] In July 1971, Zhou had a series of secret meetings with Henry Kissinger, Nixon's national security advisor, in Beijing, which resulted in Beijing and Washington simultaneously announcing that President Nixon would visit China in spring 1972.

While the Sino-American rapprochement was still being shaped, the Lin Biao incident occurred. On September 13 1971, Marshal Lin, who had been China's second-in-command and Mao's designated successor during the Cultural Revolution, boarded a plane to flee Beijing. A few hours later, the plane crashed in Mongolia. Lin's downfall represented one of the biggest political crises in the PRC's history. During the Cultural Revolution, Lin had been named Mao's "closest comrade-in-arms." His reported betrayal not only buried the myth of Mao's "eternal correctness" but also further tarnished Mao's fading "continuous revolution."

Historically, Zhou's relationship with Lin Biao had been intimate. When Lin was announced as Mao's successor, Zhou embraced it with wholehearted support. After all, Lin's name had been closely associated with Mao's Cultural Revolution. His dramatic death in a mysterious plane crash after he fell out with Chairman Mao forced Mao to reconsider the meanings of that radical experiment. Mao also had to make concrete personnel decisions to deal with the shaking of China's political structure caused by Lin's disappearance from Chinese politics. This included the return of the veteran officials who had been purged during the Cultural Revolution. All this provided Zhou with more maneuvering space and upgraded his position in the CCP's decision-making structure.

On February 12, 1972, Mao suddenly collapsed after suffering from coughing and lung infection for over a month. When Zhou rushed to Mao's quarters, the chairman was still unconscious. "Zhou was so shocked that he lost control of his bladder and bowels, soiling his pants."[53] When Mao finally regained consciousness, the first thing that Zhou told him was that "Chairman, you are still in full command of power."[54]

This, in retrospect, was a major moment in relations between the two leaders: henceforth, Zhou would be facing a Mao deeply obsessed by the fear of death. At the time, however, Mao recovered for the impending visit of US president Richard Nixon. Nixon arrived on February 21, for "the week that changed the world." A few hours after Nixon's arrival in Beijing, Mao met with him and Kissinger. Zhou had a series of meetings with them, and the Chinese-American Shanghai communiqué was signed. China's new relationship with the United States opened the door for the PRC to reenter the international community. In October 1971, the PRC claimed China's membership at the United Nations and its Security Council. Beijing also established diplomatic relations with Japan and such Western countries as Federal Republic of Germany and Britain.

But Zhou's brilliant performance in the Sino-American opening—and the spotlight that he had occupied—caused new tension in his relationship with the chairman. The ambivalence on Mao's part was further enhanced by his persistent suspicion of the premier not being one who was wholly willing to embrace his "revolutionary lincs." In May 1972, Zhou was diagnosed with bladder cancer. He would live through the last years of his life fighting against the illness and dealing with Mao's renewed criticism.

The first sign that Mao was uneasy with Zhou appeared in late 1972. In the wake of the Lin Biao affair and the rapprochement between China and America, Zhou thought it was time to return China to domestic and international normalcy. He thus tried to identify both the Lin Biao affair and the excesses of the Cultural Revolution as "ultra-leftist" in essence, so as to justify bringing China back to a more moderate path. Mao, however, disagreed, claiming that Lin's action was actually ultra-rightist in nature. This was a clear indication that Mao had no intention of allowing China to deviate from his revolutionary orbit.

But the chairman would not stop here. The trigger of Mao's renewed attack on Zhou came in summer 1973. It began with an internally circulated Foreign Ministry newsletter, which contended that between the United States and the Soviet Union there existed both competition and collaboration. Zhou praised the report. But Mao took issue with it, claiming that it had mitigated the problems between

Washington and Moscow. Zhou immediately made self-criticism and accepted Mao's views.

Yet the matter was not over. Between November 10 and 14, Kissinger again visited China. It seemed that the visit went extremely well, and Kissinger's meeting with Mao lasted for two hours and forty-five minutes.[55] Meanwhile, Kissinger's meetings with Zhou covered a wide range of areas of possible cooperation between the two countries. Before Kissinger was to depart China, he offered to establish a "secret hot line" between Washington and Beijing, which would transmit US intelligence information about any Soviet missile launch to China "in a matter of minutes." To cover the secret line, Kissinger proposed that a publicly announced "hot line," one that was similar to the ones between Washington and Moscow, could also be set up.[56]

Zhou did not give Kissinger an affirmative answer, only telling him that he would report this to Mao, and "the Chairman will make the decision." For reasons still unclear, however, Zhou probably did not report this matter to Mao. Consequently, right after Kissinger left Beijing, Zhou's troubles began. Mao charged the premier with incompetence, by not challenging Kissinger's attempt to "place China under America's nuclear umbrella." Mao now instructed the Politburo to criticize Zhou.

On November 21, the Politburo meeting began. Jiang Qing, Mao's wife, and her allies saw this as an opportunity to subdue Zhou and immediately began to criticize his "rightist surrenderism," even labeling him a "Chinese traitor." Ever since the Rectification movement, Zhou had adopted the tactic of making repeated self-criticism until Mao let him go. But this time, he refused to accept the accusation that he was a "Chinese traitor," and the meeting hit a deadlock. Following Mao's instructions, Deng Xiaoping, who had recently been brought back into China's decision-making circle, also sat in the meetings. But he did not speak until he learned that Mao was waiting for him to "stand out." Instead of accusing Zhou as a "Chinese traitor," Deng pointed out that the essence of Zhou's problem lay in that "Your position is just one step away from Chairman. To others, the Chairmanship is within sight, but beyond reach. To you, however, it is within sight and within reach."[57] After Deng's presentation, Zhou began making "self-criticism." On December 9, Zhou was asked to accompany Mao to meet the King of Nepal who was visiting China. To everyone's surprise, Mao "warmly shook hands" with Zhou, saying that "the premier remains the premier."

Mao had targeted Zhou as he was worried that the premier would outlive him and change his revolutionary line. Mao also used the Politburo meeting to test Deng, and Deng's presentation satisfied him. These incidents revealed a big dilemma Mao was facing in the last years of his life: namely, the question of his political successor. As far as political ideas were concerned, Jiang Qing and the Shanghai Gang would be ideal, but Mao knew well that they did not have the wisdom and talent to run China. He would not fully trust in anyone else (including Deng, who would be purged again a few months before Mao's death). What he finally did was to leave behind him a collective leadership composed of "factions" checking and balancing one another.

By this time, Zhou had been hospitalized for recurring cancer. He would use his remaining energy to push for something that he had striven for his whole life—to modernize China and to make it strong. In January 1975, with Mao's approval, Zhou made his last speech, announcing that China should aim to modernize its industry, agriculture, defense, and science and technology by the end of the century.[58]

VI

Zhou Enlai passed away on January 8, 1976. China was then a country significantly different from the one it was in the 1920s, when Zhou was studying in Japan and Europe and envisioning that one day "China will rise high again in the world." China, as a modern multinational state, had emerged as a recognized power on the international scene; China's age-old landlord-gentry-scholar structure had been eliminated; the "old" China's gender inequality had been changed; the Chinese people's life expectancy and education level had been significantly improved; the foundation of China's industrialization had been established; and China's tortuous path toward modernity had been opened. The achievements of the generation of the Chinese revolutionaries represented by Mao and Zhou were by no means small accomplishments.

But was Zhou, at the time of his death, in a position to celebrate with full confidence that China indeed had "risen high again in the world"? In the last decade of his life, he should have noticed the flourishing of the "Japanese miracle," and he should not have missed the emergence of the "Four Little Dragons" in East Asia. In comparison, China's record of "rise" appeared tarnished.

From the perspective of the Chinese Communist state that Zhou had devoted his life to establish and rule, even more troublesome was the legitimacy crisis it was facing. One revealing case was that three months after Zhou's death, tens of thousands of ordinary people, in the name of mourning the late premier, occupied Tiananmen Square. They made open the profound popular dismay over the economic stagnation and political cruelty conferred on them by Mao's "revolution after revolution." In response, the chairman ordered a dramatic crackdown. By doing so, Mao had virtually accepted that his revolutionary programs aimed at placing a new social order in the hearts and minds of the Chinese people had failed.

Mao died on September 9, 1976. Deng Xiaoping reemerged and unleashed in the late 1970s the "reform and opening-up" project, which has brought about phenomenal economic growth in China and profound transformations of Chinese society. As a consequence, the legitimacy of the Chinese "Communist" regime has been continuously called into serious question.

This has also tested Zhou's historical position as well as his legacies. There was a time when there existed an unusual confluence of highly positive views held by China's authorities, the general public, and academics about Zhou. Han Suyin, a Zhou biographer, even found it virtually impossible "to find faults [or] defects" in him.[59] But Zhou's image has been damaged with revelations about the negative aspects of the Chinese revolution. When authors like Jung Chang and Jon Halliday portray Mao's times as one of the darkest chapters in human history,[60] how could Zhou, who had been with Mao throughout the revolution, remain a generally positive historical figure?

It is beyond this essay's mandate to engage in the debate about how Zhou would or should be judged by history. Rather, I have attempted here to highlight some key parallels between Zhou's experience and the dilemmas and paradoxes of China's age of revolutions, so that his legacies—and their connections with "China's rise"—can be explored in an intellectually stimulating way.

To be sure, there exists no simple formula to define Zhou as a historical figure. If he left behind him a complex record mixing positives and negatives, this is because he was both the maker and the product of the successes and failures, progresses and setbacks, achievements and sufferings, and bright times and dark moments of the Chinese Communist revolution. Indeed, he should be regarded as the personification of China's tortuous path toward modernity. In Mao's shadow, he was never able to become a fully independent actor, and he had to do things even when he was deeply unwilling. But wasn't it also true that the chairman himself was the product of his environment and times—the ones that nurtured China's age of revolutions?

In the most celebratory biographies of Zhou, he was extolled as the model of virtue and high moral standards, whereas in the more critical ones, he was identified as a moral hypocrite. This discrepancy actually epitomizes the profound moral crisis entangling Chinese society. While China's age of revolutions had resulted in the breakdown of the country's traditional norms, the moral challenges facing China have greatly deepened as the result of the rampant materialism in the reform and opening-up era.

In light of this, how should we identify the meanings of Zhou's story? For me, a sensible point of departure—both in academic and intellectual senses—is to understand that the dilemmas that Zhou and his generation faced and the complicated legacies that they had bequeathed to post-Mao China have remained influential factors, continuously shaping China's path toward modernity and beyond. To comprehend these dilemmas will help us understand why China's rise has been and will continuously be a paradoxical and prolonged process.

SEVEN

SUKARNO

Anticipating an Asian Century

JAMES R. RUSH

Colonial Hybridities

AS A MAN OF HIS TIMES, Sukarno was shaped by the same large forces that shaped other leaders of Asia in the twentieth century. Global imperialism had transformed his native Java and its once-great kingdoms into a Western colony that also embraced hundreds of neighboring islands. Aggressive capitalistic exploitation brought other changes, including a vastly expanded openness to Western ideas and languages and education. In Sukarno's world and elsewhere in Asia, complex hybridities arose, creating Confucian-minded self-strengtheners in China, Westernizing Buddhist kings in Siam, Egypt-inspired Muslim reformers in South and Southeast Asia, and, eventually, revolutionaries nearly everywhere. Sukarno and his elite peers in Asia had much in common.

But in other ways, Sukarno's hybrid world view was unique to the Netherlands Indies and to Java and its deep past—and unique, of course, to his own extraordinary self. This enabled him to formulate a body of ideas—indeed one big idea—around which a coherent nationalist movement could form and, eventually, around which a nation could be created. To a very large degree, modern Indonesia has been formed around Sukarno's vision for it, just as postcolonial Asia itself has evolved in directions that he foresaw.

By the time Sukarno was born in 1901, his home island of Java had been in Dutch hands for nearly 150 years—and parts of it for much longer than that. The social station and worldview of Sukarno's Javanese father, Raden Sukemi, reflected this longstanding state of affairs. He was a government official who served under the Dutch as a grammar-school teacher and an ardent practitioner of theosophy.[1] In the family, and among the people at large, memories of Java's pre-Dutch past stirred deeply. "Father was descended from the Sultan of Kediri," Sukarno liked to say, and "I was born into the ruling class." The kingdoms of Bali, his mother's home, had come under Dutch sway more recently. Family lore had it that his maternal great grand-father had died in a historic ritual *puputan*, in which the nobles of Singaraja, rather than surrender, offered themselves up for slaughter by invading Dutch forces.[2] (These polished claims, made to his American "autobiographer" Cindy Adams when he was sixty-four and president for life, should be taken with a grain of salt. Evidently, no *puputan* occurred in Singaraja, although two such events did occur in Bali when Sukarno was a boy. Sukarno wasn't royal either. Even so, he was of *priyayi*, or ruling class, lineage on his father's side and descended from influential village gentry on his mother's.)[3]

During Sukarno's boyhood, Dutch power in Southeast Asia was still spreading. In 1903, Dutch colonial armies finally vanquished the sultanate of Aceh in Sumatra, ending a thirty-year-long struggle, and proceeded to coerce hundreds of small kingdoms of the archipelago definitively into subject status.[4] The final conquest of Bali ended in the famous *puputan*s of 1906 and 1908. By the time Sukarno was seven, Holland's eastern colony stretched five thousand kilometers from end to end. Netherlands India was virtually complete.[5] And so it was that high-born Sukarno grew into an Asian world of total white supremacy and into an ethnically multifarious society bounded by Dutch colonial rule.

Sukarno's theosophist father was also a devotee of the Mahabharata, the great South Asian epic that, with the Ramayana, had been long domesticated in Java and Bali in the *wayang* shadow-puppet theater and other popular arts. These "stories of warriors and giants, of gods, kings, princes, princesses and clowns," writes J. D. Legge, "are not merely a source of entertainment but a repository of values and a subtle exploration of mankind's relation to the universe."[6] To rural folk and the less literate, Ann Ruth Wilner tells us, these stories "are believed . . . to be history."[7] As a boy, Sukarno recognized himself in Bima, one of the heroic Pandawa brothers, who, following endless adventures and a great war called the Bharata Judha, succeeds in recovering their stolen kingdom from their usurping cousins, the Kurawas.

Bima is strong-willed, brave, and stubborn. He is the "king of war-riors."[8] In the world of the *wayang*, the defeat of the Kurawas restores balance to the cosmos and to the affairs of gods and people. Sukarno was steeped in this lore during his most impressionable boyhood years, even as he gradually entered the wider realm of the Dutch In-dies and the world beyond.

With Dutch rule came a flood of new influences and excitements that were reshaping both the white and the native world. This was especially true as the pace and intensity of industrialization and impe-rialism rose to a crescendo in the early twentieth century and the whole world awakened to modernity. ("I have been longing to make the acquaintance of a 'modern girl,'" wrote the Javanese girl Kartini in 1898.)[9] For bright and privileged young people like Sukarno, this new world was full of giddy possibilities.

Sukarno's earliest schooling occurred at the Javanese-language grammar school where his own father was a teacher. By year four, he was also learning Malay, the Indies-wide lingua franca, and, twice a week, Dutch.[10] His father realized that Dutch was the key to upward mobility in the colony and, when Sukarno was fourteen, maneuvered him into a Dutch-language primary school for European children—a privilege that his "ruling class" lineage opened to him.[11] There were also lessons at home. This paid off handsomely. A year later, Sukarno was accepted at the European Hogere Burger School (HBS) in Sura-baya, "the top academy in East Java."[12] While in Surabaya, he lodged with his father's friend Cokroaminoto, a fiery political agitator in the vanguard of the colony's proto-nationalist movement. From the unique alchemy of this new environment—Western education, na-tional awakening, and the myriad stimulations of modern life in a large colonial city—emerged the Sukarno of history: Sukarno of Indonesia.

For the Dutch themselves and fellow whites, the colonial govern-ment provided public high schools equivalent to those in Europe—five years of rigorous instruction. Dutch was the language of instruc-tion and students also learned French, English, and German. Of the three hundred or so pupils attending the Surabaya HBS in Sukarno's time, only twenty were native Indonesians! "I was surrounded on all sides by little Dutch boys and little Dutch girls," he said. Fifty years later he recounted to Adams being teased and bullied by white boys at school.[13]

Sukarno's HBS education placed him within a miniscule new elite in the colony. Between 1917 and 1927, only seventy-eight native Indonesians *in the entire Indies* passed the final HBS examinations, an average of seven per year in a colony numbering fifty-nine million.[14] (Sukarno was only one of three natives in his graduating class of fifty-two.)[15] Just as importantly, Sukarno's command of Western languages placed a new world of knowledge within his grasp. "All my time was spent reading," he said. Through books he learned of Voltaire, he said, and of Gladstone, Sidney and Beatrice Webb, Mazzini, Cavour and Garibaldi, Marx, Engels, and Lenin. And also Washington and Jefferson. "My boyhood was spent eavesdropping on America's founding fathers," he told Adams.[16]

Surabaya, where Sukarno studied, was "a bustling, noisy port town" (as he recalled it), where ships from around the world arrived to carry away Java's coffee, sugar, and tea and to deliver modern machinery and consumer goods from the West.[17] Here gathered all the polyglot ethnicities of the Dutch Indies—Javanese, Chinese, Malays, Madurese, Arabs, and Sumatrans, plus Europeans and Eurasians of all kinds. For Sukarno, it was a city of breathtaking stimulation. There were Western movies ("Mary Pickford, Tom Mix, Eddie Polo, Fatty Arbuckle") and the Theosophical Society library with treasures of Western books.[18] And most of all there was Cokroaminoto himself and the circle of young political activists who moved in orbit around him.

Political Stirrings

By the time Sukarno moved to Surabaya, anticolonial agitation in the islands had begun to take a modern shape. Prescient members of the colony's Western-educated elite (and others for whom Arabic was a window to the outside world) became attuned to political stirrings elsewhere—in India, for example, where the Indian National Congress was founded in 1885, and China, where reformist and revolutionary ideas were proliferating and spilling into Southeast Asia. (New reform-oriented Chinese organizations in the Dutch Indies became models for indigenous actors.)[19] In 1905, the already rapidly modernizing Meiji government of Japan defeated Russia in a spectacular and inspiring naval battle; and from Egypt came ideas about how colonized Muslims could restore their independence and dignity vis-à-vis the West.[20]

The earliest Indonesian organizations to reflect these new winds emphasized self-improvement and reform, such as the Javanese elite *priyayi* group formed in 1908, Budi Utomo, or Highest Endeavor.[21] More politicized groups soon emerged. Sarekat Islam (SI), the Islamic League, formed in 1912, grew from efforts by Muslim merchants in Java to organize against local Chinese competition. Under the leadership of H. O. S. Cokroaminoto, however, it grew into the colony's first quasi-mass organization tapping into myriad discontents and aggravations among the people and creating a kind of "group solidarity" mounted against the Chinese, Dutch, and collaborating *priyayi* officials.[22] By 1919, the organization claimed two million members.[23] Cokroaminoto had graduated from a Dutch academy that trained native officials but had abandoned government service for activism. He was impassioned, belligerent, and charismatic. He was also, with his wife, a boarding-house keeper. Sukarno occupied one of their smallest rooms and soon fell under Cokro's famous spell.[24]

Cokroaminoto's Surabaya home, writes Willard Hanna, was like a "Sarekat Islam asrama" where the organization's young activists gathered to thrash out their ideas and strategies.[25] Cokro's houseguests were politically eclectic and included Islam-oriented reformers such as Haji Agus Salim, alongside some of the colony's budding Marxists, including Alimin and Musso (and their Dutch mentors Asser Baars and Hendrik Sneevliet—later known as Maring in China).[26] "I loved mealtimes," said Sukarno, when "I would . . . soak up the political conversation." "Little by little," he said, "I became a fierce patriot."[27] He joined a patriotic youth organization and was soon testing his skills as a political writer.[28] He contributed hundreds of fiery articles, he says, to Cokroaminoto's own organ, the *Utusan Hindia* (Indies Messenger).[29]

But it was yet another political skill learned during these years that would separate Sukarno from his activist peers. This was speechmaking. Sukarno studied debating at the HBS and practiced at his youth club. But Cokro was the unrivaled crowd master of his day, and Sukarno says, "Wherever he went I followed. . . . I watched him throw his voice. I saw him gesture, I observed and applied." Savoring the moment fifty years later, he told Cindy Adams, "A shiver went through me when I first discovered the kind of power that could move masses."[30] He seized every opportunity to rise and speak. At a time when public speaking was the fast track to leadership, he soon became "the lion of the podium."[31]

Meanwhile, political discourse around Cokro's table and in the colony at large became hotter. Communists affiliated with the Indies

Social-Democratic Association (ISDV) and Sarekat Islam pursued a more radical agenda, especially following the October Revolution in Russia in 1917.[32] In Surabaya, they actually created soviets, prompting the colonial authorities to crush them and to expel their Dutch leaders, including Sneevliet.[33] Indonesian protégés now established a Communist wing of Sarekat Islam and, shortly thereafter, a free-standing Communist party, the first in Asia. Meanwhile, Islam-oriented activists and Western-educated reformers debated whether or not to participate in the colonial People's Council, or Volksraad (a collaborative consultative body that included 39 percent native members). These debates were complex and intense. In them lie the roots of Sukarno's obsession with synthesis and with accommodating the disparate voices of Indonesian nationalism.

In 1921, Sukarno shifted to the colony's new engineering school in Bandung (having taken Cokroaminoto's fourteen-year-old daughter as his first wife).[34] The Technical College was the only university-level institution in the Indies at the time, and Sukarno was one of eleven native students enrolled.[35] This was, he told Adams, a "passport to a white world."[36]

As Sukarno studied mathematics, physics, and mechanics, he naturally began circulating among the city's political activists. Among them were Ernest F. E. Douwes Dekker, Dr. Cipto Mangunkusumo, and Ki Hadjar Dewantara. In 1912, these three men had founded the radical Indies Party, which had demanded total independence for the Indies on behalf of both its native and Eurasian inhabitants—Dekker himself was Eurasian. The Dutch exiled them to Holland, but they had since returned. Dewantara was engaged deeply in launching a new, Tagore-inspired private school system to promote native history and values and a national spirit as a counterpart to Dutch schools. (This grew into the enormously influential Taman Siswa, or Garden of Pupils.) Sukarno, himself the son of a theosophist and *wayang* devotee, embraced Dewantara's insistence that the movement for political freedom be rooted in the authentic cultures of the people, not solely Western ideas.[37] Dr. Cipto identified the new nation-to-be as precisely Netherlands India: "No matter how great are the differences that exist in culture and history between these races," he wrote, "a great bond ties them together, that is, a common economic and political domination by a foreign power."[38] This concept conspicuously included hundreds of ethnicities and local identities as "Indonesian" that were not Javanese or Sumatran. Finally, in envisioning an independent Indonesia, Dekker rejected both Islam and secularism or communism as the basis for the new state and, instead, "thought in terms of an independent nation, multi-racial in composition but bound by its common allegiance to its homeland." For him, the national revolution itself should override "all other considerations of social conflict" and bind "the people of the Indies as a whole."[39]

By the early 1920s, "the Indies as a whole" had a new name, Indonesia. This once purely geographic term was first used in its modern sense in 1917 in a publication of Dewantara's. In 1922, Indies students in Holland changed the name of their organization from the Indies Association to the Indonesian Association; and three years later, Communists in the colony also adopted the term to become the PKI: the Communist Party of Indonesia.[40] Soon, writes Robert Elson, "no self-respecting nationalist organization or newspaper could avoid using the term."[41]

Framing Nationalism

Sukarno graduated as an engineer in May 1926. He had written a thesis on harbor construction and waterways and was offered some promising jobs and even opened an engineering office with a classmate. But this soon "slowed down until it ground to an absolute standstill."[42] Sukarno now occupied himself full time with the achievement of Indonesia.

With friends from the Technical College, Sukarno had formed a study club (Algemeene Studieclub) to debate issues of current events, political philosophy, and nationalist strategies. Sukarno's club in Bandung was one of several in the colony.[43] It is probably among his friends in the study club that Sukarno tested the arguments that he propagated in a lengthy essay in 1926 in the club's new publication, *Suluh Indonesia Muda*, the Torch of Young Indonesia.[44] In "Nationalism, Islam, and Marxism," he put forward the political idea that would catapult him to national leadership and define his career. He began with the *wayang* and Bima's son Gatutkatja, who "was born in an age of struggle . . . and now sees the light of day." The people of Asia, he then wrote, have learned that "the men who rule them today" are not really well-meaning guardians or "elder brothers" who will free them when they have "come of age." Colonization was not a civilizing mission. It was "the search for gain." This realization has "awakened the colonized people" throughout Asia and in Indonesia, too, as manifest in "the inner spirit of the people's movement . . . a movement with a single common goal . . . a Free Indonesia."[45]

All over Asia, Sukarno went on, this movement contained three elements that were often in competition with each other: nationalism, Islam, and Marxism. Only by unifying these apparently disparate elements, he wrote, would it be possible to achieve "the realization of our dreams."[46] Then he asked: "[C]an Islam, as a religion, cooperate with Nationalism, which stresses the nation, and with Marxism, which teaches materialism?" And then: "With full conviction, I answer: 'Yes.' "[47]

In the wide-ranging discussion that followed, Sukarno called upon authorities as diverse as Ernest Renan and Otto Bauer (and other European thinkers), Mohandas K. Gandhi, Muhammad Abduh, Jamal al-din Al-Afghani, Karl Marx, and the Holy Qur'an itself to argue that nationalists, Muslims, and Marxists possessed compatible beliefs when it came to achieving independence. Although some of his arguments involved a certain amount of hair-splitting ("Historical Materialism" is different from "Philosophical Materialism" and so on) and selective anecdotes, Sukarno built his argument upon areas of broad agreement.[48] In Indonesia, for example, "all elements of our movement . . . have shared for hundreds of years a 'unity of historical experience.' They are all members of 'one group, one nation.' "[49] Although we may perceive Muslims as internationalists who occupy a global Dar al-Islam, he wrote, every Muslim is obliged by his religion "to work for the welfare of the people in whose country he resides."[50] Moreover, the great Muslim reformers and modernists of the late nineteenth century and especially Jamal al-din Al-Afghani also sowed "the seeds of nationalism and love of country" among their followers across the Muslim world.[51] In Egypt, Turkey, and across colonized Africa, Islam had stirred anticolonial and nationalist movements, just as it had in Indonesia under leaders like Cokroaminoto.

And were Islam and Marxism antithetical? Not necessarily. Islam barred usury and exploitative economic practices. (Here he cited the Qur'an.) It was "openly anti-capitalistic."[52] Marx, for his part, "never ceased to defend the poor, to show them the reasons for their misery, and to prove to them that victory would certainly be theirs in the end."[53] This was something Muslims could embrace. As for Marxism's attack on religion, Sukarno argued that this arose from perceptions of European Christianity and its reactionary churches, not from Islam. In Indonesia, Islam was not the religion of power but the religion of the oppressed, "a religion of the masses 'at the bottom,'" who would "generate a struggle which in several respects is identical with the struggle of the Marxists." This being so, Indonesia's Marxists would "surely stretch out their hands and say: 'Brother, let us be one.'"[54]

It is easy to discern the romantic quality in Sukarno's hopeful arguments, as though simply believing that Indonesia's disparate young nationalists could all be brothers could make it so. But this was exactly the power of Sukarno's conception, his *one big idea*. Here we might allude to Isaiah Berlin's depiction of certain thinkers as hedgehogs, who, unlike the ever shifting foxes, "relate everything to a single central vision in terms of which they understand, think, and feel—a single universal organizing principle. . . ."[55] This was true for Sukarno. In the cause of Indonesia's freedom, he believed, many can be one.

In November of 1926 and the following two months, some of Indonesia's excited young Communists launched a grab for power. The Dutch crushed their delusionary revolution easily, executing some of its leaders, imprisoning others, and exiling 1,308 of them to a new and soon-to-be notorious prison camp at Boven Digul in Dutch New Guinea. For the time being, as M. C. Ricklefs puts it, the "PKI was dead."[56] Its eclipse and the waning influence of Cokro's residual Sarekat Islam now created an opening in the public forum. Sukarno stepped in.

On July 4, 1927, Sukarno and some friends from his study club formed the Indonesian Nationalist Party, or PNI.[57] The party was based on no one ideology or religion or social program. Its single goal was the immediate independence of Indonesia. Its members pledged themselves to noncooperation with the Dutch authorities. Sukarno was now a man in motion. He threw himself into developing his party and propagating the call for unity. As a Dutch observer wrote that same year, "There is ferment in the Indies. . . . The inner motives of the leaders differ fundamentally, but this need not and does not prevent them from working with each other for the achievement of one common goal: the overthrow of Netherlands rule."[58]

With exactly this goal in mind, Sukarno soon engineered the creation of a nationalist umbrella group of the major cooperating and noncooperating organizations.[59] This PNI-led federation sought to bridge the divisions of the movement—not only the nationalist-Islam-Marxism strains but also the Javanese and Sumatran strains, as well as the gulf separating liberal Holland-educated nationalists (such as

Mohammad Hatta and Sutan Sjahrir) and those of more local and traditional leanings. In a flurry of meetings and speeches and public writing, Sukarno became the face and voice of defiant nationalism.[60] Speaking in public halls and movie theaters, he told Cindy Adams, "I lived to intoxicate the masses."[61] A striking affirmation that the movement was getting its message across occurred in October 1928, when delegates to the All Indonesian Youth Congress meeting in Batavia swore their allegiance, in the soon-to-be-famous Youth's Oath, to "one motherland and one nation, the Indonesian nation," and to Indonesian, "the language of unity."[62] (Indonesian was none other than Malay, the ancient lingua franca of interisland trade that Holland adopted as its colonial administrative language and was subsequently embraced by young nationalists as the language of their nation-to-be.)[63]

The Indies at the moment were under a relatively liberal-minded governor general, A. C. D. de Graeff, whose regime tolerated open political speech.[64] Sukarno brashly tested the limits. Aside from his forthright calls for independence and noncooperation, he reminded his listeners that the Prophet Muhammad himself was "a great organizer" who had united previously warring tribes into "a powerful Islamic society."[65] He alluded to the ancient Javanese dream of liberation under a righteous king, the messianic *ratu adil* who would rise to lead the people against their oppressors.[66] And he stirred audiences with the messianic fantasies of Jayabaya, a legendary king who prophesied deliverance at the hands of foreigners, connecting this to contemporary anxieties about the ambitions of imperial Japan. Could it be that a great Pacific war spurred by Japan might lead to Indonesia's freedom?[67]

It was in the wake of such a speech in 1929 that a Dutch police inspector arrested him for "sowing hatred" and conspiring to overthrow "the established Netherlands Indies authority."[68] For eight weeks, working in his jail cell and using the flat bottom of a tin prison-house urinal as a desk, Sukarno prepared his defense, "Indonesia Accuses."[69] In it, he made his full case.

He did so in the voice of the Western-educated Asian, calling upon a vast array of Dutch, English, French, German, and American authorities in a manner that reveals the vigor and extent of his own self-education.[70] Imperialism was a fact of modern history, he argued. It was the process whereby European power and capital—and also Western values—were changing the entire world. Indonesia had become "an arena for the exploitation of foreign capital." Indeed, he said, "at least f1,500,000,000 worth of Indonesian wealth is removed each year."[71] The deleterious consequences of this for Holland's subjects had been documented repeatedly by the Dutch themselves and debated in the Dutch parliament.[72] Dutch colonialism had rendered Indonesians "a faceless people, a people without an identity they can call their own." And yet, in the Indies, no native subject had the right "to combat the terror of imperialism sprawling over our society and livelihoods." (Was it any wonder, he asked, subtly adopting a Western perspective, that "our people believe in and look forward to the coming of Ratu Adil," the Just King, and other messiahs?)[73]

It was self-evident, Sukarno told the court, to "the coloured people as well as the white," that "all colonial people want to be free." This was true in India, Vietnam, Egypt, Korea, the Philippines, and everywhere else in the colonized world. And this was "exactly what Indonesians want and what my party, the PNI, strives for, a 'Free Indonesia!' We have never denied this, nor the fact that we are self-consciously radical and revolutionary." And yet they did not resort to "swords, bolo knives, or bombs." Everything they did, including calls for mass action, was "to generate power within the law." On this point, Sukarno referenced the Czech-Austrian Marxist Karl Kautsky, who said, "The Socialist Party is a revolutionary party, but not a revolution-making party." By drawing upon Kautsky and other European socialists, Sukarno was attempting to disassociate himself and the PNI from the Indonesian Communists. The PNI, he said, "is emphatically not Communist."[74]

Also emerging in Sukarno's defense oration was a conceptualization of society's common people not as proletarians, as the Communists would have it, but as "little men who are peasants, laborers, traders, seaman," people who possess some property and work hard but who still live in poverty. He called these members of the honorable poor "Marhaen," after a small farmer whom he met one day—one of his much-told stories.[75]

At the end of this oration, Sukarno also addressed specific accusations against him and the party. His overarching argument was straightforward enough. Sukarno argued that Europeans and the Dutch themselves were profoundly aware that revolutionary Indonesians were playing a historic role in ending colonial oppression. And, if necessary, they were willing to pay the price: "we readily surrender our entire being to our homeland and our people . . . to Mother Indonesia."[76]

The court did require Sukarno to pay the price. He was convicted and sentenced to four years in prison.[77] For eight months he was in solitary confinement, and, even afterward when he was assigned work in the prison print shop, he was forbidden to read political works. Instead, he told Adams, "I . . . began to discover the Qur'ran" and "became a real believer." After that, he said, he no longer turned to Western sociology "for answers to how and why things are."[78]

Although Sukarno's defense oration did not convince the colonial judges, it circulated widely in the Dutch and Indonesian languages and gained sympathy for him among the liberal-minded Dutch and others in Europe—as well, of course, among his Indonesian followers. As a result, Governor General de Graeff commuted his sentence to two years, and, on the last day of 1931, he was released.[79]

Once out of prison, Sukarno found himself at loggerheads with the nationalist movement's Holland-educated leaders. Both Mohammad Hatta and Sutan Sjahrir disagreed with Sukarno's provocative grandstanding and advocated a more programmatic and education-based approach to eventual independence. "When you and the others were jailed," Hatta told him, "the entire movement fell apart. My idea is to mentor a small nucleus of an organization which will then train cadres infused with our ideology." Sukarno told Adams that he replied, "Your way takes an eternity." The two remained profoundly divided.[80] Hatta now formed an evolutionist party (again the PNI but now Pendidikan Nasional Indonesia, Indonesian National Education) and Sukarno led Partindo, the Indonesian Party.[81] Once more, he mesmerized crowds all over Java, formulating, he said, "my people's hidden feelings into the political and social terms which they would have spoken themselves if they could. . . . I became their mouthpiece."[82] Eight months later he was arrested again.

This time Sukarno was exiled, first to tiny Flores Island in eastern Indonesia and later to the sleepy harbor town of Bengkulu (Bencoolen) in southern Sumatra. He wasn't free again until 1942, when the great Pacific War finally arrived and the Japanese Imperial Army drove the Dutch from the Indies. By sending Sukarno to Flores, the Dutch isolated him not only from the public but also from the other nationalist leaders who were exiled to Boven Digul in New Guinea. Both Hatta and Sjahrir spent part of the decade there. In Flores and, after 1938, in Bengkulu, Sukarno led a low-key life with his wife Inggit befriending local people and managing financially on a small stipend, gifts from friends and supporters, and odd jobs.[83] In Flores he sold textiles door-to-door. And in Bengkulu he taught at the local Muhammadiyah school, a modernist reform-oriented Muslim organization that he now joined. He also corresponded with Ahmad Hasan, leader of a smaller modernist Islam group in Bandung, and contributed articles under pen names to a variety of publications.

As Sukarno and other radical nationalists bided their time in prison and exile, the cause of nationalism continued to deepen in Indonesia. Some cooperating nationalists remained important public figures and gained a platform by serving in the Indies Council, or Volksraad.[84] Indies-wide organizations such as Muhammadiyah, although technically "cooperative," kept the idea of Indonesia alive in their public meetings and publications. In Medan, for example, the Muhammadiyah-influenced weekly led by the popular Muslim writer Hamka, *Pedoman Masyarakat* (People's Compass), openly embraced the dream of Indonesia and published articles by leading nationalists including Sukarno.[85] Despite Dutch repression, writes Legge, "People who were once awakened to national consciousness never lost it."[86] And although often at loggerheads with other nationalists and, for long periods, out of play, Sukarno remained the beacon.

Suddenly, a New World

In the decade that followed, Sukarno rose to lead a collaborationist apparatus under Japan's Greater East Asia Co-Prosperity Sphere, harkening to the call of "Asia for Asians" and gambling that a devil's bargain with Japan would hasten independence.[87] In the process, Japan raised an Indonesian defense force and trained its officers. As the fortunes of war shifted decisively from Japan to the Allies in 1945, Sukarno and Hatta and other leading nationalists were permitted to draft a blueprint for a new Indonesian-led government.[88] It was during this process in June 1945 that Sukarno articulated a new crystallization of his core concept of national unity: Panca Sila, the five principles of Indonesian national identity. In his original formulation, these were: (1) Indonesian nationalism; (2) internationalism or humanity; (3) consensus or democracy; (4) social welfare; and (5) belief in one God. "Let us practice our beliefs, whether we are Muslims or Christians, in a civilized way," he told the gathered committee members. This "means mutual respect for one another." On the basis of these five principles, he said to loud applause, "we will build the State of Indonesia to be everlasting and eternal."[89] Two months later, on

August 17, as news of Japan's defeat reached the Indies, Sukarno and Hatta together stepped before a small crowd in Jakarta to declare Indonesia free. The next day, under a hastily completed constitution, Sukarno became president of the Republic of Indonesia.[90]

As the new republic and its leaders braced for the return of the Dutch, adjustments to the constitution orchestrated by Hatta and Sjahrir favoring a multiparty parliamentary system rendered Sukarno's position as president "largely ceremonial." A prime minister would lead the government.[91] Sukarno later complained that this was a mistaken consequence of "Dutch thinking" but at the time he acquiesced to it. He thus removed himself from the complex and laborious business of organizing and running the government but retained his role, as Legge puts it, as *the* leader of the Indonesian people, standing above party." As the young republic embarked on its revolution, Sukarno remained "indispensable as arbiter and unifier when critical moments came."[92]

Sukarno was to remain on this esteemed presidential perch for several years to come. During the revolution (1945–1949) he used his charismatic authority repeatedly to support a negotiated peace with Holland, even though it meant compromising with the hated Dutch and risking the support of the many young revolutionaries and left-wing nationalists who preferred war. He used it several times in fraught moments to finesse leadership changes as first Sjahrir, then Amir Sjarifuddin, and then Hatta formed governments as prime ministers. And in September 1948, he used it to crush an attempt by the resurgent Communist Party (PKI) led by Musso to seize control of the revolution. (In a bold maneuver, he issued a proclamation challenging the public to choose one or the other: "Sukarno-Hatta" or "PKI-Muso.")[93] During Holland's second direct military assault on the republic in December 1948, during which he, Hatta, and Sjahrir were captured, he used it again to refuse a Dutch demand to order Republican armies to stand down.

Although Sukarno cannot be said to have led the revolution—it was too disorganized, episodic, and decentralized to have had only one commanding leader—he remained the face of it. George Kahin, one of the few Americans who observed the Indonesian Revolution firsthand, witnessed Sukarno before a crowd in Yogyakarta in 1948. "I had heard that Sukarno was an eloquent orator," he writes, "but I was totally unprepared for the extent of his rapport with the crowd. He had a sort of magnetic charisma that quickly established a bond with it. . . . He spoke of self-respect, dignity and independence from the Dutch and seemed to direct a current of electricity into the crowd. . . . It was as if he were a heart pumping oxygen into and animating the Indonesian body politic."[94]

When world opinion shifted dramatically in the republic's favor after the second Dutch assault—Nehru in India hosted an All-Asia conference of outrage; the United States threatened to cut its postwar aid to Holland—and when the Dutch at last realized that in the face of ferocious revolutionary resistance it could not hold Indonesia by force, the republic did in fact win its independence through negotiations.[95] In April 1949, Holland relinquished sovereignty over the Indies (except for western New Guinea) to the United States of Indonesia, a federation of fifteen small states plus the republic. One year later, this Dutch-influenced structure gave way to a unitary state—the Republic of Indonesia, Sukarno's dream come true.

At Last, the Nation

This dream had first emerged among the young politicized activists of the 1910s and 1920s. In this dream—expressed best by Sukarno himself—the colony *was* the nation-to-be, or in Benedict Anderson's formulation, "the imagined community" of Indonesia.[96] But in fact, the leading nationalists and revolutionaries came predominantly from Java and Sumatra and from among a very small number of Western-educated and partially Western-educated elites. (Just how thin this layer of leadership was can be gauged by the fact that, in 1930, there were only 178 indigenous Indonesians studying at the university level in the entire colony.)[97] Beneath this thin layer of elites lived the vast majority of ordinary people scattered about the islands and speaking hundreds of vernacular languages. The new republic inherited all this from the Dutch along with a bare-bones infrastructure and a huge debt of some US$1.723 million.[98] Moreover, as Ruth McVey has written, "war and revolution had shaken broad layers of the society and brought them, however briefly, into political action; new sources of leadership emerged, more local and less Westernized."[99] Many glib things have been said about nation-building. But in 1950, Indonesia was clearly a nation that still needed to be built.

As president, Sukarno left the nuts and bolts of this daunting task to the republic's prime ministers and continued to play the role of high arbiter and face of the nation. Beneath him, however, the nation's extraordinary diversity immediately began to take its toll.

Sukarno had never favored full-out democracy. The democracy of his Panca Sila was not "Western" democracy but rather the democracy of consensus between leaders and followers, as practiced by the immediate successors of the Prophet Muhammad and (he truly believed) countless Indonesian villagers. But in 1945 he had accepted the party-based parliamentary formula of his "Dutch-thinking" colleagues nevertheless, with the result that, immediately, the new nation possessed twenty-nine official political parties! They ranged from ultra-conservative Muslim parties and small Christian parties to the Communist PKI.[100] In the absence of elections until 1955, leaders of these parties jostled among themselves for influence and power and competed for backing in the country's parliament made up of some 232 members.[101] No one party dominated this fragile structure, and it fell to Sukarno as president to guide the formation of coalition governments, one after another. He became—in Herbert Feith's classic formulation—Indonesia's leading "solidarity maker."[102]

At the same time, despite his misgivings, Sukarno used his personal authority to protect the party system against its opponents. A dramatic example of this occurred in September 1952, when army officers led by Colonel Abdul Haris Nasution staged a large armed demonstration in front of the presidential palace.[103] Sukarno faced them down and ordered them to disperse. They did.[104] The day was Sukarno's, but the event signaled the emergence of the army as a new player in national politics. It would soon wax strong. By 1952, it was already engaged in suppressing an internal rebellion in West Java and South Sulawesi, where the armed Darul Islam movement was mobilizing thousands of followers behind an alternative Islam-driven vision for the nation.[105]

Competition among the new country's political parties reflected genuine sociocultural cleavages in the society. There were Catholics and Protestants and Socialists, and there were Communists, too, with the PKI rising yet again under D. N. Aidit and other new leaders.[106] There were Sarekat Islamists, and there was also a large *priyayi*-based party of Sukarnoists called the PNI, or Nationalist Party, although Sukarno himself wasn't formally involved.[107] During the Japanese years, the country's two prominent prewar Muslim mass organizations, Muhammadiyah and Nadhlatul Ulama, had combined to form

Masjumi, which functioned as a political party afterward; the first postindependence government was led by a Masjumi prime minister, Mohammad Natsir. But in 1952, the Java-based, tradition-oriented Nadhlatul Ulama withdrew from Masjumi and became a party in its own right. Afterward, Masjumi carried the flag for Muhammadiyah-oriented Muslims and other modernists with substantial followings outside Java.[108]

Each of the major parties, and some more than others, had deep roots in society through pyramids of formal and casual ties that reflected class hierarchies, patron-client ties, and shared worldviews.[109] When the republic finally held elections in 1955, the Sukarnoist PNI and Masjumi each gained 22 percent of the parliamentary seats; Nadhlatul Ulama, 17.5 percent; and the PKI, 15 percent.[110] The elections were a triumph of a kind and symbolized Indonesia's coming of age as one of the world's new democracies. But in confirming Indonesia's sociopolitical divisions, they also portended more gridlock ahead.

A High Postcolonial Moment

Meanwhile, in 1955, Sukarno presided over one of the triumphal moments of his career, hosting the Asian-African Conference in Bandung. The Indonesian Republic's involvement with its Asian neighbors began during the revolution. In March 1947, Jawaharlal Nehru of soon-to-be-independent India sent an Indian plane secretly through the Dutch air blockade to bring Prime Minister Sutan Sjahrir to New Delhi for the first Asia Relations Conference and subsequently sent three tons of medical supplies to the beleaguered republic.[111] Two years later, during the crisis of the second Dutch assault, Nehru again sent a plane to rescue the republican leaders and, when the plan failed, convened the leaders of Burma, Ceylon, and Pakistan in India to condemn Holland and explore resolutions to the conflict. Consequently, on his first trip abroad as president, Sukarno paid his respects to Nehru.[112] It was during a five-country Asian prime ministers meeting in Ceylon in 1954 that Ali Sastroamidjojo, the current prime minister and long-time Sukarno ally, proposed the Asian-African Conference. Ali proceeded brilliantly to organize it. But when prominent leaders from twenty-nine newly independent countries—including Zhou Enlai, Gamel Abdel Nasser, Norodom Sihanouk, Pham Van Dong, and Nehru—all collected in Bandung in April 1955, "Sukarno, not Ali, was the featured Indonesian performer."[113]

Sukarno, ever the hedgehog, seized intuitively the large meaning of the Bandung event and expressed it powerfully in his opening address: "This is the first intercontinental conference of colored peoples in the history of mankind!" For many generations, he said, "our people have been the voiceless ones in the world . . . the people for whom decisions were made by others." Yet today, the formerly colonized "peoples of Asia and Africa, 1,400,000,000 strong [make up] far more than half the population of the world." The task, he told the delegates, "is first to seek an understanding of each other, and out of that understanding will come a greater appreciation of each other, and out of that appreciation will come collective action."[114]

Much on Sukarno's mind at the conference, and a chief concern of India's Nehru and the other sponsors, was bringing the People's Republic of China into this "understanding of each other" and mobilizing the collective influence of the new states to mitigate potential violence and war between Communist and non-Communist states (and particularly between China and the United States). On this score, the conference succeeded brilliantly in part due to the deft diplomacy of Zhou Enlai, who demonstrated "conciliatory reasonableness" in engaging conference delegates over a variety of issues.[115] Zhou convinced the delegates that China would not resolve the Taiwan crisis by resorting to war, for example. In the end, the conference "condemned colonialism in all its manifestations," and agreed that each nation possessed the right "to defend itself singly or collectively in conformity with the Charter of the United Nations."[116] The debates behind these seemingly predictable resolutions represented the kind of collective action Sukarno was calling for—they were not "made by others."[117]

In Bandung, Indonesia orchestrated a high postcolonial moment. "From Belgrade to Tokyo," writes Vijay Prashad, and "from Cairo to Dar es Salaam, politicians and intellectuals began to speak of the 'Bandung Spirit.'"[118] Sukarno, standing above the troubling dysfunctionalities of his own house, assumed the posture of an emerging world leader.

Suddenly, as Willard Hanna writes, ambassadors from around the world "headed to the palace, gilt-edged cards in hand, to advise Bung Karno that he would be welcome whenever and wherever he cared to call."[119] During the year following the Bandung Conference, Sukarno made triumphal state visits to Soviet Russia, China, Yugoslavia, Czechoslovakia, and the United States, where he was treated to a standing ovation by the United States Congress and interviewed by "one hundred ten correspondents" (as he told Cindy Adams).[120] Accompanied everywhere by an entourage of prominent Indonesians, Sukarno dazzled the crowds who gathered to greet him with his adroit speeches and public manner. Writing on the front page of the *New York Times*, Tillman Durdin described his American arrival saying: "Within an hour he had shaken hands with sidewalk welcomers, exchanged greetings with a small boy from Duluth, kissed an elderly lady, and paid tributes to Washington, Jefferson, Lincoln and United States aid."[121] In certain places, of course, the crowds were also adroitly arranged. Here is Willard Hanna describing his reception in Beijing: "He was greeted . . . by a million wildly enthusiastic welcomers, including stilt dancers, jugglers and musicians . . . , pretty girls who pelted him with flowers and just about everybody else who was ambulatory." Even so, as news and photographs of his triumphs in distant capitals reached home, Indonesians observed that their leader commanded "the admiring attention of the world audience."[122]

Guiding Democracy

Sukarno arrived back in Indonesia in October following the second of his whirlwind tours refreshed and confident. But what he had seen also disturbed him. Much of the world was far in advance of his own country. The United States was industrialized and prosperous. In Russia and China, revolutionary movements were changing life for the better.[123] Indonesia, meanwhile, seemed stalled in its postindependence experiment with parliamentary democracy. In a speech later that month, he expressed this frustration openly: "My dream," he told an assembly of youth leaders, "is that the leaders of the parties would deliberate together and then come to the decision 'let us now join together to bury all parties.'"[124]

The elections of 1955 failed to resolve the dysfunctionality of Indonesia's serial coalition governments. So, too, did the constitutional assembly that followed. Mandated to write a new constitution, it broke down along factional lines and brought forth arguments from Muslim-party members that challenged Sukarno's Panca Sila as the basis of the state. Indonesian patriots who sacrificed themselves in the revolution had not done so for Panca Sila, said assembly delegate Isa Anshari, "They fought to place Islam in the life of our society and state. They fought to establish the Sovereignty and the Law of Islam."[125] The same Muslim groups also voiced vociferous opposition to the growing influence of the country's Communist Party, to which Sukarno increasingly turned for inspiration and support. In the midst of these fissures arose other signs of disunity; in late 1956, army commanders in parts of Sumatra and Sulawesi staged local putsches by seizing control of the civil administrations in their territories.[126]

Sukarno now groped for a way to reconcile his country's divided tribes. In a formal speech before nine hundred leaders gathered at the presidential palace in February 1957, he argued that Indonesia should reformulate its democracy in line with traditional village concepts of deliberation *(musjawarah)* and consensus *(mufakat)* under the guidance of an authoritative elder, someone who "did not dictate, but led, and protected." "Indonesian democracy since ancient times," he told the crowd, "has been Guided Democracy."[127] This was Sukarno's new *konsepsi*. During the next three years Sukarno maneuvered opportunistically to achieve it, employing his constitutional powers as president (subject to his own interpretation) and his growing alliances with the army under his long-since-rehabilitated chief of staff, Abdul Haris Nasution.

All this occurred in a climate of crisis. In March 1957 occurred one of seven attempts on Sukarno's life—this one, staged at his children's school, killed eleven people.[128] The following year, regional power grabs by the army blossomed into full rebellions in which army officers, senior Muslim leaders affiliated with the Masjumi party (including the former prime minister Mohammad Natsir), and the American CIA were all complicit.[129] Nasution and his loyal forces crushed the rebellions, waxing stronger as a result and acting with great latitude throughout the country under a state of war and siege that lasted until 1962.[130] The national economy was in extreme disarray, all the worse following the seizure in 1957 of all remaining Dutch-owned banks and enterprises—many commandeered by the army—and the flight of their professional managers.[131] Cabinets continued to come and go.

The key institutional shift occurred in 1959. As the constitutional assembly debated on and on without consensus, Sukarno proposed that it abandon its two-year-long efforts in favor of restoring the country's original 1945 constitution, which favored a strong executive and provided for deliberative bodies more amenable to presidential "guidance." When the assembly failed to do so, Sukarno disbanded it by decree and, based on a "national emergency," reinstated the 1945 constitution himself. Among those who denounced him for doing so was his former vice president, Mohammad Hatta, who said Guided Democracy was "a masquerade democracy."[132] Sukarno responded by closing down the magazine that published his inflammatory article.

The following year Sukarno banned both the Socialist Party and Masjumi and disbanded the country's residual elected parliament when it declined to rubber-stamp his budget. He replaced the old parliament with an appointed one and also, in accordance with the 1945 constitution, two other deliberative bodies; these included the 616-member Provisional People's Consultative Assembly.[133] He filled these councils with representatives of so-called functional groups, including some political parties (conspicuously the PKI), the armed services and police, plus workers, peasants, youth, women, intelligentsias, and Islamic authorities.[134] These hand-picked assemblies formed the deliberative, lawmaking basis of Guided Democracy. As both president and prime minister, Sukarno was the Guide. He had seized power. He had also taken upon himself personally the awful responsibility of completing Indonesia's revolution and of achieving his vision for the nation: from many, to make one.

Culture Wars and the Power of Words

It was perhaps a natural outcome of Sukarno's great confidence and egocentricity that he should foist himself into power at this moment. The nation was not cohering. Only an act of inspired will could save it. Unlike most of his nation-founding peers in Asia, such as Nehru, Mao, and Ho, Sukarno did not lead a large, disciplined political party or movement. Although the nationalist PNI was undeniably Sukarnoist, he did not actually control it in the way that, say, Lee Kuan Yew controlled the People's Action Party in Singapore. It is true that under Guided Democracy, Sukarno wielded authoritarian tools—to arrest and detain political foes, for example, and to ban parties and publications. But as his biographer J. D. Legge argues, Sukarno used these powers sparingly. There were no concentration camps under Sukarno. His opponents were not murdered.[135] Instead, in large measure, Sukarno relied upon his personal magnetism and the power of words to bring his nation's warring tribes into consensus.

By the early 1960s, these tribes included a large and growing Communist party. Revived under its new leadership in the early

1950s, the PKI made big gains in the 1955 elections and surged in influence. Its party newspaper, *Harian Rakyat*, the People's Daily, was the largest of any party, and its influence reached deep into the countryside, especially in Java where, in the words of M. C. Ricklefs, PKI teams "repaired bridges, schools, houses, dams, public lavatories, drains, and roads, . . . eradicated pests and set up literacy courses, organized village sports and musical groups, and offered members support in times of hardship."[136] Ideologically flexible under its chairman Aidit, it sought power openly through its mass membership.[137] By the early 1960s, with 1.5 to 2 million members, it was the largest such party in the world. Through affiliated organizations of students, workers, and artists, its number of stakeholders reached to some 10 million.[138]

Sukarno had rejected communism per se in the 1920s without rejecting Communists, whose nationalism and revolutionary fervor he admired. Even the Communist putsch at Madiun during the revolution had not dissuaded him from embracing the movement as a positive force in the Indonesian revolution. Now he said, "I can never be a Communist," but "I am a friend of the Communists because the Communists are *revolutionary* people."[139] The Communists' focus on issues of social justice and the plight of the small man—his own Marhaen—also appealed to him. Under Guided Democracy, Sukarno began bringing members of the party into leadership circles and became a willing ally in advancing the party's influence. In return, the PKI became an indispensable source of support for the charismatic president—alongside, of course, the army, the PKI's most "hated and feared" opponent.[140] It was now Sukarno's mortal dilemma to nourish his support from both of these entities—using them to balance each other's power and, at the same time, keeping them from each other's throats.

Also wary and in fact profoundly alarmed at the resurgence of Indonesia's Communist Party were the country's Muslim parties and mass organizations. Some of these had made their peace with Guided Democracy and participated in its organs; this was conspicuously true of Nadhlatul Ulama (NU), the large traditionalist organization with deep roots in the Javanese countryside. The majority of PNI members were also Muslim as was Sukarno himself. (A great many PKI members were, too, at least nominally.) Sukarno now returned to his famous 1926 conception of "Nationalism, Islam, and Marxism" with a new slogan—Nasakom, meaning the amalgamation of nationalism, religion *(agama)*, and communism—to reflect his ideal of Indonesian political unity. In vigorous opposition were the majority of the country's modernist Muslims affiliated with the huge mass organization Muhammadiyah and the political party Masjumi. Masjumi had crossed Sukarno in the 1950s when some of its leaders joined the 1958 rebellions and when it publicly rejected Guided Democracy. He had banned it in 1960. Subsequently, he imprisoned some of its key leaders and intellectuals.[141] But through a network of popular organizations and publications and through the nationwide chapters of Muhammadiyah and its affiliates, the modernists remained a powerful political and social influence. And as the Communist Party grew ever stronger through its own far-flung affiliations, Muslims retaliated forcefully—demonizing communism as the enemy of Islam and, indeed, of all religion.

By 1963, this culture war had gripped the entire country. In bitter clashes between leftwing intellectuals and their opponents (who opposed ideology-driven literature and art), Sukarno's regime sided with the PKI. Journals were banned. Professors were fired.[142] Christian parties stood with modernist Muslims against the Communists and eventually the pro-Sukarno NU also found itself in angry competition with the Communists in rural Java, where the PKI began to carry out extra-legal land seizures from wealthy Muslim landlords in unilateral land-reform actions.[143]

Underlying these tensions were conditions of wrenching socioeconomic decline. By the mid-1960s, prices in Indonesia were doubling almost every week, leaving the well-to-do to fear for their property and the poor to dream of a miraculous rescue from their otherwise hopeless poverty—dreams that Sukarno now strove to embody.[144]

Rather than contain the nation's warring tribes, Sukarno's Guided Democracy unleashed a power struggle in which there were no clear procedures or rules. At the center of the maelstrom, Sukarno attempted frantically to balance the warring factions, just as the puppeteer *(dalang)* in Java's ubiquitous *wayang* shadow shows eventually brings the great war of the Bharata Judha to a peaceful end. This famous depiction of him is one that he embraced himself.[145] At the same time, he attempted to rally his followers behind great hypernationalist causes that appealed to both the Communists and the army (or at least some in the army), such as the campaign to wrest West Irian (New Guinea) from Holland and the fostering of a belligerent attitude toward Malaysia. He railed against the West and the

United States, and in 1965 he withdrew Indonesia from the United Nations. He spoke of a Peking-Hanoi-Jakarta Axis. He introduced one new slogan after another to capture his latest *konsepsi* in made-up mantra-like utterances: Nasakom; Manipol Usdek; Ampera; Nefos (new emerging forces) and so on. He took upon himself the grandiose titles of Great Leader of the Revolution and President for Life.

Sukarno did everything he could, in short, to make himself larger than life. To his secular critics, this was laughable, evidence of delusional fantasies. But to many common people of Indonesia, as Sukarno knew well, this was the key to his great authority. He cultivated a certain air of kingliness, even godliness, modeled on the story cycle of the *wayang*. His bearing was regal, his appearance immaculate; he was virile and beloved of women.[146] He was Bima. He was Arjuna. He was Yudhistira, "who brought all the neighboring kings to his kingdom."[147]

In 1965, the Australian journalist Maslyn Williams observed Sukarno among the people, much as George Kahin had done some sixteen years before. In Sukabumi, Sukarno steps down from a helicopter dressed in a "dark khaki uniform [with] the ribbons of the revolution." He is "tall, straight-backed, impressive; aware of himself and his powers." Williams writes, "I looked at the people close by and saw in their faces such devotion and joy that I was amazed; men and women, faces alive with delight, some crying with happiness, some praying."[148] An Indonesian familiar with this same phenomenon, Dr. Abu Hanifah, confirms that "these people indeed believed in Soekarno as their savior. From the devotion in their faces you could see he was their king."[149]

Living Dangerously

It didn't work. In the end, even Sukarno's exceptional charisma could not settle the roiling waters of Indonesia under Guided Democracy. Many could not be one. So even as Sukarno in August 1964 called upon his citizens to prepare for "The Year of Living Dangerously" and thundered "The Indonesian Revolution MUST GO FORWARD," many Indonesian actors, behind the scenes in what Robert Hefner has called a netherworld of "secrecy and underground alliances," were considering other options.[150]

By 1965, at exactly the time when Sukarno was regaling Cindy Adams with tales of his life and entertaining her and others at the palace with dance parties and parlor games, rumors of intrigue and coup d'état were rife among the political classes.[151] *The communists will strike. They are getting weapons from China.* And, *The CIA is goading the generals to seize power and crush the communists!* Just how complex these intrigues were is suggested by the one that actually erupted into action on September 30, 1965—the event known as Gestapu.

In this coup attempt, members of Sukarno's own palace guard and several battalion-level officers, along with the air-force vice chief and certain PKI operatives and leaders including Aidit, kidnapped and killed six senior army officers close to Sukarno—in an effort, they said, to thwart an anti-Sukarno coup by these very same officers. Three of the murders took place at Halim Air Force Base where, at one point following the outbreak of the coup, Sukarno was himself present along with his air vice chief, units of Communist youth and women's organizations (who took part in the killings), and PKI chief Aidit. Sukarno did not endorse the coup-makers, but his exact role and foreknowledge of the plot have never been sorted out—among the many mysteries of this vexed event. Nasution was meant to be killed, but wasn't. Although Nasution was the senior man, it was Brigadier General Soeharto who took charge.[152] Soeharto had risen with the army itself through the revolution and early years of independence and now commanded the troops that controlled the capital city.[153] Seizing this critical advantage, he took the initiative to stamp out the rebellion and to impose clarity upon the bewildering event.

The Communists were utterly to blame, Soeharto said. They had sought to grab power and failed. News of the murder of the generals—said falsely to have been mutilated—was broadcast widely and covered avidly by Western as well as local journalists already predisposed to believe the worst of the Communists. These deft propaganda measures elided the role of the army and other players in the coup attempt and shifted suspicion almost solely upon the Communists. In the feverish atmosphere of Indonesia's long-escalating culture wars, Soeharto now acted to lance the boil by eliminating the Indonesian Communists altogether. In doing so, he had the fervent support of the country's organized Muslims.[154]

In many regions, military commanders and their units conducted executions directly, relying on local people to identify Communists and their supporters. In others, the army stood by as local vigilantes including Muslim youth groups conducted the killings with swords and knives and farming tools, hacking their victims to death amid ambient acts of rape, torture, and mutilation. The terror lasted six months. Some half a million people were killed.[155] Meanwhile, tens of thousands of others were arrested, interrogated, and detained for indefinite periods.

De facto, Soeharto began wielding power in October 1965. But de jure he treaded cautiously, acting solicitously toward Sukarno. For more than a year afterward, Sukarno remained officially president and Great Leader of the Revolution and continued to form cabinets, even as Soeharto maneuvered to marginalize (and in some cases to imprison) his key political allies and his supporters in the military.[156] In March 1966 Sukarno officially granted Soeharto "supreme authority to restore order and facilitate the functioning of government."[157] It was only after this that the PKI and communism were officially outlawed. Sukarno never condemned them.[158] A full year passed before the Provisional People's Consultative Assembly formally removed Sukarno from office and named Soeharto acting president.[159] He became president only in 1968.

Sukarno spent the rest of his life under house arrest, in a private house in Jakarta and on the grounds of the spacious presidential palace in Bogor surrounded by vast botanical gardens, a legacy of the Dutch. He was a prisoner, a man instantly irrelevant as Soeharto and the army took hold. Soeharto reversed many of his policies—Indonesia soon rejoined the United Nations and made peace with Malaysia—but embraced others, such as Panca Sila, scorn for political parties and parliamentary democracy, consultation through functional groups, and, most of all, a fierce commitment to the nation. The New Order, as Soeharto's government called itself, would place the full weight and power of a military dictatorship—working through a façade of staged elections and appointed deliberative bodies—behind a new effort at unity. With the elimination of communism and of democracy itself, perhaps many could be one after all.

Sukarno declined rapidly in his final years. Visiting with him in 1966, Cindy Adams found him lonely, overweight, and careless of his appearance. "As the chill winds of fate blew mercilessly," she wrote, "he wrapped his tattered friendships around him like a blanket."[160] In the end, all of his wives divorced him but one.[161] He died in 1970. President Soeharto accorded him a state funeral, and Muslim leaders who had opposed him and survived him prayed over his bier and forgave him.

Now, with hindsight, we can see again the bigness of Sukarno's life. He was unquestionably the formative political actor in the creation of Indonesia. And Indonesia has endured, surviving decades of dictatorship under Soeharto to embark in the late twentieth century on a second round of democracy. Sukarno's own daughter has served as president. In assessing his role in history, it is worth remembering that he was born at the very peak of Western colonial domination in Asia. His life stood astride the entire era of modern nationalism and revolution, when a new Asia-to-be was being brilliantly improvised by protean actors like himself, who through stunning acts of political imagination and will, and even in failure, drew whole societies into the hopes and bitter truths of the postcolonial world.

EIGHT

DENG XIAOPING
AND THE CHINA HE MADE

ODD ARNE WESTAD

TOGETHER WITH CHIANG KAI-SHEK, Deng Xiaoping is perhaps the most consequential figure in China's twentieth century. Mao Zedong led a revolution, but never much liked the state he founded and led it in disastrous directions during his last twenty years in power. Zhou Enlai started out as a transformational revolutionary figure and a significant leader, but ended—after the People's Republic of China was founded in 1949—as Mao's political lapdog. Chiang led the country through twenty years of state-building and civil and foreign wars. His main accomplishment was to keep China together as a unit when dissolution and outside invasion threatened its very existence. Deng also led the country for some twenty years. His achievement was to make China richer and freer than it had been at any other point in its recent history. Both men had great flaws, but—by and large—these were the flaws of the age in which they lived. For bad and good they made China into the country it is today.

Deng Xiaoping was born in 1904 in a small village in northeastern Sichuan. His family was Hakka, an often persecuted minority group that had arrived in the area from the south around 1800. Deng's Hakka background and his family's origin in the south were important to him. According to people who knew him, he was proud to be an "outsider," a son of migrants. It made him feel special, select. It also toughened him. As are many among his people, Deng was a small man—as an adult, he stood barely five feet tall. He and his kind were looked down upon—quite literally—by other locals. All Hakka children have examples of victimization, and Deng—in spite of being the son of a landowner—was no exception. He always fought back. This pugnacity was to be characteristic of Deng throughout his life. He seemed to cultivate it, along with a certain coarseness (which could have been a way of disguising his superior class origins). Deng's mother died when he was very young. His father—himself an educated man—sent his eldest son to a Western-style school when he was seven, and from there to a school in the nearby city of Chongqing, which would prepare Deng for a work-study program in France. In 1919, not yet sixteen years old, Deng Xiaoping left Shanghai for Marseilles.[1]

Deng's seven years in France were the formative element in his life. His journeys there and back were integral elements of his awakening. Going through Hong Kong, Vietnam, Singapore, Sri Lanka, and Egypt gave him a sense of Asia that he had not had before and a sense that all Asians were being exploited by Europeans. Only Asian conquest of the most advanced forms of European modernity could rectify this injustice, Deng later wrote. In France, he worked, went to evening school, and realized that socialism was the most advanced form of modernity Europe could offer. He entered into the heady political climate of postwar France and saw a world that had the material advantages he wanted for China, but also one where everyone seemed to question established authority. At nineteen, he joined the Chinese Communist Youth League, the youth wing of the Chinese Communist Party (CCP). Wary of what he saw as the condescending attitude of French radicals to their Asian comrades, Deng mostly stayed among his fellow Chinese. It could be said that it was in France he discovered Chineseness; no longer only Hakka, or only Sichuanese, or only a southerner, he was now fully Chinese, part of a new nation with very old roots. He became a full-time revolutionary in 1925. The following year the French police were looking for him, and he absconded, quickly, through Germany to Russia.[2]

Deng stayed in Moscow for a year. This was his stage of higher education—he studied at Sun Yat-sen University, a training school set up by the Comintern to educate leaders for the Asian revolution. Being in Moscow and at an elite institution gave Deng a sense of the centrality of the movement he was part of. Stalin himself came to lecture at the university. Its students were supposed to go back to their countries and create socialist modernity there, patterned on the Soviet experiment. Deng enjoyed his stay in Moscow. He met a Chinese girl, whom he later married. As in France, he kept his distance from the Soviets and stuck mainly to his Chinese compatriots and other Asians. Deng wanted knowledge but sometimes felt uncomfortable around those from whom this knowledge emanated.[3]

When Deng Xiaoping was suddenly recalled to China by his party in January 1927, the summons may have come as a relief to the young man. He had been abroad for eight years and had learned more than anyone could have expected when he set out as a fifteen-year-old. But his was a different kind of knowledge from what Deng's family might have expected. He had first and foremost learned about society and how to change it. Marxism to Deng meant materialism, in opposition to most Chinese beliefs and ideas. His primary concern was how to make his country rich and strong. This demanded the destruction of old ways and a remaking of China in the image of the most progressive parts of the West. Given his outsider background, it was perhaps not surprising that he was also concerned with creating a Chinese people out of all of China's nationalities. In this, he thought, the Soviet Union was a practical model. But Leninism was perhaps even more important to Deng than Marxism. It told him that a determined elite could remake a country through mobilization of the masses. Social justice, it seems, was more a tool than an aim for the young Deng. It was the means through which the most talented people could be brought forth to lead the revolution.

The task Deng was brought to China to handle in 1927 was one of the most dangerous a young Communist could engage in. Feng Yuxiang, a Christian warlord in central China who reputedly liked to collectively baptize his troops with a fire-hose, had somewhat serendipitously also expressed an interest in joining the Communist cause. Although the Soviets distrusted Feng, they could not let the opportunity pass. So Deng went off to Xi'an, and right into the lion's den. He escaped by a hair's breadth when Feng, a few months later, joined Chiang Kai-shek in arresting every Communist they could put their hands on. Deng fled to Shanghai, where he joined up with those who were left in the underground CCP leadership. After a few months he became chief secretary to the Central Committee, a sign both of how impressive his comrades found him to be and of how few Communists were left. Deng was twenty-three years old. The rest of his life would be spent in high positions in the CCP. The party, in a certain way, would become his life.[4]

The rest of Deng's revolutionary career is easy to sum up. The CCP leadership in 1928 sent him to the south, to Guangxi province, where

Deng thrived as a fish in water. He helped build a strong Communist base, with at least partial control of a territory containing almost one million people. But the local soviet did not last long. It was crushed by a coalition of local forces who abhorred the radicalism of Deng and his comrades. A refugee again, he went back to Shanghai and then to Mao Zedong's soviet in the Jiangxi-Fujian borderlands, where he joined the local administration and became close to Mao himself. When the Communists were driven out from there as well in 1934, Deng joined Mao in a great escape to the north, generally referred to as "The Long March." But Deng's six years in the south confirmed his identity as a southerner, a theme he would often turn to later on.

With their new base area established in northwestern Shaanxi, Deng excelled as a Communist administrator with a particular penchant for military affairs. Mao obviously liked the plainspoken and some-what crass youth, with his intelligence, dedication to the party, and willingness to prioritize military needs. It is harder to determine exactly what Deng saw in Mao, except power. Mao Zedong was the obvious head of the party by the time they reached the north, and Deng—like most others—saw him as the savior of the rump CCP. But Deng's attachment to Mao seemed to have gone beyond reverence for the leader. Given what he later said about the chairman, it is likely that Deng was attracted by Mao's practical attitude to problem-solving, which at the time must have seemed similar to his own. Mao Zedong always surrounded his burning fervor with a great deal of practical sense. Deng would also have been attracted by Chinese Communism now having a *Chinese* leader, who made his own decisions without always consulting Moscow first.

Deng Xiaoping served in high positions throughout the war with Japan and the civil war that followed. He became a master of improvi-sation and of narrow escapes. One of his main tasks was to work as a political commissar, linking the CCP's political purpose with armies fighting in the field. He learned to appreciate the needs and deeds of warfare, and some of the commanders he worked with often sensed that he was more their man against the party hierarchy than the other way around. This closeness to the military would later stand Deng in good stead. His main efforts in battle were fighting alongside the famed CCP General Liu Bocheng all over central China during the civil war, providing relief for the hard-pressed CCP front in the north, where the main party leaders were holed up. When the CCP went on the offensive, Liu's and Deng's forces turned west, and it was their army that finally drove Chiang Kai-shek out of Sichuan—his last stand on the mainland—in December 1949.

After the victory in the civil war, as one of the most admired CCP leaders in the country, Deng chose to stay in Chongqing as mayor of the largest city in his home province, rather than heading straight for Beijing and central power, as many of those in a similar situation did. Perhaps he wanted to show his fellow Sichuanese how he had come up in the world. Perhaps, also, he sensed that he would have more freedom of action in the southwest. Deng stayed three years in Chongqing. In 1952, he moved to Beijing to become, in quick succession, vice-chairman of the party's Finance Commission, minister of finance, and chairman of the Information Commission. In 1956 he became general-secretary of the Central Committee of the CCP and head of its organization department. These appointments made Deng a key player in the inner circle that was forming around Mao Zedong. They also put him in positions that made a lot of people depend on him and his support for the advancement of their careers. He traveled extensively to visit party branches in all parts of the country. He also kept up his close relationship with many military leaders. But Deng's real preoccupation in Beijing in the 1950s was with planning and economic development. He wanted China to learn from the Soviet Union, and quickly. "Successful development," Deng said, "depends on whether the Party is good at learning (if it is, it will avoid major mistakes and get more done on less money). . . . In planning, too, we must adopt a correct guiding concept, because improper planning may lead to enormous waste."[5] He wanted a dynamic, rapidly advancing economy and shared Mao's concern that economic development was happening too slowly in the mid-1950s.[6]

Deng's message was that China's modernization was a matter of life or death for the country. There were no signs, in this period, that he distrusted the Soviet development model; quite on the contrary, he traveled around the country criticizing those who deviated from Soviet planning principles. He became known within the party as the apostle of planning, centralization, and efficiency. He also helped to win others over to his vision of socialism. Deng's supreme self-confidence, his obvious skill and intelligence, his directness, willingness to take responsibility, and if necessary to experiment, all came together in a public figure in whom most party leaders had an enormous trust. His great capacity for hard work and his never-ending optimism made him an attractive model for those who worked with him in Beijing.

In the late 1950s, Deng worked increasingly with Mao himself. His role as general secretary of course linked him with the chairman in an immediate way, but there were also signs that Deng was politically closer to Mao's thinking than were many of the other "old" leaders of the party. The younger leader revered the chairman, as did the others, but he was also attracted by Mao's spontaneity, his impatience, and his Chinese nationalism. The thought that China, which had been downtrodden and underdeveloped, could show Communists from other countries how to progress quickly toward socialism appealed to Deng over and beyond the meaning it had to leaders such as Liu Shaoqi and Zhou Enlai, Deng's political superiors.[7]

Deng's attraction to the impulsiveness of Mao Zedong led him down the road to the greatest human and political disasters of his life. Mao chose Deng to head the Great Leap Forward, the CCP's ill-conceived plan for increasing industrial production by 50 percent per year through sheer willpower and thereby catapult China into socialist high modernity. Deng was late in realizing the disastrous consequences of the Leap he had helped launch. His deflection, work-wise, to handling some of the fallout from the collapse of the Sino-Soviet alliance may have influenced his judgment. It must have been hard for a nationalist such as Deng to admit that his party had led China to disaster, while preparing what he undoubtedly saw as necessary polemics against the Soviets. He knew, of course, that no peasant was starving in the Soviet Union, whereas millions were dying in China. This might have been one reason why Mao selected him as "criticizer-in-chief" of the Soviets. By late 1961, however, Deng had joined Liu and Zhou in attempting to abate the worst consequences of the Great Leap.

Some historians see the early 1960s as a first breakthrough for Deng's reform thinking, which would only come to full fruition a decade and a half later. There is almost no evidence for this view. The Deng Xiaoping of the early 1960s is a study in political failure. Of course he was out to remedy the disastrous consequences of the Leap. After a cataclysm in which more than twenty million people died, it was necessary to feed the living and get at least part of the economy back on track. But Deng had run out of options. He had abandoned the Soviet-style incrementalism of the plan for a leap that had turned phantasmagoric. Returning to mid-1950s-style planning was not an option. Moving toward market incentives, at the same time as the CPP was furiously attacking the Soviet Union for its supposed "capitalist deviations," was no alternative either. Deng may well have uttered his famous phrase—quoting his old friend Marshal Liu Bocheng—that "It does not matter if it is a yellow cat or a black cat, as long as it catches mice" in 1962.[8] But he knew that Mao would never let go of the vestiges of the Leap—the people's communes, the eradication of private ownership, the super-radical foreign policy. Deng's fabled pragmatism in the early 1960s became a plan-less patchwork to cover up the results of the biggest disaster his party inflicted on China.

Neither is there any evidence that Deng Xiaoping ever understood the drift toward the Cultural Revolution started by the chairman in the early 1960s. The almost god-like worship of Mao, which Deng had played a key role in orchestrating, was to him probably an instrument for nation-building. In spite of his increasing instability and eccentricity, Mao had come to symbolize China (just as to some extent he still does today). This worship meant that Deng and his colleagues were led like lambs to the slaughter in the period up to 1966, when Mao decreed the start of the Cultural Revolution, the next stage of China's long sorrow. In Mao's eyes, Deng was tainted by his efforts to rescue what could be rescued after the collapse of the Leap. There was in Deng's attitude an implicit criticism of the chairman himself, Mao thought. He therefore let Deng use his famed efficiency to prepare the campaign that cost Deng his career and nearly his life.

It is often (conveniently) forgotten today that Deng Xiaoping was in the group Mao first selected to head the Cultural Revolution. As such, Deng dutifully attacked every leader who was purged before he himself was thrown into darkness in 1966. Like everyone else in the leadership, he turned on his old comrades one by one as they were singled out for criticism. He attempted to make self-criticism to be kept in the fold, stressing that the Cultural Revolution was necessary to "prevent China from ever changing color and [help China] avert the danger of revisionism and capitalist restoration."[9] But this could not save Deng from Mao's wrath. He was condemned in party propaganda as the "Number Two Capitalist Roader" in China after Liu Shaoqi, the country's president. But while Liu was killed in prison in 1969, Deng's fate was more benign. He first spent two years under house arrest in Beijing. Then he was sent to the southern province of Jiangxi to do physical labor and study "Mao Zedong Thought."

The time in Jiangxi made Deng begin to rethink China's experience under the Communist state he had helped create. He was horrified at how poor local peasants were—not much progress had been made there since 1949. He also picked up the disillusionment and despair many local leaders felt over the way things were heading in Mao's last years. When the chairman had fallen out with many of his new radical friends and brought Deng back to Beijing to serve as vice-premier in 1973, Deng was far more careful when trying to sweep up the rubble left by the Cultural Revolution than he had been after the Great Leap a decade earlier. Most of those who knew him thought he was biding his time until the chairman died. But when the memorial service for Deng's main ally, Zhou Enlai, almost turned into an attack on the regime in early 1976, Mao and the radicals turned on Deng again. This time he was lucky to escape alive.[10]

Mao's death in September 1976 changed the political picture in China almost entirely. His hand-picked successor, the colorless bureaucrat Hua Guofeng, was more afraid of the radicals than he was of the old guard, and conspired with the heads of security and of the army to have the main Cultural Revolutionaries, including Mao's widow, Jiang Qing, arrested. Even after Hua's coup, Deng had to wait nine months before he was allowed to return to his former positions. But the direction of things as far as Deng was concerned was clear. The military had made Deng's return a precondition for their support of Hua Guofeng. But neither Hua nor the marshals had expected Deng's political position to become crucial so soon after his return as vice-premier in mid-1977.

What Deng had to offer in the faction-ridden, Byzantine milieu of Chinese politics in the late 1970s and early 1980s was experience and a sense of direction. Deng had no master plan for how he wanted to proceed, but he gave voice to an overwhelming majority of party members who wanted no return to the bad old days of the Leap and Cultural Revolution and who wanted instead to stress the need for rapid economic growth. In the fall of 1977, it soon became clear that Deng's no-nonsense approach and his close links with the army gave him many advantages over all other leaders in Beijing. Where Hua Guofeng appeared leaden and vague, Deng proposed new measures that could bring immediate effect to the economy and he did so with a style and efficiency that impressed other leaders. Dressing himself in the cloak of the late Premier Zhou Enlai, Deng stressed modernization as his main theme. He carefully avoided joining any party faction, such as those who wanted a return to Soviet-style planning or those who wanted to democratize China's political life. Against the latter, he argued the need for strict party control of the changes he proposed. Against the former, he argued that while plans were necessary, they should not be restrictive or unenterprising.[11]

Most of his colleagues expected Deng to move in the same direction as what he, Zhou, and Liu Shaoqi had proposed in the early 1960s: namely, a socialist planned economy, with import of new technology, improvements in education, and limited material rewards for those who in output fulfilled the plan. They simply did not see the degree of Deng's disenchantment with centralized planning as a mechanism for growth. Already by the time of the Third CCP Central Committee Plenum in November 1978, which often is seen as symbolizing Deng's taking over from Hua Guofeng as the main policymaker within the party, Deng wanted experiments within the plan, to see whether output could be increased by giving more autonomy to the provinces, counties, and even to local factories. There is an element of Mao's impatience in Deng's policy in the late 1970s and early 1980s, although the new leader wanted to use different instruments for change. What they had in common, it could be argued, was the inordinate fear of the consequences of China lagging behind other countries in terms of development. They both concluded that the Soviet-style plan could not deliver the kind of growth they were looking for. But they drew very different implications from their conclusion.

So where did the ideas behind Deng's concepts of transformation come from? As with Mao, he did not have a specific form of society in mind. His preoccupation was with process, not end result. Deng's understanding in the late 1970s of how a market economy worked was vague (to put it mildly), and he was insistent that the party dictatorship should be kept in place. He first looked at other Asian societies and proclaimed that China needed more of what they already had: economic progress, material wealth, high technology, and stable societies and institutions. Many were dictatorships: South Korea and Taiwan, for example. Some were authoritarian states with political participation, such as Japan and Singapore. But they had all progressed much more than China in terms of economic development. Deng knew that the market had played a significant role in these transformations, but he did not know how to fit it into the Chinese scheme of things within the framework of a heavy-handed Stalinist approach that his party had practiced since its inception in 1921.

What came out was a typical Dengist muddle, though a fruitful one. When in late 1979 the new leader tried to justify his policies to visiting foreigners, he claimed that "It is wrong to maintain that a market economy exists only in capitalist society and that there is only 'capitalist' market economy." As he remarked:

> Why can't we develop a market economy under socialism? Developing a market economy does not mean practising capitalism. While maintaining a planned economy as the mainstay of our economic system, we are also introducing a market economy. But it is a socialist market economy. Although a socialist market economy is similar to a capitalist one in method, there are also differences between them. The socialist market economy mainly regulates interrelations between state-owned enterprises, between collectively owned enterprises and even between foreign capitalist enterprises. But in the final analysis, this is all done under socialism in a socialist society. We cannot say that market economy exists only under capitalism. Market economy was in its embryonic stages as early as feudalist society. We can surely develop it under socialism. Similarly, taking advantage of the useful aspects of capitalist countries, including their methods of operation and management, does not mean that we will adopt capitalism. Instead, we use those methods in order to develop the productive forces under socialism. As long as learning from capitalism is regarded as no more than a means to an end, it will not change the structure of socialism or bring China back to capitalism.[12]

There were four key supply lines of inspiration for Deng's reforms. One was elements of social change that were already underway in some parts of southern China during the 1970s. Another was the development experience of other East Asian states. A third was the impact of the Chinese diaspora. And a fourth was the relationship with the United States, which by the late 1970s had spread from the security sphere into economic and technological interaction. All of these were important to Deng. Together with the conclusions he drew from the experiments he himself cultivated in southern China, they carried him along, toward a Chinese economy and a Chinese society very different from what anyone (including Deng himself) could have imagined in 1980.

Deng regarded himself as a southerner, and he stayed in close touch with people from the region. In the years when he was exiled to Jiangxi—one of the poorest provinces in the south—he observed both directly and indirectly how local leaders struggled to break out of the confines imposed on them by Maoism and provide a better life for the people they were responsible for. Their methods included bartering between production units and illegal import of technology through Hong Kong. There is evidence that Deng continued to study these sprouts of market behavior after he returned to Beijing and especially after he was purged for a second time in 1976. Unlike the Maoists, Deng saw the desperate attempts at using market incentives to their own advantage as something positive for the region and for China. He wanted to control what was done in the provinces from Beijing after he returned to power. But he also wanted to learn from what he saw as the natural instinct of many southern Chinese to strive to become rich and to work in large family units to do so, for China's overall benefit.

Deng's first major trips abroad after returning to power in 1977 were to Southeast Asia and Japan. His reasons for going there were very clear: he wanted to observe at close range how these countries had managed to get rich quickly from a fairly low starting point. His first stop in Southeast Asia was Thailand in November 1978, where he blithely overlooked the regime's violent suppression of local Communists and appealed for unity in combating China's main enemy in the region, Vietnam. But his main pitch in Bangkok was to the local Chinese overseas community. They had an obligation, Deng told them, to help the motherland get rich and strong. Thereby they would also help the country where they were now citizens.

Of all the countries in Southeast Asia none is more important to China than Singapore. The country has a majority Chinese population, and Deng was convinced, from reading about its recent history, that China had a lot to learn from its development experience. His conversations with Singapore's leader, Lee Kwan Yew, turned into seminars on market development and social engineering. Lee, a fellow Hakka, stood for values that Deng admired: progress, order, and economic flexibility. According to Lee, Deng said, "you've done a good job in Singapore. . . . I came to Singapore on my way to Marseilles in 1920. It was a lousy place. You have made it a different place."[13]

Also in 1978, Deng visited Japan, the first top Chinese leader to do so. He was desperate to get Japan on board with assisting China's development efforts. As many other world leaders did in the late 1970s, Deng believed that Japan's economy was the most dynamic in the world. When meeting with the Japanese emperor, Deng stressed that memories of the Sino-Japanese wars should not stand between them: "Bygones should be bygones, and we must be forward-looking in the future and work in every field to develop relations of peace and friendship between our two countries."[14] No Chinese leader, before or since, had shown such willingness as Deng Xiaoping to get along with Japan, in China's own interest. Toward the end of his life, it is said, this was the topic that most preoccupied him.

Southeast Asia, with its Chinese diaspora, and Japan were crucial to Deng's attempt to break China out of its poverty and stagnation. But it was the United States that was the key global power, and Deng knew that Beijing would have to rely on Washington's cooperation if its economy were to engage more actively in international trade. He also knew that China to quite some extent relied on the United States for its security. Deng took over from Mao a somewhat simplistic strategic worldview, in which the military power of the Soviet Union was rising fast. The Soviets, he thought, were China's deadly enemies. China was militarily weak because of the excesses of the Maoist era. Beijing needed access to US military technology to improve its power, but it also needed protection from the US nuclear umbrella to balance the Soviet threat at its border. A good relationship with the United States was therefore essential both for security and economic reasons.

In the late 1970s China's relationship with the United States was paradoxical. Under Mao, the country had begun working closely with the United States on security matters, to stave off what the chairman saw as the extraordinarily dangerous threat from the Soviet Union. But the two countries still did not have normal diplomatic relations because of the close US relationship with Taiwan. Beijing and Washington could work together against Soviet interests in Africa or even Southeast Asia, but they could not exchange ambassadors. Even worse, at least for Deng, there was very little economic exchange. The Maoists wanted to keep China's relationship with the United States exclusively to the strategic sphere. They thought that engaging the Americans economically would set China on the course toward counterrevolution. Deng thought the opposite. He wanted more trade, more technology imports, and, eventually, US investments in China. He also wanted the Americans to help China open the doors to other markets for Chinese exports.

When he arrived in Washington in January 1979, Deng had already achieved much to set his stamp on the liaison. Even though he regarded the US position on Taiwan essentially as a colonial relationship, he agreed to fudge the wording on that relationship in the future in order to pave the way for full mutual recognition between the United States and China. He had agreed—or so he thought—to a tougher US approach to Soviet worldwide expansionism. And he had opened up China for technology transfers, not least in agriculture and light industry. But much still remained to be done, especially in terms of trade. Deng was eager to see for himself what the United States looked like and how it was organized. So he traveled widely during his visit. He went to the West Coast, to Texas (where he went to a rodeo and put on a ten-gallon hat—the hat looked bigger than Deng himself), to President Jimmy Carter's home state of Georgia, even to Philadelphia. He confided to a colleague that the material wealth of the United States—its shopping malls, its wheat fields, its mechanized factories—boiled him over, so that he could hardly sleep. Such was the extent of America's modernity. Deng wanted it for China.

After his visit to the United States and after squelching the main attempts at antimarket resistance at home, Deng sped up the reform plans. He introduced so-called Special Economic Zones (SEZs) in the south, where foreign companies could invest freely and export their profits, as long as they agreed to import technology and train Chinese in how to use it. He stepped up the ambitious plans to send students abroad (obviously based on his own experience as a young man). In agriculture the People's Communes, in which everything had been run and owned collectively, were gradually phased out and replaced by family farming. In the 1980s small-scale private enterprises began and foreign investment increased dramatically. By the time Deng had been in power for ten years, China had been set on a path away from the socialist planned economy and toward a market-driven form of development.

Some Chinese and foreigners expected the new Chinese leadership to begin experimenting with democracy as well. But Deng made it clear from the beginning that this was not his intention. He turned viciously on those within the CCP who had realized that the only guarantee against the return of terror and one-man rule was some form of political pluralism. Although Deng was willing to allow debate and differing points of view to a degree that would have been impossible under Mao, he insisted on the dictatorship of the party.

People's private lives were their own as long as they did not challenge power. Discussion of alternatives was permissible, as long as some degree of censorship was kept in place. Increasingly, Deng came to think of the party leaders as a kind of company that ran China under his guidance, with strict rules on confidentiality, loyalty, and obedience. The company culture decided all. As long as the brand stayed intact, and the Chinese economy grew, Deng did not care very much about the nepotism, corruption, and blatant misuse of the legal system that were by-products of the political structure that he had created.

In 1989, all of this came to a head. Hundreds of thousands of protesters in the main Chinese cities came out on the streets to proclaim their support for democracy, freedom of speech, and the rule of law. Deng was probably never in any doubt that the movement had to be crushed, and he deplored his lieutenants' feebleness in putting it down. Where some high-ranking CCP members saw a chance to break the party's links with dictatorship and oppression, as Mikhail Gorbachev had done in the Soviet Union a few years previously, Deng saw threatening chaos and disorder of a kind not unlike that of the Cultural Revolution. He felt that he had set China on the path to national and material success. It was not be derailed by demonstrators. Deng had not come through revolution, civil wars, foreign wars, Mao's campaigns, and two purges to be challenged for power by unarmed students sitting down in Beijing's main square. He unleashed the army on the protesters. About eight hundred were killed and thousands arrested.

The Tiananmen massacre and the political crackdown that followed did much to destroy Deng's reputation outside China. Inside China it was (and is) more divided. Among people who were young in 1989, some see the protests as a missed opportunity for China's democratization, and (rightly) blame Deng for destroying it. Others believe that the "stability" (read "dictatorship") that CCP rule brought made the extraordinary economic growth of the 1990s and 2000s possible, and that China would have descended into chaos without authoritarian governance. There is much that is confused about this debate. Deng did not act the way he did in 1989 to rescue China's economic growth rate. He did it because he believed very firmly in the rule of the party and because he was still a prisoner of Stalinist concepts of "subversion," "counterrevolution," "rebellious cliques," "dregs of society," "cruel enemies."[15] But neither did he use military force to turn the clock back on reform *tout court*. Deng wanted accelerated economic reform under the dictatorship of the party.

Deng Xiaoping's last hurrah turned out to be not 1989, but the tour of the south he went on three years later, in 1992, when he was eighty-eight years old. Sensing that some of the new leaders who he himself had put in place after 1989 were more skeptical, or at least more noncommittal, toward economic reform than Deng himself, he set out on a three-week, imperial-style, grand tour of the southern provinces where his policies had reached their highest levels. He went to Shenzhen, near Hong Kong, the first of the SEZs, where in 1980 there had been nothing but small fishing villages and where there was now a bustling city of several million people, the most dynamic (and most capitalist) in China. It was here that the old man (according to some who were present) should have uttered the famous words "To get rich is glorious!"[16] His formal comments were more prudent, but equally clear: "Socialism essentially aims to release and develop productive forces, wipe out exploitation and eliminate polarization between poor and rich and finally achieve common prosperity. Are such things as securities and stocks good, do they cause danger, are they things unique to capitalism, can socialism make use of them? It is permissible to judge, but we must be resolute in having a try."[17]

Deng died at home in Beijing in 1997. His legacy is mixed, though of supreme importance to China's twentieth-century history and to everyone who lives in China today. His main achievement was allowing the country to rebuild its economic strength, so that today—for the first time in over two hundred years—China is a global commercial powerhouse. He did this through his willingness to experiment, even when he himself had no idea about the outcome. What he did demanded bravery, dedication, and enormous personal strength. Through his actions, hundreds of millions of Chinese could move out of poverty and despair and lead lives of a quality that they would not have dreamed about before 1980.

But Deng failed in setting a political course for China that would have made it a better-governed country. He wanted to keep the dictatorship in place and leave the issue of political reform to his successors. His nationalism blinded him to the need to learn from others in terms of civil rights and the rule of law. The result has been the creation of an economic hyper-power with a tiny sense of self. Today's

China is not an example to others except in terms of naked economic growth. Deng Xiaoping returned, again and again, to help make China richer and stronger than he could ever had hoped for when he got on the boat to Marseilles. He also, in most ways, helped make it freer. But he did not break the vicious cycle of repression that still informs its mode of government.

NINE

INDIRA GANDHI

India and the World in Transition

SRINATH RAGHAVAN

I

OCTOBER 2009 marked the twenty-fifth anniversary of the death of Indira Gandhi. For a few days, newspapers and magazines were awash with retrospective assessments of India's third, and most controversial, prime minister. With the exception of professional sycophants and paid-up members of the Congress Party, few commentators found anything edifying in her record and legacy. The undermining of India's democracy and constitution by imposing the Emergency; the terror and repression unleashed during the Emergency through its programs of forcible sterilization and slum clearance; the assault on the independence of the Supreme Court and the press; the accentuation of regional secessionism in Assam, Kashmir, and Punjab; the drop in economic growth owing to deeply flawed antibusiness and antimarket policies; the abandoning of India's nonaligned foreign policy by tilting toward a moribund Soviet Union: the cumulative indictment was formidable indeed.

These judgments, however, sit awkwardly with public perceptions of Indira Gandhi. Opinion polls routinely throw her up as the best prime minister the country has ever had. Indeed, in a recent poll, nearly a third of the respondents voted for her—a number that placed her well ahead of her predecessors as well as successors. Such expressions of popular opinion confound her critics. They attribute it either to sheer ignorance or to wishful nostalgia. One such poll moved a well-known Indian columnist to wag her finger against "the illiterate villagers" who gave top marks to Indira Gandhi: "She was a bad leader. It was a bad time."[1] The afterlives of Indira Gandhi seem as puzzling and paradoxical as her life.

She was, after all, the daughter of Jawaharlal Nehru—the man who laid the institutional foundations of independent India and trained the country for democracy. And yet, she seemed to have little time for prevailing proprieties and a great deal of political ruthlessness. She began her prime ministerial career with an inclination to liberalize India's economy. And yet, she fortified the "license-permit-quota raj." She won a decisive victory in the war against Pakistan and went on to authorize nuclear tests. And yet, she refrained from imposing a settlement on Kashmir and from weaponizing India's nuclear capabilities. She secured dramatic majorities for her party in the elections of 1971 and 1980. And yet, she was unable to prevent the rapid dissipation of popular approbation. She created a strong centralized administrative and political apparatus. And yet, she was confronted with a range of regional reversals and revolts that she was unable to manage.

Making sense of Indira Gandhi is uneasy business. Nevertheless, her personality and the period continue to draw the attention and interest of admirers and critics alike. The shelves creak under the collective weight of biographies, memoirs, and journalistic accounts. But, for the most part, these remain exercises in condemnation or commendation. Understanding and explanation, archival research and cool interpretation remain at something of a discount. Part of the problem stems from the fact that Mrs. Gandhi was and remains a sharply polarizing figure. Part of the problem also arises from the fact that most biographers and chroniclers belonged to generations that experienced at first hand the hopes and frustrations, the upheaval and repression of the Indira Gandhi years. Unsurprisingly, when it comes to Indira Gandhi, most scholars and analysts find it difficult to slough off the accumulated layers of parti pris.

This essay attempts a fresh assessment of Mrs. Gandhi by drawing on new archival material and by placing her more firmly in the domestic and international context of her times. It is neither a capsule biography nor an intellectual history. Indeed, when it comes to an intensely political figure like Mrs. Gandhi, what matters most is not the coherence or consistency of thought, but the character and quality of her practical judgment. Indira Gandhi held the levers of the state for all but three years from 1966 to 1984. These were times of great change and churning both within India and in the wider world. Her choices and actions left a deep impress on India's politics, its economics, and its engagement with the world. In the age of Indira, the Indian people came of age. This helps explains why she remains a figure of widespread adulation as well as detraction.

II

Born on November 19, 1917, Indira Priyadarshini Nehru was the only child of Jawaharlal and Kamala Nehru. A single girl child was a rarity in her generation and in the class to which her family belonged. Then again, the family was rather distinctive. Her grandfather Motilal Nehru was an immensely successful and ambitious lawyer, who was determined to recast his family along Western mores. This not only involved changes in lifestyle and education, but also a gradual move toward a more liberal ordering within the family.[2] The public stage on which Indira's life would be enacted was also undergoing dramatic changes. She was born in a time of war, revolution, and upheaval. Western imperialism and the Bolshevik Revolution would cast a long shadow on her public life. From the outset, then, the personal and the political were closely entwined in the life of Indira Gandhi.

Indira's early years saw her family being pulled into the ruck of nationalist politics under the inspiration of Mohandas K. Gandhi. Young Indira was seeped in the nationalist ethos of her family. Just short of her thirteenth birthday, she wrote to her father that her friends had decided her future profession, hastening to add: "That is of course after we have got Swaraj [Independence]—till then every one has just one job—fighting."[3]

But the family's immersion in the nationalist movement also took its toll on Indira. With her parents and relatives in and out of prison and her mother chronically ill, Indira found herself shouldering far greater responsibilities than did most children of her age. The psychological consequences of her periodic loneliness have been the subject of much speculation by her biographers. Of greater interest, though, is the impact on her formal education. In 1931, Nehru sent her to the Pupils' Own School in Poona. This experimental school started by a young couple sought to inculcate in the students an awareness of their cultural heritage. Three years later she was sent to another unconventional educational institution: Rabindranath Tagore's Visva Bharati in Santiniketan. A year later, Indira had to leave Santiniketan and accompany her ailing mother to Europe for treatment. The time spent in these unorthodox schools, especially Santiniketan, helped her develop a taste for the visual arts and dance. But her exposure to the humanities and the sciences was limited. Jawaharlal was, of course, well aware of these shortcomings. And he took it upon himself to provide a remarkable course of epistolary education from prison. Not only did he write for her, as a series of letters, a sprawling outline of world history. He also directed her toward his own favorites in history and literature: G. M. Trevelyan, Bernard Shaw, H. G. Wells, Aldous Huxley, among others.

After her mother's death in January 1936, Indira joined Badminton School at Bristol in preparation for going up to Oxford. The following October, she joined Somerville College to read history. By her own account, she found her studies tough going. While she enjoyed history, she was soon toying with the idea of switching to Politics, Philosophy, and Economics. The problem with PPE, she admitted, was that "it means a terrible lot of work & jolly hard work too. And also I am not very good with economics."[4] Eventually it was her poor health and not her lack of application that forced her to leave Oxford without a degree. In the summer of 1939 she took ill and had to be treated for tuberculosis in Switzerland. This unconventional and interrupted education left Indira with an intellectual apparatus that was quick on the uptake but unsuited to the demands of sustained reflection. The range of her intellectual interests mirrored that of her father, but she lacked his capacity for deep engagement with ideas.

The years in England, however, exposed her to wider currents of politics. She was active in the Indian Majlis at Oxford and also moved in British radical circles. Through her father's friend and admirer, V. K. Krishna Menon, she was drawn toward socialist and anti-imperialist groups in London. The events in China, Spain, and the brewing crisis in Europe engaged her interest and energies. "Isn't the European situation perfectly sickening?" she wrote to Nehru just before the Munich agreement. "What can one say about it? Words seem so superfluous. I knew Chamberlain couldn't be up to any good when he flew to Germany."[5] Later, looking back at her radical associations in England, she would recall not the traffic of ideas but "mammoth gatherings in Hyde Park and Trafalgar Square. . . . The enthusiasm of it!"[6]

Indira's early radicalism stemmed from the Popular Front politics of that period, two main strands of which left an imprint. The first was anti-imperialism. This came almost naturally to her in relation to

India. But while in Europe she began to appreciate the wider international implications of imperialism. Leninism in international politics tended to shade into a form of "realism." And Indira Gandhi's approach to international relations was shaped by an early appreciation of the role of interests and power.

The second strand of Popular Front politics that influenced her thought was antifascism.[7] Indira's assessment of, and antipathy toward, European fascism molded her views about extremist Hindu Right organizations in India such as the Rashtriya Swayamsevak Sangh (RSS). Observing the activities of the RSS just after India's independence, she wrote to Nehru: "the growth of this organization is so amazingly like the Brown Shirts of Germany, that if we are not very quick on our toes it will grow beyond our control. . . . The recent history of Germany is too close for us to be able to forget it for an instant."[8] Her ideas about the dangers presented by clones of European fascism on the Hindu Right would influence her actions at a critical juncture in her prime ministerial tenure.

Indira's youthful dalliance with radical socialism had another, more practical fallout. During her time in England, she came in close contact with a group of bright, left-leaning Indian students: Parvathi Kumaramangalam, Mohan Kumaramangalam, and especially P. N. Haksar. The son of a senior politician from Madras, Mohan Kumaramangalam went on to become a member of the Communist Party of India (CPI). Although he quit the CPI and joined the Congress in 1967, he served as a bridge between Indira Gandhi, who was now prime minister, and an important segment of the Indian Left. P. N. Haksar, a cerebral Kashmiri Brahmin from Allahabad, was known to the family and was induced to join the new Indian Foreign Service by Jawaharlal Nehru. Subsequently, as principal secretary to the prime minister he was Mrs. Gandhi's chief strategist and advisor during her years of ascent. In England in the late 1930s, Haksar also played an important role in Indira's personal life. His flat in Primrose Hill was frequented by Indira and her boyfriend, Feroze Gandhi. Their decision to get married was met by a distinct lack of enthusiasm on her father's part. But Indira stuck to her guns and got her way.

III

When Jawaharlal Nehru took over as the prime minister of independent India in 1947, Indira had been married to Feroze for five years and was the mother of two boys. Yet she moved into the prime minister's residence, took over its management and became her father's social hostess. Gradually and reluctantly she was drawn into the world of politics. Accompanying her father on numerous international visits, she gained experience of diplomacy at the highest levels and met several important world leaders. At home, she began to take an interest in the intrigues and machinations within the Congress Party—things that her father thoroughly disliked—and to get the measure of the party as an institution.

Although Indira refused to become a member of Parliament, she campaigned for the party during the general election of 1957. Two years later, at the initiative of Nehru's senior colleagues, she was elected president of the Congress. In retrospect, her tenure as the party's president stands out primarily for her role in orchestrating the downfall of the recently elected Communist Party of India government in the state of Kerala. Though she was not the prime mover in this episode—her father and the home minister, G. B. Pant, arguably played a more important role—it showed how far she had swung from the left-wing radicalism of her youth. This episode is usually seen as an early indicator of an antidemocratic, not to say authoritarian, streak in her politics. Yet Mrs. Gandhi showed little will to power during these years. In fact, she declined a second term as president. Just prior to Nehru's death in 1964, she was even contemplating moving to England to be with her boys. One of the main reasons she accepted a cabinet portfolio under Nehru's successor, Lal Bahadur Shastri, was her need for a salary. It was Shastri's sudden demise in January 1966 that catapulted her into the prime minister's office.

Her elevation as prime minister was by no means a smooth affair. In fact, there was a strong contender for the office: the senior Congressman Morarji Desai, who had earlier been passed over in Shastri's favor but was now determined to wrest his due. In the event, the party bosses—a group of five regional heavyweights, collectively known as the Syndicate—piloted Indira's candidature. Paradoxically, it was her political weakness and ideological indistinctness that led them to believe that she would be a pliable prime minister. Her ability to borrow the sheen of Jawaharlal Nehru was seen as an added advantage. Mrs. Gandhi's initial months in office seemed to bear out the Syndicate's assessment. She was diffident and inarticulate in Parliament, leading one of her harsh opponents to brand her *"goongi gudiya,"* the Dumb Doll. Her handling of policy matters was equally tentative.[9]

Very soon, though, she began to demonstrate a degree of political finesse and decisiveness that was entirely unanticipated. Following the Congress Party's poor showing in the general and state elections of 1967, she moved against her former patrons, split the party, and took it on a left-ward course. These moves by Mrs. Gandhi are usually attributed to a "logic of survival."[10] Indeed, some accounts go so far as to claim that she was an empty vessel filled by the ideas and ideology of her advisors.[11] Furthermore, it is argued that by wrecking the old Congress Party and by centralizing power in her own hands, she set in motion a process of rapid institutional decay. This, in turn, left her incapable of handling mounting popular protests against her government within a democratic framework, so leading to the imposition of the Emergency.[12]

Whatever the utility of these arguments in explaining the onset of the Emergency, it does not satisfactorily account for the reasons why Mrs. Gandhi made these moves in the first instance. For one thing, it implicitly assumes that the undivided Congress Party—which relied on strong regional leadership to tend and deliver "vote banks" and to transmit information from local to national levels—could have continued on its old course in the post-Shastri period. For another, while Indira Gandhi was concerned about her survival, her actions were also underpinned by a wider set of political assessments and judgments.

In her broad approach to political and economic issues, Indira Gandhi was her father's daughter. She believed both in the framework of political economy instituted by Nehru and in the objectives that he wished to pursue. But she also thought that the Congress Party was not geared toward achieving these goals. The regional bosses, she believed, held too much countervailing power and thwarted the achievement of the progressive ideas envisioned by Nehru. Nor, she thought, was the Congress effective as a conveyor belt of popular aspirations. At the height of the language movements of the 1950s, she wrote to her father: "you are tending more and more to accept almost without question, the opinions of certain people with regard to certain parts of the country. Morarjibhai for Bombay, Gujerat, Maharashtra etc, Bidhan Babu for Bengal, Bihar, Kamaraj for Tamilnad.

These are very fine men and our top leaders, but no one is big enough or detached enough to be the only word on matters of their area."[13] Transforming the internal character of the Congress Party was critical to bringing about larger changes in Indian polity, economy, and society.

A corollary to this was Mrs. Gandhi's belief that her father had not been sufficiently assertive in overcoming the resistance of his senior colleagues. During the Kerala crisis, she wrote to a friend that Nehru was "incapable of dictatorship or roughshodding over the views of his senior colleagues."[14] A close advisor recalled that Indira suspected that her father's weakness lay in goodness and that she was determined not to be hamstrung by "what she called public-school morality, and she did not mind her critics calling her amoral and ruthless."[15]

A second assessment on Mrs. Gandhi's part was regarding the surge in popular participation in politics and the rising expectations of the people. During the Nehru years, the state had insinuated itself to an unprecedented degree into Indian society. From employment and education to food and water, the state took it upon itself to provide for, improve, and regulate the lives of the Indian people. This led to greater awareness among the people of the importance of politics. The number of people casting their vote in general elections almost doubled between 1952 and 1967.[16] Further, economic development over the previous decade had led to increasing levels of disparity and heightened expectations. As Mrs. Gandhi observed, "we are at a stage of development . . . where the gap between expectations and resources for meeting them is at the widest. Political awareness is also coming up sharply."[17] Related to this was the fact that many traditionally marginalized groups were gradually becoming politically active and unwilling to conform to the particular caste and patronage politics of the Congress Party. Mrs. Gandhi was broadly aware of these trends, but they became stark after the elections of 1967. The regional grandees of the party suffered humiliating defeats at the polls, and their much-vaunted electoral machine was shown to be obsolescent.

The final assessment pertained to the immediate challenges confronting the government. The economic impact of the recent wars with China and Pakistan was compounded by the failure of two successive monsoons. The economy was in dire straits, and large parts of the country were on the verge of starvation. In this context, the institutional weaknesses of the Congress Party and constraints on the executive seemed more debilitating than ever. Mrs. Gandhi wrote to Haksar a few weeks into her premiership:

> The state of affairs is quite extraordinary here. . . . When I am depressed, which is often, I feel I must quit. At other times, that I must fight it out even if the results are negligible. . . . Congress as a party is dormant and inactive. . . . As I see it we are at the beginning of a new dark age. The food situation is precarious, industries are closing. There is no direction, no policy on any matter. . . . As a child I wanted to be like Joan of Arc—I may yet be burnt at the stake.[18]

These considerations led Mrs. Gandhi after the elections of 1967 to contemplate a dramatic transformation of the Congress Party. In these elections, the Congress's vote share dropped four percentage points from 1962, and its share of seats in Parliament dipped to 283 in a house of 520. The party lost power in eight major north Indian states and the southern Indian state of Tamil Nadu. The only consolation for Mrs. Gandhi was that the stalwarts of the Syndicate were trounced in their own constituencies. Sensing that the party was at its weakest, Mrs. Gandhi decided to go for a complete organizational makeover. By this time, Haksar had joined her as the principal secretary and helped her forge a clear and workable strategy. Over the next eighteen months or so, Mrs. Gandhi adopted a two-pronged approach based on her prior assessments. On the one hand, she decided to force a showdown with the party elders and cut them to size. Eliminating opposing power blocs and centralizing power in her hands would be the first step toward remaking the Congress Party. Toward this end, she took on her senior colleagues in a series of confrontations, culminating in her opposition to the party's candidate for election as president of India.

On the other hand, she projected a more left-wing stance on policy matters. This was essential to developing alliances with progressive elements within the Congress and with the Communist Party of India (CPI). The original CPI had split into two factions some years ago, so enabling Mrs. Gandhi to reach out to the pro-Soviet CPI, which tended to follow the mother party's sympathetic stance toward Congress rule in India. This would allow her to tap into much wider bases of popular support, especially among the lower orders of society. As Haksar told her, she needed to "project more assertively [her] own ideological image directly to the people over the heads of colleagues and party men."[19] Populist measures were rolled out to buttress her socialist credentials: social control and subsequently nationalization of banks, abolition of constitutionally guaranteed privy purses for India's erstwhile princes, restrictions on large businesses, and so forth.

This strategy was executed with considerable dexterity and an impeccable sense of timing. The outcome was exactly as she had desired. In late 1969, the Congress Party was split. The masterstroke was her decision to call for national elections in 1971, a year ahead of schedule. This broke the link between the national and provincial elections and so fixed the electorate's attention on national as opposed to local issues. Pitted against her party, Congress (R), was a hastily cobbled-together coalition comprising the Congress (O), the right-wing Jana Sangh, the pro-business Swatantra, the socialists, and a smattering of regional parties. This self-styled "Grand Alliance" adopted the slogan "*Indira Hatao*" (Remove Indira). The lady responded with "*Garibi Hatao*" (Remove Poverty). Mrs. Gandhi's electoral strategy paid off handsomely. She won by a margin that exceeded that of her father's best performance. Congress (R) returned to power with 352 out of 518 seats. The next largest party garnered a pitiable twenty-five. Her standing was further bolstered by the adroit handling of the East Pakistan crisis that erupted in March 1971 and that ended in December with a decisive military victory over Pakistan and the creation of Bangladesh. In the state elections held the following year, Mrs. Gandhi's party swept all thirteen states that went to the polls.

By 1972 Mrs. Gandhi had consolidated her hold over the party and her standing among the people. Even in hindsight, it is difficult to argue that her assessments about the state of the party and country were erroneous. She had rightly identified that India was undergoing deep-seated transitions and that the old Congress Party was incapable of shepherding it through this period of change. The argument that by breaking the party she ushered in a period of institutional decay overlooks the fact that the undivided Congress was already in a state of terminal decline. That said, Mrs. Gandhi's principal failing lay in her inability to consider how the enormous powers at her disposal could be used to revitalize the party along new lines. To be sure, some steps were taken to promote provincial leaders from the lower castes and to encourage the Youth Congress. But this succeeded only to a limited extent—mainly in the southern states of Karnataka and Kerala.

In consequence, Mrs. Gandhi found herself increasingly embroiled in the affairs of regional Congress outfits. As early as December 1970, she wrote to Haksar: "The situation is not an easy one for me as I do not have any one to help with the follow up. . . . There has been hardly a night when I have had more than 2 or 3 hours in bed."[20] The upshot of it was increasing centralization and the vesting of power in trusted bureaucrats and technocrats as opposed to elected officials. Worse, Mrs. Gandhi came over time to rely on her family to run party affairs. Initially, she turned to her younger son, Sanjay, who along with his cronies in the Youth Congress, lumpenized the high reaches of the party. Following Sanjay's demise in a plane crash, she looked to her elder son, Rajiv, to step into party affairs. In so doing, Mrs. Gandhi not only turned the Congress Party into a family firm but provided a model for many regional parties to emulate. The abortive attempt to overhaul the Congress Party highlights an important facet of her political judgment: it seldom stretched beyond the medium-term and sometimes fell short of it.

The institutional weakness of the party and excessive concentration of power in the hands of the prime minister are important to explaining why, when faced with popular protests from 1974 onward, Mrs. Gandhi chose to suspend democracy and impose the Emergency. But the Emergency was also the outcome of a contest between two sets of ideas that had been brewing throughout Mrs. Gandhi's tenure, if not earlier still.

First, there was the uneasy coexistence between the notions of the state and of democracy. As Sunil Khilnani has argued, "The Emergency is best regarded as the parodic version of the desire to return the Indian state to the hands of a do-good elite."[21] This, as we have seen, flowed from the failure of Indira Gandhi's efforts to recast the institutional structures of her party and its relationship with the state. The bureaucratic elite was most enthusiastic in its reception of the Emergency. One such confidante, B. K. Nehru, applauded the imposition of the Emergency as a "*tour de force* of immense courage." "The Emergency should be taken advantage of while it lasts," he advised her in September 1975, to install "a strong executive at the centre capable of taking tough, unpleasant and unpopular decisions."[22]

Second, there was the struggle between the ideas of democracy and constitutionalism. These are by no means entirely compatible: the former precipitates popular expectations and enthusiasms, while the latter seeks to impose a grid of rules and procedures on public life. The radical policies adopted by Mrs. Gandhi resulted in a prolonged standoff with the Supreme Court of India. A key point of contention was the competence of the Parliament to amend the fundamental rights enshrined in the Constitution, especially the right to property. The ramifications of this question for land reforms had made it a bone of contention between the government and the courts during the Nehru years. In 1967, the Supreme Court delivered a verdict asserting that the fundamental rights were part of the basic structure of the Constitution and hence could not be amended by Parliament. In 1970, the Supreme Court held that the nationalization of banks was in violation of the fundamental rights guaranteed in the Constitution. Later that year, the Court delivered a heavier blow by holding the government's abolition of the privy purses of the princely rulers unconstitutional and invalid. In the wake of Mrs. Gandhi's massive electoral victory, the Constitution was amended in December 1971 to restore to Parliament the power to amend the fundamental rights. This, in turn, was challenged in the Supreme Court, which took a complex position on the question—but one that was seen as a defeat for Mrs. Gandhi. This spurred her to move an even stronger set of constitutional amendments during the Emergency that aimed at an enormous concentration of power in the prime minister's hands. A tame Supreme Court would go on to endorse these changes to the Constitution, although they were subsequently repealed by the next government.

By claiming at once that she stood for the supremacy of the people and that the will of the people was represented in her person, Mrs. Gandhi was moving toward "a Jacobin conception of direct popular sovereignty."[23] It is against this backdrop that her response to the popular protests must be understood. Beginning with students' protests in Gujarat against inflation and corruption, it rapidly transmuted into a wider campaign for reform. Under the leadership of the veteran Gandhian, Jayaprakash Narayan ("JP"), the movement spread to other parts of the country, drawing in diverse social groups and an unlikely assortment of political parties. In particular, the movement was imparted considerable strength by the cadres of the Hindu Right: the RSS, the Jana Sangh, and their affiliated student organizations.

The JP juggernaut unnerved Indira Gandhi. She rightly believed that the movement was aimed at her personally, though she remained oblivious of the fact that this was the price to be paid for her drive toward personalization. She also saw the movement through the historical prism of 1930s Europe: as fascist in the composition of its core rank-and-file and in its drive to overthrow an elected government. Critics believed that this was a rhetorical device to crush the opposition with force. But well before the JP movement had come to the fore, Mrs. Gandhi had insisted that her antipathy to proto-fascist groups on the Hindu Right was "not a put-on show, it is something that has gone deep into my being, because I have seen what it did to a whole people, how in one country a whole people could not resist a small party who in the name of democracy overthrew democracy."[24] Her overweening sense of legitimacy coupled with her fears about the nature of the opposition led Mrs. Gandhi to proclaim the Emergency.

The suspension of democratic procedures and civil liberties during the Emergency—and the ensuing excesses with slum clearances and population control, particularly under the malign inspiration of Sanjay Gandhi—are well known. But this period of Indian history raises several questions that are yet to be seriously tackled. Two of these are especially relevant to any assessment of Indira Gandhi: Why did Mrs. Gandhi refrain from a wholesale modification of the Constitution and the political system in ways that would have made her position unassailable? And why did she decide to call for free and fair elections in early 1977?

In fact, a number of ideas and proposals were afloat among her advisors on using the Emergency for pushing through far-reaching changes to the country's political structure. The most detailed of these was advanced by B. K. Nehru (a cousin of Indira and the Indian high commissioner to London), who argued that "democratic institutions copied from Great Britain . . . have not been able to provide the answer to our needs." Among other things, he suggested a directly elected presidency with a single seven-year term and complete separation of executive and legislative branches, weakening the federal structure by ensuring that governors of states would be "de facto agent[s] of the Centre." B. K. Nehru urged her to "make these fundamental changes in the Constitution now when you have 2/3rd majority."[25] The prime minister's close political advisors in the party developed these suggestions in a manner that "twisted the Constitution in an unambiguously authoritarian direction."[26] Ironically, it was the galloping enthusiasm of her advisors that gave Mrs. Gandhi pause.

Standing at the cusp of almost absolute power seems to have made her more sensitive to its potentialities and dangers.

The decision to end the Emergency and to call for fresh elections is equally puzzling. In fact, the opposition initially saw the move as aimed at perpetuating Mrs. Gandhi's rule. Various reasons have been proffered for why Mrs. Gandhi confounded this expectation: that she was misled into believing that she would actually win the elections (though there is some evidence to the contrary); that she was swayed by the criticism from friends of India across the world; that she realized that the Emergency had not paid the expected dividends. In the absence of any documentary evidence, this remains a tantalizing question.

In the event, Mrs. Gandhi and her party were decisively routed at the polls. The newly formed Janata Party, which united her adversaries from across the political spectrum, came to power with a thumping majority. But from the beginning it was beset with internal contradictions and factional conflicts. The larger problem was that the Janata government focused its energies on fixing Indira Gandhi rather than fixing the country. The unstable coalition fissured in less than three years, paving the way for another general election. In retrospect, an important—arguably the main—consequence of the Emergency and the Janata interlude was the respectability attained by the Hindu Right. Over the following decade, "Hindutva" would become a major political force to reckon with.

Meantime, Indira Gandhi had donned sackcloth and ashes and had gone back to wooing her key constituencies in the lowest orders. The Janata Party's proven incompetence helped in no small measure. In the elections of 1980, Mrs. Gandhi's party outdid its performance in the elections of 1971, winning 353 seats in all. Her second term in office (1980–1984) was marked by a desire to recapture the center ground of politics. There was a subtle move toward the right involving adopting the slogans and themes of Hindu chauvinism. This was an attempt to outflank parties to the right of the Congress such as Bharatiya Janata Party (successor of the Jana Sangh) and the Lok Dal—very like her effort to marginalize the Marxist Left by courting the CPI and other progressive political forces in the late 1960s.[27] This move paid some dividends in the state elections of 1982 and after. In fact, during the local elections of 1983 in Delhi, the RSS cadres worked in support of the Congress Party rather than the BJP. But in the longer run, Mrs. Gandhi's moves contributed to the communalization of Indian politics in the late 1980s and early 1990s.

The larger problem confronting her was a reassertion of the claims of regional autonomy. Here, Mrs. Gandhi was reaping the whirlwind. The structural factors driving these crises stemmed from her earlier policies and approaches. One of these was the unevenly directed policy of economic development. This included, but was not restricted to, the regionally skewed effects of the Green Revolution (discussed in the next section). Regions such as Punjab that had benefited from this policy wanted greater autonomy in managing their own affairs. Regions such as Assam that had been neglected demanded greater redistribution of resources. The other factor was Mrs. Gandhi's centralizing instinct, which ensured that no regional leadership within or outside the Congress Party could challenge her but which also resulted in a backlash couched in the idiom of regional pride.[28]

Mrs. Gandhi mismanaged a series of challenges in the states of Karnataka and Andhra Pradesh; in Kashmir and Assam; finally, and fatally, in Punjab. Her failure stemmed from an understandable belief that preemptive strikes had worked for her in earlier crises. It also arose from her inability to understand the nature and magnitude of the problems confronting her. She saw these crises as externally supported threats to India's unity and integrity, and failed to grasp the political economy and the psychology of these movements—a failure that she eventually paid for with her life.

IV

Indira Gandhi's views on economic growth and development were shaped largely by the circumstances confronting India during her years in power. She had a broadly defined economic philosophy, which she had imbibed from her father and from her extensive travels across the country. The main components of this economic philosophy were national self-reliance, modernization, and the removal of poverty. However, unlike Jawaharlal Nehru she had no clearly worked-out design for converting these large ideas into actual policies. From the outset, her approach to economic issues was pragmatic.[29] She admitted that she knew little about economic policy but was prepared to learn from her advisors.[30] Yet her pragmatism could easily shade into expedience; for economic questions were also the terrain on which many of her political conflicts were played out.

The planned economy in the Nehruvian mold had focused on state-led industrialization and cooperative forms of agriculture. The latter, Nehru had hoped, would generate pressures from below to alter the rural property order dominated by the landed castes. His expectations were belied. The cooperative system failed to boost agricultural productivity, never mind achieving any political effects. This, in turn, generated little by way of rural surpluses for public investment in industries.[31] By the time Nehru died in 1964, the shortcomings of his model of planning were evident. India was increasingly dependent on foreign aid, especially in food. The successive failures of the monsoon in 1965 and 1966 pushed the country to the brink of starvation.

Internal calamity was compounded by external pressures. The United States—the main source of food grain imports—insisted that India abandon its experiment in cooperative agriculture and adopt technology-intensive methods that went by the label of the Green Revolution. Prodded by the United States, the World Bank urged India to undertake sweeping reforms not only in agriculture, but also in liberalizing imports and relaxing controls on industrial licensing. As part of this package, the bank and the International Monetary Fund called for steep devaluation of the Indian rupee.

Mrs. Gandhi was loath to look to the West for increased aid, not least because it cut against her preference for self-reliance. As she wrote to Haksar in early 1966, "Brave words notwithstanding, there is anxiety to go to America, who will I have no doubt give PL 480 food aid and everything at a price. The manner of execution will be so deft and subtle that no one will realise it until it is too late and India's freedom of thought and action will have both been bartered away."[32] But India's food import requirement had escalated from four million tonnes to ten million tonnes a year. So she had little choice but to seek American assistance. President Lyndon Johnson pledged a generous aid package but insisted on the devaluation of the rupee as an essential first step toward sanctioning aid.

On returning to Delhi, Mrs. Gandhi consulted a small group of economic advisors, all of whom supported the move.[33] On June 5, 1966, she announced a 35 percent devaluation of the rupee. The public response to the decision was virulent. She was charged both with undermining India's economy and with selling out to the Americans. Worse, the expected aid package failed to materialize. Johnson's pledge was wrecked by the parsimony and pettifogging of his officials.[34] Mrs. Gandhi quietly placed the rest of the reform package on hold. The episode colored her economic outlook by reinforcing the importance of nondependence.

Her views were further fortified by American policy on food aid. President Johnson insisted that India should modernize its agriculture by adopting the Green Revolution. To ensure India's compliance, Johnson adopted a short-tether approach. The United States would only release grain required for one month at a time, while closely monitoring Indian reforms.[35] This "ship-to-mouth" policy was deeply resented by Mrs. Gandhi. It convinced her that achieving self-sufficiency in food was of paramount importance. The prime minister threw her weight behind the efforts of her minister of agriculture, C. Subramaniam—a key advocate of the Green Revolution.

The decision to support the Green Revolution proved momentous. The approach called for the use of imported high-yielding strains of staple crops and chemical fertilizers, the availability of assured water supply, and mechanized harvesting equipment—all of which depended on the provision of government subsidies and support.[36] The adoption of the new agriculture strategy paid rich dividends, though unequally distributed. Between 1965–1966 and 1971–1972, the production of wheat doubled. However, the yield and output of paddy—India's largest food grain crop—did not rise as significantly. The Green Revolution thus largely benefited the wheat growing states of Punjab, Haryana, and western Uttar Pradesh. This, as noted in the previous section, had long-term implications for relations between the central and state governments during Mrs. Gandhi's tenure. Yet, it is important to note that India's GDP also rose, growing at 6 percent a year from 1967–1968 to 1970–1971, although industrial performance remained sluggish.

Regional disparities apart, there were important social consequences. In areas where it succeeded, the Green Revolution enhanced the power of the rich and middle peasantry. These were the only groups that possessed the requisite economic muscle to take advantage of the agricultural strategy promoted by the government. The disparity between them and the rest of the rural population increased dramatically. The rise of the middle peasantry, most of whom belonged to the so-called Backward Castes (though superior to the Scheduled Castes to which most poor peasants and laborers belonged), had major political implications as well. Since the 1950s, they had been unhappy with the Congress Party for its excessive reliance on the landed elites who also hailed from the upper castes. Their clout enhanced by the Green Revolution, the middle peasantry began moving away from the Congress—a shift that was heralded by the departure of Charan Singh from the Uttar

Pradesh Congress to form the Bharatiya Kranti Dal in 1967. Their growing political profile, in turn, ensured that agricultural subsidies became an entrenched feature of the Indian economy.

Following the elections of 1967, Mrs. Gandhi sought to move further to the left in her politics. This led her to adopt more radical economic policies such as nationalizing domestically owned commercial banks and passing the Monopolies and Restrictive Trade Practices Act that closely regulated the functioning of business houses. This shift also reflected personnel changes in the prime minister's secretariat. Her first principal secretary, L. K. Jha, was eased out because Mrs. Gandhi believed that he had misled her into accepting devaluation. Jha was a liberal on economic issues. By contrast, Haksar, who replaced Jha, was a committed socialist. He emphasized the need to nationalize banks, to develop the public sector with a new managerial cadre "animated by the desire to serve the community," and to introduce a monopolies law.[37]

This "socialist" phase in economic policy continued until 1973 and involved nationalization of insurance companies and coal industry, takeover of the management of several "sick" companies, the passage of a Foreign Exchange Regulation Act that comprehensively controlled foreign investment in India. Mrs. Gandhi also introduced a slew of central government schemes to assist landless laborers, and small and marginal farmers to increase their income and consumption. This signaled an entirely new approach to promoting economic and social welfare. These policies promised economic redemption for targeted groups. And in so doing, they transformed these and other groups' expectations of the Indian state. The centrality of these schemes to Mrs. Gandhi's political strategy threw open the state to a profusion of new demands, thereby widening and deepening Indian democracy in quite unexpected ways. They also left a deep imprint on the Indian state's approach to welfare and poverty alleviation schemes.

But the reality was that even a substantial diversion of developmental resources toward the most impoverished groups could only marginally affect inequalities of income and consumption. Then, too, the Indian state simply did not command such resources. What was worse, an economic crisis loomed on the horizon. It stemmed from a combination of the Bangladesh refugee crisis and war with Pakistan, the ensuing termination of American aid, the renewed failure of monsoons, and the international oil crisis of 1973. This triggered high inflation and led to a rapid slide in balance of payments. At its height from mid-1973 to September 1974, inflation in India rose at an annual rate of about 33 percent. This also played an important role in touching off the popular antigovernment protests that snowballed into the JP movement leading to the Emergency.

The Indian government's response to the crisis had three strands.[38] By late 1972, it was clear to Mrs. Gandhi that the economic situation was steadily worsening.[39] From mid-1973, the government began cutting down its expenditure and tightening monetary policy. In July 1974, Mrs. Gandhi introduced an extremely tough package of anti-inflationary policies—fiscal, monetary, and income-policy measures—by means of a supplementary budget and by ordinances. Many of her senior colleagues and left-leaning advisors warned her that these measures would be politically unpopular. But she fully backed her team of liberal economic advisors and officials, led by Manmohan Singh (later prime minister of India).[40] By the end of 1974, inflation had been tamed, and it remained low until the second oil crisis of 1979.

Further, Mrs. Gandhi swallowed her pride and approached the IMF for assistance. The $925 million financed largely from the IMF's low-conditionality facilities helped stabilize the current account of the balance of payments. As a consequence of this experience, the Indian government began strengthening its balance of payments position and foreign exchange reserves in 1975. From 1976–1977 to 1978–1979, India's foreign exchange reserves increased by more than $5 billion.[41] Finally, Mrs. Gandhi went in for a quiet, de facto devaluation of the Indian rupee. The earlier fiasco with devaluation ruled out any formal move. But Mrs. Gandhi understood the advantages of a weaker currency. After the Nixon administration took the dollar off gold in August 1971, the rupee was pegged to the sterling until 1975. The sterling, of course, was weak during this period, and the nominal effective exchange rate of the rupee fell by 20 percent from 1971 to 1975. In consequence, Indian exports remained competitive through the period of high inflation.[42] The devaluation of the 1970s marked the beginning of India's slow reintegration with the world economy.

The crisis of 1973–1974 marked an important turning point in Indira Gandhi's economic policy—a development that remains underappreciated. The received wisdom is that she shackled the Indian economy in a thicket of controls and stunted its growth. This reading is qualified and supplemented by a series of studies that assert that during her second term Mrs. Gandhi adopted an approach that was more open and congenial to businesses, primarily by relaxing the industrial licensing system. This shift was "attitudinal" and not reflected in substantive policy changes. And it was driven primarily by her desire to garner political support from businesses. Nevertheless, it pushed India on to a high growth trajectory.[43]

This widely accepted account, however, misreads the economic data and the policy of Mrs. Gandhi. For a start, this reading of growth rates in the 1970s and early 1980s overlooks the fact that in 1979, owing to the second oil shock, the Indian economy shrank considerably. The growth rate in 1979 was negative 5.2 percent—the highest-ever drop in India's GDP since Independence. If the year 1979 is excluded, India's growth from 1975 to 1978 averaged a healthy 6 percent—a figure that is comparable to the "boom" of the 1980s. In other words, India's economy entered a high growth trajectory in the mid-1970s, not the early 1980s or later still.[44] This increase in GDP per capita from the mid-1970s was paralleled by an increase in total factor productivity (TFP). In other words, India's higher growth was driven not by an increase in capital or labor, but by an increase in the productivity of both. The increase in TFP was spurred by a marked revival in fixed capital formation, both in its public and private components. In particular, there was a spectacular rise in the private equipment investment rate since the mid-1970s. This was partly the outcome of the earlier "socialist" decision to nationalize banks, which resulted in a considerable deepening of the financial sector.[45] But clearly the "animal spirits" of Indian businesses were already rising in the mid-1970s, and the "pro-business" shift took place around this time.

The trigger for this shift was provided by the botched attempt in 1973 to nationalize the wheat trade—a move that was undertaken on the advice of Mrs. Gandhi's left-leaning advisors and that ended up exacerbating the food crisis and the problem of inflation.[46] By this time, she had also begun to solicit advice from business leaders on spurring industrial growth. In late 1972, J. R. D. Tata submitted a memorandum entitled "Suggestions for Accelerating Industrial Growth," which called among other things for a streamlining of industrial licensing processes, ensuring reliable supply of industrial inputs (power, raw material, and labor), and the overcoming of the bias against larger houses reflected in the Monopolies Act.[47]

Such ideas were voiced from closer quarters starting in late 1974. A fascinating exchange of letters between Mrs. Gandhi and B. K. Nehru sheds light on the pro-business shift undertaken subsequently. In a missive of December 1974, Mrs. Gandhi observed that "solely profit motivated functioning is harmful and our industrialists even reduce production in order to get higher profits." She went on to note that the Pugwash group of economists had said that "in the present conditions there can be no economic growth which ignores social justice."[48] B. K. Nehru replied that India had adopted "anti-production policies— in the quest for 'social justice.'" He urged her to adopt the slogan of "Utpadan Barhao" (increase production) instead of "Garibi Hatao" (remove poverty). The present crisis and discontent in India stemmed from the fact that "in our attempt to create 'social justice' through laws, regulations, controls, quotas, licenses and permits what we have succeeded in doing is really to establish unadulterated 19th century capitalism without simultaneously permitting it to increase production. . . . Does 'social justice' mean equality in poverty or growth in the size of the national cake which may continue to be divided in unequal portions—if necessary?" All other objectives, insisted B. K. Nehru, should be "subordinated to this one objective of increased production."[49]

Mrs. Gandhi answered that she "did not intend to pick a quarrel or begin an argument" and that she was "slightly annoyed." Nevertheless she wrote: "Give concrete suggestions for 'Utpadan barhao.'"[50] In response B. K. Nehru wrote that "Harmful, cumbersome physical controls must be abolished and not [merely] streamlined. . . . Only industrialists, traders, politicians and administration benefit from controls not the consumer." He also asked her to avoid focusing solely on welfare programs. "Employment and not subsidy or charity is the answer to poverty and employment is generated by increasing production." He suggested greater involvement of industry and business leaders in the government's economic committees and reforming of the economic administrative system.[51]

In May 1975, a special cabinet committee was established to begin an export-promotion drive, and a number of measures toward this end were instituted. These included an automatic increase in production capacity of 25 percent over a five-year period for major export-oriented engineering industries; automatic import licenses for these industries; provision of financial incentives; and so on. All this marked a sharp departure from earlier policies adopted by Mrs. Gandhi.[52]

With the onset of the Emergency, Mrs. Gandhi announced a Twenty Point Program of economic and social change. The components of this program relating to industry fit quite snugly with the ideas suggested by J. R. D. Tata and B. K. Nehru. Facilitating and accelerating private-sector activity was a key part of the government's economic agenda during the Emergency. Certain measures taken earlier to rein in labor unrest—the ruthless putting down of the railway strike in 1974 and the freeze in the wages of organized sector workers as part of the anti-inflation package—worked in the interests of the business sector.

This pro-business tilt was continued and intensified in her last term in office. This was symbolized by an unprecedented dinner in her honor hosted in an elite Delhi hotel in 1980. Her host was Dhirubhai Ambani, India's largest producer of polyester. Reliance ranked in the top fifty industrial houses in 1980 but would be among the five largest by 1984.[53] During these years, Mrs. Gandhi's economic policy was focused on raising the profitability of industrial and commercial establishments by easing restrictions on capacity expansion, removing price controls, and reducing corporate taxes. The public sector enterprises, too, were urged to shed their flab and become competitive. Indeed, during this period many such units achieved impressive turnarounds. Another important development during this period was the liberalization of electronics imports, particularly of computers. This provided the basis for the subsequent expansion of the telecom and software industries.[54]

Nevertheless, both in the mid-1970s and the early 1980s, Mrs. Gandhi did not initiate far-reaching economic reforms of the kind that took place in the 1990s. She remained satisfied with the successes in managing crisis and with short-term achievements. And she was unable to appreciate the prospects of liberalization policies in achieving high growth and reducing poverty.[55] Besides, the policies previously adopted had resulted in the mushrooming of politically influential groups—big and small industrialists, rich and middle peasants, government professionals and the labor aristocracy—that demanded subsidies from the state and brought to bear conflicting pressures on it. In consequence, the state's role in the economy ended up being more regulatory than developmental—a state of affairs that in many ways continues to date.[56]

V

Indira Gandhi's approach to international affairs was continuous with the framework of nonalignment laid down by Jawaharlal Nehru. She too believed that India should, as far as possible, steer clear of the superpower confrontation while developing a capability for autonomous strategic action. But the context in which she had to pursue these objectives was quite different from those of the Nehru years. For one thing, India's own security environment had markedly deteriorated owing to wars with China and Pakistan in 1962 and 1965, respectively. Besides, following the 1965 war with Pakistan, the United States had imposed a military embargo on both countries, and in consequence India was forced to move closer to the Soviet Union for its military and strategic economic requirements. For another, by the late 1960s the Cold War alliances led by the United States and the Soviet Union were undergoing important changes. The Sino-Soviet split had become irrevocable, and the US alliance system was strained by the Vietnam War and differences over economic issues. Finally, these years marked the beginning of increasing interdependence in world politics—a trend that was sharply underlined by the collapse of the Bretton Woods system and the oil shocks of the 1970s. The international system was thus in a state of flux, and it bore down on India in unprecedented ways.

As seen earlier, Indira Gandhi was forced early on to turn to the United States for aid and assistance. An invitation from President Lyndon Johnson to visit Washington afforded an opportunity to do so. Mrs. Gandhi was determined to seek American assistance without appearing to be a supplicant. Johnson's aide Robert Komer claimed that she had "vamped" the president. Johnson himself announced at a party in her honor that he would ensure that "no harm comes to this girl." Johnson pledged a generous aid package; Mrs. Gandhi declared that "India understood America's agony over Vietnam."[57] On her way back to India, Mrs. Gandhi met the Soviet premier, Alexei Kosygin, exchanging little more than platitudes. The thaw with America was palpable. But the Johnson administration's subsequent response on food and economic aid soured the relationship. Mrs. Gandhi also grew censorious of US actions in Vietnam. The American honeymoon was soon at an end.

Following the election of Richard Nixon as president, Mrs. Gandhi sought to pick up the threads, hoping that the United States would accord India greater importance in the wake of the debacle in Vietnam. Contrary to these expectations, the Nixon administration chose to revivify its relations with Pakistan. For Pakistan's new military dictator, General Yahya Khan, emerged as the main conduit for reaching out to China. The Nixon administration's "tilt" toward Pakistan during the Bangladesh crisis of 1971 and its decision to send an aircraft carrier to the Bay of Bengal during the war gravely harmed US-India relations. The latter also made Mrs. Gandhi more responsive to calls from the Indian scientific establishment for conducting a nuclear test. The nuclear tests of May 1974 were a further setback to relations with the United States, for Washington not only imposed strict sanctions on technology transfer but also created the Nuclear Suppliers Group to prevent the growth of India's nuclear capabilities, both civilian and military.

India's relations with the Soviet Union were not unproblematic. Following the successful mediation between India and Pakistan at Tashkent in early 1966, the Russians basked in the warmth of their newfound influence in South Asia. Indeed, they began to take their role as peacebroker between India and Pakistan rather seriously. In July 1968, Kosygin wrote to Indira Gandhi expressing hope that the two neighbors would be able to make significant progress in normalizing their relations. Mrs. Gandhi gently but firmly replied that there was no scope for third-party mediation on the core problems between India and Pakistan. She asked Kosygin to "exercise your growing influence with Pakistan and persuade them to start direct discussions with us with the object of normalising our relations."[58]

Around the same time, Moscow dropped yet another bombshell by announcing military sales to Pakistan. The quantum of arms sold to Pakistan was small in comparison to what India had got, but the reaction in India was decisively negative. The episode pointed the need to shore up ties with the Soviet Union. But it also underscored the importance of looking for other ways of improving India's external environment.

This led Mrs. Gandhi to tentatively explore the opportunities for a rapprochement with China—notwithstanding the lingering concerns about China following the war of 1962. In early 1969, she publicly expressed willingness to talk to China without preconditions and hoped that the boundary dispute could be settled. Beijing rebuffed her statement as "hypocritical," but Chinese officials began to make appearances on public functions in New Delhi. In May 1970, Mao greeted the India chargé d'affaires in Beijing at the May Day celebrations. The Indian official reported to New Delhi that Mao had said, "We cannot keep on quarreling like this. We must try and be friends again. . . . We will be friends again some day. We are ready to do it today."[59] The Bangladesh crisis put paid to the prospects of an early Sino-Indian rapprochement. Nevertheless, even at the height of the crisis, Mrs. Gandhi sought to reach out to Beijing by writing directly to Premier Zhou Enlai. The Chinese stood by Pakistan, but refused to extend unconditional support to the Yahya regime. Well before the war began, they advised Yahya Khan to seek a political settlement in East Pakistan and made it clear that they would not embroil themselves in an India-Pakistan war. In the aftermath of the war, India and China resumed their efforts to find some way of thawing the relationship. In 1975, Mrs. Gandhi appointed an ambassador to China—the appointment had been vacant since 1961—and so took the first step in the long road toward a rapprochement with China.

Meantime, the Sino-Soviet clashes along the Ussuri River in March 1969 led Moscow to regard India in more favorable light, as a potential counterweight to China in Asia. Within weeks, Moscow approached New Delhi with the idea of a bilateral treaty of friendship and cooperation. Mrs. Gandhi's advisors—Haksar, the ambassador to Moscow, D. P. Dhar, and the foreign secretary, T. N. Kaul—felt that India should seize this opportunity to restore the exclusivity of its relationship with the Soviet Union. Mrs. Gandhi agreed that the treaty would help in bolstering ties with Moscow. But she was more concerned about the potential implications of such a treaty and wanted to move gingerly.

To begin, she was worried about the domestic political fallout of a treaty. While some sections on the Left—especially the pro-Soviet CPI—might welcome it, the rest of the political spectrum was likely to react negatively. Further, she was concerned about the international reaction. Relations with the Americans were already at a low ebb. But the United States was providing much-needed food aid and was closely involved in launching the Green Revolution to spur India's food production. Furthermore, Mrs. Gandhi was unwilling to abandon the central tenet of nonalignment: the need to avoid being ensnared into military alliances. She was clear, therefore, that the treaty should be carefully drafted to avoid the impression that India had become a Soviet ally.

When Kosygin broached the idea in a meeting in May 1969, Mrs. Gandhi's response was cautious. "Firstly," she told Kosygin, "it would not be appropriate to have any phraseology in the Treaty which might be misunderstood and construed as a shift from our stand of non-alignment." Secondly, "the Treaty should not contain anything which might be construed—even though we may not mean it that way—by others as directed against a third party. Such a thing would not be appropriate."[60] In the event, although a draft of the treaty was finalized in the summer of 1969, Mrs. Gandhi decided against inking it.

The idea of a treaty was revived by India in May 1971 following the outbreak of the East Pakistan crisis. The treaty was eventually signed in August 1971. There were two reasons for concluding it at this point. First, India was keen to ensure that Moscow supported its stance on the crisis. In fact, the Soviet Union had been rather reluctant to back India.[61] Second, the Sino-American rapprochement dramatically changed the context in which this treaty was being considered. On July 15, 1971, President Richard Nixon announced the breakthrough with the People's Republic and his own forthcoming trip to China. Two days later, Kissinger met the Indian ambassador, L. K. Jha, and told him that if China intervened in an India-Pakistan war, the United States would be unable to help India. Noting Kissinger's message to Jha, Foreign Secretary Kaul told the prime minister that it "changed the whole perspective in which the Soviet proposal has to be considered." The treaty, he emphasized, "does not conflict with our conception of non-alignment."[62] It was at this point that Mrs. Gandhi overcame her lingering doubts about the treaty and speedily moved forward to conclude it.

Her adroit management of the Bangladesh crisis and her decisiveness in the war against Pakistan were undoubtedly the high points of Mrs. Gandhi's prime ministerial career. But her handling of the postwar negotiations with Pakistan remains underappreciated. It is commonplace now to assert that Mrs. Gandhi won the war but lost the peace: that she failed to use the historic opportunity presented by the victory against Pakistan to impose a final settlement on Kashmir. Mrs. Gandhi was, in fact, acutely aware that a punitive settlement would only prepare the ground for further conflict in South Asia. She was convinced by Haksar's observation that "historians now say that if those who sat around the table at Versailles to conclude a peace with Germany defeated during the First World War had acted with wisdom and not imposed upon Germany humiliating terms of peace, not only [the] rise of Nazism would have been avoided but also the seeds of the Second World War would not have been sown."[63]

In negotiating the Simla Accord with Zulfikar Ali Bhutto, Mrs Gandhi sought to treat a defeated Pakistan on the basis of equality and respect. The accord not only laid the basis for a stable India-Pakistan relationship but also precluded the possibility of external intervention in bilateral disputes. More importantly, by converting the cease-fire line in Kashmir to a line of control that would gradually assume "the characteristics" of an international border, it prepared the ground for an eventual settlement of the Kashmir dispute. Bhutto agreed that "an agreement will emerge in the foreseeable future. It will evolve into a settlement. Let there be a line of peace; let people come and go; let us not fight over it."[64] It did not quite work out like that. Bhutto quickly backed away from this understanding and reverted to a traditional anti-India stance. By mid-1974, it was clear that neither Bhutto nor Mrs. Gandhi had the political will and capital to forge a lasting settlement. Yet the assumption that Mrs. Gandhi could have forced a settlement on Pakistan overlooks the weakness of Bhutto's own domestic position and Mrs. Gandhi's desire to avoid behaving in a manner that was "contrary to our interests, contrary to our traditions, contrary to our long devotion to international peace and cooperation."[65] The agreement in Simla was arguably Indira Gandhi's finest hour.

By the time Mrs. Gandhi returned to office in 1980, a host of other regional challenges had cropped up. The revolution in Iran, the Soviet invasion of Afghanistan, the transfer of Diego Garcia to the United States, and the increasing American naval presence in the Indian Ocean: all contributed to a marked deterioration in India's security environment.

The most serious foreign policy challenge was the Soviet intervention in Afghanistan. Mrs. Gandhi privately urged the Soviet leadership to pull out of Afghanistan; but she refused openly to condemn their intervention. This put India in a tight spot. Its image with the Afghan people and its standing with the other nonaligned countries seemed in jeopardy. A larger problem was the Reagan administration's decision to provide arms to Pakistan in exchange for its services in the anti-Soviet jihad in Afghanistan. Above all, India now required American support to obtain much-needed economic assistance from international financial bodies. Mrs. Gandhi's visit to Washington in July 1982 ensured a long-overdue, if limited, rapprochement in US-India relations. Indira Gandhi was in the midst of a diplomatic effort aimed at convincing the superpowers to exercise restraint in Afghanistan and to consider a "regional solution," when she was cut down by her assassins' bullets on October 31, 1984.

VI

Looking back at the Indira Gandhi years, it is understandable why they lend themselves to easy moralizing about the dangers and corruption of overweening power. Her peculiar combination of great power and great insecurity inflicted deep blows to the Indian body politic. But Indira Gandhi's tenure in office should not be reduced to a morality play. For better and for worse, her policies and choices redefined Indian politics, economics, and international relations. Mrs. Gandhi held the reins of power at a time when India was undergoing far-reaching changes in each of these domains—changes that she grappled with and accelerated. Her actions and policies deepened as well as distorted Indian democracy, spurred as well as constrained the Indian economy, enhanced as well as redefined India's position vis-à-vis its neighbors and the wider international system.

Leadership in a time of transition requires courage and decisiveness. And even Mrs. Gandhi's sharpest critics would not deny that she possessed these qualities. But dealing with such far-reaching changes also calls for more than ordinary levels of political judgment. And it is on this terrain that Indira Gandhi will have to be evaluated by the historian.

Mrs. Gandhi had a sharp instinct for the crucial problems of her times and a sharper instinct for acquiring the requisite power to tackle them. She could be a superb manager of crises and was seldom hesitant to act under conditions of uncertainty. But she lacked the capacity to reflect on the background conditions under which her choices would play out and on the probable consequences of her actions. (It is in this, and not in her autocratic disposition, that she crucially differed from her father, Jawaharlal Nehru.) Mrs. Gandhi's intellectual outlook seldom seemed to range beyond the middle distance. Thus she often found herself wielding power but not knowing how best to use it to achieve the desired outcomes. Even when moderately successful (as in her economic policy), she was unable to conceive of the longer-term potentialities in a process or situation. Although she could be detached and aloof as a person, she found it difficult to step back and critically reflect on her own position and decisions. Worse, she failed to recognize that many of the problems that she confronted were the progeny of her own earlier choices. Ultimately, Indira Gandhi's greatest failure lay in her inability to get the measure of her own transformative impact on India.

TEN

SINGAPORE'S LEE KUAN YEW

Traveling Light, Traveling Fast

MICHAEL D. BARR

WHEN "HARRY" LEE KUAN YEW WAS A LAW STUDENT at Cambridge University in the late 1940s, he was a formidable personality who tended to make a lasting impression on many of his fellow students. Half a century later one of those fellow students described the Harry Lee of his memory in these terms:

> There is a phrase in an essay by Shaw, I think, that describes the Harry I knew perfectly. I cannot put my finger on the quotation precisely, but in describing a particular historical hero of his, he said that he was essentially a man who would have suited the modern world, because like modern man he wanted to move fast, and he who wants to move fast, travels light, unencumbered by the heavy luggage of doctrine, whether political or religious.[1]

To the best of my knowledge, Lee never knew he was thought of in these terms, but if he had, I am sure he would have embraced the description because it encapsulates the self-image that he has projected throughout his public life. He elevated this self-perception to the status of a declared operating principle—"pragmatism"—which scholars have subsequently identified as Lee's ideology.[2] In 1989 Garry Rodan argued that even "pragmatism" was a populist vehicle for a more sophisticated ideology that he identified as "scientism," an idealization of cold, impartial logic as the operating principle of governance.[3] Yet the story is not as simple as these labels suggest. How, for instance, to account for Lee's purported enthusiasm for socialism from the 1940s to the first half of the 1960s, and his attachment to "Asian," "Confucian," and "Chinese" values, which has persisted since the mid-1980s?[4]

The truth is that Lee was never a coldly logical thinking machine. He was beset with prejudices about race, gender, elitism, the nature of progress, and—not least—the quality of his personal gene pool.[5] The difference between him and most political leaders is that at his peak he possessed a rare gift for political judgment and capacity. On the one hand, he had no time for hopeless dreams. He declared in 1966 that he was interested in only one test of an idea: "the sheer test of its applicability."[6] Democracy itself was one of the ideas that he regarded as being an experiment under consideration—an experiment that he judged was failing before his eyes in the mid-1950s, in contrast to his perception of the wonderful utility of Chinese-style communitarianism.[7] On the other hand, if there was a way to build a scenario for success based upon his own prejudices, he was clever enough and energetic enough to create the edifice of ideas by which it could be rationalized and justified in terms of pragmatism.[8]

The Life and Political Thought of Lee Kuan Yew

Lee's political thought developed in tandem with the late-colonial and early postcolonial history of his generation.[9] He was born in 1923, the eldest son of a well-to-do *baba* family in colonial Singapore. The *babas* were a community of English- and Malay-speaking Chinese that had been at home in Singapore, Penang, and Malacca (together constituting the British colony of the Straits Settlements) for generations. In colonial Singapore *babas* were respected and did well because they were useful to British colonial and business interests, but they held themselves aloof from the Chinese-speaking community with whom they had little in common. Between his social advantages, the relentless encouragement of his strong-willed mother, and his natural intelligence and energy, young Harry Lee flourished in the colonial education system. In this cosy little society Lee learned about the blessings that the British brought to the world and the wonders of social and scientific progress, and he acquired the self-confidence that comes with knowing that he was one of the best of the brightest in a meritocratic, elitist system. He knew from the age of twelve that he was special, and he and his mother looked forward to a prosperous future for him.

Two events disturbed Lee's world and were fundamentally important in determining the sort of man he was to become. The first was the Great Depression, which shattered any complaisance he may have had about his destiny. He did not begin to doubt himself, but he no longer took for granted the world around him. His family lost its fortune, reducing them to relatively humble means as they moved in with relatives, and Lee became a typical "Depression child," acquiring the pessimistic conservatism and insecurity about the future that is typical of so many who lived through that period. The second pivotal event was the Japanese Occupation of Singapore. Lee did not have a good war, though it must be said that it could have been much worse. His mother accepted the patronage of a wealthy Chinese harbor-front contractor to protect and support her family,[10] and Lee himself accepted a job with the Japanese Propaganda Department. In the early days of the Occupation he suffered the humiliations of a couple of beatings at the hands of Japanese occupiers and a daily dice with arbitrary execution, all of which built a determination in him to avoid being so dependent and subservient ever again. In this period his faith in the wonderful British was shattered, though not his faith in progress. Upon the return of the British after the war, he became conscious, seemingly for the first time, of the racism that was inherent in colonial society, and came to despise it whenever he recognized it.[11] It was unfortunate for the later development of Singapore that he allowed this element of his social cognition to atrophy as he came to see the world and his own society through a racial prism that was substantially of his own creation, but was in critical ways drenched in the colonial racial stereotypes that he had earlier found so repulsive.

His mother had saved to send him to England to study, but the intervention of the war meant that he had to rebuild his fortune through sharp business dealings and a willingness to seize any opportunity that presented itself.[12] With a substantial nest egg in hand, he set sail for England, where he not only received an excellent Cambridge law degree but managed to woo and marry Kwa Geok Choo, a Chinese-Singaporean heiress who was also a Cambridge law graduate. She was soon to become his unfailing rock of emotional stability and, during the crucial early years of his political career, his main source of financial stability.

From his arrival in England, Lee's biography becomes increasingly indistinguishable from the development of his political thought. He began a course of study at Cambridge that was to provide him with a lifelong belief in the power of the state to transform, drive, and manage society from above. It was a period in which dons at Cambridge put great faith in the radical power of the law to improve society and push aside burdens of tradition, and the entire curriculum was directed to developing this insight into a practical, working reality.[13] "Historical Introduction to the English Legal System" was taught by R. M. Jackson and was substantially devoted to reconstruction and reform. Lee's friend and fellow student, David Allan, had trouble conveying to me in an interview the excitement that this course caused among the students, but some of it was captured in the preface to the 1953 edition of Jackson's book. It explained that this edition was very different to the 1939 edition because most of the reforms advocated in the earlier edition had been implemented in the late 1940s. That is to say, Lee was able to read about the implementation of reforms in the newspapers as they were studying the proposal of those reforms in their textbooks and in the classroom.[14]

The power of these experiential lessons proved to be enduring for the rest of his very long life. These lessons in the law were reinforced by his newfound faith in socialism, which he acquired both from his personal exposure to the generosity of the newborn British welfare state, and from the socialist and Labour Party associations that he developed while he was a student. His faith in socialism was, however, founded more in romanticism than in ideology, and it did not last long. In fact before he had even left Britain, it had been replaced by an extreme aversion to anything that smacked of the welfare state.[15] This antipathy developed into an ideological obsession and came to form the basis of a major overhaul of the health and welfare system of Singapore in the 1980s.[16] Yet the romanticism behind his socialist idealism proved deeper than his affiliation with socialism itself. Even while his faith in socialism was still alive, his romanticism had already found another, parallel outlet that was to serve him well in government: Arnold Toynbee's *A Study of History*. Toynbee was the most fashionable pop-intellectual among the undergraduates in Cambridge immediately after the war,[17] and he wrote of civilizations rising and falling with the fortunes of elites, whom he termed "creative minorities."[18]

Toynbee's idea of the creative minority fed and provided an intellectual framework for a natural disposition in Lee toward elitism. Decades later Goh Keng Swee told me that Lee quoted Toynbee in cabinet meetings from their earliest days in government. Lee was particularly taken with Toynbee's "Challenge and Response" thesis, whereby ruling elites retain their creative edge (or not) according to how effectively they responded to crises.[19] This vision of constant struggle and achievement fed his natural temperament, which, as he noted in a speech delivered in 1965, made him doubt that he could ever be comfortable in "a placid society."[20] It also provided the framework for what became his standard use of brinkmanship and the use of crises to force desired political outcomes, as well as to shape and train his colleagues, subordinates, and successors. Between graduation and his return to Singapore he found another focus for his romanticism in the image of strong, forceful Germans working together under strong leadership to reconstruct their nation after the war.[21] This image was formed during his and Geok Choo's honeymoon in Europe,[22] and it is significant mainly because it proved to be a foretaste of his propensity for thinking of nations, races, genes, and cultures in collective and visionary terms, and of analyzing problems through such conceptual prisms.

Lee returned to Singapore in 1950 with a conviction that he and his fellow "returned students"—Asian graduates of English universities—had a duty to take leading roles in the anticolonial movement so as both to guide Singapore to independence and to save it from communism. He entered legal practice in 1950 and used his position to build a loose network of left-wing social, industrial, student, and political organizations that would subsequently become his political base. He joined up with fellow "returned students," and in 1954 they set up the People's Action Party (PAP). Lee and most of his colleagues were lapsed socialists by this stage, but they judged that it was necessary to identify with socialism to appeal to their anticolonialist, working-class constituents. They went a step further and formed a united front with local Communists and militant leftists in order to tap their much larger and better-organized political base. The PAP contested Singapore's first popular elections in a very limited fashion—nominating just enough candidates to establish an opposition presence in the new Legislative Assembly. It then swept the race in the subsequent elections in 1959, the first to be held with a full universal franchise and which introduced complete self-government on domestic matters.

The next few years were mayhem as Lee led Singapore into Malaysia as a constituent state in September 1963, and then led it out again in August 1965, by which mechanism it became an independent republic.[23] In the meantime he and his colleagues had broken their alliance of convenience with the left wing of the PAP, and in 1963 Lee ordered a security sweep that destroyed the Left and the Communists as political forces, leaving the now-conservative PAP to comfortably win the general elections of that year. Two permanent legacies of this period are that it confirmed in Lee's mind the colonial racial stereotypes about Malay "sluggishness" and Chinese superiority,[24] and that it left Singapore as an independent, but vulnerable microstate.

With Singapore finally independent, Lee successfully led it down a path of intense economic development and increasingly tight social and political control, both of which were to become hallmarks of his rule, and which are the focus of much of the subsequent sections of this chapter. Although the PAP has stayed continuously in power to the present day (holding all seats in Parliament from 1968 to 1981 and almost all seats thereafter), the character of the government, and Lee Kuan Yew's role within it, has changed dramatically. The government of the 1960s and 1970s was dominated by a collective leadership of the original "old guard" leaders—the "classes of 1959 and 1963," so to speak—but by the early 1980s Lee had acquired the authority of an autocrat due to a spate of retirements (some of which were forced) among his old colleagues. He used the opportunity to shift the Singapore political and social landscape in two directions that were dear to his heart: he moved "Chineseness" to the center of the Singaporean national identity, and he enhanced the elitist character of the education system.[25]

In 1984 the family legacy in government seemed assured when his eldest son, Lee Hsien Loong, entered Parliament and began rising quickly through the cabinet. In 1990 Lee Kuan Yew stepped down as prime minister but retained effective control of policy matters as senior minister in a government led by his immediate successor, Prime Minister Goh Chok Tong. The year 1990 also saw the appointment of Lee Hsien Loong as deputy prime minister and the public acknowledgement that he would succeed Goh as premier "in due course."[26] Lee Hsien Loong probably would have become prime minister some time during the 1990s except that he was diagnosed with cancer in 1992. Goh took the chance offered by Lee Hsien Loong's misfortune to build a power base to rival that of the two Lees, but as soon as Lee Hsien Loong had fully recovered from cancer at the beginning of 1998, the Lees reestablished their hegemony over politics with remarkable ease. In 2003 a senior member of the elite described to me how Lee Hsien Loong had marginalized Goh Chok Tong from real power, even though Goh was still, at that time, prime minister. When Lee Hsien Loong officially became prime minister in 2004, Lee Kuan Yew remained in the cabinet as "minister mentor." He tried to continue as the "power behind the throne," but time and tide were against him, and he suffered a slow decline in his power. Yet his ultimate political demise came only in 2011 when he was implicated in the PAP's exceptionally poor showing in the general elections of that year, after which he finally stepped down from the cabinet. At the age of ninety, he remains a member of Parliament and commands more respect and influence than direct power.[27]

For Lee, the distribution of talent and energy and intelligence among peoples, both as individuals and as collectives, explained the world. Race had always formed an important element of his understanding of the hierarchies of the talented. When he looked out over civilizational history and contemporary global politics, he saw strong societies being led by natural elites.[28] The critical point here is that his social cognition saw the world in hierarchies, where elites ruled and others served to the best of their abilities. He was circumspect about such thoughts in the 1950s, but once Singapore separated from Malaysia, he was suddenly liberated to speak his mind on elitism, if not yet on race. The social "pyramid," said Lee late in 1966, consisted of "top leaders" at the apex, "good executives" in the middle, and a "highly civic-conscious broad mass" at the base. The role of each of these social strata was distinct, requiring "qualities of leadership at the top, and qualities of cohesion on the ground." Lee supplemented his imagery of the pyramid with that of a military organization, and argued that after the leaders come the "middle strata of good executives," because "the best general or the best prime minister in the world will be stymied if he does not have high-quality executives to help him carry out his ideas, thinking and planning." Finally comes "the broad base" or the "privates." They must be "imbued not only with self but also social discipline, so that they can respect the community and do not spit all over the place."[29]

Democracy and constitutionality demanded routine genuflections, but neither was important to Lee.[30] It so happened that in the first decade and a half of Singapore's independence, the country's very survival was a matter of serious doubt,[31] and for someone who had only ever considered democracy to be an "experiment" bequeathed by the British on their former colonies[32] and who sought to highlight crises and challenges as a matter of political technique, this was a golden opportunity. The 1970s was the dark decade for Singapore's democracy, as Parliament, political parties, the news media, the trade unions, and the ethnic and language associations succumbed to the hegemony of the PAP, and dissidents were detained, bankrupted, or marginalized.[33] Lee was clearly comfortable rationalizing the use of repressive practices—including the detention without trial or charge of political opponents for years at a time, along with beatings, sleep deprivation, induced coldness, and intimate humiliations—to the point where it became standard government practice in the 1960s and 1970s, and was still an option at the end of the 1980s when he stepped down as prime minister.[34]

Today a government attack on political opponents is more likely to take the form of litigation and civil action than actual detention without trial—though it needs to be noted that the threat of detention remains, and the courts have not been of any help in upholding even the most basic natural rights of defendants or the most elemental of judicial procedures when it is a political case.[35] The political process Lee created under himself and bequeathed to his successors was therefore supine and compliant. The fact that it has also been stable and economically successful brings us to perhaps Lee's most significant legacy: the legitimation of a new and repressive form of political entity. It was described at the time by Thomas Bellows as the "dominant party system"[36] and by Chan Heng Chee as an "administrative state" and "one-party dominance."[37] Years later Chua Beng Huat would call it "illiberal, communitarian democracy."[38] Today Andreas Schedler describes it as "Electoral Authoritarianism," which she identifies as part of an emerging new form of governance that is challenging democracy across the globe.[39] Regardless of the labels and the analytical prism used, in Singapore's case we are talking about a marriage of repression and capitalism that promises to be a model for the more clever dictators of the twenty-first century.

Economic Growth and Development

Lee is most positively regarded on both the local and the global stage for his ideas about economic growth and development. Indeed, when finding a title for the second volume of his memoirs, Lee chose this achievement as his primary boast—having taken Singapore "from third world to first."[40] Yet the truth is that he was not the primary mover in this field of endeavor. His early finance ministers, Goh Keng

Swee, Hon Sui Sen, and Lim Kim San, led the way,[41] all the time under the guidance of a Dutch economist called Albert Winsemius, who really should be called the father of Singapore's economic development.[42] There is an implicit consensus in the scholarly literature that Lee's substantive contribution in this field was to provide the political conditions to enable these other leaders to devise plans and implement them,[43] but the final result is such a clear reflection of his ideological convictions and personal traits that it seems to me that this assessment grossly understates his real importance in this field.

Let us consider just three salient points. First we can consider the nimbleness of the Singapore economy as it jumps at opportunities and defies conventional wisdoms. It did not start off this way. In the 1950s and 1960s Singapore was pursuing a conventional program of economic development through Import Substitution Industrialization (ISI). This program followed the economic orthodoxy of the day, and indeed was the mandatory course of action for receiving World Bank loans. Upon Singapore's separation from Malaysia in August 1965, Singapore suddenly had a domestic market of less than two million people, making ISI unsustainable. Winsemius advised a switch to Export Oriented Industrialization (EOI), having ensured years earlier that the economy already had the tools needed to run an EOI-based economy.[44] It was not Lee's idea to make this switch, and he was not the primary manager of such economic matters, but he embraced the logic and became its most effective public champion—in the process establishing Singapore as a pace-setter for Japan, the other Asian "tiger economies," and eventually China.[45] Then in 1968, when Singapore's continued existence was in doubt and the EIO program was still in its infancy, he put his weight behind a plan to establish Singapore as the financial center of Southeast Asia (by taking advantage of the gap between the closure of the San Francisco and the opening of the Zurich stock exchanges half a day later) and in the process completed the world's first twenty-four-hour-a-day money and banking market. Again, this was not Lee's idea. It was Winsemius's proposal, and even he had to have the mechanics of the plan explained to him by a friend who was vice president of the Bank of America,[46] but it was Lee who embraced it, ran with it, and drove it. Later, in the 1980s, when Ezra Vogel was busy declaring that Japan was "number one,"[47] but Singapore's collective memory was still traumatized by the Japanese Occupation, Lee opened the country not only to Japanese investment, but to every fad associated with

Toyota-ism in an effort to improve standards and increase production levels.[48]

Second, consider that the vehicle for this nimbleness was persistently the state, an investment and management vehicle not usually associated with this virtue. It was fortunate that Lee found himself in charge of a microstate that lends itself to sudden changes of direction. If he had been in charge of China, Japan, or Indonesia, it is extremely doubtful that he could have exercised such versatility through the levers of state power—a point that severely limits the "Singapore model" of development as a template for emulation. After initially operating through companies and statutory boards fully owned and directly managed by government ministries, the government settled on its preferred model, which was the government-linked company (GLC): wholly or partially government-owned; given preferential treatment in domestic markets; given enough independence to act like a business in day-to-day affairs, but with more than enough government control to make it a reliable political tool.[49] Eventually the government consolidated its GLCs into two major sovereign wealth funds: Temasek Holdings, designed to house Singapore-based companies, and the Government of Singapore Investment Corporation (GIC) for direct offshore investments, which between them have become the country's most important tools of patronage and power.[50] The size and ubiquity of the government in business and society means that it has dealt itself a powerful hand when it comes to handling domestic politics. Once we include the set of Statutory Boards, one of which owns and manages the housing of more than 80 percent of Singaporeans, we reach a situation where it is near-impossible to live or work in Singapore without bumping into government. Reliable estimates put government equity in the Singapore economy at 60 to 70 percent.[51] One direct outcome of this state-driven enterprise has been the marginalization of local small and medium-sized enterprises (SMEs). Today this outcome is regretted, but originally it was an intended effect. SME ownership was drawn mainly from Chinese families who operated independently of government patronage,[52] and one of Lee Kuan Yew's most basic political instincts when confronted with capacity for independent action is to take control, to co-opt, or to marginalize.[53] (In the case of the Chinese SMEs he did all three.) This propensity to utilize the state as his preferred instrument of economic development—including Singaporean investment overseas—complements this political methodology.

A third feature of Singapore's economic development model that is distinctively Lee is the attention to managerial professionalism. It was both a strength and weakness. It enabled him and a select group of civil servants to manage the GLCs with cutting-edge efficacy (though not necessarily high levels of efficiency or productivity) while facilitating the levels of control that Lee demanded of any institution of power.[54] The personal attention that Lee and his inner circle have paid to professionalism and managerialism over several decades of stable rule has enabled "Singapore Inc.," as it is now known,[55] to avoid the typical problems of corruption, ineptitude, and inefficiency that are routinely associated with government enterprise, especially in developing countries.[56] These positive legacies are real but should not be overstated. It is intrinsic to the system Lee created that there is very little accountability at the upper levels of government, administration, and government-linked business, in contrast to high levels of accountability at the lower levels, so mistakes by members of the elite are routinely papered over and those responsible protected from public scrutiny.[57] There has also been a remarkable prevalence of family networks in Singapore Inc. and the public sphere more generally (especially Lee's family), but there is no active concept of conflict of interest operating anywhere in the Singapore public sphere.[58] Yet even with such question marks hovering, the achievements are remarkable, and the presence of serious blemishes should not obscure their significance.

One of the blemishes in the system was famously identified by Paul Krugman in 1994, when he compared Lee Kuan Yew's Singapore with Stalin's Soviet Union:

> All of Singapore's growth can be explained by increases in measured inputs. There is no sign at all of increased efficiency. In this sense, the growth of Lee Kuan Yew's Singapore is an economic twin of Stalin's Soviet Union growth achieved purely through mobilization of resources. Of course, Singapore today is far more prosperous than the USSR ever was—even at its peak in the Brezhnev years—because Singapore is closer to, though still below, the efficiency of Western economies.[59]

Since then this theme has been developed further. In 2002 Peter Robertson contrasted the record of Singapore with the other "tiger" economies:

Much of the capital accumulation in South Korea, Taiwan and Hong Kong was due to productivity growth. The direct and indirect effects of productivity growth account for half the growth in Korea and two-thirds of Taiwan's growth over a 30-year period. Only in Singapore is the [measure of productivity growth] too small to have much impact on capital accumulation.[60]

The essence of this criticism is that Singapore's increased outputs and wealth are almost entirely due to increased inputs of capital and labor.

The inputs of capital were drastically increased mainly by two distinct sets of measures. The first set was domestic in nature: appropriating most domestic savings through a compulsory Central Provident Fund that in the mid-1980s took 50 percent of wage earners' salaries,[61] a Post Office Savings Bank through which most remaining domestic household savings were enlisted in the service of the government, and by assiduously building and husbanding government surpluses. The second set looked outward, providing tax and myriad other incentives to attract Multinational Corporations (MNCs) to set up factories and eventually regional bases in Singapore.[62]

The increase in labor inputs was achieved by pushing almost the entire adult population, male and female, into a new waged, industrial workforce, then increasing workers' hours of work per week, and finally by importing labor from less developed parts of Asia.[63] The creation of a waged workforce was driven substantially by the government's housing program. It bulldozed *kampongs,* squatter villages, and shop houses—all of which supported life to varying degrees of comfort and hygiene at very low cost—and replaced them with high-rise rented flats with conservancy fees, running water, and electricity, all of which needed to be sustained by a steady income.[64] Parallel to the simple expedient of increasing the volume of labor, the government also set out to improve the workforce's skill set by spreading and improving the quality of education and by attracting "foreign talent."[65]

In this enterprise of economy-building, Lee was crystal clear that the needs of capital were paramount, and labor played a subordinate role.[66] This privileging of capital gave Lee an affinity with neoliberalism, but he was no liberal. He was a free trader because Singapore relied upon free trade. He upheld the nearly unfettered right of capital to be mobile simply because Singapore needed foreign capital. But he was a state capitalist operating in a neoliberal international environment. His government not only intervened in the economy but micromanaged it and dominated it as no self-respecting neoliberal ever would. He also used an extraordinary level of state intervention to pass many benefits of the national prosperity to the ordinary worker so that they felt a commitment to and a sense of solidarity with their country. A liberal may be able to find common ground with the objectives and some of the final outcomes, but Lee's methods were more akin to those of an authoritarian socialist than those of a democratic liberal.[67]

In 1970 Lee argued that the major preconditions for economic development were: capital accumulation; a disciplined, skilled workforce; management; engineering; and administrative "digits."[68] His insight was undoubtedly correct for the Singapore of 1970, but that model is much less useful today.[69] He and his successors have tried to find alternative models—they have exercised their minds to develop creativity in the population, and to rent the best minds in the world in fields such as biotechnology, all in an effort to break out of the Krugman dilemma. They have found real difficulties in breaking out of old ways because with the old model of tightly controlled, state-led economic development came the justification for the privileged position of the ruling elite and its political and social control. It seems that whenever they are able to point to significant achievements in this regard—such as the successful creation of a well-endowed "knowledge hub" of universities, research institutes and professional schools—it is due more to the depth of the government's pockets than the creativity of Singaporeans. These limitations should not be laid exclusively at the feet of Lee Kuan Yew, but the symbiotic linkage between the political system and the economic system is his personal creation: this was part of his political genius and has become the burden of his legacy.

The Cultural Politics of Nation-Building

If there was one element of Singaporean life in which Lee Kuan Yew was the prime driver, it was building the country's national identity. Interestingly, however, he was not the first prime mover. That honor goes to Singapore's first minister for culture and master wordsmith, S. Rajaratnam. Singapore's third president, C. V. Devan Nair, has also been credited as a national myth-maker,[70] but both men and the visions they represented were subsequently overwhelmed by Lee.

In the heyday of Rajaratnam and Devan Nair as mythmakers—a period that stretched from the 1950s to the early 1970s—the national culture and identity swirled around images of a Singaporean melting pot of races and cultures, all pulling together and defying the odds to build a better future. This was hardly surprising since both men were Indians and therefore members of one of Singapore's smaller ethnic communities. During this period Chineseness was marginalized in the national narrative, as was Sir Stamford Raffles because using him as a starting point made the Singapore story a British-cum-Chinese story. In 1969 Lee was busy playing down the importance of Raffles in Singapore's history, and a contemporary editorial in the Chinese newspaper *Sin Chew Jit Poh* dismissed the "discovery [sic]" of Singapore by Raffles as "a historical accident" that merely "accelerated the growth of Singapore." Education Minister Ong Pang Boon warned against giving "too much" emphasis to the personal contribution of Raffles, preferring to "play up the meritorious services rendered by our pioneering forefathers" and the "industry of the various races" of Singapore.[71]

By the 1980s, something had changed. Both Chineseness and Raffles were becoming prominent in the Singapore story, and Lee was being presented increasingly as a new Raffles.[72] Some of the drivers of this change were circumstantial: Singapore had left Malaysia; it was no longer facing existential threats; it was thriving. Yet part of the change was due to shifts in the thinking and emotional resonances of Prime Minister Lee, which took on disproportionate significance because of the dramatic increase in his personal power in the same period. In the early 1980s Lee was almost the last active member of the original "old guard" that came to power in 1959, and so he was able to dominate a younger and less secure cabinet as he never could in the 1960s and 1970s.[73] Paradoxically, he took this chance to start stepping back from day-to-day management of the country, but this was merely an indication of the supreme confidence with which he was wielding power by this time.[74]

Lee treated his newfound power as an opportunity to indulge those of his private prejudices that he thought were useful and politically viable. The most notable of these was his belief in the superiority of "Chinese culture," "Chinese values" and Chinese people. Hence, at the beginning of the 1980s, the state began sponsoring a Sino-centric concept of nation in which the Chinese were expected to share, and the minority races expected to mimic. The country had been built on the twin myths of multiracialism and meritocracy, but by the early 1980s government leaders were just as comfortable upholding the supreme place of Chinese culture and virtues as they were in insisting on the importance of multiracialism. In this vision multiracialism equaled peace, whereas Chinese values equaled prosperity.

This bifurcated thinking became a fundamental dynamic in the new multiracialism, and it was created almost single-handedly by Lee in the 1980s and 1990s.[75] It came to dominate public space through the education system and the media,[76] as well as in the use of Chinese ethnicity (race), and not just "Chinese culture," as a basis for career promotion and elite selection.[77] The effect of these moves was to shift Singaporean society from one that provided a reasonably equitable balance among the various ethnic and religious communities, to one in which being Chinese and speaking Mandarin and English provided the keys to worldly success. Nowhere was this more visible than in the tertiary student population and in the various Public Service Commission (PSC) scholarships, which were and are the key to entering the elite. Despite the non-Chinese making up around 23 percent of the population at all relevant times, we find that:

- ethnic Chinese make up 92.4 percent of local university students and 84.0 percent of polytechnic students;[78]
- after 1980, the proportion of non-Chinese among the President's Scholars (the high-water mark of elite production) more than halved from an already-low figure of 8.8 percent (1966–1980) to 3.8 percent (1981–2010);[79]
- for the twenty-four years from 1990 to 2013, there were only four non-Chinese President's Scholars out of ninety-one (4.4 percent)—and one of these non-Chinese studied Higher Mandarin at Chinese schools;[80]
- for the entire forty-three years in which the prestigious Singapore Armed Forces Overseas Scholarship (SAFOS) has been awarded (1971–2013), only 6 (2.8 percent) out of the 213 that I have been able to identify by race are non-Chinese.[81] Over the twenty-four years from 1990 to 2013, I can positively identify only 5 (3.4 percent) of 148 SAFOS winners as non-Chinese.

If we focus on all types of PSC overseas merit scholarships from 2002–2012, we find that 21 (4.2 percent) out of 500 were non-

Chinese.[82] These skewed outcomes are not accidental. They are the result of systemic discrimination in favor of Chinese throughout the education system from kindergarten onward, which culminates in an opaque selection process at PSC scholarship level.[83]

How do we reconcile this ethnonationalism with Lee's early and notionally ongoing advocacy of multiracialism and meritocracy? Some may suggest that they were never anything more than political conveniences, but Lee deserves more credit than that. We know that he grew up and was educated in a genuinely multiracial environment, and there is every reason to think that this experience profoundly influenced his social cognition. The contradiction between these positions exposes an obvious tension in his thinking, but the tension becomes less pronounced if we refine our account of his childhood experiences of multiracialism and meritocracy thus: Harry Lee—a Chinese—excelled in a multiracial and meritocratic environment, matriculating ahead of all other members of his cohort throughout Malaya. He was, in fact, a Chinese who had emerged supreme in a multiracial environment. With the benefit of hindsight, we can recognize in this experience the model for Lee's vision of multiracialism and meritocracy. This need not have resulted in systemic discrimination against non-Chinese, but put this way it is not difficult to see how Chinese supremacism could be imperfectly reconciled with notions of multiracialism and meritocracy. There is an expectation that when "meritocracy" operates in a multiracial environment in the social milieu of Singapore, it will, in the normal course of events, produce a Chinese hegemony, and Lee built a system that was designed to facilitate this outcome.[84]

Yet Lee went further than merely presuming Chinese hegemony. He also wanted to share his personal virtues—what he saw as his "Chinese" virtues and values—with Singaporeans, so that they could be uplifted. He was convinced—and has said so on many occasions—that what he regards as "Chinese culture," "Chinese virtues," and "Chinese values" are the key to the material success of Singapore.[85] Alongside his faith in the importance of genes, he was also a passionate believer in the pivotal role of culture, nurturing, and social engineering in determining life outcomes.[86] Thus he sought to impose his sense of Chineseness onto the population, making Chinese culture, art, language, and mores central elements of the state and society. He had indeed come far from the idealism of the 1950s.

It must be conceded, however, that even though this racial favoritism suited his personal prejudices, there was also a ruthlessly practical dimension operating: Lee was plugging Singapore into the rise of China. The most important dynamic in his thinking—and the purest sense in which he lived up to his ideal of being a pragmatist—was that if there was not a credible likelihood of being on the winning side, then he could not see the point. No matter how strong was his prejudice, if it was not likely to prove useful he would park it out of sight, waiting until he found a way to use it. For instance, regardless of the strength of his prejudices about the supremacy of the ethnic Chinese gene pool and Chinese culture,[87] if China had been just entering its century of humiliation during the first decades of his rule, rather than just getting ready to emerge from it, he would never have turned his gaze to China. But with the rise of Deng Xiaoping at the end of the 1970s, China was indeed readying itself to rise, and Lee's vision and his prejudices helped him to recognize this earlier than most—and his position in the government of a country that was nearly 80 percent ethnic Chinese and situated on the meeting point of the Indian and Pacific Oceans enabled him to do something about it. He was convinced that China's chances had been squandered, not just by the "century of humiliation," but by the incompetence of the Great Leap Forward and the mindless excesses of the Cultural Revolution. Yet even before the Cultural Revolution came to an end and Deng had defeated the Gang of Four, his antennae were already sensitive to the opportunities that could be available in a new China. It is notable that Lee himself identifies 1982 or so as the period in which he became convinced (correctly as it turned out) that China was on the cusp of emerging as a major economic force, but his visits to China began in the mid-1970s, and his fascination with what he thought of as "Chinese values" and Chineseness had been growing since the 1950s and emerged as a direct force in his domestic politics by the late 1970s.[88] So central did China become in his global thought—and his vision of Singapore's future—that in the early 1990s he took Singapore out on a diplomatic limb with his "Asian Values" diplomacy that was intended to blur the politics of human rights and democracy by using arguments of cultural relativism. The story was told to me in an interview with Bilahari Kausikan, a permanent secretary with the Singapore Ministry of Foreign Affairs, who was adamant that the entire international "debate" on "Asian Values" had nothing to do with Singapore and "everything to do with China":

The Asian values debate began when there was a new Democratic administration [in Washington] who . . . seemed to be trying
to be define their approach to China on the basis of democracy
and human rights and trying to set up to change China. . . . They
couldn't change China but they could sure as hell cause a hell of
a lot of confusion . . . in an effort to do so. Now that lasted I
would say for about three years of the first Clinton Administration and then I guess reality set in and they started restructuring
their relationship with China in a different way. Once that happens, I mean for people like us, in Singapore who went into this
debate in a purely instrumental way . . . there's no reason to participate anymore so we all stopped writing about it and stopped
talking about it.[89]

This episode was not a direct and personal intervention by Lee, but it
was a logical—perhaps even a necessary—outcome of the logic of the
China card that he had begun playing back in 1982. By the 1990s,
China was too central to Lee's vision for the region and for Singapore
to allow amateurs in important positions to muddy the waters. These
days Singapore is trying desperately to build two-way human exchanges with China in an effort to capitalize properly on what was
started thirty years ago: for instance, by bringing cohorts of school
and university students from China to Singapore on scholarships, and
building cohorts of bilingual, bicultural Singaporean-Chinese entrepreneurs who can work and live in China.[90]

The Idea of Singapore

Lee Kuan Yew's vision for Singapore is derived partly from the economic imperatives in which Singapore finds itself: a city-state utterly
dependent upon its capacity to survive and profit from the whimsical
currents of the global economy. The politics of the region have also
helped to form his vision: a small, developed microstate flourishing in
a region dominated by large, developing states. Yet in perhaps its
most decisive way, the idea of Singapore emerges from Lee's imagination as a manifestation of his own personality and drives.

The "idea" of Singapore is powerful and omnipresent in his mind
and now in Singaporean society. "Singapore" the idea is, very simply,
the best: a tiny Chinese beacon of talent-driven achievement in a
Southeast Asian sea of mediocrity and a global ocean of giants. It

navigates its way through the shoals and reefs of global politics and economics with the nimbleness of a speed boat, changing tack to confront new challenges and meet new opportunities. It has become a small but integral node in a network of "global cities" that are home to and generators of innovation, progress, and new global elites.[91] It is "a renaissance city" of culture, refinement, vitality, and ideas—a welcoming environment that makes foreign elites feel welcome.[92] If I may adapt a metaphor that is in constant use in Singapore, it is a country that "punches above its weight."[93] This is a catchphrase born of complacent confidence, and the worrying thing is that it is usually used without any hint of an acknowledgment that Singapore's "weight" is so slight and its size so tiny that any admiration and any lessons need to be severely tempered by a reality check. An alternative and slightly more modest variant of this expression is that Singapore is a "success"—an eternally vulnerable success, always at risk of falling off its perch, and only ever saved by the cleverness of its leadership (the elite), but always a success.[94]

The "success" theme is linked inextricably to Lee's perception of elitism and "talent" and dates right back to 1964, when Singapore's claims to success in any meaningful sense were, to say the least, audacious, yet he attributed success to the fact that in the late colonial era Singapore had acted as a magnet for talent from Malaysia and that contemporary Singapore was benefitting from that legacy:

> The success story of Singapore, of the last few years, was one achieved to a large extent by men from Malaya. Seven out of nine Singapore Ministers came from Malaya, seven out of nine Permanent Secretaries came from Malaya, four out of six judges are from Malaya. So also most of Singapore's trade union leaders and business executives have come from Malaya. For many years there was a drift of talent to Singapore.[95]

Lee has anthropomorphized the country and imposed his own personality onto it. In the idea of Singapore, the romantic and the pragmatist in Lee have found common ground. The two biggest powers in the world have both looked to Singapore as a model. Singapore is an example to China of how to marry economic development and authoritarianism.[96] The Americans have had a much more problematic relationship with Singapore, but there is ample evidence of admiration, beginning with Richard Nixon and continuing, surprisingly, into the Clinton administration, which in its early years was seriously considering the Singapore health system as a potential model for its own health reform program.[97]

The litany of role-model seekers who look to Singapore[98] is both a testament to the undoubted achievements of Singapore and to its capacity for self-promotion. And lest anyone doubts that Lee deliberately sets out to present Singapore and his personal legacy—much the same thing—as models to be admired, one only needs to take a glance at the opening credits of his memoirs, in which thirty-three international political and business leaders take turns in heaping praise on Lee and his achievements. It must have taken a significant amount of determination and manpower to solicit these testimonials to "the Singapore story." These witness statements were not just invited to feed an ego—though this motive cannot be discounted. They are evidence of Lee's success in showing the way to others: effectively, his success in teaching by example, even if it as an example acted out in a microstate so small that all lessons learned there need to be taken at a huge discount. There is a deep-seated drive in Lee toward didacticism that emerges persistently in his speeches, interviews, and the pattern of his public life, and he has bequeathed this impulse onto his idea of Singapore. He once described school and the schoolteachers of his childhood as being "the beginning and an end of life,"[99] so it should not be entirely surprising that didacticism has always been present in his model of politics.[100] In 1966 he gave an address to an assembly of school principals:

> In my experience—both as a pupil in school and in universities, and subsequently in trying to teach people at large simple political ideas—the most important person is the man who is in charge of the boy. . . . For effective teaching—such as explaining to an ignorant audience the simple A.B.C. of currency or reserves backing, and why our currency could be sound if we do this or that—one really has to give of oneself. The process demands effort and nervous energy.[101]

Didacticism was thus a vital element of his approach to domestic politics and his idea of Singapore. At a personal level he takes particular delight in being idolized in China and Britain, these being the two great recipients of his affection and admiration at different stages of his life and the two centers of his global political thought. He is particularly proud of having played a role in the thawing of hostilities between the PRC and Taiwan in the early 1990s and maintains a posture as an active commentator on cross-strait affairs.[102] These achievements are reflected onto Singapore, and he in turn enjoys the reflected glory from public recognition of his country's many achievements and successes.

Lee Kuan Yew in the Twenty-First Century

Lee is now at the end of his long and successful life, and after more than half a century in office, he has only recently relinquished the last of his executive roles. By the end he was clearly out of touch with the changing attitudes of his own constituency in Singapore, which is why his son forced him to retire in May 2011. History will no doubt confirm how much he has contributed to public discourse and ideas— particularly to the politics of economic development and to recognition of the importance of professional management. Some of his prescience has today become common wisdom: welcoming international capital; the idea and best practice of state capitalism at a time when regional economic unions and liberal capitalism are lurching from crisis to crisis; seeking export markets wherever they can be found; and the importance of a rising China. Even his persistence in thinking in terms of ethnic communities and structuring society through this prism may turn out to be an enduring legacy. And who knows? His very effective utilization of communalism to feed national success, even at the relative expense of minority groups, could yet prove to be visionary, as distasteful as this idea sounds. In among all these legacies it seems likely that one of the more significant and powerful of them might be the legitimacy he has lent to authoritarianism as a political system, and the example he has created for the world's more intelligent and sophisticated dictators—those willing to seek a long-term marriage between a strong state at least bordering on dictatorship and capitalism.

Within his tiny former fiefdom of Singapore, his legacy will be enduring, well beyond his own lifetime. Lee himself, however, has now become stuck in deep grooves of thought laid by half a century of active leadership, and he is not traveling as light as he used to do. How could he, in his nineties? But the ideas that he sowed in his relative youth (from his thirties to his fifties), when his mind was more nimble, will be with Singaporeans for a long time. He has implanted the ideal of a meritocracy deeply into the national psyche even if the reality is a highly flawed distortion of the ideal. He built an education system that is elitist and in many ways unfair to significant sections of the population, but which produces high-caliber outputs that make excellent professionals, and then set up a system of importing more expertise.[103] As a direct consequence, the society he leaves behind has an extraordinarily high regard for education and professionalism.[104] This is the core of his positive legacy.

As his legacy becomes part of history rather than part of contemporary politics, we can expect the critical interrogation of it to intensify, producing increasingly candid assessments that acknowledge the flaws within the achievements and the foibles within the brilliance. Some of these negatives are relatively incidental to his achievements, but others seem to be intrinsic either to his vision or to the reality of his achievement. Many of these failings reflect deep-seated impulses on his part. On the one hand, his disrespect for democracy, human rights, rule of law, and for any idea with which he disagrees is intrinsic to his political vision and praxis, as is his systemic privileging of Chinese people and "Chinese values." On the other hand, it remains to be seen whether his willful persistence in creating a cozy network of personal contacts and family members to run and profit from the instruments of state capitalism are central to his method of operation. These practices were and continue to be so endemic that his claims to have been running the country through a system of meritocracy are easily challenged.[105]

One of the other fundamental challenges that his system faces, and that it has been trying to overcome for nearly two decades with indifferent success, is the production of educational, social, and political systems that conspire to stultify the imagination and engender a culture of bland and sterile conformity.[106] The government has been trying to introduce a significant degree of diversity into the education system in an effort to stimulate entrepreneurial individualism and creativity, but it faces a problem: the same features that make Singapore an outstanding success by its own terms also serve to cramp independence of imagination. This conundrum leads to an even more fundamental impasse: the ruling elite wants independent thought and creativity in business and enterprise, but not in politics.[107] There is a basic contradiction between the demands of capitalism in a knowledge-based economy and the demands of authoritarian rule, and they may prove to be irreconcilable in the long term.

Lee Kuan Yew is a colossal figure in modern Asian history. Whether he is regarded as a hero or a villain will ultimately depend on the values of future generations casting judgment. For my part, I think that Singaporeans have paid a high price for Lee's vision. He has produced prosperity, but at the cost of leaving behind him a sterile, soulless, racist society that has little respect for ordinary human values, let alone human rights. It is run by an exclusive professional class that at the higher levels endures almost no accountability and suffers no interrogation about conflicts of interest, while reaping financial rewards of such magnitude that one can perhaps consider it a form of legal corruption. I realize that Singaporeans could have done much worse, but personally, I think they deserved better.

ELEVEN

ZULFIKAR ALI BHUTTO

In Pursuit of an Asian Pakistan

FARZANA SHAIKH

I

ON APRIL 26, 1945, Zulfikar Ali Bhutto, then a high school student in Bombay, wrote his first and possibly only letter to Muhammad Ali Jinnah. In it he laid bare his understanding of Jinnah's yet-to-be-realized national cause and swore undying loyalty to it. "Musalmans," he declared,

> should realize that the Hindus can never and will never unite with us, they are the deadliest enemies of our Koran and our Prophet. You Sir, have brought us under one platform and one flag. . . . Our destiny is Pakistan, our aim is Pakistan. . . . Nobody can stop us, we are a Nation by ourselves and India is a sub-continent. . . . Being still in school I am unable to help the establishment of our sacred land. But the time will come when I will even sacrifice my life for Pakistan.[1]

Indeed, for Bhutto the fact that the creation of Pakistan in 1947 entailed the sacrifice of millions of lives was cause for celebration. In another passionate letter to the student magazine of the University of Southern California, where he had arrived as a freshman just weeks after the Partition of India, he claimed:

> A few million more will shed a greater quantity of blood but will not molest in any measure the celestial rise of my

Asia. Ideals grow quickly when watered by the blood of martyrs.[2]

More than three decades later, Bhutto was faced with putting his words to the test. He rose to the occasion. In one of his last letters written to Pakistan's military ruler, General Zia ul Haq, who had refused to commute his death sentence (carried out on April 4, 1979), Bhutto renewed his bond with the ideal he believed he was dying for. "My blood is in the blood of Pakistan. I am a part of its dust, a part of its aroma"—a part of a land blessed with "my Islam and the Islam of the poor and exploited masses of Pakistan."[3]

These statements, spanning almost forty years of a tumultuous political career, encapsulate some enduring features of Bhutto's political vision. His implacable hostility to a caste-bound "Hindu India," which he judged as the antithesis of Muslim self-determination; his dreams of an ascendant Asia free from colonial domination; and his vision of an egalitarian order held together by "Islamic socialism"— all would come to be associated with his legacy. At its heart lay his prescriptions for Pakistan as "one of the beacon lights in the array of independent Asian states" that were often inconsistent and sometimes radically at odds with the direction of his politics.[4]

This essay tracks the evolution of Bhutto's thinking from an articulate exponent of decidedly Western values to the would-be conscience of the Afro-Asian Third World and putative champion of a classless society inspired by Islam. Critical to this process was the importance Bhutto attached to the notion of economic justice as the basis of an equitable global order. It served as the wellspring of an intellectual and political trajectory that reshaped his understanding of the struggle against economic exploitation and of Pakistan as a lead player and engine of Asian unity.

Today Bhutto is most vividly recalled as the founder of Pakistan's leading (and most controversial) political dynasty, and as a leader whose compromises paved the way for the steady Islamization of the state. What has received much less attention, however, is Bhutto's bold foreign policy vision. This sought to chart a course for Pakistan away from its status as a "client state" of a US-dominated Western alliance toward the rank of an autonomous player on the global scene, with the capacity freely to choose its international partners and redirect its loyalties.[5] At least as important was Bhutto's ambition to carve a niche for Pakistan as an Asian power, whose territorial roots in Asia would come to define it almost as much as its Islamic purpose.

II

Zulfikar Ali Bhutto was born in Larkana, in the southern province of Sindh in present-day Pakistan, on January 5, 1928, to Sir Shahnawaz Bhutto and his second wife, Khursheed, née Lakhi Bai.[6] As the scion of one of Sindh's wealthiest families, whose vast landholdings were said to have defeated even the census officials of the raj,[7] the young Zulfikar enjoyed a life of unparalleled privilege. Although drawn to an increasingly cosmopolitan lifestyle, the Bhuttos owed strong allegiance to Shi'ism and were known to be generous benefactors of local Sufi saints. Like many Sindhi families, the Bhuttos worshiped regularly at the shrine in Sehwan Sharif of Lal Shabaz Qalandar, the thirteenth-century patron saint of Sindh. This iconic saint exercised a profound effect on Bhutto, who would rely on his appeal to strengthen his populist discourse and, later, to project his vision of Pakistan as a nation rooted in strong regional cultures rather than in the standardized rules of textual Islam.

Bhutto's father, Shahnawaz, was prominent in Indian politics. Although devoid of formal education, he was knighted for his services to the British Empire in 1925 and was appointed in 1934 to serve as the first Muslim member of the Governor's Council in Bombay. Shahnawaz won plaudits from Jinnah for his role in securing the recognition of Sindh as an autonomous province following its separation from Bombay in 1936. He was praised again by Jinnah for trying to win the accession of the princely state of Junagadh to Pakistan—an exercise that ended in failure after its ruling nawab was forced to abdicate and surrender his state to India. These early experiences of his family's proximity to the centers of power left an important mark on Bhutto, who would call on them in his grooming for high office.

Bhutto's father was determined to ensure for his son the best education possible. He was well placed to pursue this plan: as a high-ranking member of the Governor's Council, he easily managed to secure a place for his son at Bombay's elite institution, the Cathedral Boy's School, where he was enrolled in 1937. Here young Zulfikar's lavish lifestyle made an impression and was judged, even by the standards of his affluent peers, to be particularly ostentatious. Bhutto's close childhood friend, Piloo Mody (later a member of the Indian Parliament), recalls how Bhutto pursued a "carefree life devoted to much pleasure." Mornings were often spent playing tennis, badminton, and squash or swimming in the pool; afternoons were frittered away at local theaters, while evenings were used up relaxing by the pool before dinner and "a stroll till about midnight." Others among Bhutto's group of friends were also impressed by his "good English'" and his fine taste in "clothes and good food."[8]

It is perhaps no surprise that, with these distractions, Bhutto failed in his first attempt to qualify for admission to Oxbridge. Mody believes that the setback was a reflection of Bhutto's "lack of early grounding in education . . . and discipline" rather than any lack of aptitude.[9] Indeed, Bhutto's natural wit and brilliance set him apart from many of his fellow students, who had no doubt his talents would take him far ahead of them. In September 1947, after a successfully passing his Ordinary-level examination the year before, Bhutto headed to the University of Southern California (which at the time enjoyed something of a reputation among his peers as a "school for playboys"). Following a short spell as a freshman, he transferred to the University of California at Berkeley and graduated with a degree in political science in 1950.

It was while at Berkeley that Bhutto is said to have fallen under the spell of the eminent jurist Hans Kelsen, who was then professor of international law at the university. Kelsen's realist dictum that a norm becomes valid when backed by the full force of the state apparently made a great impression on Bhutto, who, some have since argued, used it to justify his authoritarian style of politics.[10] While this claim is hard to substantiate, what is not in doubt is that Bhutto's exposure to Western education fueled a voracious and lifelong appetite for the legal and political writings of European thinkers, which left a lasting imprint on his political outlook. From Machiavelli to Metternich, Hobbes to Hume, Talleyrand to Toynbee—none escaped his attention.

There is little evidence however at this (or any other) time of Bhutto's sustained intellectual interest in the works of Asian or Muslim thinkers. The exception appears to have been Jawaharlal Nehru, whose writings he absorbed.[11] What he made of them as a young man remains generally unreported, although Piloo Mody recalls that during their long discussions at the Willingdon Sports Club in Bombay, while Bhutto was still at Cathedral High, Bhutto had confessed to him that "Nehru's socialist thinking appealed to his mind." By the time Bhutto reached Berkeley, he had grown disillusioned with Nehru, who, he claimed, once "wrote and spoke like a socialist" but had changed upon becoming prime minister.[12]

Nevertheless, it is clear that Nehru had made his mark on the young Bhutto. Writing in the 1960s, he called Nehru a "peerless knight'" among Indian intellectuals. Nehru's deep knowledge of history, his commitment to liberal values and his fluency in the cultures of both East and West were all worthy of admiration. So too were his skills as a diplomat in which he excelled "to the point of dangerous perfection." Bhutto also acknowledged Nehru's singular triumph in articulating the idea of nonalignment, which he believed had won for India self-respect and freedom from foreign influence.

Yet, according to Bhutto, Nehru suffered from deep flaws and a "mass of contradictions"—contradictions that he, Bhutto, may well have recognized in himself. Among the failings singled out by Bhutto were Nehru's arrogance and his profound contempt for India's neighbors. He also denounced as a sham Nehru's love of democracy and his commitment to secularism, while Nehru's attempt at "royal control," Bhutto claimed, had destroyed India's bureaucracy and weakened the Congress Party, leaving India irreparably damaged.[13]

Thus, while Bhutto intensely admired some aspects of the Indian leader, he greatly disliked others. It is plausible that Bhutto saw himself, or at least hoped in time to project himself, as Pakistan's answer to Nehru—urbane, well read, widely traveled, a committed patriot, and yet a man of the world, who would (almost single-handedly) assure for his country an honored place in the comity of nations.

The architects of Muslim civilization escaped the critical scrutiny and close reading Bhutto reserved for Nehru and his ideas. Although several of Bhutto's biographers have noted his youthful zeal in support of a pan-Islamic order, his engagement at the time appears to have been more politically inspired than fueled by intellectual curiosity. The broad achievements of Muslim civilization were, however, a source of pride. In a rousing speech at the University of Southern California, Bhutto waxed eloquent about "the opulent heritage of Islam" and its contribution to the arts and sciences. He also drew attention to the power of Islamic civilization to unify Muslims in the face of global dissension. "An Islamic Federation even at its weakest," he argued, would make all Muslims more secure, although such a federation, he emphasized "would not be based on a theocratic principle." With the kind of rhetorical flourish that would become his hallmark,

Bhutto declared: "Destiny demands an Islamic association, political reality justifies it, posterity awaits it, and by God we will have it."[14]

It was at this time that Bhutto became familiar with the personality and ideas of Napoleon Bonaparte, who would emerge as his most enduring role model and the object of his impressive collection of Napoleona, said to be one of the best in the world.[15] It was apparently Sir Shahnawaz who sparked his son's interest in the French emperor by presenting him on his twenty-first birthday in 1949 with a five-volume leather-bound biography of Napoleon by the American historian William Sloane, which was first published in 1896. Curiously, Shahnawaz was also instrumental in introducing young Bhutto to the works of Karl Marx: *The Communist Manifesto* was another birthday gift from father to son. It too would remain a lasting source of inspiration.

Bhutto would later recall that "from Napoleon I imbibed the politics of power. From the pamphlet [*The Communist Manifesto*] I imbibed the politics of poverty."[16] But, according to one of Bhutto's close confidantes, the real roots of his revulsion against economic injustice lay closer to home. The humiliation of his mother, Khurshid, a low-caste Hindu convert of modest origins, at the hands of her husband's aristocratic clan had made a deep impression on him. Many years later Bhutto bitterly recalled the unfair treatment meted out to his mother, observing that "poverty was her only crime."[17]

For the moment, however, it was not so much the discourse of poverty but the prospect of power that preoccupied young Bhutto. Like many of his contemporaries, Bhutto had set his sights on Oxbridge as a necessary port of call to realize his political ambitions. Encouraged by his father, he set sail for Oxford, where he arrived in the fall of 1950 to study law at Christ Church College under the tutorship of the historian Hugh Trevor-Roper, with whom Bhutto forged a lifelong friendship.

In a revealing account written after Bhutto's execution in 1979, Trevor-Roper remembered his young ward's success in mastering Latin in two rather than the customary three years.[18] There was, however, little sign of Bhutto's later engagement with social and political radicalism.[19] On the contrary, what struck Trevor-Roper about Bhutto during his years in Oxford was his "great sophistication," his Westernized outlook, and his considerable means to indulge his "epicurean tastes" and fondness for "good living." But behind this cultivated veneer lay a personality that, the historian claimed, had already begun to show the fundamental traits that many would later associate with Bhutto and his political style—"vast ambition, acute personal sensitivity, great pride, even vanity."[20]

III

Bhutto returned to Pakistan, now a married man,[21] at the end of 1953. Armed with his Oxford degree in jurisprudence and with powerful connections at his disposal, the bright young barrister (Bhutto had been called to the bar at Lincoln's Inn in 1953) was quickly snapped up by the best legal chambers in Karachi. Yet it was clear from the outset that Bhutto had set his sights on a political career. But he soon found that the ideals he had nurtured abroad, and that he hoped to realize upon his entry into the corridors of power, would be hard to accommodate in a country that had become more unstable during his absence. Plagued by political intrigues, still bereft of a constitution (that would have to wait until 1956), and vulnerable to a new web of foreign influences, Pakistan bore little resemblance to "the beacon light" of Asia that Bhutto had envisioned as a young man.

In a country locked in a tight alliance with Western powers to protect itself against India, Bhutto's youthful dreams of Asian unity seemed a distant prospect. In a state increasingly beset by a fierce constitutional struggle over its relation to Islam, his clarion call for a pan-Islamic federation sounded dangerously rash. More importantly, with Jinnah's Muslim League, which had led the movement for an independent Pakistan, now in terminal decline, Bhutto's hopes of mounting a campaign for extensive economic and social change looked doomed to failure.

It took little time for Bhutto to become aware of these constraints. In 1954, following Pakistan's accession to the US-sponsored South East Asian Treaty Organization (SEATO), he observed that

> the authors of our foreign policy have rejected both the imminence of neutrality [in the conflict between the West and the Soviet Union] and the emergence of a united Third Force [capable of establishing a balance between the great powers].[22]

Nor did the country's constitutional paralysis escape his notice. In 1955 he berated the "frenzied bouts" of Pakistan's constitutional lawmakers and condemned them as sanguine enthusiasts little versed in the science of fundamental laws [who] aired their views about an "Islamic Constitution," and in their naive quest to give Pakistan something entirely "new," vagueness reigned supreme.[23]

A year later he turned on the Muslim League, blaming it for severing its "contact with the masses, with their feelings and their problems," and for failing "to serve the interests of the common man."[24] It was now becoming clear to Bhutto that his ambition to project Pakistan as the embodiment of Asian self-determination, pan-Islamic solidarity, and egalitarian socialism would have to wait.

Nonetheless, in 1954 Bhutto threw himself into the campaign against a proposal to amalgamate Pakistan's four western provinces (Sindh, Baluchistan, Punjab, and the North West Frontier Province) into a single unit, to be designated as "West Pakistan" and become constitutionally on par with "East Pakistan." The aim of this "One-Unit" plan was to neutralize the Bengali population of East Pakistan, whose absolute majority was regarded as a threat by Pakistan's dominant Punjabi elites.

Bhutto denounced the scheme, claiming that it represented a patent breach of the federal institutional arrangements Jinnah had envisaged for Pakistan. He also used his opposition to express his strong attachment to his Sindhi roots, which had sensitized him over time to the appeal of local cultural identities.[25] In a stinging denunciation he condemned the "One-Unit" plan as "invidious" and warned that it would result in "the liquidation of the smaller units [of Pakistan]. . . . [T]hus the ancient land of Sind, which took shape in the [prehistoric Indus Valley] civilization of Moenjo Daro [2600 BC] . . . will wither into a mere pensioner of the Punjab."[26]

As it happened, once the "One-Unit" proposal went through, Bhutto quickly made his peace with it. At stake was nothing less than the prospect of a ministerial appointment. Bhutto was lucky to have among his patrons General Iskander Mirza, a close family friend, who had held power as governor general before assuming the post of president in 1956. It was Mirza who gave Bhutto his first opportunity to shine on the world stage by choosing him (although still without an official position) as head of Pakistan's delegation to a UN Conference on the Law of the Sea in 1957—a post to which he was reappointed in 1958. Both occasions enabled Bhutto to display his sharp legal mind and to try and break new ground in his interpretation of the postwar world.

The forum he chose was the special (sixth) committee of the UN General Assembly, which was deliberating on a comprehensive definition of aggression. In his address to the committee in October 1957, Bhutto argued strongly in favor of extending the legal definition of aggression to include not only direct armed aggression, but also "indirect economic aggression." The latter, he declared, was of particular concern to Pakistan as well as to other states, whose geographical position had left them vulnerable to more powerful neighbors. With a clear eye to the simmering Indus waters dispute between India and Pakistan (which was not resolved until 1961), Bhutto pressed for a separate article to be included in the draft resolution before the committee. He proposed that its wording should state "clearly and unambiguously that economic or indirect aggression is perpetrated if lower riparians are deprived of their natural rights in the use of rivers that flow through two or more countries." Any such interference, he claimed, insofar as it threatened his (or any other) country with "total annihilation" demanded to be condemned as "the most invidious form of aggression."[27] Bhutto's tour de force clearly made an impression at home. In October 1958 he was formally invited to join General Ayub Khan's new military regime as minister of commerce and energy development.[28]

IV

If Bhutto had any qualms as a self-professed democrat and student of law about becoming party to a military coup, he showed—at the time—few signs of it. On the contrary, he took to his portfolio with gusto and moved with alacrity to stretch its remit to foreign affairs.

It was, of course, no secret that the position Bhutto most coveted was that of foreign minister—a position that was to elude him until 1963. However, his keen understanding of international affairs and the fact that he enjoyed the confidence of Ayub, who is said to have admired Bhutto's "first rate mind,"[29] encouraged him to risk some bold initiatives that were well beyond his brief and that his more experienced cabinet colleagues regarded with consternation.

Bhutto was preoccupied with the question of Pakistan's membership of, and dependence on, a string of US-sponsored Western security alliances against the Communist bloc. He was convinced that these would reduce Pakistan to the status of a satellite and dilute its Asian identity by cutting it adrift from its neighbors, notably Communist

China. These concerns deepened with Bhutto's urgent plea to craft a more "authentic" foreign policy based on what he called his nation's "psychic urges." It involved restoring Pakistan to its rightful place as

> a member of the Third World . . . [and as] a nation inhabiting the heart of Asia, of a people authentically Asian in their personality, of a country situated in the immediate proximity of China and the Soviet Union and of a society sharing the culture and civilization of the Middle East.[30]

The relentless pursuit of this vision, often in defiance of official foreign policy, brought Bhutto into confrontation with his cabinet colleagues. The alarm bells first rang in late 1959 after it emerged that Bhutto, in his capacity as energy minister, had invited Soviet Prime Minister Nikita Khrushchev to send a team to prospect for oil in Pakistan's southern province of Baluchistan—a move that was widely construed as a pointed rebuff to the US oil company, Hunt Oil, which had just abandoned its interest in the project. Bhutto's apparently unauthorized invitation to Khrushchev met with stiff resistance in the cabinet. Among his strongest critics was Ayub's pro-Western foreign minister, Manzur Qadir, who seems not to have been consulted. Qadir warned that Bhutto's actions could gravely compromise Pakistan's standing as a Western ally and would amount to a breach of its obligations as a member of the US-sponsored anti-Soviet security alliance, the Central Treaty Organization (CENTO). Ayub was more ambiguous. Although himself a strong advocate of a pro-Western policy, he was clearly seduced by Bhutto, whose eloquence and expertise in foreign affairs he regarded as invaluable assets with which to strengthen his regime. In November 1960, after weeks of verbal sparring with his cabinet colleagues, Bhutto finally won Ayub's backing to go ahead and negotiate an oil agreement with the Soviet Union.[31]

Bhutto's determination to reach out to the Communist bloc has since been judged, even by his critics, as a major turning point that demonstrated Pakistan's capacity to reduce its dependence on the West and diversify its foreign policy options. In retrospect it would certainly be reasonable to assume that Bhutto aimed for nothing less than to raise Pakistan from its status as a "client state" of a US-dominated Western alliance to the rank of a country that was master of its fate, altering the contours of the global order in a manner comparable today to that of a "pivotal state." A key part of this exercise was Bhutto's attempt to deepen Pakistan's relations with China—a move that also met with a hostile reception among his pro-Western cabinet peers, who were anxious not to jeopardize gains flowing from Pakistan's membership in the US-sponsored SEATO. But this time they reacted more vigorously. In September 1960, Foreign Minister Qadir ordered the withdrawal of Bhutto's "discretionary powers" after learning that, as head of his country's UN delegation, Bhutto had decided to abstain rather than oppose a resolution on China's membership in the United Nations.

Bhutto justified his action, which also incurred the wrath of the United States, by claiming that it aimed to resolve inconsistencies in Pakistan's policy toward Communist China. He emphasized that it was absurd for Pakistan to recognize China (which it had done in 1950) while simultaneously opposing China's membership in the United Nations. He argued that without China's friendship, Pakistan stood no chance of emerging as a key player in the Third World, which he now envisioned as the vital bloc to mediate conflicts between the two superpowers, the United States and the Soviet Union.[32] Bhutto's pleas fell on deaf ears. The cabinet not only vetoed his suggestion to back China's membership of the United Nations but expressed serious doubts about his enthusiasm for a policy of Afro-Asian "neutralism," fearing that it would open the way for Nehru to exercise "Indian hegemony" over Pakistan.[33]

The border conflicts between India and China in the late 1950s gave Bhutto a further opportunity to press his case in favor of expanding Pakistan's relations with China. By doing so, Bhutto hoped to consolidate an independent pan-Asian bloc that would not only neutralize the debilitating bipolar rivalry between the United States and the Soviet Union but, in time, possibly even supersede the India-led Non-Aligned Movement (NAM), which he believed had excluded Pakistan from playing its part in Asian affairs.

Bhutto was now on stronger ground. The famous Panch Shila agreement, which assumed the permanence of Sino-Indian friendship, had broken down. While its collapse was seen by Bhutto mainly as confirmation of the fundamental instability of superpower politics, he seized on the possibilities it offered to small countries like Pakistan that could take advantage of a fast-changing scenario by seeking fresh international alignments. In years to come this belief in the volatility of international alliances, including the fluidity of Cold War "bi-polarity," would help Bhutto react with alacrity to the sudden rupture in relations between the Soviet Union and China or the unexpected rapprochement between the United States and China.

For the moment, however, Bhutto was savoring the quiet satisfaction of having persuaded his cabinet colleagues of the importance to Pakistan of what he called "the China factor." His campaign was boosted by Ayub's decision to open talks between Pakistan and China in early 1961, which aimed to formalize a boundary agreement between the countries and strengthen bilateral relations. In 1962 Pakistan's new foreign minister, Mohammad Ali Bogra, who was also known for his pronounced pro-Western views, was instructed by Ayub to travel to China to continue these discussions. They were interrupted just weeks later by the outbreak of war between India and China. The perceptible pro-Chinese shift in Pakistan triggered by this event was vigorously endorsed by Bhutto, who now basked in glory as the chief architect of Pakistan's China policy.

Bhutto wasted no time in strengthening its foundations. In an address to the National Assembly in November 1962, he came down strongly on China's side and accused India of intransigence.[34] But Bhutto took care to emphasize that his country's support for China was not the beginning of another formal alliance. Rather it was consistent with his country's sovereign and independent status. "Our friendship," he emphasized, "is not tainted by any form of bargain or barter. . . . China has assured us that our membership of the pacts with the West is in no way incompatible with our friendship with China."[35] Pakistan's relations with China were, therefore, "an independent factor in our foreign policy, and not contingent on any other."[36] Here, in essence, were the elements of what in years to come would be described by Bhutto as his policy of "bilateralism," which rested on the notion that "friendship towards one power entails no unfriendliness towards another."[37]

v

With seismic changes afoot in the neighborhood, Bhutto could hardly wait to put his policy in practice. Indeed, his first act as foreign minister—a post to which he was appointed in January 1963—was to sign a formal border agreement with China. It led to his first meeting with Mao Zedong in March 1963, setting in motion one of the most enduring partnerships in Asia.[38] Happily for Bhutto, the stage was also set for a major reappraisal of Pakistan's membership in the Western alliance and its relationship with the United States. The decision by the United States to rush arms to India to counter the Chinese threat had provoked widespread anger in Pakistan. In July 1963, Bhutto announced to a stunned National Assembly that an Indian invasion of Pakistan would be regarded as an attack on the territorial integrity of China.[39] Many, not least in India, believed that Bhutto's announcement signaled an imminent (if not formal) Sino-Pakistan alliance against India. But this was soon shown, in the words of one member of the National Assembly, to be no more than a figment of Bhutto's "romantic imagination," which had wanted to read more than was warranted into Chinese professions of friendship.[40] In retrospect, this conjecture now sounds plausible for not only did China fail to come to Pakistan's assistance in its war against India in 1965;[41] it actively refrained from any direct involvement in the war between India and Pakistan in 1971, which precipitated the breakup of Pakistan.

Bhutto's strenuous efforts to reorient his country's foreign policy away from its dependence on the West were not limited merely to expanding ties with China. Long before he assumed charge of the foreign ministry, Bhutto had already moved to forge close links with Muslim countries in the Afro-Asian Bloc such as Algeria and Indonesia, which were strongly opposed to Western policies. But Pakistan's membership in CENTO meant that its relations with key Arab states, especially those active in the nonaligned movement such as Egypt, were distinctly cool. The ruling Baath Socialists in Iraq and Syria, who had chosen to pursue radical agendas, were judged meanwhile to be too close to the Soviet Union for Pakistan to risk espousing their causes. However, the struggle for Algerian independence offered Bhutto an ideal opportunity to reset Pakistan's relations with the Muslim world and to ensure that the espousal of revolutionary and pan-Islamic causes would become a defining element of his foreign policy agenda. In 1959, while still commerce minister, he had made an impassioned plea at the United Nations in support of "the people of Algeria" against "French imperialism."[42] Bhutto's statement caused fury in Western capitals, where it was seen to be in open breach of Pakistan's responsibilities as a member of CENTO. He was undeterred. In 1961, now convinced of the importance of Algerian independence as a vital anticolonial and pan-Islamic cause, Bhutto reiterated his support and called on the United Nations "to acclaim the entrance of that brave nation."[43]

Bhutto understood that his aspirations to become the standard-bearer of a new Afro-Asian bloc would not carry any weight unless he first burnished his nationalist credentials by taking on India. For Pakistan's political and military establishment had long suspected that the discourse of Afro-Asian solidarity was a guise to promote India's leadership of the Third World, now institutionalized as the Non-Aligned Movement (NAM).[44] These concerns prompted Bhutto to turn his attention to the question of "Indian hegemony" and thus dispel speculation that he was ready to compromise Pakistan's national interests in the service of an agenda driven by Pakistan's archrival in Asia.

The still-unresolved dispute over Kashmir provided Bhutto with a suitable platform. It has been suggested that Bhutto used his position as foreign minister to aggressively proclaim "total mistrust of Indian promises as well as intentions" and to vow "never to give up on Kashmir."[45] A sympathetic biographer claims that "for many years Bhutto reveled in his reputation as a 'hawk' in relations with India," and that his "appointment as external affairs minister in 1963 was taken as an indication to the Indians of a tougher line in Indo-Pakistan relations than had hitherto been followed by Ayub."[46]

It seems clear that Bhutto was encouraged by the outcome of the 1962 Sino-Indian War, which exposed India's military weakness. It is also possible that, in late 1962, when Bhutto accepted Nehru's invitation to tea in New York during a break in UN meetings that they both attended, he was aware that the spirit of his great foe had already been broken by India's broken relationship with China.[47] These perceptions, combined with his characteristic political recklessness, may well have encouraged Bhutto to push for a military campaign against India to try and wrest control of Kashmir.

Bhutto had spent months carefully preparing his opening salvo. In July 1963, shortly after his appointment as foreign minister, he declared: "Kashmir is to Pakistan what Berlin is to the West"[48]—the implication being that Kashmir was a colonized territory that needed to be liberated and made free. Earlier in 1962 he had rejected as "sinister" a proposal by Nehru for a "No War Pact," dismissing it as a ploy to conceal India's aggressive designs against Pakistan. But as foreign minister, Bhutto was also keen to demonstrate his skills as a diplomat. During much of 1962–1963 he was engaged in lengthy negotiations with his Indian counterpart, Swaran Singh, to persuade India to recognize Kashmir's special status as a disputed territory. Although he failed in this endeavor, he pointed to it as proof of his diplomatic acumen and sincerity to find a solution to the problem of Kashmir.[49] In an interview with the BBC in London in 1964, he reiterated this position, saying, "we have discussed it [Kashmir] a hundred and nine times and we are going to discuss it for the hundred and tenth time and we are prepared to discuss it for a thousand times."[50]

Bhutto worked assiduously to raise international awareness of Pakistan's claim to Kashmir. In 1963 he lobbied leaders in Washington and London to try and win support for Pakistan's position but made little headway. However, he scored a significant success when he obtained China's endorsement of a plebiscite in Kashmir during a visit to Pakistan by Zhou Enlai in the spring of 1964. But his greatest coup came soon afterward, in April 1964, when he secured the backing of President Sukarno of Indonesia, Nehru's erstwhile non-aligned partner, who came out publicly in support of Pakistan's position on Kashmir. Sukarno may well have been responding to flattery, for he had emerged by that time as something of a role model for Bhutto, who made no secret of his admiration for Sukarno and his anti-imperialist agenda. Their close friendship strongly suggests that Bhutto looked to Sukarno as a key ally to help forge his new vision of Asian unity, hoping it would supersede Nehru's version of "Asian non-alignment," which Bhutto criticized as divisive in nature.[51]

Bhutto still faced the challenge of confronting India if he was to be taken more seriously within Pakistan. With typical bravado he chose the riskiest option, namely, instigating an armed rebellion in Indian-held Kashmir in September 1965. The idea of sending poorly trained "freedom fighters" into Kashmir on the assumption that they would overwhelm conventional Indian forces may well have borne the mark of Bhutto's characteristic impatience with detailed planning and preparation. Yet, Ayub's military strategists (some of whom worked closely with Bhutto) must be held equally culpable of underestimating India's readiness to widen the conflict beyond Kashmir and launch retaliatory attacks against Pakistan.

Today opinion is divided over Bhutto's role in precipitating the war with India and leading Ayub to preside over a military debacle. Among his political supporters there is no doubt that Bhutto was exceptional among Pakistani leaders in demonstrating the lengths to which he was prepared to go to defend the "just cause of Kashmir and its people."[52] His detractors, by contrast, have condemned him not only for leading Pakistan on to a disastrous military adventure that failed to "liberate" any part of Kashmir, but for cynically exploiting the debacle to engineer Ayub's downfall and make his own bid for power.[53] Outsiders, such as Sir Morrice James—at the time Britain's high commissioner to Pakistan—have offered more complex assessments of Bhutto's actions. His impressions, conveyed to the Commonwealth Relations Office in 1965 and recalled in his memoirs, are worth quoting at length. "Bhutto" he wrote,

> certainly had the right qualities for reaching the heights—drive, charm, imagination, a quick and penetrating mind, zest for life, eloquence, energy, a strong constitution, a sense of humour and a thick skin. Such a blend is rare anywhere, and Bhutto deserved his swift rise to power.... But there was—how shall I put it?—a rank odour of hellfire about him. It was a case of *corruptio optima pessima*. He was a Lucifer, a flawed angel ... his triumphs came too easily for his own good. Lacking humility he thus came to believe himself infallible, even when yawning gaps in his own experience (e.g. of military matters) laid him—as over the 1965 war—wide open to disastrous error. Despite his gifts I judged that one day Bhutto would destroy himself—when I could not tell. In 1965 I so reported in one of my last despatches from Pakistan as British High Commissioner. I wrote by way of clinching the point that Bhutto was born to be hanged. I did not intend this comment as precise prophecy of what was going to happen to him, but fourteen years later that was what it turned out to be.[54]

Bhutto was tempted to use the glare of publicity generated by his flamboyant personality to draw attention to Pakistan's case for Kashmir. At the same time, he clearly believed that in so doing, he was articulating the dominant vision of Pakistani nationalism in which the struggle over Kashmir was symptomatic of a deeper divide between Hinduism and Islam—a divide expressed in Hinduism's urge to dominate and Islam's instinct to liberate.[55] The idea of "political, cultural and economic hegemony," he declared, "has become a part of the tradition which modern India has inherited" from its Hindu tradition, which "as a semi-religious concept ... demands the end of Pakistan."[56] The mission to liberate Kashmir was, therefore, part of a larger project of resistance against the absorption of Muslims by "Greater Bharat" (the Sanskrit appellation for India), whereby Pakistan stood as an exemplar of Muslim self-determination and engine of Muslim emancipation.

What is curious about this articulation of Pakistani nationalism is how crudely rendered it was for a politician of Bhutto's sophistication and how poorly judged as an excuse for war on the part of one so widely admired for his talents as a diplomat. It was odder still for Bhutto, a politician from Sindh, where the issue of Kashmir had played little part in shaping political consciousness and where the tug of regional roots had proved more tangible than loyalty to putative Muslim causes such as the "liberation" of Kashmir.[57] Yet, Bhutto instinctively understood that he could not afford to ignore the cause of Kashmir if he was to consolidate his status as a leader of national standing in Pakistan. Without it, this politician from Sindh, however talented, stood little chance of success in breaking into the stronghold of state power dominated by Punjab's military-bureaucratic complex.

VI

Bhutto's political ambitions to secure national leadership now took center stage. In June 1966 he resigned as foreign minister after months of tension with Ayub and his cabinet over the conduct of the war. He had prepared the ground for his resignation through the skillful manipulation of public opinion in the aftermath of the 1966 Tashkent Declaration signed by India and Pakistan, which formally brought the war to an end. Denouncing the declaration as a humiliation for Pakistan, for which he held Ayub and his government responsible, he now careened through a dizzying round of mass public meetings, mainly in West Pakistan, where millions drank his heady brew of populist politics. Deep and widespread public disenchantment with Ayub's policies ensured that Bhutto's timing was perfectly judged.

With a group of left-wing politicians and thinkers in tow—chief of whom were Dr. Mubashir Hasan, a well-known activist and engineer by training, and J. A. Rahim, a career diplomat and theoretician— Bhutto rallied his followers to mount an unprecedented campaign against Ayub with the aim of transforming Pakistan. In December 1967 he announced the creation of the Pakistan People's Party (PPP) and proclaimed its three-pronged motto: "Islam is our Faith, Democracy is our Polity and Socialism is our Economy." The motto was a carefully planned and direct response to the frustration spawned by Ayub's brand of secularism, his restrictions on participatory politics, and his policies of unfettered capitalism that had resulted in acute disparities in wealth.

The PPP signaled the onset of a new style of mass politics that promised to break the mold of the established party system that had held sway in Pakistan since its inception. The failure of the Muslim League to transform itself from a national movement into a broad-based political organization with support that cut across regions and classes had exposed its shallow roots. Within a decade of independence the institutional weakness of the Muslim League had taken its toll, leaving it ridden with factionalism—a party still in thrall to personalities rather than programs. Disenchanted by its performance, some rank-and-file members compared it to "a virtuous lady who has fallen on hard times and is forced by circumstances to become a courtesan . . . and handmaiden of every charlatan who came to seize the reins of power in Pakistan."[58]

The political vacuum created by the decline of the Muslim League was occupied by parties with pronounced ethnic agendas. While some of these parties were based on the same pattern of patron-client ties that characterized the league, they were nonetheless able to draw on a robust tradition of popular regionalism that had long predated the creation of Pakistan. Among the leading contenders in this field were the pro-Pashtun National Awami Party, which enjoyed support in the country's northwestern regions, and the Bengali-dominated Awami League, which held sway in East Pakistan. Both were to prove formidable challengers to Bhutto's PPP. No less impressive for their reach were Pakistan's pro-Islamic parties. Although some, like the revivalist Jamaat-i-Islami, were initially handicapped by their historical opposition to Jinnah and his vision of Pakistan, the state's repeated and extravagant claims to be acting in the name of "Islam" eventually gave them the space to enter the debate and define its terms. Even if many religious parties therefore failed to make an impression on the average voter, their rhetoric and capacity to mobilize street power in "Islamic Pakistan" remained a force to be reckoned with.

The style and tone of the PPP's Foundation Documents left no doubt about Bhutto's intention to correct the problem of Pakistan's weakly institutionalized party system and address his country's social, political, and economic crises.[59] With an eye to fundamental systemic change, he appealed directly to the electorate, promising to empower the poor. His party's ten Foundation Documents were unusual and notable for their mix of styles, alternating between the language of high lyricism (poets, including Faiz Ahmed Faiz, Hanif Ramay, and Khurshid Hasan Meer had a strong presence in the PPP) and more prosaic instructions on how to plan a revolution. Document 4, entitled "Why Socialism was Necessary for Pakistan," represented the heart of the party's credo. It focused squarely on the question of Pakistan's underdevelopment and held up socialism as the only solution to Pakistan's multiple crises. It also proposed the nationalization of industrial enterprises, although there was no suggestion of the wholesale expropriation of private property. With an eye to the establishment of a "classless society," it called for the "elimination of feudalism and landlordism," a minimum wage for all workers, and the protection of the workers' right to strike.

The authors of the PPP's Foundation Documents were clearly aware that the reference to socialism, which Bhutto's critics among religious parties equated with "godless communism," needed clarification to avoid any suggestion that it was un-Islamic. Document 7 thus equated the struggle against "oppression, exploitation and slavery" with "jehad" and called on "the masses of Pakistan to unite . . . until this land brightens up with the divine light of God." Nor were regional concerns, notably those centering on the political alienation of the Bengali majority in East Pakistan, ignored. Document 10 recognized the growing divide between Pakistan's two wings, expressing sympathy for the relative poverty of East Pakistan and its "exploitation" by West Pakistan. However, it stopped short of endorsing the Awami League's confederal Six-Point program by calling instead for "the nationalisation of all the major industries in West Pakistan."

Despite this appeal to Pakistan's Bengali constituency, the PPP's Foundation Documents failed to resonate in East Pakistan. There, a combination of economic deprivation, political disaffection, and anger at being left undefended by the Pakistan army during the 1965 war had taken their toll and raised unprecedented questions about the merits of continuing the province's union with West Pakistan. But Bhutto would brook no obstacle now in his single-minded pursuit of power. And he had no doubt that the most potent threat to his ambitions at this time came from the Bengali leader, Sheikh Mujibur Rahman, who was head of the popular Awami League in East Pakistan.

In a suggestion full of ominous overtones that would later be used to justify the massacre of thousands of Mujib's followers in East Pakistan in 1971, Bhutto claimed at the inauguration of his party that the Awami League was more influenced by Indian "political philosophy" than by Pakistani ideas and ideals.[60] By contrast, he declared, the PPP was an authentically national party that was free of the influence of "other countries" and that sought "a Pakistani interpretation" of a solution to the country's problems. Elaborating on this theme, Bhutto explained that

> we are wedded to certain basic principles. We have said that Islam is our faith . . . it is the basis of Pakistan. There is no controversy on that and if any party were not to make Islam as the pillar of its ideology, then that party would not be a Pakistani party. It would be an alien party.[61]

This is not to say that Bhutto was working to break up the country he wished to lead—indeed, there were many occasions before 1971 when he sided with Mujib in calling for greater Bengali autonomy and for the rights of the Bengalis to be recognized. Rather, it is to underscore Bhutto's abiding conviction that he more than any other leader was destined (in the manner of Napoleon) to steer a united Pakistan.

In fact, Bhutto's ambitions for himself extended beyond Pakistan. With Nehru dead, Sukarno effectively neutralized by a military coup, and Zhou Enlai now preoccupied with the onset of the Cultural Revolution in China, the way lay open for Bhutto to stake his claim as head of a new generation of Asian leaders. He believed that changes in the political contours of Asia afforded opportunities that could be used to his advantage. The relationship between the two Asian giants— India and China—lay in ruins after 1962, while strains between the United States and Pakistan following the 1965 Indo-Pakistan War had widened cracks in the Western alliance. The time was ripe for a fresh commitment to the idea of Afro-Asian and Third World unity based on new realities. Bhutto seized the moment by promising to repair the divisions between the "non-aligned" and "aligned" group of countries and to underscore the common condition shared across the Third World—namely, underdevelopment.

In a rousing speech to a gathering of Pakistani students in London in August 1966, Bhutto made a strong bid for the leadership of a reinvigorated and unified Third World.[62] Pakistan, he claimed here, was "the handsomest offspring of self-determination" in Asia.[63] It had no need to be intimidated by India's size and military strength. Without so much as a hint of irony, less than a year after threatening to wage a "thousand year war" against India,[64] Bhutto exhorted "the people of India and the people of Pakistan" to acknowledge their "common history" and to lay the foundations of a freshly imagined Asian unity. "We are a part of the same geography," he declared, "the same geographical compulsions, the same geo-political factors. We share poverty. We are part of the same music and march of Afro-Asian solidarity."[65]

Bhutto further argued that Asia as a continent was bound by a common historical experience, namely, colonialism. He was directly inspired here by General de Gaulle's vision of European unity. For just as de Gaulle had worked to bring Europe together after the divisions unleashed on the continent by Hitler's aggression, so too had it become imperative for Asia to seek strength in a common heritage and to turn its back on divisions now that colonial rule was over. "Once you remove domination," Bhutto argued,

> the common factors come into operation. And that is why I believe . . . General de Gaulle espouses a great idea when he talks about [a] European Europe. As there must be a European Europe, there must be an Asian Asia.[66]

In this self-determined Asia, Pakistan was ready to play its part for, as Bhutto emphasized, "our place is in Asia and nowhere else . . . we have to forge our future in Asia."[67]

Nor was Pakistan's place in Asia defined only by a shared history and geography; it also stemmed from a shared state of underdevelopment. "We are the proletariat of the world," Bhutto declared, and "we are asking for a better life. Our people deserve it. For centuries they have lived in misery, squalor, filth and poverty."[68] Bhutto concluded by highlighting the qualities required of a leader fit to guide "dear Asia," which combined the skills of

> a mathematician . . . to calculate . . . a musician and romanticist . . . to know the tempo of the time and the rhythms of revolution . . . [and] an architect [to] build for the present as well as for the future.[69]

Bhutto's new vision for Asia was grounded in the evolving partnership between Pakistan and China, which he believed would determine the future of the continent. "Any development, any progress in Asia," he declared, "must take the China factor into account." And Pakistan, he argued, enjoyed a unique capacity to facilitate this "China factor." "We have a common boundary. . . . They [China] are our immediate neighbours. We look at each other face to face every day. We must have some understanding." He emphasized that it was Pakistan that had first recognized the global importance of China. It was Pakistan that demonstrated that no problem in Asia, or indeed globally, could be solved without China. There was no better proof of this than his country's support for China's membership in the United Nations.[70]

Bhutto's London speech brought into sharp relief two key themes in his political discourse, which would resurface in the run-up to his stunning election victory in 1970: Pakistan as an exemplar of the Afro-Asian struggle for economic justice and Pakistan as an expression of a predominantly Asian identity. In his book, *The Myth of Independence*, published in 1969 and now judged to be broadly representative of Bhutto's worldview on the eve of his bid for power in Pakistan, he wrote:

> Pakistan has a moral obligation . . . to strive for a more equitable economic and social international order. Afro-Asian unity is a powerful force for emancipation and Pakistan, as a member of the Afro-Asian community, has to be in the vanguard of the Afro-Asian movement. It can be justly demanded from Pakistan that she should continue to identify herself with the aspirations of the people of these continents. [71]

The spirit of these words with their strong accent on Pakistan's role in alleviating inequality in Asia and its claim to be a lead player in Afro-Asian affairs was echoed in Bhutto's election campaign, which was launched in 1970, following Ayub's resignation in March 1969.

By this time, Bhutto had emerged as a serious contender for power, at least in West Pakistan, where his defiance of Ayub's increasingly authoritarian regime had enhanced his status as a champion of the democratic rights of the dispossessed. A period of incarceration in 1968–1969, ordered by Ayub, added to his political allure, while his outfit of choice on the hustings—a red Mao cap and a green Chinese-style jacket—raised his standing as the "voice of the people's revolution." This image was reinforced by the power of his oratory and the novelty of his slogan, *"roti, kapra, makan"* (food, clothing, and shelter), which he tirelessly invoked to promote his party's election manifesto.[72]

Like the Foundation Documents, the PPP's election manifesto placed a strong emphasis on economic equality and distributive justice as the basis of its socialist credo, which was consciously equated with the Islamic idea of *musawat* (the Arabic term for "equality") to loosen its association with atheistic socialism. Indeed, some have argued that Bhutto's election manifesto showed much greater sensitivity than the party's Foundation Documents to the importance of reconciling the PPP's socialist program with "the spirit of Islam" by downplaying the party's commitment to a secular socialist order.[73] Bhutto himself was certainly concerned not to lose ground to pro-Islamic parties such as the Jamaat-i-Islami, which had mounted a strong campaign against him on grounds of his alleged preference for secularism.[74] How seriously Bhutto took the threat by the religious Right can be gauged by his election speeches, which are littered with allusions to Islamic history and tradition. At times he openly flaunted his Islamic credentials as if to underscore his Muslim over his Pakistani identity. "The first principle [of the PPP]," Bhutto reminded his opponents,

> is that Islam is our religion. . . . We are proud of the fact that we are Muslims. We shall wage a jihad for the cause of Islam, not only in Pakistan, but anywhere in the world if required. . . . The ideology of Pakistan means that the Muslims of Pakistan should do their duty to Muslims who are in trouble anywhere in the world.[75]

VII

These professions of high moral conduct were about to be tested.

In late 1969, the army chief, General Yahya Khan, who had assumed power following the resignation of Ayub earlier in the year, ordered elections. They were held in December 1970 and hailed as Pakistan's first democratic polls since independence; they were also notable for abandoning the "One-Unit" principle of parity of representation between East and West Pakistan and allocating to East Pakistan a majority of seats in the National Assembly (the lower house of parliament).

The outcome of polls proved to be a cruel blow for Bhutto. For although his party won 81 out of 138 seats in West Pakistan, it had no representation in East Pakistan, where it had failed to put up any candidates. Here, the Awami League won a landslide victory by securing 160 out a total of the 162 seats allocated to the province and gaining complete control of the provincial assembly as well as a clear majority in the National Assembly. However, in a mirror image of the PPP's performance, it failed to win any seats in West Pakistan (although unlike the PPP it had fielded seven candidates in the western provinces). The elections precipitated a constitutional crisis. The failure of the PPP and the Awami League to reach a power-sharing agreement after protracted and bitter negotiations in early 1971 led to a brutal military crackdown in the eastern wing that would spell the end of a united Pakistan before the year was out.

Bhutto's role in the crisis was particularly controversial. Although he later claimed he had always favored a political settlement, his own account of the crisis put him on record as having supported military action in East Pakistan.[76] It was used by his critics to accuse him of sacrificing Pakistan to wrest power at all cost: one of Yahya's ministers is said to have warned that "if Bhutto did not assume power within a year he would literally go mad."[77] Bhutto's supporters by contrast maintained that he was manipulated by the military, which had no intention of handing over the reins of government to politicians.[78] What seems beyond question is that Bhutto emerged from the crisis politically damaged and compromised by his part in appearing to have rejected the democratic rights of the Bengali majority. Later Mujib would tell several West Pakistani political leaders that he had been "incensed at Bhutto's arrogance and presumptuousness, at his cavalier attitude toward a constitutional settlement."[79]

Bhutto defended himself against these charges by falling back on the language of a "One-United West Pakistan"—a scheme he had strongly opposed in the 1950s—to argue that conceding the Bengalis' right to rule went against the spirit of constitutional "parity" between the country's two wings.[80] But his offer to reach a settlement with Mujib, which would have left East and West Pakistan under the respective control of their dominant parties, based on the formula "*Idhar hum, udhar tum*" ("Us here, you there"), was denounced as a cynical ploy to satisfy his thirst for power.[81]

Meanwhile, Pakistan's military action and the civil insurrection in East Pakistan triggered a major humanitarian crisis. The conflict resulted in the deaths of thousands of civilians and forced an estimated four million Bengali refugees to flee to India. Their arrival and the risk of political instability along its northeastern border prompted India to intervene and end the crisis by force. In early December full-scale hostilities erupted between the two countries, resulting in an unqualified military victory for India. Pakistan lost a third of its army and surrendered more than ninety thousand of its troops, who were taken as prisoners of war. On December 16, East Pakistan declared its independence as the republic of Bangladesh.[82]

Controversy over Bhutto's questionable conduct in precipitating the conflict was soon overwhelmed by the much larger crisis that now engulfed the truncated state of Pakistan and especially its most powerful institution—the army. Its military defeat and widespread popular anger against the high command offered Bhutto a golden opportunity to claim the supreme position that he had coveted for so long. On December 20, 1971, he returned home from New York, where he had been delegated to represent Pakistan at the United Nations, to assume the post of president and chief martial law administrator; he would be named prime minister in 1973.

It is somewhat ironic that among the first tasks facing Bhutto, who had come to be known for his famous threat to wage "a thousand years' war against India," was to make peace. In July 1972 he flew to Simla to meet the Indian prime minister, Indira Gandhi, and to sign an agreement that committed both sides to settle their differences through "bilateral negotiations" and to respect the 1971 cease-fire line in Kashmir as a new "line of control" (LOC). Although the agreement raised fears that Bhutto had compromised Pakistan's long-held position on Kashmir as an international rather than a bilateral issue, and that by accepting the new LOC he had effectively recognized the status quo in Kashmir, Bhutto moved swiftly to crush the speculation. Rejecting claims that he had been forced to negotiate from a position of weakness, he told the National Assembly that he had in fact triumphed by refusing Indian pressure to sign a "no war pact" and to accord recognition to Bangladesh. The National Assembly accepted his argument and endorsed his position; it voted unanimously in favor of the Simla Agreement and chose in the process to overlook Bhutto's failure to persuade India to release ninety-three thousand Pakistani prisoners of war still in its custody.[83]

In early 1973 Bhutto was confronted with a serious challenge from the pro-Pashtun National Awami Party (NAP), which headed the provincial governments in the North West Frontier Province (now Khyber-Pakhtunkhwa) and Baluchistan. It demanded greater provincial autonomy—a demand Bhutto met with derision. But fearing that the threat posed to his power could intensify, he used the full might of the state to crush the dissenters and to dismiss the provincial governments. In 1975 he took the ultimate step of formally banning the NAP, which, ironically, much like Mujib's Awami League, shared Bhutto's broadly secular and left-of-center economic programs. Even in Punjab, where he enjoyed solid support, Bhutto's authoritarian style of leadership took its toll when he appeared to endorse the callous methods employed against political dissidents by local PPP bosses, leaving his erstwhile comrades angered and dispirited. He summed up the growing mood of disenchantment in a memo in August 1973, noting: "Pistols to the right of us, pistols to the left of us, pistols all around us."[84]

Rural Sindh—the bastion of the PPP—alone stood by him. Here Bhutto's land reforms had been popular, and his strong support for the promotion of Sindhi language and culture were widely welcomed. But his decision to elevate Sindhi to the status of an official language also created bitter divisions. The acrimony was particularly sharp between native Sindhi speakers and the powerful, mainly urban-based Urdu-speaking elite in the province, commonly known as *mohajirs* (migrants), who represented Muslims who had arrived from India after Partition. They were resentful of Bhutto's attempts to strengthen a more territorially defined expression of Pakistani identity based on regional "folk" cultures, which they feared would dilute the nexus between Urdu as "a Muslim language" and Pakistan's distinctive Islamic personality.

Bhutto was sensitive to these concerns. But he was also aware that the separation of East Pakistan, which had called into question the country's founding ideology, demanded a fundamental reappraisal of Pakistan's raison d'être. One of the ways he sought to address this dilemma was to emphasize that Pakistan was a territorial rather than an ideological construct. Traditions grounded in regional cultures gradually replaced the language of Islam as the dominant features of an evolving Pakistani identity. Bhutto's advocacy of the folk cultures of Pakistan, especially of his native Sindh, was an expression of this endeavor. However, the contradictions between his defense of Sindhi identity and his earlier disregard of Bengali rights, as well as his subsequent treatment of demands for greater Baloch and Pashtun autonomy, clearly escaped him. He fell back on the language he had once used to oppose the "One-Unit" scheme and argued that respect for diverse regional identities, which privileged land, language, and culture, most faithfully reflected the original vision of Pakistan as a coherent multicultural nation. The new constitution promulgated in 1973, for which he was widely credited as the author, sought to embody these values by granting far-reaching political and cultural rights to Pakistan's federating units.

It is perhaps no coincidence that this emphasis on regions and territories as the defining features of Bhutto's "new Pakistan" should have converged neatly with his growing interest in locating Pakistan more firmly as an integral part of the larger continent of Asia. But the discourse of Islam was still too pronounced a feature of Pakistan[85] for Bhutto to ignore it completely or to be indifferent to its potential to serve as political capital. The opportunity presented itself at a star forum of Islamic luminaries where Bhutto hoped to burn brightest. The event—the second pan-Islamic summit held in Lahore in February 1974—was attended by more than thirty-eight Muslim heads of state and served as Bhutto's grandest stage yet. His purpose was twofold: to advertise his personal dedication to the cause of Islam and neutralize critics who accused him of "godless socialism"; and to widen the basis of the grand coalition of the Third World he hoped one day to lead by extending it to the Muslim world.[86]

The basis of this new coalition combined a radical economic strategy with a broad commitment to values that, he declared, were best mediated by Pakistan and, by extension, Bhutto himself. "The Third World," he stated,

> has emphasized, time and again, that poverty and affluence cannot co-exist. . . . The [Arab-Israeli] war of last October [1973] has, however, precipitated a chain of events and created an environment in which the developing countries can at last hope to secure the establishment of a more equitable economic order. . . . This may well be a watershed in history. . . . The Third World can now participate in the economic and financial councils of the world on an equal footing with the developed world.[87]

Bhutto himself bid for leadership of this new coalition by seeking to portray Pakistan as the perfect embodiment of the link between East and West. With a flourish that drew on his interpretation of Quranic verses, he observed: "In being called the midmost nation or the People of the Middle, we [Muslims] are charged with the mission of mediating conflicts." Pakistan, as a state neatly poised between East and West Asia, was best placed to assume this leadership and bridge the gap between the "materialistic West" and the "spiritual East." For, as he reminded his audience, "Islam rejects such dichotomies. . . . [A] true Muslim is at once Eastern and Western, materialistic and spiritual."[88]

This pointed engagement with the discourse of Islam was, of course, nothing new to Bhutto. As a young man he had been emotionally swayed by the fervor of pan-Islamism and later as Pakistan's foreign minister had vigorously advocated Muslim causes from Algerian independence to Palestinian self-determination. However, Bhutto's fresh emphasis on Pakistan's putative Islamic purpose must be understood in the context of mounting controversy at home, where he faced criticism from religious parties, which accused him of eroding Pakistan's Islamic identity by promoting a secular agenda. Bhutto had responded by ensuring that his new constitution consolidated the Islamic character of the state by making it mandatory for both the head of state and the head of government to be Muslim. In 1974, under pressure from pro-Islamic parties, he gave his consent to a measure with lasting repercussions—the declaration of members of the country's heterodox Ahmadi community as non-Muslims, stripping them of the rights reserved for Muslim citizens. The recognition of Bangladesh, which was universally opposed by religious parties, also weighed heavily on Bhutto who was keen to normalize relations with the new state. The Islamic summit with its high rhetoric of Muslim solidarity gave him the sanction he needed by disarming his critics who claimed that recognizing Bangladesh would be tantamount to damaging Pakistan's Islamic founding ideology.

As part of this showcasing of the country's Islamic identity, Bhutto sought the backing of the rich Muslim states of the Middle East to finance the development of a nuclear weapons program for Pakistan. The explosion of a nuclear device by India in May 1974 had shocked Bhutto, who vowed his people would "eat grass" rather than be the victim of India's "nuclear blackmail." The Islamic summit served as an opportunity to garner support and harden his defiant stance against India. Claiming that the Muslim world was entitled to its own "Islamic bomb," he later recalled his reasons for appealing to his Muslim partners:

> The Christian, Jewish and Hindu civilizations have this [nuclear] capability. The Communist powers also possess it. Only the Islamic civilization was without it, but that position was about to change.[89]

This newfound dedication to the cause of Islam did not deflect Bhutto from his long-standing engagement with the question of Asia's under-development. His phrase "the myth of independence" was designed precisely to show how political independence, whether for Pakistan or for any other developing country, would amount to little unless these countries also found the means to break free from the shackles of poverty and inequality. For Bhutto those means lay in the radical ideologies of the Left. Their early appeal during his days as an idealis-tic young student abroad had matured and had now come to exercise a decisive influence on him as he worked for Pakistan to take its place in the Asian struggle for a more equitable global order.

The evolution in Bhutto's thinking was reflected in two key articles written in 1976, when, as Pakistan's prime minister, he took the lead in calling for a fresh approach to address the disparity between rich and poor nations.[90] Its success, he argued, would depend upon recog-nizing the "imperative of unity" among developing countries. The aim was to highlight the imbalances of the *global economic order* rather than to emphasize the power relations of the *global political order* with their concomitant system of "alignments" and "non-alignments."[91] While he acknowledged the contribution of the nonaligned movement in keeping alive issues of economic justice at the international level, Bhutto criticized it for sapping "the collective strength of the Third World" by excluding a large number of developing countries.[92] Differ-ences in political systems and "external outlook," he argued, could no longer be allowed to stand in the way of "our common struggle against exploitation. . . . On this issue there is no division between the so-called aligned and the so-called non-aligned; there exists only the difference between the developed and the underdeveloped."[93]

These concerns, especially the urgency to rethink the question of "non-alignment" as the defining principle of Afro-Asian foreign pol-icy, resurfaced in Bhutto's ideas for a policy of "bilateralism."[94] It in-volved building relations between two states without prejudice to a third—a policy, Bhutto believed, that all Afro-Asian countries, the "aligned and the non-aligned," could readily subscribe to. It was justified by international changes, which Bhutto claimed spelled the end of "bipolarity," that is to say, the rivalry between the United States and the Soviet Union. Among the changes he pointed to was the creation of the United Nations, the end of Western colonialism, and, most significantly, the rise of China. The emergence of these countervailing forces, Bhutto suggested, had made nonalignment redundant. While he recognized that nonalignment had served a useful purpose as "a balancing force," there was

> a canker in the rose ... generated by the assumed or professed leadership of the group on non-aligned states by one or more powers that have sought to use non-alignment as a lever for their own diplomacy in pursuance of their own chauvinistic ends.[95]

The man he held responsible for arrogating to himself this mantle of leadership was none other than Nehru. His "historic contribution" and "enduring service to peace," Bhutto argued, would have remained intact had Nehru not

> sought to graft on the [nonaligned] movement the tendency to hammer away at other Third World countries that had chosen, for compelling reasons, to be aligned with one or other of the great powers.[96]

But most damaging of all to Nehru's legacy, Bhutto claimed, was

> the lamentable fact that India engaged itself in a major international dispute with its neighbour Pakistan [in 1971], in which it actively sought, and depended upon, the support of a superpower [the Soviet Union through the 1971 Indo-Soviet Treaty of Friendship].[97]

Against the background of the divisions caused by the abuse of nonalignment, Bhutto now proposed a fresh and more inclusive response that he hoped would "be perceived as an enlargement and evolution, and not as a negation, of the concept of non-alignment."[98] The key lay in "bilateralism"—a concept he freely admitted to drawing from Pakistan's own experience. It held that vulnerable countries in Afro-Asia, which needed to protect their national interest by formal alliances with great powers, could, if necessary, do so without compromising the larger cause of Afro-Asian unity. Pakistan served as a model. Its alliance with the United States, while intrinsically consistent with Pakistan's self-interest [was] untainted by any dishonourable motive, [was] directed against no other power's legitimate interests and [did] not fetter Pakistan's standpoints nor hamper its loyalty to the causes of Asia and Africa.[99]

Here then was the moral high ground occupied by Pakistan. India, by contrast, stood condemned for its "plot" to reincorporate Pakistan in 1947 and for its "invasion" of East Pakistan in 1971. By highlighting these differences, Bhutto hoped to make a compelling case for his and his country's claim to honorably steer a united Asia.[100]

However, the growing opposition to Bhutto at home soon drowned out these high-minded ideals. By early 1977, it was clear that Bhutto faced not only the wrath of pro-Islamic religious parties, but also widespread disaffection within the very constituencies that had once supported him. His economic policies, which had led to the large-scale nationalization of hundreds of private enterprises, alienated his supporters among the urban middle classes, including businessmen and small traders, who had grown increasingly hostile to his style of politics.[101] Meanwhile, the perception that he had used his populist policies to tighten his personal grip on power lost him the backing of the professional classes and students, who were once among his key defenders.[102] His attempts to reform Pakistan's overextended bureaucracy, his reliance on the security forces to enforce compliance, and his decision to turn to a largely discredited rural coalition of wealthy landlords to shore up his government, all contributed to his sagging popularity.

In a surprise move Bhutto announced fresh elections for March 1977. They were won, rather too handsomely, by the PPP, which gained control of 155 out of 200 seats in the National Assembly. The results were immediately contested by opposition parties, which alleged widespread electoral malpractice and called for Bhutto's resignation. Although most observers had expected that, despite stiff opposition, the PPP would win a majority of seats, many were taken aback by the scale of the ruling party's gains.[103] Even Bhutto is said to have experienced a sense of "deep foreboding" on that long election night of "ballot-stuffing and re-stuffing, of counting and re-counting and discounting."[104] The weeks that followed were marred by violent protests, which Bhutto sought to calm, to no avail, by agreeing to a dialogue with opposition parties to negotiate a political settlement. In what was seen by many as a desperate attempt to curry favor with the pro-Islamic lobby, he also announced a series of "Islamic measures" that banned alcohol and prohibited gambling.

By June 1977 it was clear that the breakdown of trust between Bhutto and the opposition was irreversible. Bhutto himself had come to believe that he was the victim of a conspiracy orchestrated by the United States, which was working to engineer his downfall and prevent Pakistan from emerging as a nuclear-armed and independent Islamic state. Neither factor was cited as a cause of the bloodless military coup led by the army chief General Zia ul Haq, who finally deposed Bhutto on July 5, 1977. Instead, in keeping with time-honored traditions that had justified earlier military coups in Pakistan, Zia blamed quarreling politicians for setting back the process of democracy. More than two years would elapse before Bhutto, arrested and facing charges of murdering a political opponent, was found guilty by the courts and sentenced to death. Appeals for clemency at home and abroad were rejected by General Zia on grounds that justice had been done to a man of whom he was quoted by Roedad Khan, a close confidante and member of his inner circle, to have said: "It is either his [Bhutto's] neck or mine."[105] In an interview some years later with Bhutto's biographer, Stanley Wolpert, Khan also claimed Zia had said: "I have not convicted him, and if they hold him guilty, my God, I am not going to let him off."[106]

IX

Although Bhutto's foreign policy prescriptions, notably his tireless campaign to lay the foundations of a long-lasting and productive Sino-Pakistan alliance, broke new ground, they clearly failed to stem the tidal wave of domestic opposition that eventually brought him down. The loss of key international allies (both Mao Zedong and Zhou Enlai had died within months of each other in 1976), the indifference of conservative Arab leaders wary of Bhutto's radical discourse, and Bhutto's profound differences with the United States over the development of Pakistan's nuclear weapons program appeared to seal his fate. When he was led to the gallows in April 1979, there were no protests to mark the brutal end of a man whose extraordinary political career had touched the lives of millions. Yet, more than thirty years later, it is Bhutto's legacy that remains an index of the sense of self-worth many Pakistanis believe they and their country are entitled to. It also serves of course as a poignant reminder of just how far Pakistan has moved away from that legacy.

A key part of this legacy was to affirm Pakistan's national autonomy by freeing it from dependence on foreign powers. This, Bhutto argued, called for a more multifaceted foreign policy that would help ease pressure on small states like Pakistan and prevent them from becoming party to the ideological confrontation between superpowers. Today little remains of that legacy, compromised as it is by decades of Pakistan's active role as a "front-line state" in the service of the United States and its allies in the war against "Soviet communism" and, more recently, against "terror." However, Bhutto's influence lingers on in one important respect, namely, in the steady expansion of Pakistan's remarkable relationship with China. Its significance for Pakistan lies not only in demonstrating the country's power to diversify its foreign relations if it should so choose, but in securing for Pakistan an enduring presence in Asia. Both were fundamental components of Bhutto's legacy and both continue to define Pakistan.

Bhutto's quest for a clearly defined "Asian Pakistan" has proved to be more difficult to realize. Ultimately, he was defeated by the contestation over Pakistan's identity and the still-unresolved conflict between Pakistan's "native" roots in Asia and its "ideational" sources in "Islam." Bhutto's attempt to project Pakistan as a territorial entity grounded in local regional histories and cultures rather than as an ideological construct informed by Islam represented a bold move to privilege his country's Asian identity. Yet, he was unable to forge a viable political consensus in support of his vision. And while the discourse of underdevelopment and Third World solidarity may have helped him to gloss over this incipient tension, the ever-present appeal of Islam as a key component of Pakistan's ideology meant that Bhutto was forced to moderate his call for pan-Asian unity with a plea to deepen his country's ties to a global Muslim community.

Bhutto was of course complicit in accentuating this tension and in contributing to the erosion of his legacy. While his ideas of economic equality and justice offered a powerful alternative in reimagining Pakistan's national purpose, he lacked the political will to reorient his discourse and make it a reality. For even as he sought to free Pakistani nationalism from a rigid adherence to the narrative of Islam, he proceeded to reanchor it in that very discourse by casting "Islamic socialism" as the guiding principle of his new national polity.

In Pakistan today, Bhutto is chiefly remembered—especially among the younger generation—for launching a tradition of dynastic politics that has arguably deepened their country's national malaise. The fact that his daughter, Benazir Bhutto, and son-in-law, Asif Ali Zardari, have both been at the helm of power for extended periods and that his grandson, Bilawal Bhutto, is being actively groomed to succeed them has reinforced the impression that Bhutto's contribution lay primarily in ensuring the political dominance of his family. Yet, as shown here, his larger-than-life personality and the sheer scale of his ambition also made him a thinker and politician of considerable originality and daring, whose views and policies were compelling to some yet distasteful to others.

NOTES

ACKNOWLEDGMENTS

NOTES ON CONTRIBUTORS

CREDITS

INDEX

NOTES

INTRODUCTION

1. Y. R. Chao, "With Bertrand Russell in China," available at http://digital commons.mcmaster.ca/cgi/viewcontent.cgi?article=1706&context=russelljournal.

2. Bertrand Russell, *The Problem of China* (1922; repr. London: George Allen and Unwin, 1966), 9.

3. Ibid., 77–78, 166–167.

4. Ibid., 241ff. See also Peter Zarrow, "'The Problem of China': A Revisitation," *China Beat* (blog), November 25, 2008, http://thechinabeat.blogspot .in/2008/11/problem-of-china-revisitation.html.

5. For a sampling of the now numerous works in this genre, see Kishore Mahbubani, *The New Asian Hemisphere: The Irresistible Shift of Global Power to the East* (New York: Public Affairs, 2008); Fareed Zakaria, *The Post-American World* (New York: W. W. Norton, 2009); Martin Jacques, *When China Rules the World: The Rise of the Middle Kingdom and the End of the Western World* (London: Penguin, 2011).

6. Stephen N. Hay, *Asian Ideas of East and West: Tagore and His Critics in Japan, China, and India* (Cambridge, MA: Harvard University Press, 1970).

7. George McTurnan Kahin, *Nationalism and Revolution in Indonesia* (Ithaca, NY: Cornell University Press, 1952); John K. Fairbank, *The United States and China* (Cambridge, MA: Harvard University Press, 1948); Stanley Wolpert, *Tilak and Gokhale: Reform and Revolution in the Making of Modern India* (Berkeley: University of California Press, 1963).

1. GANDHI, INDIA, AND THE WORLD

1. On the broader political and historical background to this ordinance, see Bala Pillay, *British Indians in the Transvaal: Trade, Politics and Imperial Relations, 1885–1906* (London: Longman, 1976), and Iqbal Narain, *The Politics of*

Racialism: A Study of the Indian Minority in South Africa down to the Gandhi-Smuts Agreement (Delhi: Shiva Lal Agarwal and Co., 1962).

2. This account of the September 11 meeting is based on reports in *Indian Opinion*, September 15 and 22, 1906; *Collected Works of Mahatma Gandhi* (New Delhi: Publications Division, 1958–2004, hereafter CWMG), 5: 419–423, 439–443; *Natal Mercury*, September 12, 1906.

3. *Times*, November 10, 1906.

4. News reports in L/P&J/R/5/118, India Office Records, Asia and Pacific Collections, British Library, London.

5. CWMG, 12: 602–603; Robert A. Huttenback, *Gandhi in South Africa* (Ithaca, NY: Cornell University Press, 1971), 319–321.

6. See *Report of the Indian Enquiry Commission* (Cape Town: Government Printers, 1914).

7. Amales Tripathi, *The Extremist Challenge: India between 1890 and 1910* (Bombay: Orient Longman, 1967); Peter Heehs, *The Bomb in Bengal: The Rise of Revolutionary Terrorism in India, 1900–1910* (Delhi: Oxford University Press, 1993).

8. For more on Gandhi's debt to Tolstoy, see Ramachandra Guha, *Gandhi before India* (London: Allen Lane, 2013), 286–289, 337–340.

9. H. J. Wolstenholme to Smuts, May 14, 1909, in W. K. Hancock and Jean van der Poel, eds., *Selections from the Smuts Papers: Volume II: June 1902–May 1910* (Cambridge: Cambridge University Press, 1966), 568–573.

10. Gandhi to G. A. Natesan, c. October 30, 1909, CWMG, 9: 506–507.

11. CWMG, 12: 213–314.

12. Jacques Pouchepadass, *Champaran and Gandhi: Planters, Peasants, and Gandhian Politics* (New Delhi: Oxford University Press, 1999); David Hardiman, *Peasant Nationalists of Gujarat* (New Delhi: Oxford University Press, 1981).

13. Ravinder Kumar, ed., *Essays on Gandhian Politics: The Rowlatt Satyagraha of 1919* (Oxford: Clarendon Press, 1971).

14. Gail Minault, *The Khilafat Movement: Religious Symbolism and Political Mobilization in India* (New York: Columbia University Press, 1982).

15. Sumit Sarkar, *Popular Movements and Middle Class Leadership in Late Colonial India* (Calcutta: K. P. Bagchi and Sons, 1983).

16. CWMG, 12: 416.

17. Shahid Amin, "Gandhi as Mahatma: Gorakhpur District, Eastern UP, 1921–2," in Ranajit Guha, ed., *Subaltern Studies III* (New Delhi: Oxford University Press, 1984).

18. CWMG, 42: 398–399.

19. Thomas Weber, *On the Salt March* (New Delhi: HarperCollins India, 1998).

20. M. R. Phatak, ed., *Source Material for a History of the Freedom Movement in India: Volume III: Mahatma Gandhi, Part III, 1929–1931* (Bombay: Government of Maharashtra, 1969), 11.

21. *Time Magazine*, March 24–May 5, 1930.

22. R. J. Moore, *Churchill, Cripps, and India, 1939–45* (Oxford: Clarendon Press, 1979).

23. Gyanendra Pandey, ed., *The Indian Revolution in 1942* (Calcutta: K. P. Bagchi and Sons, 1988); Francis G. Hutchins, *Spontaneous Revolution: Gandhi and the Quit India Movement* (New Delhi: Manohar, 1973).

24. Dhananjay Keer, *Veer Savarkar* (Bombay: Popular Prakashan, 1966).

25. Walter Andersen and Shridhar D. Damle, *The Brotherhood in Saffron: The Rashtriya Swayamsewak Sangh and Hindu Revivalism* (Boulder, CO: Westview Press, 1987); D. R. Goyal, *Rashtriya Swayamsewak Sangh* (Delhi: Radhakrishna Prakashan, 2000).

26. Peter Hardy, *The Muslims of British India* (Cambridge: Cambridge University Press, 1972).

27. Presidential Address to the annual session of the All-India Muslim League, Lahore, March 23, 1940, in Jamil-ud-din Ahmad, ed., *Some Recent Speeches and Writings of Mr. Jinnah,* 4th ed. (Lahore: S. Muhammad Ashraf, 1946), 176–180. There are many biographies of Jinnah, of which the best remains Stanley Wolpert's *Jinnah of Pakistan* (Delhi: Oxford University Press, 1985).

28. Eleanor Zelliot, *From Untouchable to Dalit: Essays on the Dalit Movement* (New Delhi: Manohar, 2001); Valerian Rodrigues, ed., *The Essential Writings of B. R. Ambedkar* (New Delhi: Oxford University Press, 2002).

29. K. T. Shah, "Principles of National Planning," in Iqbal Singh and Raja Rao, eds., *Whither India?* (Baroda: Padmaja Publications, 1948); Nariaki Nakatozo, "The Transfer of Economic Power in India: Indian Big Business, the British Raj, and Development Planning, 1930–1948," in Mushirul Hasan and Nariaki Nakatozo, eds., *The Unfinished Agenda: Nation-Building in South Asia* (Delhi: Manohar, 2011).

30. The locus classicus of this view remains R. P. Dutt, *India Today* (London: Victor Gollancz, 1940).

31. A useful overview of the last years of British rule is Sucheta Mahajan, *Independence and Partition: The Erosion of Colonial Power in India* (New Delhi: Sage Publications, 2000).

32. D. G. Tendulkar, *Mahatma: Life of Mohandas Karamchand Gandhi* (2nd ed., 1963; repr. New Delhi: Publications Division, 1990), 8:112.

33. CWMG, 90: 495–496.

34. Rajni Bakshi, *Bapu Kuti: Journeys in Rediscovery of Gandhi* (New Delhi: Penguin India, 1998).

35. Sudarshan Kapur, *Raising Up a Prophet: The African-American Encounter with Gandhi* (Boston: Beacon Press, 1992); Nico Slate, *Coloured Cosmopolitanism: The Shared Struggle for Freedom in the United States and India* (Cambridge, MA: Harvard University Press, 2012).

36. Anil Nauriya, *The African Element in Gandhi* (New Delhi: National Gandhi Museum, 2006); Mary Benson, *The African Patriots: The Story of the African National Congress of South Africa* (Chicago: Encyclopaedia Britannica Press, 1964); E. S. Reddy and Fatima Meer, eds., *Passive Resistance 1946: A Selection of Documents* (Durban: Institute of Black Research, 1996); Leo Kuper, *Passive Resistance in South Africa* (New Haven, CT: Yale University Press, 1957).

37. Speech by Oliver Tambo in New Delhi on November 14, 1980, copy in Accession Number 1995-M-129, Box 3, E. S. Reddy Papers, Yale University; Nelson Mandela, *Long Walk to Freedom* (London: Little, Brown and Company, 1994), 97–98 and passim; "Mandela and Gandhi on the Hill," http://www.southafrica.info/mandela/mandela-gandhi.htm. See also André Brink, "Mahatma Gandhi Today," in his *Writing in a State of Siege* (New York: Summit Books, 1983).

38. Quoted in Peter Popham, *The Lady and the Peacock: The Life of Aung San Suu Kyi* (London: Rider, 2011), 90.

39. CWMG, 35: 461.

40. Ibid., 37: 243.

41. Ibid., 31: 478.

42. Ibid., 59: 187.

43. Ramachandra Guha, *How Much Should a Person Consume? Environmentalism in India and the United States* (Berkeley: University of California Press, 2006); Ramachandra Guha, *Environmentalism: A Global History* (New York: Addison Wesley Longman, 2001).

44. *Transvaal Leader*, January 13 and 15, 1908.

45. Leung Quinn, "A Chinese View of the Transvaal Trouble," *Indian Review*, June 1910.

46. See Edgar Snow, *Red Star Over China* (New York: Grove Press, 1968), 94.

47. Liu Xiabao, *No Enemies, No Hatred: Selected Essays and Poems*, ed. Perry Link, Tienchi Martin-Liao, and Liu Xia (Cambridge, MA: Harvard University Press, 2012), 288.

2. CHIANG KAI-SHEK AND CHINESE MODERNIZATION

1. Mao Zedong also cut off his pigtail at eighteen.

2. As early as 1924, the perceived value in China of a Japanese education had become "quite low." Between 1854 and 1953, 20,906 Chinese were educated in the United States—most in engineering. Y. C. Wang, *Chinese Intellectuals and the West, 1872–1949* (Chapel Hill: University of North Carolina Press, 1966), 119–120.

3. Qin Xiaoyi, ed., *Zong Tong Jiang gong da shi chang pain chu gao* [Preliminary draft of President Chiang's Chronological Biography], 12 vols. (Taipei: Chung Chang Cultural and Educational Foundation, 1978), 5: 1857. When World War II began, the Indian National Congress refused to support the United Kingdom in the war effort until it promised full independence, but it did not sabotage that effort.

4. Or as usually referred to, the "Three People's Principles."

5. Sun Zhongshan (Sun Yat-sen), *Guo fu zhuanshu* [Complete works of the Founding Father of the Republic] (Taipei: Institute of National Defense, 1960), 798–799; Pichon P. Y. Loh, *The Early Chiang Kai-shek: A Study of His Personality and Politics, 1887–1924* (New York: Columbia University Press, 1971), 36–38.

6. Loh, *Early Chiang*, 60–65.

7. Japan continued to rule Taiwan as it had since the 1895 Sino-Japanese War and its seizure of the island.

8. Chiang Kai-shek, *China's Destiny and Chinese Economic Theory* (New York: Roy Publishers, 1947), 231.

9. Ibid., 96, 146, 233, 235.

10. Morris L. Bian, *The Making of the State Enterprise System in Modern China* (Cambridge, MA: Harvard University Press, 2005), 46, 51–53.

11. In the second year of the war, Wang would defect to Japan.

12. William C. Kirby, *Germany and Republican China* (Stanford, CA: Stanford University Press, 1984), 3.

13. Arthur N. Young, *China and the Helping Hand, 1937–1945* (Cambridge, MA: Harvard University Press, 1963), 4.

14. Kirby, *Germany*, 86

15. Utilizing its share of the "Boxer Indemnity," the US government provided scholarships to 1,300 Chinese students for study in the United States. See Young, *Helping Hand*, 4, and Wang, *Intellectuals*, 177. By 1937, 75 percent of returned Western-trained engineers and others were employed in key positions in government and business. Wang, *Intellectuals*, 174.

16. Bian, *Enterprise*, 48–53.

17. Kirby, *Germany*, 206.

18. Bian, *Enterprise*, 73.

19. Fifty thousand were combat planes. Walter J. Boyne, ed., *Air Warfare, An International Encyclopedia* (Santa Barbara, CA: ABC-CLIO Inc., 2002), 433.

20. Bian, *Enterprise*, 32.

21. Kirby, *Germany*, 77.

22. The term "Nanjing Decade" generally refers to the period 1927–1937 in all of the Republic of China, including Nationalist-, warlord-, Communist-, and Japanese-controlled areas.

23. Wang, *Intellectuals,* 434–435.

24. Kirby, *Germany,* 79.

25. Zhaojin Ji, *A History of Modern Shanghai Banking* (Armonk, NY: M. E. Sharpe, 2003), 174–178.

26. F. F. Liu, *A Military History of China, 1924–1949* (Princeton, NJ: Princeton University Press, 1956), 101–102.

27. Young, *Helping Hand,* 5–9.

28. Parks M. Coble Jr., *The Shanghai Capitalists and the Nationalist Government, 1927–1937* (Cambridge, MA: Harvard University Press, 1986), 172–205. Coble, pp. xi–xiv, cites Lloyd E. Eastman, "New Insights into the Nature of the Nationalist Regime," *Republican China* 9, no. 2 (February 1984): 8–18. Also see Ji, *Modern Shanghai Banking,* 140–160.

29. Ji, *Modern Shanghai Banking,* 176.

30. Coble, *Capitalists,* 244–245.

31. Ibid., 208, 232–233.

32. Ibid., 1–11.

33. Arthur N. Young, *China's Wartime Finance and Inflation, 1937—1945* (Cambridge MA: Harvard University Press 1965), 5.

34. Kirby, *Germany,* 210.

35. Of the ten projects: one involved the construction of the Central Steel mill; three had to do with mining and processing of strategic minerals; one was concerned with iron mining and a copper smelting and refinery plant; one aimed at coal mining in five locales; another planned the construction of a coal liquification plant and development of oil fields at four sites; one focused on the mining and processing of zinc, lead, and copper; one was committed to the manufacture of chemicals for munitions manufacture and a plant to produce alcohol for fuel mixtures; one was scheduled for construction of a machine manufacturing works to build engines as well as entire power plants and machine tool plants; and finally the last was programed to build a factory assigned to make electric wire, light bulbs, vacuum tubes, telephone equipment, electrodes, etc. All the projects were part of the Sino-German economic exchange. Kirby, *Germany,* 206–217.

36. Bian, *Enterprise,* 63–64.

37. Chiang explained this theory years later to General George Marshall. Larry I. Bland, *Papers of George Catlett Marshall* (Baltimore: Johns Hopkins University Press, 2003), 5:750–751.

38. Chiang Kai-shek, *China's Destiny and Chinese Economic Theory,* 259.

39. Kirby, *Germany,* 79.

40. Young, *Helping Hand,* 40.

41. See the National Palace Museum's website at http://www.npm.gov.tw.

42. Young, *Helping Hand,* 30–33.

43. Young, *Finance,* 349, table 49.

44. Ibid., 356, table 58.

45. Bian, *Enterprise,* 166.

46. William Kirby, "The Nationalist Experience," in Denis Fred Simon and Merle Goldman, eds., *Science and Technology in Post-Mao China* (Cambridge, MA: Harvard University Press, 1989).

47. Bian, e-mail to author, January 2013.

48. Bian, *Enterprise,* 153–179.

49. Ibid., 34–33.

50. Ibid., 153, 160–161, 166.

51. Ibid., 52–54, 63, 65, 70, 95.

52. Ibid., 61.

53. Ibid., 43–44.

54. Ibid., 56.

55. Ironically, the intelligence came from the Soviet spy in Tokyo, Richard Sorge, who knew the chief of Chiang's personal security, Walthur Stennis, and visited him at least once in Chongqing. Stennis, it turned out, was also a KGB spy. Stalin believed neither Sorge nor Chiang. Jerrold Schecter and Leona Schecter, *Sacred Secret* (Washington, DC: Brassey's, 2002), 15–16.

56. The money went to build airfields and provide food, housing, and other services in support of what would eventually consist of thirty thousand American military personnel.

57. Young, *Helping Hand,* 351, 403, 442.

58. Herbert Feis, *The China Triangle: The American Effort in China from Pearl Harbor to the Marshall Mission* (Princeton, NJ: Princeton University Press, 1953), 195, 204.

59. A prediction made in a conversation with General George Marshall. Bland, *Papers,* 5:751–752; *Foreign Relations of the United States,* vol. 10, *The Far East: China* (Washington, DC: US Government Printing Office, 1946), 315.

60. For example, PLA offices in North Korea employed two thousand railcars to transship Soviet military material to PLA forces in Manchuria. Michael M. Sheng, *Battling Western Imperialism: Mao, Stalin, and the United States* (Princeton, NJ: Princeton University Press, 1997), 155–156. See also Yang Kweisong's definitive *Mao Zedong yu Mosike de enen yuanyuan* [Mao and Moscow: Favors and grievances] (Nanchang: Jiangxi People's Press, 1999), 157–163, 184, 190, 191–195.

61. American Embassy Airgram, A-29, September 30, 1967, National Archives RG59, /50/65/6, shelf 4, 1967–1969, China Policy File, China box 1984.

62. According to later Taiwan Government figures, in the infamous "2/28 Incident" on Taiwan and its aftermath, some 28,000 Taiwanese were killed.

63. Chiang Diaries, Hoover Institution, Stanford, December 25, 30, 1949, box 47, folder 20.

64. *Far Eastern Economic Review* 8, no. 4 (January 26, 1950): 116; ibid., 9, no. 11 (September 14, 1950): 307. After six months of free exchange, Chiang set a limit on the weekly purchase of gold.

65. *Far Eastern Economic Review* 27, no. 15 (October 8, 1959): 585.

66. The JCRR worked briefly on the mainland, then moved to Taiwan in 1949, where it supervised the land reform program, agricultural improvement, and educational and health projects.

67. From 1962 to 1965, when I served as a young US diplomat in Taipei, my job was to get to know the native Taiwanese community and report on their leaders, conditions, complaints, political activity, and opinions. It was widely recognized by most politically aware Taiwanese at the time, including oppositionists, that Chiang had gained significant popularity in the rural areas.

68. Taiwan Cement Corporation, Taiwan Pulp & Paper Corporation, Taiwan Tea Corporation, and Taiwan Industry and Mining Corporation

69. Murray A. Rubenstein, ed., *Taiwan, A New History* (Armonk, NY: M. E. Sharpe, 1999), 327.

70. Chiang Diaries, Hoover, June 3 and August 30, 31, 1951, box 49, folder 2, September 31 and October 11, 31, 1951, box 49, folder 4.

71. Richard Hughes, "Portrait of Chiang on his Mountain Top," *New York Times Magazine,* September 28, 1958.

72. Chiang Diaries, Hoover, March 11, 17, 31 and April 6, 1953, box 50, folder 15.

73. Bruce Dickson, "Lessons of Retreat: The Reorganization of the Kuomintang on Taiwan, 1950–1952," *China Quarterly* 133 (March 1993): 63.

74. Ibid., 64, 68.

75. Hung Mao-tien, *Great Transition: Political and Social Change in the Republic of China* (Stanford, CA: Hoover Institution Press, 1989), 23.

76. Peter Chen-main Wang, "A Bastion Created, a Regime Reformed, an Economy Reengineered, 1949–1970," in Murray A. Rubenstein, ed., *Taiwan: A New History* (Armonk, NY: M. E. Sharpe, 1999), 325.

77. Ibid., 331–335.

78. The indirect evidence of Zhou's briefing Chiang on the Washington/Beijing secret discourse is dramatically evident in Chiang's diaries beginning in early 1969. At that time, Chiang understood that Nixon intended to "sell out" Taiwan as the price of détente with the People's Republic. Chiang knew that Nixon was going to Beijing long before that venture or the 1971 Kissinger visit to that city were publicly known. See Jay Taylor, *The Generalissimo: Chiang Kai-shek and the Struggle for Modern China* (Cambridge, MA: Harvard University Press, 2009), 600–607.

79. Min S. Yee, *Boston Globe*, May 6, 1968. The program, penetrated by the CIA, was closed down after Chiang Ching-kuo's death in 1988.

1. The standard biographies of Ho Chi Minh in English are William J. Duiker, *Ho Chi Minh: A Life* (New York: Hyperion, 2000); Pierre Brocheux, *Ho Chi Minh: A Biography* (New York: Cambridge University Press, 2007); Jean Lacouture, *Ho Chi Minh: A Political Biography* (New York: Vintage Books, 1968). My book *Ho Chi Minh: The Missing Years 1919–1941* (London: Christopher Hurst, 2001) is an examination of his pre-power political career.

2. Quinn-Judge, *Ho Chi Minh*, 180–181, 185.

3. Ibid., 184.

4. Ibid., 171.

5. See, for example, David Marr, *Vietnam 1945: The Quest for Power* (Berkeley: University of California Press, 1995), 184–194.

6. David Marr, "Beyond High Politics," in Christopher E. Goscha and Benoit de Tréglodé, eds., *Naissance d'un Etat-Parti: Le Vietnam depuis 1945* [Birth of a party-state: Vietnam since 1945] (Paris: Les Indes Savantes, 2004) 37–46.

7. Ho Chi Minh, *Le procès de la colonisation française* [The trial of French Colonialism] (1925; repr. Pantin: Le Temps des Cerises, 1998).

8. "Declaration of Independence of the Democratic Republic of Viet Nam," in *Breaking our Chains: Documents of the Vietnamese Revolution of August 1945* (Hanoi: Foreign Languages Publishing House, 1960) 94–97.

9. Philippe Devillers, *Histoire du Viet-Nam de 1940 à 1952* [History of Vietnam from 1940 to 1952] (Paris: Editions du Seuil, 1952), 200.

10. Ibid., 220.

11. Ibid., 225.

12. Brocheux, *Ho Chi Minh,* 121.

13. Ibid.

14. Devillers, *Histoire du Viet-Nam,* 306–310.

15. Stein Tonnesson, *1946: Déclenchement de la guerre d'Indochine* [The outbreak of the war in Indochina] (Paris: Editions L'Harmattan, 1987), 37.

16. Devillers, *Histoire du Viet-Nam,* 311.

17. Francois Guillemot, "Au cœur de la fracture vietnamienne: L'élimination de l'opposition nationaliste et anticolonialiste dans le Nord du Vietnam (1945–1946)" [At the heart of the Vietnamese fracture: The elimination of the nationalist, anticolonialist opposition in North Vietnam], in Goscha and de Tréglodé, eds., *Naissance d'un Etat-Parti,* 191–193.

18. Bui Diem, with David Chanoff, *In the Jaws of History* (Boston: Houghton Mifflin Company, 1987), 41.

19. Guillemot, "Au cœur de la fracture vietnamienne," 194–195.

20. Devillers, *Histoire du Viet-Nam,* 312.

21. Ibid.

22. Ibid., 313.

23. Tonnesson, *1946*, 39.

24. *New York Times,* January 11, 1947, 3.

25. *Ho Chi Minh Bien Nien tieu su,* 4 [Ho Chi Minh, Biographical Chronology] *(1946–1950)* (Hanoi : NXB Chinh tri quoc gia, 1994), 27.

26. Ibid., 29.

27. Ibid., 39.

28. Ibid., 31.

29. See Yoki Akashi, "Lai Teck: Secretary General of the Malayan Communist Party, 1939–1947," *Journal of the South Seas Society* 49 (1994): 57–103. This biography resembles that of "Truong Phuoc Dat" as described in his statement to the French police in Archives d'Outre-Mer, Aix-en-Provence; Service de Protection du Corps Expéditionnaire, 367, "Declarations faites par Truong Phuoc Dat le 22 mai, 1933" [Statement of Truong Phuoc Dat, 22 May, 1933].

30. Truong Chinh, "The August Revolution," in *Primer for Revolt: The Communist Takeover in Viet-Nam*, intro. by Bernard Fall (New York: Frederick A. Praeger, 1963), 39–43.

31. It is notable that Ho Chi Minh had assigned another trainee of the British, Le Gian, to oversee the reorganized national police in February 1946. A collection of essays on Phan Boi (Hoang Huu Nam) printed in 2003 includes one by Le Gian. See Cong Thanh, ed., *Phan Boi—Hoang Huu Nam, Nha tri thuc cach mang, nguoi cong su tin cay cua Bac Ho* [Phan Boi—Hoang Huu Nam, a revolutionary intellectual, a trusted minister of Ho Chi Minh] (Danang: NXB Danang, 2003).

32. Le Van Hien, *Nhat Ky cua mot Bo Truong* [A minister's journal] (Danang: NXB Danang, 1995), 1:80.

33. Ibid., 1:82–83.

34. Robert Shaplen, *The Lost Revolution* (New York: Harper Row, 1965), 49–54.

35. Mark Philip Bradley, *Imagining Vietnam and America: The Making of Postcolonial Vietnam, 1919–1950* (Chapel Hill: University of North Carolina Press, 2000), 149.

36. RGASPI (Russian State Archive for Social and Political History), Collection 17 (Central Committee of CPUSSR), 128, 404. Report in Russian from the diary of Soviet representative A.G. Kulazhenkov, on a conversation with Pham No Mach, September 9, 1947.

37. Le Van Hien, *Nhat Ky cua mot Bo Truong*, 1:254–255.

38. Ibid, 1:262.

39. Ibid, 1:264.

40. Ibid., 1:279.

41. Ibid., 1:396–397.

42. David G. Marr, *Vietnam: State, War and Revolution, 1945–1946* (Berkeley: University of California Press, 2013), epilogue, 572.

43. Georges Boudarel, *La Bureaucratie au Vietnam* [Bureaucracy in Vietnam] (Paris: L'Harmattan, 1983), 70–72.

44. Le Van Hien, *Nhat Ky cua mot Bo Truong*, 1:382.

45. Ibid., 1:463.

46. Ibid., 1:402.

47. Yang Kuisong, "Mao Zedong and the Indochina Wars," paper delivered at the Cold War International History Project meeting, *New Evidence on China, Southeast Asia, and the Vietnam War*, Hong Kong, January 2000, 4–5n9.

48. Christopher Goscha, "Le contexte asiatique de la guerre franco-vietnamienne: Réseaux, relations et économie" [The Asian context of the French-Vietnam War: Networks, relations and economy] (PhD dissertation, Ecole Pratique des Hautes Etudes, 2000), 680.

49. Balazs Szalontai, "Political and Economic Crisis in North Vietnam, 1955–56," *Cold War History* 5, no. 4 (November 2005): 397, citing a Hungarian embassy report of May 10, 1950.

50. Chen Jian, *Mao's China and the Cold War* (Chapel Hill: University of North Carolina Press, 2000), 44.

51. Le Van Hien, *Nhat Ky cua mot Bo Truong*, 2:290.

52. Ibid., 2:370.

53. Ibid., 2:371–372.

54. Edwin E. Moise, *Land Reform in China and North Vietnam: Consolidating the Revolution at the Village Level* (Chapel Hill: University of North Carolina Press, 1983), 230–234.

55. *Nhan Dan*, March 25, 1951, cited in Thai Quang Trung, *Collective Leadership and Factionalism* (Singapore: Institute of Southeast Asian Studies, 1985), 20.

56. Le Van Hien, *Nhat Ky cua mot Bo Truong*, 2:373.

57. Hoang Van Hoan, *Giot Nuoc trong Bien Ca* [A drop in the ocean] (Beijing: NXB Tin Viet Nam, 1986), 357.

58. *Van Kien Dang 1954* [Documents of party history], Report to the Sixth Party Plenum, July 15, 1954, 167–168.

59. Moise writes that "As laws and decrees became more moderate during 1955, the actual conduct of the land reform campaign was becoming more radical" (*Land Reform*, 1983).

60. Ngo Dang Tri, *80 Nam Dang Cong San Viet Nam (1930–2010)* [80 years of the Vietnamese Communist Party (1930–2010)] (Hanoi: NXB Thong Tin va Truyen Thong, 2010), 362.

61. *New York Times*, August 10, 1957, 6.

62. Mari Olsen, *Changing Alliances: Moscow's Relations with Hanoi and the Role of China, 1949–1964* (Oslo: Faculty of Arts, University of Oslo, 2005), 224.

63. Martin Grossheim, "'Revisionism' in the Democratic Republic of Vietnam: New Evidence from the East German Archives," *Cold War History* 5, no. 4 (November 2005): 454–455.

64. Information on the Institute of Marxism-Leninism comes from the documents on display at what is now renamed the Ho Chi Minh Academy of Administration and Politics in Hanoi. For a discussion of the 1967–1968 purge, see Sophie Quinn-Judge, "The Ideological Debate in the DRV and the Significance of the Anti-Party Affair, 1967–68," *Cold War History* 5, no. 4 (November 2005): 479–500.

65. Nguyen Nghia, "Cuoc hop nhat cac to chuc cong san dau tien o Viet Nam va vai tro cua dong chi Nguyen Ai Quoc" [The unification of the first Vietnamese Communist groups and the role of Nguyen Ai Quoc], *Nghien Cuu Lich Su* 59 (1964): 6–7.

66. In a recently discovered letter written in 1921 to a French Protestant pastor, a young Ho Chi Minh writes in a way possibly influenced by Tagore: "I believe that only one philosophy, one principle, one religion exists for everyone, because only one Truth exists . . . we name it according to what we see and how we are able to see it: Confucianism or Buddha for Orientals, and Christ for Occidentals." At the time, he was already a member of the French Communist Party. See "Ho Chi Minh: An Unpublished Letter by Ho Chi Minh to a French Pastor," with comments by Pascal Bourdeaux, *Journal of Vietnamese Studies* 7, no. 2 (Summer 2012): 2.

4. MAO ZEDONG AND CHARISMATIC MAOISM

1. Joan Judge, *Print and Politics: "Shibao" and the Culture of Reform in Late Qing China* (Stanford, CA: Stanford University Press, 1996).

2. There is a wealth of scholarship on the May Fourth movement, including key works such as Tse-Tung Chow, *The May 4th Movement: Intellectual Revolution in Modern China* (Cambridge, MA: Harvard East Asia Monographs, 1960); Vera Schwarcz, *The Chinese Enlightenment: Intellectuals and the Legacy of the May Fourth Movement of 1919* (Berkeley, CA: University of California Press, 1986). An attempt to bring together some of these threads of interpretation about the movement and its legacy is Rana Mitter, *A Bitter Revolution: China's Struggle with the Modern World* (Oxford: Oxford University Press, 2004).

3. See Mitter, *A Bitter Revolution*, 129–133.

4. Chen Tu-hsiu (Chen Duxiu), "Call to Youth," in John Fairbank and Ssu-yu Teng, eds., *China's Response to the West: A Documentary Survey* (Cambridge MA: Harvard University Press, 1979), 240.

5. See, for instance, James Pusey, *China and Charles Darwin* (Cambridge, MA: Council on East Asian Studies, Harvard University, 1983).

6. Lu Xun, "Diary of a Madman," in *Call to Arms* (Beijing: Foreign Languages Press, 1981), 4.

7. Stuart Schram, ed., *Mao's Road to Power* (Armonk, NY: M. E. Sharpe, 1992), 1:125.

8. Ibid., 1:125–126.

9. Prasenjit Duara, *Rescuing History from the Nation: Questioning Narratives of Modern China* (Chicago: University of Chicago Press, 1995). See also John Fitzgerald, *Awakening China: Politics, Culture, and Class in the Nationalist Revolution* (Stanford, CA: Stanford University Press, 1998).

10. Rebecca Nedostup, *Superstitious Regimes: Religion and the Politics of Chinese Modernity* (Cambridge, MA: Harvard East Asia Center, 2010).

11. On alternative political parties, see for instance Roger Jeans, ed., *Roads Not Taken: The Struggle of Opposition Parties in Twentieth-Century China* (Boulder, CO: Westview, 1992).

12. Schram, *Mao's Road,* 1:421.

13. Ibid., 1:423.

14. Pei-yi Wu, *The Confucian's Progress: Autobiographical Writings in Traditional China* (Princeton, NJ: Princeton University Press, 1990).

15. Rana Mitter, *Forgotten Ally: China's World War II, 1937–1945* (Boston: Houghton Mifflin Harcourt, 2013), ch. 4.

16. This is necessarily a brief summary of a very complex life. For more details, see Alexander Pantsov and Stephen Levine, *Mao: The Real Story* (New York: Simon and Schuster, 2012).

17. As ever, brief summaries of this sort do scant justice to the highly complex and sophisticated debates that have been conducted on the origins of the Chinese Communist revolution and the nature of Mao's contribution to the rural revolution.

18. Mao Zedong, tr. Roger R. Thompson, *Report from Xunwu* (Stanford, CA: Stanford University Press, 1990).

19. Among the most sophisticated analyses are the various works by Stuart Schram; one illustrative example is Stuart Schram, *Mao Zedong: A Preliminary Reassessment* (Hong Kong: Chinese University Press, 1983).

20. See, e.g., Frederick Teiwes, with Warren Sun, "From a Leninist to a Charismatic Party: The CCP's Changing Leadership, 1937–1945," in Tony Saich and Hans van de Ven, eds., *New Perspectives on the Chinese Communist Revolution* (Armonk, NY: M. E. Sharpe, 1995).

21. Hans van de Ven, "Introduction," in Saich and Van de Ven, *New Perspectives,* xx.

22. David Apter, "Discourse as Power," in Saich and Van de Ven, *New Perspectives,* 195.

23. CCP Central Committee, "Decision Concerning the Great Proletarian Cultural Revolution," in Michael Schoenhals, ed., *China's Cultural Revolution,*

1966–69: Not a Dinner Party (hereafter NADP) (Armonk, NY: M. E. Sharpe, 1996), 33.

24. Ibid., 36.

25. Ibid., 37.

26. Red Flag, "In Praise of the Red Guards," in NADP, 45.

27. Zhou Enlai, "Mao Zedong Thought Is the Sole Criterion of Truth," in NADP, 27.

28. Lin Biao, "Lin Biao zai qingzhu wuchanjieji wenhua da geming qunzhong dahui shang de jianghua" [Lin Biao's speech celebrating the mass meetings for the Great Proletarian Cultural Revolution (August 1966)], in Song Yongyi et al., eds., *Chinese Cultural Revolution Database* (Hong Kong: Chinese University Press, 2006), section 3 (1966), document 14, available at http://www.chineseupress .com/chinesepress/promotion/cultural-revolution-cd-new2006/e_revolution.htm (hereafter CCR).

29. The new wave of studies from post-1949 archives shows how local level society often changed less than the centralized state claimed. See, e.g., Neil Diamant, *Revolutionizing the Family* (Berkeley: University of California Press, 2000).

30. "Zhesi baowei wuchanjieji zhuanzheng" [Vow to maintain to the death the dictatorship of the proletariat], in CCR, section 6 (1966), document 5.

31. "Ba weida de Mao Zedong sixiang de huoju gaogao jueqi" [Raise high the great torch of Mao Zedong thought], in CCR, section 6 (1966), document 18.

32. "Wo gei Mao zhuxi daishangle hong xiuzhang" [I put on my red armband for Chairman Mao], in CCR, section 6 (1966), document 42.

33. "Hongse kongbu wansui" [Long live red terror], in CCR, section 6 (1966), document 105.

34. "Women de duiwu xiang taiyang" [Our troops face the sun], in CCR, section 6 (1966), document 133.

35. "Mao zhuxi jianle women 'Hong weibing'" [Chairman Mao saw us "Red Guards"], in CCR, section 6 (1966), document 41.

36. Bei Guancheng, "I saw Chairman Mao!!!," in NADP, 148–149.

37. Song Yongyi et al., eds., *Chinese Cultural Revolution Database,* 1st ed. (Hong Kong: Chinese University Press, 2002), section 6 (1967), document 18. My translation uses capitalization of "Your" as the respectful *nin* rather than normal *ni* as is used for "you."

38. Ibid., section 6 (1967), document 67.

5 · JAWAHARLAL NEHRU

1. Quoted in Alan Brinkley, *The Publisher: Henry Luce and His American Century* (New York: Alfred A. Knopf, 2010), 275.

2. Guido Samarani, *Shaping the Future of Asia: Chiang Kai-shek, Nehru, and China-India Relations during the Second World War Period* (Working Paper Number 11, Centre for East and South-East Asian Studies, Lund University, 2005).

3. Jawaharlal Nehru to Madame Chiang Kai-shek, a four-page handwritten letter datelined "Somewhere in India, December 26 1942," in IOR, R/3/1/296, Asia, Pacific and Africa Collections, British Library, London.

4. The standard and still unsurpassed life remains the three-volume work by Sarvepalli Gopal, *Jawaharlal Nehru: A Biography* (London: Jonathan Cape, 1975–1984).

5. These letters are quoted in P. D. Tandon, *The Unforgettable Nehru* (New Delhi: National Book Trust, 2003), 67–68.

6. Jawaharlal Nehru, *An Autobiography: With Musings on Recent Events in India,* 2nd ed. (London: The Bodley Head, 1938), 41.

7. Ibid., 130.

8. Jawaharlal Nehru, *The Discovery of India* (Calcutta: The Signet Press, 1946), 403–405, 687.

9. Ibid., 427.

10. Nehru, *An Autobiography,* 406.

11. Tibor Mende, *Conversations with Mr. Nehru* (London: Secker and Warburg, 1956), 129–132.

12. There are many editions of this book, of which I would recommend M. K. Gandhi, *Hind Swaraj and Other Writings*, ed. Anthony Parel (Cambridge: Cambridge University Press, 1997), in part for its excellent, context-setting introduction by the editor.

In 1945, Gandhi and Nehru exchanged letters about *Hind Swaraj,* with the former defending the essence of what he had written thirty-five years previously, and Nehru dismissing it as out of tune with the economic and scientific requirements of the modern nation that India had to become. See Gandhi to Nehru, October 5, 1945, Nehru to Gandhi, October 9, 1945, in Uma Iyengar and Lalitha Zackariah, eds., *Together They Fought: Gandhi-Nehru Correspondence, 1921–1948* (New Delhi: Oxford University Press, 2011), 449–452.

13. Nehru, *The Discovery of India,* 47, 307, 330.

14. Rajmohan Gandhi, *The Good Boatman: A Portrait of Gandhi* (New Delhi: Viking, 1995), 387.

15. These letters are reproduced in Durga Das, ed., *Sardar Patel's Correspondence, 1945–50* (Ahmedabad: Navajivan Press, 1971–1974), 6:8–31.

16. Rajmohan Gandhi, *Patel: A Life* (Ahmedabad: Navajivan Publishing House, 1991), 490.

17. Gopal, *Jawaharlal Nehru,* 2:309.

18. Jawaharlal Nehru, *Letters to Chief Ministers*, ed. G. Parthasarathi (New Delhi: Jawaharlal Nehru Memorial Fund, 1985–1989), 1:2, 49–50. (Hereafter cited as LCM.)

19. Ibid., 3:375–376, 535–536.

20. See Nehru, *An Autobiography*, 454–455.

21. *Report of the States Reorganization Commission* (Delhi: Manager of Publications, 1955); Robert D. King, *Nehru and the Language Politics of India* (New Delhi: Oxford University Press, 1997).

22. LCM, 3:381.

23. Speech to Associated Chambers of Commerce of India, Calcutta, December 14, 1957, copy in G. D. Birla Papers, Nehru Memorial Museum and Library, New Delhi (hereafter NMML).

24. Chitra Sinha, *Debating Patriarchy: The Hindu Code Bill Controversy in India, 1941–1956* (New Delhi: Oxford University Press, 2012).

The reform of Hindu personal laws was an important first step toward the common civil code promised in the Constitution. However, given the sensitive aftermath of Partition, Nehru (and Ambedkar) deemed it prudent not to extend the core of this legislation to the Muslim minority. They left this for the future, when they hoped the Muslim community would be more amenable to progressive social reform. This moment came in 1985, when, in the Shah Bano case, the Supreme Court asked a Muslim husband who had abandoned his wife to continue paying her an allowance, commenting further that it was past time that the constitutional promise of a common, gender-sensitive, civil code be finally redeemed.

Despite many Muslim intellectuals and activists being in favor of the Supreme Court judgment, and himself having a solid two-thirds majority in Parliament, the then-prime minister, Rajiv Gandhi, had a law passed overturning the court verdict. See Niraja Gopal Jayal, *Democracy and the State: Welfare, Secularism and Development in Contemporary India* (New Delhi: Oxford University Press, 1999), ch. 3.

25. Nirmal Nibedon, *Nagaland: The Night of the Guerillas* (New Delhi: Lancer, 1983); A. Lanunungsang Ao, *From Phizo to Muivah: The Naga National Question in North-east India* (New Delhi: Mittal Publications, 2002).

26. Michael Brecher, *The Struggle for Kashmir* (New York: Oxford University Press, 1953).

27. Cable to State Department by Loy Henderson, quoted in Ajit Bhattacharjea, *Kashmir: The Wounded Valley* (New Delhi: UBS, 1994), 196–197.

28. Nehru to C. Rajagopalachari, July 31, 1953, File 123, Fifth installment, Rajagopalachari Papers, NMML.

29. Sheikh Abdullah, *Flames of the Chinar: An Autobiography*, abr. and trans. Khushwant Singh (New Delhi: Penguin India, 1993); Ramachandra Guha, *India after Gandhi: The History of the World's Largest Democracy* (London: Macmillan, 2007), ch. 12.

30. *Memorandum Outlining a Plan of Economic Development for India*, Parts One and Two (Harmondsworth: Penguin Books, 1945).

31. See Daniel Yergin and Joseph Stanislaw, *The Commanding Heights: The Battle for the World Economy* (New York: Simon and Schuster, 2002), chaps. 2–3.

32. M. Visvesvaraya, *Reconstructing India* (London: P. S. King and Sons, 1920); M. Visvesvaraya, *Planned Economy for India* (Bangalore: Bangalore Press, 1936).

33. A. H. Hanson, *The Process of Planning: A Study of India's Five-Year Plans, 1950–1964* (London: Oxford University Press, 1966).

34. G. D. Birla to M. O. Mathai, September 11, 1954, Birla Papers, NMML.

35. Birla to Mathai, April 26, 1955, Birla Papers, NMML.

36. Letter of October 2, 1952, LCM, 3:114–115.

37. LCM, 3:204–205.

38. Ibid., 3:205–206.

39. Letter of June 5, 1955, LCM, 4:186–187.

40. Note of October 10, 1955, repr. in V. N. Balabubramanyam, *Conversations with Indian Economists* (London: Macmillan, 2001), 198–201.

41. Quoted in Sarvepalli Gopal, "The Mind of Jawaharlal Nehru," in Srinath Raghavan, ed., *Imperialists, Nationalists, Democrats: The Collected Essays of Sarvepalli Gopal* (Ranikhet: Permanent Black, 2013), 194.

42. *Asian Relations: Being a Report of the Proceedings and Documentation of the First Asian Relations Conference, New Delhi, March–April 1947* (New Delhi: Asian Relations Organization, 1948).

43. LCM, 3:15–16.

44. Ibid., 3:588–590.

45. See notes of conversations in File 6, Subimal Dutt Papers, NMML.

46. Letter of January 27, 1953, LCM, 3:235–236.

47. LCM, 4:210.

48. Letter of March 15, 1954, LCM, 3:506.

49. Nehru to G. D. Birla, May 21, 1954, Birla Papers, NMML.

50. LCM, 5:285.

51. "Record of Talks between Prime Minister of India and Prime Minister of China, 20th to 25th April 1960," Subject File 24, P. N. Haksar Papers, First and Second Installments, NMML.

52. This is a necessarily brief summary of a complicated conflict that has spawned a large literature of specialist works, the best of which include Dorothy Woodman, *Himalayan Frontiers: A Political Review of British, Chinese, Indian and Russian Rivalries* (London: Barrie and Rockcliff, 1969); Steven A. Hoffman, *India and the China Crisis* (Delhi: Oxford University Press, 1990); Srinath Raghavan, *War and Peace in Modern India: A Strategic History of the Nehru Years* (London: Palgrave Macmillan, 2010).

53. LCM, 5:547–553.

54. Walter Crocker, *Nehru: A Contemporary's Estimate* (New York: Oxford University Press, 1966), 178. For a more detailed discussion of Abdullah's peace mission to Pakistan, see Guha, *India after Gandhi*, ch. 16.

55. Gopalkrishna Gandhi, in a conversation with the present writer in the late 1990s.

56. Mendes, *Conversations with Mr. Nehru*, 123–126.

57. Quoted in Gopal, *Jawaharlal Nehru*, 3:20.

58. Craig Baxter, *The Jana Sangh: A Biography of an Indian Political Party* (Bombay: Oxford University Press, 1971).

59. T. J. Nossiter, *Communism in Kerala: A Study in Political Adaptation* (Berkeley: University of California Press, 1982); T. J. Nossiter, *Marxist State Governments in India* (London: Pinter, 1988).

60. C. Rajagoplachari, *Satyam Eva Jayate: A Collection of Articles Contributed to Swarajya and Other Journals from 1956 to 1961* (Madras: Bharathan Publications, 1961); Rajmohan Gandhi, *Rajaji: A Life* (New Delhi: Penguin Books India, 1997); H. L. Erdman, *The Swatantra Party and Indian Conservatism* (Cambridge: Cambridge University Press, 1967).

61. Jayaprakash Narayan, *A Plea for Reconstruction of Indian Polity* (Kashi: Akhil Bharat Sarva Seva Sangh Prakashan, 1959); Allan and Wendy Scarfe, *J.P.: His Biography* (New Delhi: Orient Longman, 1975); Ajit Bhattacharjea, *Unfinished Revolution: A Political Biography of Jayaprakash Narayan* (New Delhi: Rupa and Co., 2004).

62. Rammanohar Lohia, *The Caste System* (1964; repr. Hyderabad: Rammanohar Lohia Vidyalaya Nyas, 1979); Indumathi Kelkar, *Dr. Rammanohar Lohia: His Life and Philosophy* (New Delhi: Anamika Publishers, 2009).

63. There is no biography of Kripalani. My account is based on my analysis of his contributions to parliamentary debates and on a conversation with Gopalkrishna Gandhi, who knew him well.

64. See H. V. Kamath, *Last Days of Jawaharlal Nehru* (New Delhi: Shipra Publications, 1977).

65. The arguments in this concluding section draw upon two previous essays of mine: "The Dynasty in Myth and History," and "Verdicts on Nehru: The Rise and Fall of a Reputation," both reprinted in Ramachandra Guha, *Patriots and Partisans* (New Delhi: Allen Lane, 2012).

66. C. P. Srivastava, *Lal Bahadur Shastri: A Life of Truth in Politics* (New Delhi: Oxford University Press, 1995).

67. Nehru to C. D. Deshmukh, April 16, 1956, in Subject File 67, Deshmukh Papers, NMML.

68. Michael Brecher, *Succession in India: A Study in Decision Making* (London: Oxford University Press, 1966); Anand Mohan, *Indira Gandhi: A Personal and Political Biography* (New York: Meredith Press, 1967).

69. Janardhan Thakur, *All the Prime Minister's Men* (New Delhi: Vikas Publishing House, 1977); Vinod Mehta, *The Sanjay Story: From Anand Bhavan to Amethi* (Bombay: Jaico, 1978); Emma Tarlo, *Unsettling Memories: Narratives of India's Emergency* (Delhi: Permanent Black, 2003).

70. The clipping I have of this essay does not carry the date; it was published most likely in the first months of 1992.

71. In a personal conversation with this writer.

6. ZHOU ENLAI AND CHINA'S "PROLONGED RISE"

1. *Zhou Enlai waijiao wenxuan* [Selected diplomatic papers of Zhou Enlai] (Beijing: Zhongyang wenxian, 1990), 120–125.

2. Li Ping et al., eds., *Zhou Enlai nianpu, 1898–1949* [A chronological record of Zhou Enlai, 1898–1949] (Beijing: Zhongyang wenxian, 1989), 22.

3. Jin Chongji et al., *Zhou Enlai zhuan, 1898–1949* [A biography of Zhou Enlai, 1898–1949] (Beijing: Zhongyang wenxian, 1998), 43–44.

4. Li Ping et al., eds., *Zhou Enlai nianpu, 1898–1949*, 40–41.

5. *Zhou Enlai shuxing xuanji* [A selected collection of Zhou Enlai's correspondence] (Beijing: Zhongyang wenxian, 1988), 23–24.

6. Ibid., 24.

7. Ibid., 46–49.

8. *Mao Zedong xuanji* [Selected works of Mao Zedong] (Beijing: Renmin, 1965, 1977), 1:3–11, 13–46, 49–58, 101–111.

9. Jin et al., *Zhou Enlai zhuan, 1898–1949*, 266, 285–286.

10. Gao Wenqian, *Wannian Zhou Enlai* [Zhou Enlai's later years] (Hong Kong: Mingjing, 2002), 26–42.

11. Ibid., 51–61.

12. Odd Arne Westad, *Cold War and Revolution* (New York: Columbia University Press, 1993), ch. 2.

13. *Mao Zedong xuanji*, 4:1191–1192; *Renmin ribao* [People's Daily], January 4, 1947.

14. Ibid., 4:1477–1478.

15. *Zhou Enlai waijiao wenxuan*, 1–7, 48–57.

16. *Mao Zedong xuanji*, 4:1486–1520.

17. *Zhou Enlai waijiao wenxuan*, 8–10.

18. Qi Dexue et al., *Kangmei yuanchai zhanzheng shi* [A history of the war of resisting America and assisting Korea] (Beijing: Junshi kexue), 1:90–91.

19. Chen Jian, *China's Road to the Korean War* (New York: Columbia University Press, 1994), ch. 6.

20. *Jianguo yilai Mao Zedong wengao* [Mao Zedong's manuscripts since the founding of the Republic] (Beijing: Zhongyang wenxian, 1987–1993), 1:550.

21. *Zhou Enlai junshi wenxuan* [Selected military papers of Zhou Enlai] (Beijing: Renmin, 1997), 4:137.

22. *Mao Zedong xuanji*, 5:101–106; *Zhou Enlai junshi wenxuan*, 4:292–307.

23. Xiong Huayuan, *Zhou Enlai chudeng waijiao wutai* [Zhou Enlai's debut on the world scene] (Shenyan: Liaoning renmin, 1999), 140–141.

24. Pei Jianzhang et al., *Zhonghua renmin gongheguo waijiaoshi* [A diplomatic history of the People's Republic] (Beijing: Shijie zhishi, 1994), 337.

25. *Zhou Enlai waijiao wenxuan*, 134.

26. Wu Lengxi, *Shinian lunzhan* [Ten Year Debates] (Beijing: Zhongyang wenxian, 1998), 6.

27. Chen Jian, *Mao's China and the Cold War* (Chapel Hill: University of North Carolina Press, 2001), ch. 6.

28. *Cold War International History Project Bulletin* 6–7 (Winter 1995/96): 153–154.

29. *Jianguo yilai Mao Zedong wengao*, 5:484–576.

30. Li Ping, *Kaiguo zongli Zhou Enlai* [The First Premier Zhou Enlai] (Beijing: Zhongyang dangxiao, 1994), 354–358.

31. Ibid., 360–361.

32. Xin Ziling, *Mao Zedong quanzhuan* [A complete biography of Mao Zedong] (Hong Kong: Liwen, 1993), 4:102–105.

33. Jin et al., *Zhou Enlai zhuan, 1949–1976*, 424–425.

34. Li Ping et al., *Zhou Enlai nianpu, 1949–1976*, 2:243–245.

35. Chen Jian, *Mao's China and the Cold War*, ch. 7.

36. Chen Jian, "The Tibetan Rebellion of 1959 and China's Changing Relations with India and the Soviet Union," *Journal of Cold War History* 8, no. 3 (Summer 2006): 54–101.

37. Minutes of meetings between Zhou and Nehru, April 1960, Nehru Memorial Museum and Library, New Delhi.

38. *Jianguo yilai Mao Zedong wengao*, 10:195–198.

39. Editorial Group, *Zhongyin bianjie ziwei fanji zuozhan shi* [A history of operations in the war for self-defense on the Sino-Indian borders] (Beijing: Junshi kexue, 1994), especially chs. 4–5.

40. Han Huanzhi et al., *Dangdai zhongguo jundui de junshi gongzuo* [The military affairs of the contemporary Chinese Army] (Beijing: Zhongguo shehui kexue, 1989), 1:617.

41. *Zhongyin bianjie ziwei fanji zuozhan shi*, 179–180.

42. *Mao Zedong on Diplomacy* (Beijing: Foreign Language, 1993), 388.

43. Speech at the Tenth Plenary Session of the Party's Eighth Central Committee, September 26, 1962.

44. Tong Xiaopeng, *Fengyu sishi nian* [Forty years of storms] (Beijing: Zhongyang wenxian, 1996), 2:219–220, 221.

45. Zhou's presentation at the CCP Politburo enlarged meeting, May 21, 1966.

46. Li Ping et al., *Zhou Enlai nianpu, 1949–1976*, 3:440.

47. *Zhou Enlai waijiao wenxuan*, 462–464.

48. *Jianguo yilai Mao Zedong wengao*, 12:516–517.

49. Yang Kuisong, "The Sino-Soviet Border Clash of 1969," *Cold War History* 1, no. 1 (August 2000): 25–31.

50. Chen Jian, *Mao's China and the Cold War*, ch. 9.

51. Xiong Xianghui, "The Prelude to the Opening of Sino-American Relations," *Zhonggong dangshi ziliao* 42 (June 1992): 56–96.

52. Jin et al., *Zhou Enlai zhuan, 1949–1976*, 1096–1097.

53. Li Zhisui, *The Private Life of Chairman Mao* (New York: Random House, 1994), 560.

54. Zhou Bingjian, *Wo de bofu Zhou Enlai* (My Uncle Zhou Enlai) (Shenyang: Liaoning renmin, 2000), 330.

55. *Foreign Relations of the United States, 1969–1976* (Washington, DC: United States Government Printing Office, 2007), 18:380–400.

56. Memorandum, Zhou Enlai with Kissinger, November 13, 1973, 10:00 p.m.–12:30 a.m.; Memorandum, Zhou Enlai with Kissinger, November 14, 1973, 7:35–8:25 a.m. National Security Archive.

57. Gao, *Wannian Zhou Enlai*, 463–464, 472.

58. Li Ping et al., *Zhou Enlai nianpu, 1949–1976*, 691.

59. Han Suyin, *Eldest Son* (New York: Kodansha America, 1991), v.

60. Jung Chang and Jon Halliday, *Mao: The Unknown Story* (New York: Anchor Books, 2005). Chang and Halliday also present a very negative picture of Zhou in the book.

7. SUKARNO

1. Sukarno, *Sukarno: An Autobiography as told to Cindy Adams* (New York: Bobbs-Merrill, 1965), 21; hereafter cited as *Sukarno/Adams*. Adams, an American journalist living in Jakarta, interviewed Sukarno at length between 1964 and 1965 and fashioned his memoirs from the interviews. On theosophy in Indonesia, see Laurie J. Sears, *Shadows of Empire: Colonial Discourse and Javanese Tales* (Durham, NC: Duke University Press, 1966), 125–128.

2. *Sukarno/Adams*, 19. On *puputan*, see H. M. van Weede, "The Balinese *Puputan*," in Eric Tagliacozzo and Tineke Hellwig, eds., *The Indonesia Reader* (Durham, NC: Duke University Press, 2009), 262–264.

3. See Bob Hering, *Soekarno: Founding Father of Indonesia, 1901–1945* (Leiden: KITLV Press, 2002), 14–21, for a discussion of the myth and reality of Sukarno's family history. On the *puputan*, see 21, n. 55. Soekarno is the Dutch-era spelling of the latter-day Sukarno. Both are correct. Sukarno signed his name "Soekarno."

4. In part by converting old protectorate treaties with native rulers into new treaties of submission, the so-called Short Contracts. See J. S. Furnivall, *Netherlands India: A Study of Plural Economy* (Cambridge: Cambridge University Press, 1944), 236.

5. The exception was New Guinea, added in the 1920s. See Adrian Vickers, *A History of Modern Indonesia* (Cambridge: Cambridge University Press, 2005), 13–14.

6. J. D. Legge, *Sukarno: A Political Biography* (Singapore: Archipelago Press, 2003), 32. Legge is the authoritative biographer of Sukarno.

7. Ann Ruth Wilner, *The Spellbinders: Charismatic Political Leadership* (New Haven, CT: Yale University Press, 1984), 66.

8. See Wilner, *Spellbinders*, 66–69.

9. See Raden Ajeng Kartini, "A Pioneer of Women's Rights" in Tagliacozzo and Hellwig, eds., *Indonesia Reader*, 140.

10. *Sukarno/Adams*, 28.

11. This was the Europeesche Lagere School, or ELS. See *Sukarno/Adams*, 28–29; and Bernhard Dahm, *Sukarno and the Struggle for Indonesian Independence* (Ithaca, NY: Cornell University Press, 1969), 28.

12. *Sukarno/Adams*, 30.

13. Ibid., 43. Other native students at the HBS remembered nothing of the kind, however. Hering, *Soekarno*, 77. Sukarno also told Adams that he had schoolboy fantasies of making love to white girls. "It was the only way I knew to exert some form of superiority over the white race."

14. Dahm, *Sukarno*, 30. Population figure is from the 1930 census. In Bernhard Dahm, *History of Indonesia in the Twentieth Century* (New York: Praeger, 1971), 84. Legge gives slightly different figures, saying in the first twenty-eight years of the twentieth century, only 279 Indonesians graduated—an average of ten per year. See Legge, *Sukarno*, 38.

15. Hering, *Soekarno*, 95.

16. *Sukarno/Adams*, 39.

17. See Helen Churchill Candee, "Helen Churchill Candee Observes the 'Conquering Race Eating His Mid-day Snack,' " in James Rush, ed., *Java: A Travellers' Anthology* (Oxford: Oxford University Press, 1996), 137–138. See also Vickers, *Modern Indonesia*, 70.

18. *Sukarno/Adams*, 27, 39.

19. On the new Chinese organizations in the Indies, see James R. Rush, *Opium to Java: Revenue Farming and Chinese Enterprise in Colonial Indonesia, 1860–1910* (Ithaca, NY: Cornell University Press, 1990), 245–247. See also Lea Williams, *Overseas Chinese Nationalism; The Genesis of the Pan-Chinese Movement in Indonesia, 1900–1916* (Glencoe, IL: Free Press, 1960).

20. Dahm, *History*, 20. See also Nadav Safran, *Egypt in Search of Political Community: An Analysis of the Intellectual and Political Evolution of Egypt, 1804–1952* (Cambridge, MA: Harvard University Press, 1961), ch. 5, "Reformist Islam."

21. See Vickers, *Modern Indonesia*, 73; and M. C. Ricklefs, *A History of Modern Indonesia since c. 1200*, 3rd ed. (Houndmills, Basingstoke, Hampshire: Palgrave, 2001), 208–209.

22. Ricklefs, *History*, 211.

23. Ricklefs cautions that "the true number probably never exceeded half a million"—a very large number in any case (ibid., 210).

24. *Sukarno/Adams*, 34.

25. Willard Hanna, *Eight Nation Makers* (New York: St. Martin's Press, 1964), 7.

26. See Legge, *Sukarno*, 65–66; *Sukarno/Adams*, 40; Hanna, *Nation Makers*, 7–8; Hering, *Soekarno*, 79–83.

27. *Sukarno/Adams*, 40, 41.

28. Legge, *Sukarno*, 67.

29. *Sukarno/Adams*, 49. Sukarno told Adams that he used the pen name Bima, but his biographer Legge found no articles by such a person in the *Utusan*! Legge, *Sukarno*, 68, n. 7. Hering, *Soekarno*, 91–95, discusses several of his *Utusan Hindia* articles without mentioning a pen name, but he does confirm that Sukarno was known to friends as Bima at the time (83). Perhaps this is another example of Sukarno, at sixty-four, polishing his story for his American interlocutor.

30. *Sukarno/Adams*, 48.

31. Hanna, *Nation Makers*, 12.

32. For the ISDV, Indische Sociaal-Democratische Vereeniging, see Dahm, *History*, 51.

33. Ricklefs, *History*, 219.

34. This was a *kawinan gantung*, or hanging marriage, implying that it was not consummated due to the bride's young age. Hering, *Soekarno*, 90.

35. *Sukarno/Adams*, 53. A law and medical school followed in 1924 and 1925. See Furnivall, *Netherlands India*, 373, 377.

36. *Sukarno/Adams*, 53, 51.

37. Dewantara was highly influenced by Rabindranath Tagore. See R. E. Elson, *The Idea of Indonesia* (Cambridge: Cambridge University Press, 2009), 51.

38. In ibid., 34.

39. Legge, *Sukarno*, 82, 84.

40. Partai Komunis Indonesia, PKI. See Elson, *Idea*, 44–45; and 1–4 for the origins of the term.

41. Ibid., 44.

42. *Sukarno/Adams*, 69–72, 77.

43. Ibid., Legge, *Sukarno,* 90–91. The Dutch name reveals the elite character of these groups.

44. Soekarno, *Nationalism, Islam, and Marxism* (1926), trans. Karel H. Warouw and Peter D. Weldon, with an introduction by Ruth T. McVey (Ithaca, NY: Cornell Modern Indonesia Project Translation Series, 1970). The Cornell translation identifies the article as having been published in *Suluh Indonesia Muda* in 1926. Legge believes that this periodical actually began in 1927, replacing the Bandung club's earlier *Indonesia Muda* when the Surabaya and Bandung clubs combined their periodicals. See Legge, *Sukarno,* 108.

45. Soekarno, *Nationalism,* 35–36.

46. Ibid., 36.

47. Ibid., 38.

48. Ibid., 38, 60. Sukarno said, for example, that in China, nationalists and Communists were collaborating—in fact they still were in 1926, but not after April 1927 (41).

49. Ibid., 40.

50. Ibid., 43.

51. Ibid., 48.

52. Ibid., 60.

53. Ibid., 53.

54. Ibid., 61.

55. Isaiah Berlin, *The Hedgehog and the Fox: An Essay on Tolstoy's View of History* (New York: Simon and Schuster, 1953), 1.

56. Ricklefs, *History,* 125.

57. Originally Perserikatan, or association, but changed to Partai in 1928, hence Partai Nasionalis Indonesia. See Legge, *Sukarno,* 107.

58. M. W. F Treub, *Het gist in Indie* (Haarlem: H. D. Tjeenk Willink en Zoon, 1927), 23, quoted in Ruth T. McVey, "Nationalism, Islam, and Marxism: The Management of Ideological Conflict in Indonesia," in Soekarno, *Nationalism,* 1.

59. Called the Association of Political Organizations of the Indonesian People, or PPPKI, Permufakatan Perhimpunan-perhimpunan Politik Kebangsaan Indonesia. See Legge, *Sukarno,* 105.

60. Ibid., 108.

61. *Sukarno/Adams,* 86.

62. "Youth Oath," in Tagliacozzo and Hellwig, eds., *Indonesia Reader,* 269–270.

63. See A. Teeuw, *Modern Indonesian Literature* (Dordrecht, Holland: Foris Publications, 1986), 4–9.

64. Legge, *Sukarno,* 120; *Sukarno/Adams,* 88.

65. *Sukarno/Adams*, 89.

66. This messianic figure was sometimes associated with historical figures such as Diponegoro and Cokroaminoto. See Sartono Kartodirdjo, *Ratu Adil* (Jakarta: Sinar Harapan, 1984).

67. Dahm, *Sukarno*, 6–7, 120; *Sukarno/Adams*, 93.

68. His PNI colleagues Gatot Mankupradja, Supriadinata, and Maskun were also arrested at the time. *Sukarno/Adams*, 93, 94, 105. See also Soekarno, *Indonesia Accuses! Soekarno's Defence Oration in the Political Trial of 1930*, ed. and trans., with introduction by Roger K. Paget (Kuala Lumpur: Oxford University Press, 1975), lxxiii. The full charges are in "Introductory Documents," lxxiii–lxxx.

They included the assertion that the PNI was "from the beginning of its existence . . . an organ for the secret continuation of the Indonesian Communist Party."

69. "Indonesia Menggugat" or, probably in the original Dutch, "Indonesië klaagt aan!" There is some disagreement about which language the original draft was written in. See Soekarno/Paget, *Indonesia Accuses*, xviii–xx.

70. See Paget's discussion, ibid., lviii.

71. Ibid., 31. On the subject of Dutch colonialism, Sukarno cites authorities as varied as Pieter Veth, Clive Day, Thomas Stamford Raffles, H. T. Colenbrander, and C. Snouck Hurgronje.

72. He references, inter alia, the journalist Pieter Brooshooft, author of "The Ethical Policy in Colonial Politics"; the economist J. H Boeke; and the sociologist Bertram Schrieke. Soekarno/Paget, *Indonesia Accuses*, 32–38. Ibid., 41, 46–47, 51.

73. Ibid., 41, 46–47, 51.

74. Ibid., *Indonesia Accuses*, 49, 52, 69, 70, 72, 74, 75.

75. The story is told in *Sukarno/Adams*, 61–63; and also in Soekarno, *Marhaen and Proletarian*, trans. Claire Holt (Ithaca, NY: Cornell Modern Indonesia Project Translation Series, 1960), 6–7. See also Dahm, *Sukarno*, 143–144.

76. Soekarno/Paget, *Indonesia Accuses*, 141.

77. His codefendants were sentenced to shorter prison terms. See Soekarno/Paget, *Indonesia Accuses*, Document E: "The Verdict," lxxix.

78. *Sukarno/Adams*, 113–114.

79. Ibid., 115.

80. Ibid., 117, 118. See also Dahm, *History*, 67–69.

81. Partindo had been founded while Sukarno was still in jail.

82. *Sukarno/Adams*, 121.

83. Sukarno's marriage to Cokroaminoto's daughter didn't flourish, and Sukarno implied to Cindy Adams that it was never consummated. They divorced after a few years, and Sukarno married Inggit, the spouse of his Bandung landlord,

who became his first real wife. Several others followed. On Inggit, see *Sukarno/Adams,* 56–59.

84. Two key figures were Mohammad Husni Thamrin and Sutardjo Kartohadikusumo.

See Dahm, *History,* 71–73; Ricklefs, *History,* 239–240.

85. See Sukarno's "Propaganda Islam didalam Pendjara," *Pedoman Masjarakat,* March 9, 1938.

86. Legge, *Sukarno,* 119.

87. This bargain included recruiting Indonesian menial laborers, called *romusha,* to build wartime infrastructure projects in occupied Southeast Asia. Many thousands died and Sukarno spoke bitterly about it to Adams years later, saying "I shipped them to their deaths." *Sukarno/Adams,* 192.

88. See Legge, *Sukarno,* 208–217. The BPKI or Badan Penjelidik Usaha Persiapan Kemerdekaan Indonesia.

89. See "Explaining Panca Sila," Speech by Sukarno in June 1945, in Tagliacozzo and Hellwig, eds., *Indonesia Reader,* 305–308; quotation from 307 and 308.

90. Hatta became vice president. In the preamble of the constitution containing Sukarno's Panca Sila, "belief in one God" was made the first principle, to appease some Muslim nationalists whose proposal that, constitutionally, Muslims should be bound by Islamic law, or *shariah,* was voted down by Sukarno, Hatta, and other "secular nationalists." On this, see Elson, *Idea,* 113.

91. Legge, *Sukarno,* 240.

92. Ibid., 241; *Sukarno/Adams,* 264.

93. See Radik Utoyo Sudirjo, ed., *Album Perang Kemerdekaan 1945–1950* (Jakarta: Badan Penerbit Almanak Rep. Indonesia, 1981), 206: "Pilih Sukarno-Hatta atau PKI-Muso!!" Musso, an early Indonesian Communist, returned during the revolution after having spent years abroad in the Soviet Union. Rex Mortimer, *Indonesian Communism under Sukarno* (Ithaca, NY: Cornell University Press, 1974), 41.

94. George McT. Kahin, *Southeast Asia: A Testament* (London: Routledge-Curzon, 2003), 45.

95. See Sudirjo, *Album,* 226: "Konperensi Asia untuk Merundingkan Soal Indonesia." Legge, *Sukarno,* 262.

96. During the wartime planning, Sukarno had momentarily entertained the idea of a wider Indonesia to include ethnically akin Malaya and British territories on the north coast of Borneo but had ultimately decided against it. See Legge, *Sukarno,* 216–217. Benedict Anderson, *Imagined Communities,* rev. ed. (London: Verso, 2006).

97. Furnivall, *Netherlands India,* 377. See McVey, "Management of Ideological Conflict," 6, on the postindependence nationalist leadership.

98. See Kahin, *Testament,* 121.

99. McVey, "Management of Ideological Conflict," 7.

100. See Sudirjo, *Album*, 369, which lists the twenty-nine officially recognized parties of 1945.

101. These people, collectively, represented what Ruth McVey calls the "nationalist Establishment." See McVey, "Management of Ideological Conflict," 7. See also Herbert Feith, *The Decline of Constitutional Democracy in Indonesia* (Ithaca, NY: Cornell University Press, 1962), 128.

102. Ibid., 24–25, 34. Feith contrasted "solidarity makers" with Dutch-educated "administrators," who possessed "administrative, legal, technical, and foreign language skills such as are required for the running of a modern state."

103. See Harold Crouch, *The Army and Politics in Indonesia* (Ithaca, NY: Cornell University Press, 1978), 29–30. Among the issues in this semi-coup was the restructuring of the army under modernizing officers who found themselves at odds with many in the revolutionary old guard.

104. See *Sukarno/Adams*, 266–267; Legge, *Sukarno*, 284.

105. See Ricklefs, *History*, 279, 297. This rebellion simmered on into the early 1960s.

106. The other key figures were Njoto, M. H. Lukman, and, Sudisman. See Rex Mortimer, *Indonesian Communism under Sukarno* (Ithaca, NY: Cornell University Press, 1974), 29.

107. On the PNI, see Feith, *Decline*, 139–143.

108. See ibid., 134–139. Sukarno, who is almost always described as a "secular nationalist," joined Muhammadiyah while in Bengkulu and considered himself a modernist Muslim.

109. The classic analysis of this is Clifford Geertz, *The Religion of Java* (Glencoe, IL: Free Press, 1960) alongside his *The Social History of an Indonesian Town* (Cambridge, MA: MIT Press, 1965). See also Robert Jay, *Religion and Politics in Rural Java* (New Haven, CT: Yale Southeast Asia Studies, 1963).

110. Ricklefs, *History*, 304.

111. Sudirjo, *Album*, 162, 132. Interview with Lakshmi Chand Jain, September 2, 1989, Manila.

112. Ibid., 226, 298. Nehru returned the honor the following year. See also Kahin, *Testament*, 87.

113. In the words of Willard Hanna, an astute and skeptical Sukarno watcher. Hanna, *Nation Makers*, 70.

114. George McT. Kahin, *The Asian-African Conference* (Ithaca, NY: Cornell University Press, 1956), 36–38, 50. See also Richard Wright, *Color Curtain: A Report on the Bandung Conference* (Cleveland: The World Publishing Company, 1956), 136–139. Vijay Prashad has written that "Sukarno's speech was the most powerful brief for Third World unity" at the conference. Vijay Prashad, *The Darker Nations: A People's History of the Third World* (New York: The New Press, 2008), 34.

115. Quoting George Kahin, who was an official observer at the conference. See Kahin, *Conference*, 3; and also 36–38; 4–5.

116. Ibid., 3.

117. Indeed, underlying bland phrases such as "colonialism in all its manifestations" and "singly and collectively" lay very intense disagreements among the delegates. See ibid., 11–32.

118. Prashad, *Darker Nations*, 45.

119. Hanna, *Nation Makers*, 71.

120. *Sukarno/Adams*, 275. Hanna, *Nation Makers*, 72; Legge, *Sukarno*, 300.

121. Tillman Durdin, "Sukarno Captivates Washington," *New York Times*, May 17, 1956, 1. The following day, Durdin described Sukarno's address in fluent English to a joint session of the US Congress and confirms the standing ovations he had bragged to Adams about. See Tillman Durdin, "Sukarno Decries U.S. Military Aid as Harming Asia," *New York Times*, May 18, 1956, 1. Sukarno's gala arrival is captured in the British Pathé newsreel "President of Indonesia Gets Capital Honours 1956." See http://www.britishpathe.com/video/president-of -indonesia-gets-capital-honours/query/Soekarno.

122. Hanna, *Nation Makers*, 71–72.

123. See his comments in Soekarno, *Marhaen*, 21–22.

124. In Legge, *Sukarno*, 301.

125. See "Islam Versus the Secular State in Indonesia," in Harry J. Benda and John Larkin, eds., *The World of Southeast Asia* (New York: Harper and Row, 1967), 252.

126. Legge, *Sukarno*, 324; Ricklefs, *History*, 308–309.

127. "The Political Manifesto" in Benda and Larkin, eds., *Southeast Asia*, 250; Legge, *Sukarno*, 321.

128. *Sukarno/Adams*, 272–273; Legge, *Sukarno*, 332; Kahin, *Testament*, 156.

129. See George McT. Kahin and Audrey Kahin, *Subversion as Foreign Policy* (New York: The New Press, 1995).

130. Travel accounts of the period describe the ubiquitous military and its sometimes violent and capricious behavior. See "Frank and Helen Schreiber Search for the Indies of Old, 1963" in Rush, ed., *Java*, 224–225; and "Maslyn Williams Seeks the Truth in Sukarno's Indonesia," in Rush, ed., *Java*, 227, where Williams describes Kemayoran Airport: "Young men in uniform are at every gateway and entrance. . . . All of them carry automatic rifles."

131. Legge, *Sukarno*, 332; See Willard Hanna, "The Economics of Incongruity," *Bung Karno's Indonesia*, AUFS Southeast Asia Series, 7, no. 19 (1961): 3. Hanna speaks of the government's "sheer genius for mismanagement."

132. Mohammad Hatta, "Demokrasi Kita," *Panji Masyarakat*, May 1960. Hatta had resigned as vice president in 1956.

133. The MPRS, Majelis Permusyawaratan Rakyat Sementara.

134. See Legge, *Sukarno*, 355.

135. Some detainees were tortured, evidently. Rosihan Anwar, *Sebelum Prahara* (Jakarta: Sinar Harapan, 1981). One political detainee under Sukarno, M. Yunan Nasution, described the relative civility of Sukarnoist incarceration in *Kenang-Kenangan DiBelakang Terali Besi Di Zama Rezim Orla* (Jakarta: Bulan Bintang, 1967), 103–107. These included tennis, swimming, Ping Pong, books, and family visits.

136. Ricklefs, *History*, 302.

137. On the flexibility of the PKI, see Mortimer, *Indonesian Communism*, 157, who wrote that the party's political categories were so flexible that they "could be given almost any meaning required in a specific political context."

138. Donald Hindley, *The Communist Party of Indonesia* (Berkeley: University of California Press, 1964), 285. Hindley says between 7.8 and 12 million people were members of Communist-affiliated mass organizations in 1963.

139. Quoted in Odd Arne Westad, *The Global Cold War* (Cambridge: Cambridge University Press, 2005), 187. *Sukarno/Adams*, 294.

140. Crouch, *Army*, 34.

141. These included Mohammad Roem, Mohammad Natsir, M. Yunan Nasution, and Hamka.

142. H. B. Jassin, for example, leader of the non-Communist Cultural Manifesto group and Indonesia's leading literary critic, lost his post at the national university. See Rosihan Anwar, *Prahara*, 408–409, 413, 475, 528.

143. See Vickers, *Modern Indonesia*, 154–155; Jean Gelman Taylor, *Indonesia: Peoples and Histories* (New Haven, CT: Yale University Press, 2003), 354.

144. See Ricklefs, *History*, 338; Vickers, *Modern Indonesia*, 152.

145. See Sears, *Shadows*, 222–223.

146. Women were a frequent subject of braggadocio (and affection) in his conversations with Cindy Adams. See Cindy Adams, *Sukarno, My Friend* (Jakarta: Gunung Agung, 1971), which describes their working relationship and how Sukarno often fretted over how to manage his many wives.

147. Sears, *Shadows*, 29, 219–220.

148. "Maslyn Williams Seeks the Truth," in Rush, ed., *Java*, 241–243.

149. In Sears, *Shadows*, 220. Historian and *wayang* scholar Laurie Sears agrees that Sukarno can be seen as "a paradigmatic Javanese monarch fitting into earlier patterns of Javanese political authority" (219). Christopher Koch captures Sukarno's charismatic hold over the people in *The Year of Living Dangerously*, his novel depicting 1965 in Indonesia.

150. Robert Hefner, *Civil Islam: Muslims and Democratization in Indonesia* (Princeton, NJ: Princeton University Press, 2000), 45.

151. See Adams, *My Friend*. In this book, Adams is seen dancing with PKI chief Aidit at the presidential palace, in the photograph section following p. 104.

152. Ricklefs, *History,* 345–346, provides a succinct account of Soeharto's rise.

153. Ibid., 339–341. There is now a large literature on this event. Legge, *Sukarno,* takes up much of it in an appendix, p. 459. See also Robert Cribb, *The Indonesian Killings, 1965–1966* (Clayton, Australia: Monash University Press, 1990); and Douglas Kammen and Katheringe McGregor, eds., *The Contours of Mass Violence in Indonesia, 1965–68* (Honolulu: University of Hawaii Press, 2012).

154. Not to mention the United States. See Bradley Simpson, *Economists with Guns: Authoritarian Development and US-Indonesia Relations, 1960–1968* (Palo Alto, CA: Stanford University Press, 2008).

155. This is a best estimate by scholars. See, Ricklefs, *History,* 347 (500,000); Taylor, *Indonesia,* 359 (800,000). See also Robert Cribb, "The Mass Killings of 1965–1966," in Tagliacozzo and Hellwig, eds., *Indonesia Reader,* 346 (150,000–500,000).

156. Legge, *Sukarno,* 446, 454.

157. Ricklefs, *History,* 349.

158. Legge, *Sukarno,* 458.

159. Ricklefs, *History,* 353; see also Elson, *Idea,* 244.

160. Adams, *My Friend,* 303.

161. Legge, *Sukarno,* 456.

8. DENG XIAOPING AND THE CHINA HE MADE

1. There is still no good biography of Deng in his younger years. The best overview is probably in Zhonggong zhongyang wenxian yanjiushi, eds., *Deng Xiaoping nianpu* [Deng Xiaoping chronology], vol. 1 (Beijing: Zhongyang wenxian, 2009). The recollections of Deng's friend Chen Pu, in *Zaonian wangshi* [Events of early years] (Beijing: Zhonggong dangshi, 1995) are also very useful.

2. For a very interesting overview of Deng's activities seen by his Kuomintang rivals in France, see Zhang Shaojie, *Wo yu Deng Xiaoping xinian de enyuan: yijiuersi zhi yijiuerqi BeiFa qianhou Bali de Guo-Gong fengyun* [The conflicts between me and Deng Xiaoping in the early years: Activities of the Guomindang and the CCP in Paris before and after the Northern Expedition, 1924–1927] (Taibei: Liming wenhua, 1993).

3. Deng's time in Moscow is also still very under-researched. A decent overview is in A. V. Pantsov and D. A. Spichak, "Den Siaopin v Moskve (1926–1927): ideynoye stanovleniye revolyutsionera i budushchego reformatora [Deng Xiaoping in Moscow (1926–1927): The ideological shaping of a revolutionary and future reformer], *Problemy Delnego Vostoka* 4 (2011): 151–160.

4. Ezra F. Vogel, *Deng Xiaoping and the Transformation of China* (Cambridge, MA: Belknap Press of Harvard University Press, 2011), is quite good on

this period, even though this standard biography in English is rather weak overall on Deng's early years.

5. April 8, 1957, speech to cadre in Xi'an, *Deng Xiaoping wenxuan* [Selected works of Deng Xiaoping], vol. 1 (Beijing: Renmin, 1983), 174.

6. Some of his friends' recollections are in Yu Jundao and Zou Yang, eds., *Deng Xiaoping jiaowang lu* [Records of Deng Xiaoping's associates] (Chengdu: Sichuan renming, 1996).

7. Remarkably, there is no good book on the relationship between the two men. The Chinese literature is either sensationalist or awkwardly politically correct. Some of the memoir literature is useful, as are some recent biographies, such as Ding Xiaoping, *Zhonggong zhongyang diyizhi bi: Hu Qiaomu zai Mao Zedong Deng Xiaoping shenbian de rizi* [First Pen of the Central Committee: Hu Qiaomu's Days alongside Mao Zedong and Deng Xiaoping] (Beijing: Zhongguo qingnian, 2011).

8. July 7, 1962, speech on agricultural questions, in *Deng Xiaoping wenxuan*, 1:304.

9. Quoted in Roderick MacFarquhar and Michael Schoenhals, *Mao's Last Revolution* (Cambridge, MA: Belknap Press of Harvard University Press, 2006), 138.

10. There is, fortunately, the beginning of a literature on Deng's southern exile. Ling Buji, *Deng Xiaoping zai Gan nan* [Deng Xiaoping in Southern Jiangxi] (Beijing: Zhongyang wenxian, 1995), gives the "official" view, but with much good detail on Deng's exile to an area he had known during the war years. Huang Wenhua and Guan Shan, *Deng Xiaoping Jiangxi mengnan ji* [A record of Deng Xiaoping's dangerous stay in Jiangxi] (Hong Kong: Mingxing, 1990), shows how Deng survived the most dangerous part of his banishment.

11. A very good overview is Liu Jianhui, ed., *Shiyi jie san zhong quanhui qianhou de Deng Xiaoping* [Deng Xiaoping in the time around the 3rd Plenary Session of the 11th Central Committee] (Beijing: Zhonggong zhongyang dangxiao, 2004).

12. November 26, 1979, conversation with Frank B. Gibney, vice-chairman of the Compilation Committee of Encyclopaedia Britannica and others, in *Deng Xiaoping wenxuan*, 2:280.

13. Lee Kwan Yew, *The Singapore Story* (New York: Prentice Hall, 1999).

14. Quoted in Vogel, *Deng Xiaoping and the Transformation of China*, 300.

15. June 9, 1989, speech to martial law units, Beijing Domestic Television Service, June 27, 1989; Foreign Broadcast Information Service (FBIS), 8–10.

16. There is no documentary evidence for Deng uttering the famous quotation. It is, however, widely quoted by CCP historians in Guangdong province, some of whom insist that Deng first used the phrase on his visit to Shenzhen in 1992.

17. Quoted in *Renmin Ribao* [People's Daily], January 25, 2002.

1. Tavleen Singh, "Dreaming a Bad Dream," *Indian Express*, May 3, 2009.

2. Sunil Khilnani, "States of Emergency," *New Republic*, December 17, 2001, 41.

3. Indira to Jawaharlal Nehru, October 3, 1932, in Sonia Gandhi, ed., *Freedom's Daughter: Letters between Indira Gandhi and Jawaharlal Nehru 1922–39* (London: Hodder & Stoughton, 1989), 55.

4. Indira to Nehru, January 21, 1938, ibid., 361.

5. Indira to Nehru, September 21, 1938, ibid., 400.

6. Indira to Nehru, May 1, 1943, in Sonia Gandhi, ed., *Two Alone, Two Together: Letters between Indira Gandhi and Jawaharlal Nehru 1940–1964* (London: Hodder & Stoughton, 1992), 190.

7. For a brilliant, if tendentious, analysis of antifascist politics, see, François Furet, *The Passing of an Illusion: The Idea of Communism in the Twentieth Century* (Chicago: University of Chicago Press, 1999), chs. 7–9.

8. Indira to Nehru, December 5, 1947, *Two Alone, Two Together*, 548.

9. I. G. Patel, *Glimpses of Indian Economic Policy: An Insider's View* (New Delhi: Oxford University Press, 2002), 108.

10. Sudipta Kaviraj, "Indira Gandhi and Indian Politics," in his *Trajectories of the Indian State* (Ranikhet: Permanent Black, 2010), 173.

11. Katherine Frank, *Indira: The Life of Indira Nehru Gandhi* (New York: Houghton Mifflin, 2002), 312.

12. This argument about institutional decay and popular mobilization (the framework is borrowed from the work of Samuel Huntington) has wide currency in the political science literature on the Indira Gandhi years. See, for instance, Stanley Kochanek, "Mrs. Gandhi's Pyramid: The New Congress," in Henry C. Hart, ed., *Indira Gandhi's India* (Boulder: Westview, 1976); James Manor, "Parties and the Party System," in Partha Chatterjee, ed., *State and Politics in India* (New Delhi: Oxford University Press, 1997); Myron Weiner, *The Indian Paradox: Essays in Indian Politics* (New Delhi: Sage, 1989), 220–221, 226–227; Lloyd Rudolph and Susanne Rudolph, *In Pursuit of Lakshmi: The Political Economy of the Indian State* (Chicago: University of Chicago Press, 1987).

13. Indira to Nehru, April 23, 1956, *Two Along, Two Together*, 614–615.

14. Dorothy Norman, ed., *Indira Gandhi: Letters to an American Friend 1950–1984* (New York: Harcourt Brace Jovanovich, 1985), 57.

15. P. N. Dhar, *Indira Gandhi, the "Emergency," and Indian Democracy* (New Delhi: Oxford University Press, 2000), 123.

16. See table 7.1 in Weiner, *The Indian Paradox*, 196.

17. "Indira Gandhi on the Role of the Public Sector: Interview with P. N. Dhar," *Citizen and Weekend Review* 1, no. 22 (1970), reproduced in P. N. Dhar,

The Evolution of Economic Policy in India: Selected Essays (New Delhi: Oxford University Press, 2003), 205.

18. Indira Gandhi to Haksar, n.d. (c. late February 1966), Correspondence with Indira Gandhi, Haksar Papers (I & II Installments), Nehru Memorial Museum and Library (NMML).

19. Cited in Ramachandra Guha, *India after Gandhi: The History of the World's Largest Democracy* (New York: HarperCollins, 2007), 436.

20. Indira to Haksar, December 1970, Correspondence with Indira Gandhi, Haksar Papers (I & II Installments), NMML.

21. Khilnani, "States of Emergency," 44.

22. B. K. Nehru to Indira Gandhi, September 9, 1975, Correspondence with Indira Gandhi, B. K. Nehru Papers, NMML.

23. Sunil Khilnani, *The Idea of India* (New York: Farrar, Straus and Giroux, 1997), 48.

24. Speech at the Institute of Democracy and Socialism, New Delhi, May 21, 1970, *The Years of Endeavour: Selected Speeches of Indira Gandhi, August 1969–August 1972* (New Delhi: Publications Division, 1975), 50.

25. B. K. Nehru to Indira Gandhi, September 9, 1975, Correspondence with Indira Gandhi, B. K. Nehru Papers, NMML.

26. Dhar, *Indira Gandhi*, 336–337.

27. Manor, "Parties and the Party System," 111–116.

28. For a useful overview, see, T. V. Sathyamurthy, "Impact of Centre-State Relations on Indian Politics: An Interpretative Reckoning, 1947–1987," in Chatterjee, ed., *State and Politics in India*, 232–270. Also see Khilnani, *The Idea of India*, 50–52.

29. Dhar, *Indira Gandhi*, 106–109.

30. Patel, *Glimpses of Indian Economic Policy*, 134.

31. The best overview is Francine Frankel, *India's Political Economy: The Gradual Revolution* (New Delhi: Oxford University Press, 2005).

32. Indira Gandhi to Haksar, n.d. (c. late February 1966), Correspondence with Indira Gandhi, Haksar Papers (I & II Installments), NMML.

33. Patel, *Glimpses of Indian Economic Policy*, 112–115.

34. For an account from Washington's perspective, see John P. Lewis, *India's Political Economy: Governance and Reform* (Delhi: Oxford University Press, 1995), 146–147.

35. Kristin K. Ahlberg, "'Machiavelli with a Heart': The Johnson Administration's Food for Peace Program in India, 1965–66," *Diplomatic History* 31, no. 4 (September 2007): 665–700.

36. On the implementation of the Green Revolution, see C. Subramaniam, *The New Strategy in Indian Agriculture: The First Decade and After* (New Delhi: Vikas Publishing House, 1979).

37. Haksar to Indira Gandhi, July 9, 1969, Subject File 42; Haksar to Indira Gandhi, November 18, 1969, Subject File 143, Haksar Papers (I & II Installment), NMML.

38. The best account of the crisis is Vijay Joshi and I. M. D. Little, *India: Macroeconomics and Political Economy, 1964–1991* (Washington, DC: The World Bank, 1994), 105–128.

39. Haksar to Manmohan Singh (chief economic adviser, Department of Economic Affairs) enclosing a note on the state of economy, October 6, 1972, Subject File 54, Haksar Papers (I & II Instalment), NMML.

40. Manmohan Singh, "Her Economic Leadership," in G. Parthasarathi and H. Y. Sharada Prasad, eds., *Indira Gandhi: Statesmen, Scholars, Scientists and Friends Remember* (New Delhi: Indira Gandhi Memorial Trust, 1985), 291. Also see Inder Malhotra, *Indira Gandhi: A Personal and Political Biography* (London: Hodder & Stoughton, 1989), 154.

41. Joshi and Little, *Macroeconomics and Political Economy*, 125.

42. Patel, *Glimpses of Indian Economic Policy*, 170–171; Joshi and Little, *Macroeconomics and Political Economy*, 56.

43. Dani Rodrik and Arvind Subramanian, "From 'Hindu Growth' to Productivity Surge: The Mystery of Indian Growth Transition," *IMF Working Paper* (March 2004); Atul Kohli, *Poverty amid Plenty in the New India* (Cambridge: Cambridge University Press, 2012), 27–32, 97–106; Arvind Virmani, "India's Economic Growth: From Socialist Rate of Growth to Bharatiya Rate of Growth," *ICRIER Working Paper* (2004); Arvind Panagariya, *India: The Emerging Giant* (New Delhi: Oxford University Press, 2008), 47–93. Also see Brad DeLong, "India since Independence: An Analytic Growth Narrative," in Dani Rodrik, ed., *In Search of Prosperity: Analytic Narratives on Economic Growth* (Princeton, NJ: Princeton University Press, 2003).

44. Baldev Raj Nayar, "When Did the 'Hindu' Growth Rate End?," *Economic and Political Weekly*, May 13, 2006, 1888; Kunal Sen, "Why Did the Elephant Start to Trot? India's Growth Acceleration Re-Examined," *Economic and Political Weekly*, October 27, 2007, 38–39.

45. This is convincingly laid out in Sen, "Why did the Elephant Start to Trot?" Also see Joshi and Little, *Macroeconomics and Political Economy*, 118.

46. Prem Shankar Jha, *India: A Political Economy of Stagnation* (New Delhi: Oxford University Press, 1980), 171.

47. Howard L. Erdman, "The Industrialists," in Hart, ed., *Indira Gandhi's India*, 136–137.

48. Indira Gandhi to B. K. Nehru, December 30, 1974, B. K. Nehru Papers, NMML.

49. B. K. Nehru to Indira Gandhi, January 17, 1975, ibid.

50. Indira Gandhi to B. K. Nehru, March 1, 1975, ibid.

51. B. K. Nehru to Indira Gandhi, n.d. (March 1975), ibid.

52. Nayar, "When Did the 'Hindu' Growth Rate End?," 1887–1888.

53. Hamish MacDonald, *Polyester Prince: the Rise of Dhirubhai Ambani* (London: Allen and Unwin, 1998) 48–49.

54. Dinesh C. Sharma, *The Long Revolution: The Birth and Growth of India's IT Industry* (New Delhi: HarperCollins, 2009).

55. Dhar, *Indira Gandhi*, 265.

56. Pranab Bardhan, *The Political Economy of Development in India,* 2nd ed. (New Delhi: Oxford University Press, 1998); P. N. Dhar, *Evolution of Economic Policy in India* (New Delhi: Oxford University Press, 2003), 98–115.

57. Sunil Khilnani, "Looking for Indira Gandhi," *Seminar* 540 (August 2004), available at http://www.india-seminar.com/2004/540/540%20sunil%20khilnani .htm; Frank, *Indira*, 297.

58. Indira Gandhi to Kosygin, July 20, 1968, Subject File 135, P. N. Haksar Papers (III Installment), NMML.

59. Cable from Indian Embassy in Beijing to Prime Minister and External Affairs Minister, May 1, 1970, Subject File 29, Haksar Papers (I & II Installments), NMML.

60. Record of conversation between Indira Gandhi and Kosygin, May 6, 1969, Subject File 140, Haksar Papers (III Installment), NMML.

61. Srinath Raghavan, *1971: A Global History of the Creation of Bangladesh* (Cambridge, MA: Harvard University Press, 2013), ch. 5.

62. Note to Prime Minister and Foreign Minister by T. N. Kaul, August 3, 1971, Subject File 49, Haksar Papers (II Installment), NMML.

63. Comments on Simla Conference by Haksar, n.d., Subject File 181, Haksar Papers (III Installment), NMML.

64. Cited in Dhar, *Indira Gandhi*, 192.

65. Comments on Simla Conference by Haksar, n.d., Subject File 181, Haksar Papers (III Installment), NMML.

10. SINGAPORE'S LEE KUAN YEW

1. Michael Lever, an undated letter to Michael Barr, received June 5, 1996.

2. Kenneth Paul Tan, "The Ideology of Pragmatism: Neo-liberal Globalisation and Political Authoritarianism in Singapore," *Journal of Contemporary Asia* 42, no. 1 (2012): 67–92.

3. Garry Rodan, *The Political Economy of Singapore's Industrialization: National State and International Capital* (Kuala Lumpur: Forum, 1989), 89–91.

4. Michael D. Barr, "Lee Kuan Yew's Fabian Phase," *Australian Journal of Politics and History* 46, no. 1 (2000): 109–124; Michael D. Barr, "Lee Kuan Yew and the 'Asian Values' Debate," *Asian Studies Review* 24, no. 3 (2000): 309–334;

Michael D. Barr, "Harmony, Conformity or Timidity? Singapore's Over-achievement in the Quest for Harmony," in Julia Tao, Anthony Cheung, Li Chenyang, and Martin Painter, eds., *Governance for Harmony in Asia and Beyond* (London: Routledge, 2010), 73–102.

5. Michael D. Barr, *Lee Kuan Yew: The Beliefs behind the Man* (London: Curzon Press, 2000), 8–10, 201; Michael D. Barr, "No Island Is a Man: The Enigma of the Lee Kuan Yew Story," *Harvard Asia Quarterly* 11, nos. 2/3 (2008): 45–56.

6. Lee Kuan Yew, "We Must Move Forward—In Close, Conscious and Organised Co-Operation," Address to Delegates' Conference, National Trades Union Congress, *The Mirror* 2, no. 41 (October 10, 1966), 4.

7. Barr, "Lee Kuan Yew and the 'Asian Values' Debate," 323.

8. Ibid., 309–334.

9. The account of Lee's life and the development of his political thought in the following section is derived from Barr, *Lee Kuan Yew*, especially chapter 2, "Father of the Nation," 7–48, with particular acknowledgment of my intellectual debt to James Minchin and his book, *No Man Is an Island: A Portrait of Singapore's Lee Kuan Yew*, updated ed. (North Sydney: Allen & Unwin, 1990).

10. Minchin, *No Man Is an Island*, 35.

11. Barr, *Lee Kuan Yew*, 13, 14.

12. Minchin, *No Man Is an Island*, 35.

13. Barr, *Lee Kuan Yew*, 58–61.

14. This passage is taken almost verbatim from ibid., 58, 59.

15. Interview with Goh Keng Swee, October 1, 1996.

16. Michael D. Barr, "Singapore: The Limits of a Technocratic Approach to Health Care," *Journal of Contemporary Asia* 38, no. 3 (2008), 395–341; Michael D. Barr, "Medical Savings Accounts in Singapore: A Critical Inquiry," *Journal of Health Politics, Policy and Law* 26, no. 3 (2001): 707–724; Ian Holliday, "Productivist Welfare Capitalism: Social Policy in East Asia," *Political Studies* 48 (2000): 706–223; and Lee Kuan Yew, *From Third World to First: The Singapore Story: 1965–2000: Memoirs of Lee Kuan Yew* (Singapore: Singapore Press Holdings and Times Editions, 2000), 239–241.

17. Interview with David Allan (a friend of Lee's from his Cambridge days), June 3, 1996. See fuller accounts in chs. 2 and 3 of Barr, *Lee Kuan Yew*.

18. It is doubtful that Lee ever read the full twelve volumes of *A Study of History*, or even the two-volume abbreviation. According to David Allan, however, the one-volume abbreviation was read by almost everyone in Cambridge at that time. During my interview with him in 1996, Allan walked over to the bookshelf in his office in the Bond University Law School and showed me his old copy that he had bought as an undergraduate.

19. Interview with Goh Keng Swee, October 1, 1996.

20. Barr, *Lee Kuan Yew*, 7.

21. Lee in Han Fook Kwang, Warren Fernandez, and Sumiko Tan, *Lee Kuan Yew: The Man and His Ideas* (Singapore: Times Editions and The Straits Times Press, 1998), 173.

22. Ibid.

23. The story of Singapore's entry and departure from Malaysia are told in great detail, but from a partisan Singaporean perspective, in Albert Lau, *A Moment of Anguish: Singapore in Malaysia and the Politics of Disengagement* (Singapore: Times Academic Press, 1998). This was an important episode in both Singapore's and Lee Kuan Yew's history, but space precludes more than a passing reference here.

24. Barr, *Lee Kuan Yew*, 111, 112, 185–187.

25. Michael D. Barr and Zlatko Skrbiš, *Constructing Singapore: Elitism, Ethnicity and the Nation-Building Project* (Copenhagen: Nordic Institute of Asian Studies, 2008), ch. 5.

26. Diane K. Mauzy and R. S. Milne, *Singapore Politics under the People's Action Party* (London: Routledge, 2002), xii.

27. The analysis in this paragraph is derived directly from Michael D. Barr, *The Ruling Elite of Singapore: Networks of Power and Influence* (London: I. B. Tauris, 2014), chs. 4, 6, and 8.

28. Barr, "Lee Kuan Yew and the 'Asian Values' Debate."

29. Barr, *Lee Kuan Yew*, 110.

30. For an authoritative and very readable account of how the Constitution is superficially respected, but in fact treated as a pliable and lowly instrument of power by the elite, see the collection of essays in Li-ann Thio and Kevin Y. L. Tan, eds., *Evolution of a Revolution: Forty Years of the Singapore Constitution* (London: Routledge-Cavendish, 2009).

31. Among the many foreign observers who doubted Singapore's viability was John Howard, who was later to become prime minister of Australia. See *Straits Times*, April 16, 1986. For Lee Kuan Yew's account of his perception that Malaysia was waiting for Singapore to fail so that it would have to return on Malaysia's terms, see Lee Kuan Yew, *The Singapore Story: Memoirs of Lee Kuan Yew* (Singapore: Prentice Hall, 1988), 663. Also see Lee, *From Third World to First*, 19, 20.

32. Lee in Singapore Legislative Assembly, *Proceedings of the Legislative Assembly*, November 24, 1955, column 1757. Cited in a more complete form in Barr, *Lee Kuan Yew*, 109.

33. Barr, *The Ruling Elite of Singapore*, ch. 3; Rodan, *The Political Economy of Singapore's Industrialization*.

34. Detainees from the 1960s and 1970s include radicals with Communist associations such as Lim Chin Siong, and militant but hardly radical trade union

leaders such as Tan Jing Quee and Michael Fernandez. The final round of detentions under Lee's direct watch was the roundup of the alleged Marxist Conspirators including, most notably, Vincent Cheng and Teo Soh Lung—in fact a group of Catholic social activists, some people from alternate theater, and a few others. Details of some of these can be found in Michael Fernandez and Loh Kah Seng, "The Left-Wing Trade Unions in Singapore, 1945–1970," in Michael D. Barr and Carl A. Trocki, eds., *Paths Not Taken: Political Pluralism in Post-War Singapore* (Singapore: National University of Singapore Press, 2008), 206–226; C. C. Chin, "The United Front Strategy of the Malayan Communist Party in Singapore, 1950s–1960s," in Barr and Trocki, eds., *Paths Not Taken,* 58–77; Michael D. Barr, "Marxists in Singapore? Lee Kuan Yew's Campaign against Catholic Social Justice Activists in the 1980s," *Critical Asian Studies* 42, no. 3 (2010): 335–362; Tan Jing Quee and Jomo K. S., eds., *Comet in Our Sky: Lim Chin Siong in History* (Kuala Lumpur: INSAN, 2001); Teo Soh Lung, *Beyond the Blue Gate: Recollections of a Political Prisoner* (Petaling Jaya, Malaysia: Strategic Information and Research Development Centre, 2010); and Francis T. Seow, *To Catch a Tartar: A Dissident in Lee Kuan Yew's Prison* (New Haven, CT: Yale University Southeast Asian Studies, 1994). This is not even remotely a complete account of detentions during Lee's premiership.

35. See, Francis T. Seow, *Beyond Suspicion: The Singapore Judiciary* (New Haven, CT: Yale University Southeast Asian Studies, 2006).

36. Thomas Bellows, *The People's Action Party of Singapore: Emergence of a Dominant Party System,* monograph series no. 14 (New Haven, CT: Yale University Southeast Asian Studies, 1970).

37. Chan Heng Chee, *Politics in an Administrative State: Where Has the Politics Gone?* (Singapore: Department of Political Science, University of Singapore, 1975); and Chan Heng Chee, *The Dynamics of One Party Dominance: The PAP at the Grass-Roots* (Singapore: Singapore University Press, 1976).

38. Chua Beng Huat, *Communitarian Ideology and Democracy in Singapore* (London: Routledge, 1995).

39. Andreas Schedler, ed., *Electoral Authoritarianism: The Dynamics of Unfree Competition* (Boulder, CO: Lynne Rienner, 2006).

40. The full title is *From Third World to First: The Singapore Story: 1965–2000: Memoirs of Lee Kuan Yew.*

41. The stories of these men are told in various publications: Lam Peng Er and Kevin Y. L. Tan, eds., *Lee's Lieutenants: Singapore's Old Guard* (St. Leonards, NSW: Allen & Unwin, 1999); Asad-ul Iqbal Latif, *Lim Kim San: A Builder of Singapore* (Singapore: Institute of Southeast Asian Studies, 2009); Ian Patrick Austin, *Goh Keng Swee and Southeast Asian Governance* (Singapore: Marshall Cavendish Academic, 2004); Irene Ng, *The Singapore Lion: A Biography of S. Rajaratnam* (Singapore: Institute of Southeast Asian Studies, 2010); Ooi Kee

Beng, *In Lieu of Ideology: An Intellectual Biography of Goh Keng Swee* (Singapore: Institute of Southeast Asian Studies, 2010).

42. Barr, *Lee Kuan Yew*, 145.

43. See, for example, Gavin Peebles and Peter Wilson, *Economic Growth and Development in Singapore: Past and Future* (Cheltenham, UK: Edgar Elgar, 2002), 34, 35; Diane K. Mauzy and R. S. Milne, *Singapore Politics under the People's Action Party* (London: Routledge: 2002), 66, 67; and Jean E. Abshire, *The History of Singapore* (Santa Barbara: Greenwood, 2011), 7.

44. Peebles and Wilson, *Economic Growth and Development in Singapore*, ch. 2; Lee, *From Third World to First*, ch. 4; Rodan, *The Political Economy of Singapore's Industrialization*, ch. 4.

45. "China Sees Singapore as a Model for Progress," *New York Times*, August 9, 1992; National Heritage Board (Singapore), "Factsheet on Deng Xiaoping Marker," released November 14, 2010; available at http://www.news.gov.sg (accessed March 14, 2012).

46. Lee, *Third World to First*, ch. 5.

47. Ezra F. Vogel, *Japan as Number One: Lessons for America* (Cambridge, MA: Harvard University Press, 1979).

48. See, for instance, Lee Kuan Yew, "The Way to Better Job Security," *Mirror* 18, 22 (November 15, 1982): 1, 5, which calls for such Japanese innovations as Quality Control Circles and Work Improvement Teams, based on Japanese Fault Free Circles. Also see Lee, *From Third World to First*, chs. 31 and 32.

49. See Peebles and Wilson, *Economic Growth and Development in Singapore*, 12, 16, 44, 45; Ross Worthington, *Governance in Singapore* (London: Routledge Curzon, 2003), ch. 5; and Barr, *The Ruling Elite of Singapore*, chs. 4 and 7.

50. Barr, *The Ruling Elite of Singapore*, ch. 7.

51. Peebles and Wilson, *Economic Growth and Development in Singapore*, 16.

52. Sikko Visscher, *The Business of Politics and Ethnicity: A History of the Singapore Chinese Chamber of Commerce and Industry* (Singapore: National University of Singapore Press, 2007).

53. See Barr, *The Ruling Elite of Singapore*, especially ch. 3.

54. The mechanisms of control are a subject of study in their own right and cannot detain us in this short chapter. For further reading see Worthington, *Governance in Singapore*, especially chs. 4 and 5; Barr, *The Ruling Elite of Singapore*; and Werner Vennewald, "Technocrats in the State Enterprise System of Singapore," Working Paper no. 32, Asia Research Centre, Murdoch University, November 1994.

55. Linda Low and Douglas M. Johnston, eds., *Singapore Inc. Public Policy Options in the Third Millennium* (Singapore: Eastern Universities Press, 2003).

56. Barr, *The Ruling Elite of Singapore*, ch. 6.

57. Ibid., ch. 7.

58. Ibid.; Natasha Hamilton-Hart, "The Singapore State revisited," *Pacific Review* 13, no. 2 (2000): 208, 209.

59. Peebles and Wilson, *Economic Growth and Development in Singapore*, 59.

60. Peter E. Robertson, "Why the Tigers Roared: Capital Accumulation and the East Asian Miracle," *Pacific Economic Review* 7, no. 2 (2002): 269.

61. Ministry of Trade and Industry, Singapore, *The Singapore Economy: New Directions, Report of the Economic Committee* (Singapore: Government Printing Office, 1986).

62. Peebles and Wilson, *Economic Growth and Development in Singapore*, ch. 2; Lee, *From Third World to First*, ch. 4; Rodan, *The Political Economy of Singapore's Industrialization*, ch. 4; John Drysdale, *Singapore: Struggle for Success* (Singapore: Times Books International, 1984), 416 (appendix; chart 4).

63. See Drysdale, *Singapore: Struggle for Success*, 418 (appendix; chart 6); Rodan, *The Political Economy of Singapore's Industrialization*, chs. 4 and 5; and Tilak Abeysinghe and Keen Meng Choy, *The Singapore Economy: An Econometric Perspective* (London: Routledge, 2009), ch. 5.

64. Christopher Tremewan, *The Political Economy of Social Control in Singapore* (London: Macmillan Press; New York: St Martin's Press, 1994); Iain Buchanan, *Singapore in Southeast Asia: An Economic and Political Appraisal* (London: Bell, 1972).

65. Pang Eng Fong, *Education, Manpower and Development in Singapore* (Singapore: Singapore University Press, 1982).

66. Rodan, *The Political Economy of Singapore's Industrialization*; Goh Keng Swee, *The Economics of Modernization* (Singapore: Federal Publications, 1972, 1995), ch. 10.

67. Throughout this chapter I am using "liberal" in the classical English sense, not in the modern American sense whereby it refers to loosely leftist politics.

68. *Sunday Mail*, November 15, 1970.

69. Indeed, the government's persistence with the 1970s model of increasing inputs was a major factor in feeding the backlash against the government in the 2011 elections. The government's problems in that election arguably stemmed mostly from infrastructure shortcomings created directly or indirectly from the extremely high levels of foreign workers in the country. Singapore is only 682.7 square kilometers in area, with a total citizen population of 3.23 million, and a noncitizen population of another 1.85 million. A particularly strong surge in immigration levels began in 2005, stressing housing, transport, education, and water infrastructure. See Michael D. Barr, "Singapore's Immigration Dilemma," *Asian Currents*, October 2010, 15–17.

70. Hong Lysa, "Making the History of Singapore: S. Rajaratnam and C. V. Devan Nair," in Lam and Tan, eds., *Lee's Lieutenants*, 96–115.

71. Barr and Skrbiš, *Constructing Singapore*, 24 and ch. 2.

72. Ibid., ch. 2.

73. Ibid., 92; and Barr, *The Ruling Elite of Singapore*, ch. 4.

74. Michael D. Barr, "Perpetual Revisionism in Singapore: The Limits of Change," *Pacific Review* 16, no. 1 (2003): 77–97.

75. Barr and Skrbiš, *Constructing Singapore*, ch. 5.

76. Ibid., chs. 5–9.

77. Ibid., ch. 10; Barr, *The Ruling Elite of Singapore*, ch. 5.

78. Jason Tan, "Education in Singapore: Sorting Them Out?" in Terence Chong, ed., *Management of Success: Singapore Revisited* (Singapore: Institute of Southeast Asian Studies, 2010), 298. (These figures include overseas students so the implications to be drawn from them are not quite as dramatic as they appear at first glance.)

79. Barr and Skrbiš, *Constructing Singapore*, 215, supplemented by new information found at the Public Service Commission (PSC) Scholarships website, available at http://www.pscscholarships.gov.sg (accessed March 19, 2014). Racial identification is made by using the name of the recipient as a guide. Chinese names are sufficiently distinctive to make this a very reliable means of distinguishing Chinese from non-Chinese.

80. Ibid.

81. Ibid., 217, supplemented by new information found at the Public Service Commission Scholarships website. I do not have racial information on all SAFOS recipients.

82. PSC Scholarships website.

83. Eddie Teo, "An Open Letter from the Chairman," at the PSC Scholarships website; Han Fook Kwang, Zuraidah Ibrahim, Chua Mui Hoong, Lydia Lim, Ignatius Low, Rachel Lin, and Robin Chan, *Lee Kuan Yew: Hard Truths to Keep Singapore Going* (Singapore: Singapore Press Holdings, 2011), 132, 133.

84. Barr and Skrbiš, *Constructing Singapore,* especially chs. 5–10.

85. See Michael D. Barr and Jevon Low, "Assimilation as Multiracialism: The Case of Singapore's Malays," *Asian Ethnicity* 6, no. 3 (2005): 161–182.

86. Barr, *Lee Kuan Yew*, ch. 5.

87. Michael D. Barr, "Lee Kuan Yew: Race, Culture and Genes," *Journal of Contemporary Asia* 29, no. 2 (1999): 145–166.

88. See Han et al., *Lee Kuan Yew: Hard Truths*, 76; Lee Kuan Yew, *From Third World to First*, 640–159; Barr, *Lee Kuan Yew*, ch. 5; and Barr and Skrbiš, *Constructing Singapore*, ch. 5.

89. Interview with Bilihari Kausikan, Singapore, April 15, 2003.

90. Barr and Skrbiš, *Constructing Singapore*, 187, 224, 225.

91. At this point the distinction between Lee's ideas and those of his successors begins to blur, but in any case there is no doubt that the kernel of the ideas of his successors is found in Lee's pioneering vision. In 2004 Brenda

Yeoh expressed doubt that Singapore had really achieved the status of a global city, preferring to describe it as a "wannabe global city." She noted the oddity of a city's leadership consciously setting out to achieve the status of a global city. See Brenda S. A. Yeoh, "Cosmopolitanism and Its Exclusions in Singapore," *Urban Studies* 41, no. 12 (2004): 2431–2445. It is notable that Singapore rates barely a mention in literature on global cities that does not originate in Singapore. See, for instance, Saskia Sassen, *The Global City: New York, London, Tokyo,* 2nd ed. (Princeton, NJ: Princeton University Press, 2001); and Allen J. Scott, ed., *Global City-Regions: Trends, Theory, Policy* (Oxford: Oxford University Press, 2001). Yet such invocations are common in literature generated from within Singapore. See, for instance, Selvaraj Velayutham, *Responding to Globalization: Nation, Culture and Identity in Singapore* (Singapore: Institute of Southeast Asian Studies, 2007); and Karl Hack and Jean-Louis Margolin, with Karine Delaye, eds., *Singapore from Temasek to the 21st Century: Reinventing the Global City* (Singapore: National University of Singapore Press, 2010).

92. Kenneth Paul Tan, ed., *Renaissance Singapore? Economy, Culture, and Politics* (Singapore: National University of Singapore Press, 2007).

93. "How Singapore Punches above Its Weight" (reporting Lee Kuan Yew), *Straits Times,* July 22, 2011; Andrew T. H. Tan, "Punching above Its Weight: Singapore's Armed Forces and Its Contribution to Foreign Policy," *Defence Studies* 11, no. 4 (2012): 672–697; T. S. Andy Hor, "Singapore National Institute of Chemistry—Helping Singapore Punch above Its Weight," editorial, *Chemistry—An Asian Journal* 6, no. 5 (2011): 1112–1114. These three sources have been chosen because they are recent and in each case the title is sufficient to convey the message. There is also a plethora of other references to Singapore punching above its weight from cabinet ministers, journalists, and academics. The expression came into common parlance during the 2000s, but its usage dates back to the 1990s.

94. See, for instance, F. J. George, *Successful Singapore: A Tiny Nation's Saga from Founder to Accomplisher* (Singapore: SSMB, 1992); Karnail Singh Sandhu and Paul Wheatley, eds., *Management of Success: The Moulding of Modern Singapore* (Singapore: Institute of Southeast Asian Studies, 1989); Drysdale, *Singapore: Struggle for Success.*

95. Lee Kuan Yew, "Mass Rally at Suleiman Court, Kuala Lumpur," March 22, 1964, cited in Lee Kuan Yew, *The Winds of Change* (Singapore: Ministry of Culture, 1964).

96. "Cracks Appear in the Singapore Model," *People's Daily Online, English Edition,* May 23, 2011, available at http://english.people.com.cn/90001/90780/91345/7388168.html; "Singapore: A Model for China?," *Christian Science Monitor,* May 26, 2004.

97. See Barr, "Medical Savings Accounts in Singapore," 709–711.

98. See, for example, Lee Kuan Yew, "Can Singapore's Experience Be Relevant to Africa? *Keynote Address by Senior Minister Lee Kuan Yew,*" in Singapore International Foundation, *Can Singapore's Experience Be Relevant to Africa? Report on the Conference on "The Relevance of Singapore's Experience for Africa" Organized Jointly by the Africa Leadership Forum and the Singapore International Foundation, in Singapore, 8–10 November 1993* (Singapore: Singapore International Foundation and Africa Leadership Forum, 1993), 1–21.

99. Lee Kuan Yew, *New Bearing in Our Education System* (Singapore: Ministry of Culture, [n.d., c. 1966–1967]), 7.

100. Barr, *Lee Kuan Yew,* 102–104.

101. Ibid., 102.

102. See, for example, "Catching Up with an Old Friend," *Today,* April 1, 2011; "MM Lee Pays Visit to President Ma," *Straits Times,* April 1, 2011; "Lee Kuan Yew Warns on Unification," *Taipei Times,* December 1, 2010.

103. A detailed study of the faults and weaknesses of Singapore's meritocracy and its education system is beyond the scope of this chapter, but they are interrogated at length in two of my books: Barr and Skrbiš, *Constructing Singapore,* and Barr, *The Ruling Elite of Singapore.*

104. I am not suggesting, of course, that Lee can take credit for being the first to recognize the importance of education. In many ways his approach typifies Chinese cultural attitudes all over the world, but he did take a particular and very close interest in the education system, and he and his various education ministers from the late 1970s onward (particularly Goh Keng Swee and Tony Tan) fully deserve credit for implementing an education revolution.

105. Barr and Skrbiš, *Constructing Singapore,* chs. 5–7.

106. Barr, "Harmony, Conformity or Timidity?"

107. Ibid. To be fair, it must be acknowledged that some scholars who cannot be regarded as being close to the government are more optimistic about recent developments in the Singapore education system. See in particular Karl Hack, "Remaking Singapore, 1990–2004: From Disciplinarian Development to Bureaucratic Proxy Democracy," in Hack and Margolin, eds., *Singapore from Temasek to the 21st Century,* 345–383.

11. ZULFIKAR ALI BHUTTO

1. Quoted in Stanley Wolpert, *Zulfi Bhutto of Pakistan* (Karachi: Oxford University Press, 1994), 25.

2. See Bhutto's letter to the Icebox in *Newsweek* magazine on October 11, 1948, reproduced as frontispiece in Zulfikar Ali Bhutto, *Politics of the People: A Collection of Articles, Statements and Speeches,* vol. 1, *Reshaping Foreign Policy, 1948–1966,* ed. Hamid Jalal and Khalid Hasan (Rawalpindi: Pakistan Publications, n.d.).

3. Quoted in Wolpert, *Zulfi Bhutto*, 324–325.

4. Quoted in Salman Taseer, *Bhutto—A Political Biography* (London: Ithaca Press, 1979), 29.

5. See, Hasan Askari-Rizvi, "Pakistan," in Robert Chase, Emily Hill, and Paul Kennedy, eds., *The Pivotal States: A New Framework for U.S. Policy in the Developing World* (New York: W. W. Norton, 2000), 64–87. See also Christophe Jaffrelot, *La relation Pakistan-Etats Unis: un patron et son client au bord de la rupture*, Les etudes du CERI, no. 187, September 2012, 47, available at http://www.sciencespo.fr/ceri/fr/content/la-relation-pakistan-etats-unis-un-patron-et-son-client-au-bord-de-la-rupture.

6. Bhutto's younger sister, Benazir, died at age fourteen. Two older half-brothers from his father's first wife predeceased him; his older half-sister, Manna, survived him.

7. See Fatima Bhutto, *Songs of Blood and Sword: A Daughter's Memoir* (London: Jonathan Cape, 2010), 8.

8. Piloo Mody, *Zulfi, My Friend* (Delhi: Thomson Press, 1973), 25–26.

9. Ibid., 27.

10. Kelsen's strong influence over Bhutto's authoritarian style of politics is most clearly suggested in Shahid Javed Burki, *Pakistan under Bhutto, 1971–1977* (Basingstoke: Macmillan, 1988), 83–85. Others have questioned whether Kelsen exercised much influence over Bhutto. See Anwar H Syed, *The Discourse and Politics of Zulfikar Ali Bhutto* (Basingstoke: Macmillan, 1992), 249–250. In complete contrast, the distinguished historian and biographer Stanley Wolpert regards Kelsen as a key influence, who actually sharpened Bhutto's appreciation of the value of "democratic freedoms as the surest key to justice." See Wolpert, *Zulfi Bhutto*, 31.

11. Taseer, *Bhutto*, 29.

12. Mody, *Zulfi*, 49.

13. See Zulfikar Ali Bhutto, "Nehru: An Appraisal," in Zulfikar Ali Bhutto, *The Quest for Peace: Selections from Speeches and Writings, 1963–1965* (Karachi: Pakistan Institute of International Affairs, 1966), 61–75.

14. See Bhutto's speech, "The Islamic Heritage," University of Southern California, Los Angeles, April 1, 1948, in Bhutto, *Politics of the People*, 1: 7–18.

15. The size and precise contents of Bhutto's collection of Napoleona are difficult to establish as much of it remains in his original residence at 70 Clifton in Karachi, which is at the center of a family dispute between Bhutto's rival heirs—namely, the family of his murdered eldest son, Murtaza, who currently occupies the house and descendants of his eldest daughter, former Prime Minister Benazir Bhutto, who was assassinated in 2007. It is understood that before her death Benazir had repeatedly tried to acquire her father's library collection but was apparently thwarted in her attempts by Murtaza's heirs. See Declan Walsh,

"Broken Blood-line," *The Guardian*, January 11, 2008, available at http://www
.guardian.co.uk/politics/2008/jan/11/women.pakistan.

What is known, on the basis of information provided by Bhutto's respected biographer Stanley Wolpert, who had access to the library, is that in 1965 a wealthy Sindhi benefactor and admirer of Bhutto had arranged for Bhutto to purchase thousands of leather-bound first-edition volumes dedicated to Napoleon along with hundreds of memorabilia, including porcelain busts and paintings, from another avid collector of Napoleona, one Khan Bahadur Ullamah Ikanah, for the sum of Rs40,000. Today they are said to enjoy pride of place among more than ten thousand volumes that make up Bhutto's library. See Wolpert, *Zulfi Bhutto*, 98.

16. Quoted in Wolpert, *Zulfi Bhutto*, 31.

17. See Taseer, *Bhutto*, 21.

18. Zulfikar Ali Bhutto, *My Execution* (London: Musawaat Weekly International, 1980), 7.

19. See the introduction by Hugh Trevor-Roper in Zulfikar Ali Bhutto, *The Third World: New Directions* (London: Namara Publications, 1980). However, others, including Wolpert, claim that Bhutto regularly described himself as a "socialist" while still at Berkeley. See Wolpert, *Zulfi Bhutto*, 35. Bhutto's fellow student at Berkeley, Piloo Mody, also believed that Bhutto saw himself as a socialist, although he claims that Bhutto often muddied his liberal reasoning by drawing "unwarranted socialist conclusions." See Mody, *Zulfi, My Friend*, 49–50.

20. See Trevor-Roper's introduction in Bhutto, *The Third World*.

21. Bhutto had married Nusrat Ispahani in September 1951 after an ardent courtship that began during one of Bhutto's visits home to attend the wedding of his elder half-sister, Manna, in Karachi in September 1949. Born in Ispahan, Iran, in 1929, Nusrat was the daughter of a wealthy Iranian businessman who had left India and settled in Karachi. Bhutto's marriage to Nusrat was his second. When he was thirteen, he had agreed to an arranged marriage to an older first cousin, the wealthy Ameer Begum, to whom he remained married owing, it is said, to pressure from his family, which was reluctant to dissolve a union that had brought it significant gains in property. Bhutto had four children by Nusrat: the eldest, Benazir, who was born in 1953, became Pakistan's first woman prime minister in 1989 and was assassinated in Rawalpindi in December 2007. His three other children were Murtaza, born in 1954, Sanam, born in 1957, and Shahnawaz, born in 1958. Bhutto's two sons were killed in tragic circumstances—Shahnawaz, after being allegedly poisoned in Cannes in 1985 and Murtaza during an armed ambush in Karachi in 1986. Sanam, the sole survivor, lives in London. Nusrat died in Dubai in 2011. Bhutto, his wife Nusrat, and their three children are all buried in the family mausoleum in Garhi Khuda Bakhsh, near Naudero, in Sindh.

22. Z. A. Bhutto, "Treaties of Self-Defence and Regional Arrangement," November 1954, in Bhutto, *Politics of the People*, 1:48.

23. Bhutto, "The Essentials of a Constitution' (for the magazine *Vision*), May 1955, ibid., 64.

24. Bhutto, "A Development for Democracy," December 1956, ibid., 66, 67.

25. By all accounts, Bhutto's extended sojourn in the West, which sharpened his Western demeanor and added luster to his already developed cosmopolitan style, did little to rupture his links with his ancestral roots in Sindh. Unlike many of his peers (and predecessors, including Jinnah), he would combine a firm grasp of English with fluency in his native language, Sindhi. In later years he would develop his skills as a formidable public orator in Urdu. Initially, when his command of Urdu was mocked by critics, he had retaliated with typical bravado: "There are only two languages in Pakistan—the language of the exploited and the language of the exploiters. . . . I am going to speak to you in the language of the exploited." See Taseer, *Bhutto*, 84.

26. Quoted in Wolpert, *Zulfi Bhutto*, 47–48.

27. See Z. A. Bhutto, "Defining Aggression," Address to the Sixth Committee of the UN General Assembly, October 25, 1957, in Bhutto, *Politics of the People*, 1:88. The Sixth Committee failed to reach agreement on a definition of aggression, and it was not until December 1974 that a consensus resolution was finally adopted by the UN General Assembly. None of Bhutto's recommendations was incorporated in the final resolution. See UN General Assembly, Resolution 3314, Definition of Aggression, December 17, 1974, available at http://unispal.un.org/UNISPAL.NSF/0/023B908017CFB94385256EF4006EBB2A.

28. The invitation to Bhutto to join "the next cabinet" following planned elections had, in fact, already been extended by President Iskandar Mirza in the summer of 1958. In October 1958 Mirza was deposed from power in a military coup staged by General Ayub Khan, who formed a new cabinet that included Bhutto. See Wolpert, *Zulfi Bhutto*, 57.

29. Ibid., 65. There is some indication to suggest however that Ayub's interest in Bhutto stemmed not only from admiration of his young minister's intellect, but also from a keen sense that the Bhutto family name could be politically useful, especially in Sindh, where Ayub faced opposition from local political heavyweights. Ayub may also have been led to think that Bhutto's relative lack of political experience would make him easier to mold in his own image. Ibid., 59. Contemporary accounts suggest that Ayub had confided to some Western diplomats that he regarded Bhutto as his successor, although he believed that Bhutto still needed time to mature. See Shuja Nawaz, *Crossed Swords: Pakistan, Its Army and the Wars Within* (Karachi: Oxford University Press, 2008), 201. None of this can be conclusively substantiated as Ayub in his autobiography, *Friends not Masters*, published after Bhutto's exit from his cabinet in

1966, makes no reference whatsoever to Bhutto or to his contribution as a minister.

30. Zulfikar Ali Bhutto, "Bilateralism," in Bhutto, *The Third World*, 40.

31. Many years later Bhutto recalled the hostility of his cabinet colleagues, who were opposed to the Soviet oil agreement. In a conversation with his biographer Salman Taseer, he claimed: "The terrain was roughened for me by my own government." He then detailed the many administrative obstacles placed in his way by Qadir and the Foreign Ministry to try and subvert the agreement. See Taseer, *Bhutto*, 43. As for Ayub, after a meeting with President John F. Kennedy in the summer of 1961, he withdrew from any further expansion in relations with the Soviet Union. The Soviets for their part may well have lost interest by that time, having failed to find any oil in Baluchistan. See Syed, *The Discourse and Politics of Zulfikar Ali Bhutto*, 34–35.

32. Wolpert, *Zulfi Bhutto*, 66.

33. Ibid.

34. See Bhutto's speech to the National Assembly of Pakistan, November 26, 1962, in Zufikar Ali Bhutto, *Foreign Policy of Pakistan: A Compendium of Speeches Made in the National Assembly of Pakistan, 1962–64* (Karachi: Pakistan Institute of International Affairs, 1964) 42–52.

35. Ibid., 34, 35.

36. See Bhutto's speech to the National Assembly of Pakistan, December 4, 1962, in ibid., 72.

37. Bhutto spelled out this policy in his pamphlet "Bilateralism," published in 1976, which attempted to chart a *via media* between the principle of nonalignment, on the one hand, and the pursuit of multilateral alliances with the superpowers, on the other. See Bhutto, *The Third World*, 31–59.

38. The meeting itself has remained controversial as India has since repeatedly accused Pakistan of ceding territory (two thousand square miles of the Aksai Chin region of Ladakh in disputed Jammu and Kashmir) that it did not actually control and that rightfully belonged to India. Bhutto and successive Pakistani leaders have since insisted that no part of Jammu and Kashmir could be regarded as an "integral" part of India and that the 1963 boundary agreement between Pakistan and China had actually improved the climate of peace in the region.

39. See his speech to the National Assembly of Pakistan on July 17, 1963, in Bhutto, *Foreign Policy of Pakistan*, 75.

40. Quoted in Syed, *The Discourse and Politics of Zulfikar Ali Bhutto*, 37.

41. That Pakistan was still ultimately dependent on the United States for military assistance against India had been confirmed by none other than Bhutto, who took up the question with President John F. Kennedy during Bhutto's first visit to the United States as foreign minister in October 1963.

42. However, it is worth noting that, on the issue of Algeria's independence, Bhutto was not breaking new ground. In fact, Pakistan was one the first countries formally to recognize the provisional government of Algeria in September 1958.

43. See Z. A. Bhutto, "Impressions of the United Nations," Address at the Pakistan United Nations Association, Karachi, May 22, 1961, in Bhutto, *Politics of the People*, 1:142.

44. The Non-Aligned Movement was formalized in Belgrade in September 1961 at the Conference of Heads of State or Government of Non-Aligned Countries. India's prime minister, Jawaharlal Nehru, was a founding member of NAM; other key players were President Josip Broz Tito of Yugoslavia, President Gamal Abdel Nasser of Egypt, President Sukarno of Indonesia, and President Kwame Nkrumah of Ghana.

45. Wolpert, *Zulfi Bhutto*, 75.

46. Taseer, *Bhutto*, 50.

47. Bhutto's meeting with Nehru in 1962 was his second and last encounter with the Indian prime minister. Bhutto was said to have first met Nehru in Bombay when still a boy living in grand style with his parents atop Malabar Hill, where Nehru's sister, Krishna Nehru Hutheesingh, was a next-door neighbor. See Wolpert, *Zulfi Bhutto*, 21.

48. See Bhutto's "Reply to Nehru and [Krishna] Menon," Statement at Lahore, July 14, 1963, in Bhutto, *Politics of the People*, 1:192.

49. See Bhutto's speech to the National Assembly of Pakistan, July 24, 1963, ibid., 1:198.

50. See Bhutto's interview with the BBC, January 30, 1964, ibid., 1:211.

51. In 1964 Bhutto called for a fresh pledge to uphold the principles of the 1956 Bandung Conference (the precursor of the Non-Aligned Movement) and to reflect the changed context in Asia and Africa, where "old disputes persist and new frictions have arisen" (a scarcely veiled reference to the Indo-Pakistani conflict over Kashmir and the 1962 Sino-Indian War). See Bhutto on "The United Nations and World Peace," Address at the Lion's Club, Karachi, November 1963, ibid., 1:209.

52. Salman Taseer, one of Bhutto's staunchest supporters and most sympathetic biographers, conveys something of the mood among Bhutto's supporters at the time. He observes that Bhutto's speeches at the United Nations at the height of the war, although "full of exaggerated hyperbole, tautology and emotionalism . . . was an apt articulation of their [the Pakistani masses'] eighteen years of sorrow, frustration and hurt. Over Kashmir, they had repeatedly been driven up one cul-de-sac after another and Bhutto's speech was lauded for its defiance." Taseer, *Bhutto*, 63. For a more recent confirmation of the mesmeric effect of Bhutto's speeches, see Z. A. Bhutto, *Meri siyasi bible: Bhutto key afkar* [My political bible:

Bhutto's thoughts], ed. Maula Bukhsh Chandio (Islamabad: National Book Foundation, 2011).

53. This charge was most directly leveled against Bhutto by Air Marshal Asghar Khan, who served under Ayub as his Air Force chief and who was to become one of Bhutto's most inveterate political opponents. See Asghar Khan, *The First Round* (Lahore: Taabaar Publishing House, 1978) and his *We've Learnt Nothing from History: Pakistan, Politics and Military Power* (Karachi: Oxford University Press, 2005).

54. Sir Morrice James, *Pakistan Chronicle* (London: Hurst, 1993), 75.

55. Zulfikar Ali Bhutto, *The Myth of Independence* (London: Oxford University Press, 1969), 162–175.

56. Ibid., 174–175.

57. This is not to say that Islam was irrelevant to the regional culture of Sindh. Indeed, some scholars have argued that from the 1950s and 1960s, the regional character of Sindh, which was hitherto defined by its geographical separateness, came increasingly to acquire a markedly religious complexion under the influence of Sindhi nationalists such as G. M Syed, who promoted the idea of Sindh as a spiritual land of Sufi mysticism, and, of course, Bhutto himself, who relied on the Sufi culture of Sindh to project his own version of Pakistani nationalism based on egalitarian values. See Oskar Verkaaik, "The Sufi Saints of Sindhi Nationalism," in Michel Boivin and Matthew A. Cook, eds., *Interpreting the Sindhi World: Essays on Society and History* (Karachi: Oxford University Press, 2010), 196–215. Nevertheless, the importance of Kashmir as a foreign policy issue, let alone a "Muslim question," has rarely figured in the political culture of Sindh in contrast to other parts of Pakistan, notably Punjab. See Mehtab Ali Shah, *The Foreign Policy of Pakistan: The Ethnic Impacts on Diplomacy, 1971–1994* (London: I. B. Tauris, 1994).

58. Rao Rashid, *Snobs and Spices: The True Face of Pakistani Politics* (Lahore: Jamhoori Publications, 1996), 29.

59. See *Foundation Documents of the Pakistan People's Party* (Lahore: Pakistan People's Party, 1967). For detailed discussions of the party's founding ideology, see Philip Jones, *The Pakistan People's Party: Rise to Power* (Karachi: Oxford University Press, 2003), 220–230, and Syed, *The Discourse and Politics of Zulfikar Ali Bhutto*, 60–64. For a more colorful account of the events around the launch of the party, see Taseer, *Bhutto*, 87–90.

60. Quoted in Wolpert, *Zulfi Bhutto*, 116.

61. See Bhutto, "Starting with a Clean Slate," address to the Muzzafargarh Bar Association, January 17, 1968, in Zulfikar Ali Bhutto, *Politics of the People: A Collection of Articles, Statements and Speeches,* vol. 2, *Awakening the People, 1966–1969,* ed. Hamid Jalal and Khalid Hassan (Rawalpindi: Pakistan Publications, n.d.), 44.

62. See Bhutto's address to the All Pakistan Students Federation, Conway Hall, London, August 13, 1966, ibid., 2:4–15.

63. Ibid., 2:5.

64. See Bhutto's speech to the UN Security Council, September 22, 1965, in Bhutto, *Politics of the People,* 1:236–243.

65. See Bhutto's address to the All Pakistan Students Federation, Conway Hall, London, August 13, 1966, in Bhutto, *Politics of the People,* 2:10.

66. Ibid., 2:7.

67. Ibid., 2:12.

68. Ibid., 2:8.

69. Ibid., 2:14.

70. Ibid., 2:10.

71. Bhutto, *The Myth of Independence,* 114.

72. For a comprehensive account of the PPP's early years, see Jones, *The Pakistan People's Party,* 98–137.

73. See Shahid Javed Burki, *Pakistan under Bhutto, 1971–77* (Houndsmill, Basingstoke: Macmillan Press, 1988), 53. Bhutto did not just point to Islam to back up his socialist credo. Jinnah too was marshaled in defense of his party's socialist program, although Bhutto's grounds here were somewhat shakier given Jinnah's fervent attachment to private property. But never one to be deterred by inconvenient facts, Bhutto declared: "I am not the first one to talk of Islamic equality. I did not originate the idea. If you study your history, and if you go through the speeches of the Quaid-i-Azam Mahomed Ali Jinnah, who founded this country, [he] promised that there would be Islamic socialism." See Z. A. Bhutto, "A People's Economy," public speech at Bannu, April 26, 1970, in Zulfikar Ali Bhutto, *Politics of the People: A Collection of Articles, Statements and Speeches,* vol. 3, *Marching Towards Democracy, 1970–1971,* ed. Hamid Jalal and Khalid Hasan (Rawalpindi: Pakistan Publications, n.d.), 82.

74. Bhutto, *Politics of the People,* 3:82.

75. See Bhutto's public speech, "A Long March for People's Rights," Abbottabad, April 19, 1970, ibid., 3:62.

76. See, Z. A. Bhutto, *The Great Tragedy* (Karachi: Pakistan People's Party, 1971).

77. R. Sisson and Leo Rose, *War and Secession: Pakistan, India and the Creation of Bangladesh* (Berkeley, CA: University of California Press, 1990), 57.

78. Hasan Zaheer, *The Separation of East Pakistan: The Rise and Realization of Bengali Muslim Nationalism* (Karachi: Oxford University Press, 1994), 147.

79. Sisson and Rose, *War and Secession,* 70.

80. He argued: "there should be no question of majority or minority. If they are in a majority there, we are in a majority here. Pakistan consists of two parts.

Both parts have to prosper equally." See "A Compromise Is Possible," Karachi, March 14, 1971, in Bhutto, *Politics of the People,* 3:191.

81. For Bhutto's robust defense of his own position during the political and constitutional crisis following the 1970 general election, see Bhutto, *The Great Tragedy.*

82. For one of the best detailed accounts of the conflict, see Srinath Raghavan, *1971: A Global History of the Creation of Bangladesh* (Cambridge, MA: Harvard University Press, 2013).

83. Their release was secured in 1973, though without Pakistan meeting the condition set by India, namely, the recognition of Bangladesh. That would have to wait until the Islamic Summit in Lahore in 1974, when Bhutto cast the gesture as an act of Muslim solidarity.

84. Quoted in Anwar H. Syed, "The Pakistan Peoples and the Punjab," *Asian Survey* 31, no. 7 (July 1991): 111.

85. Farzana Shaikh, *Making Sense of Pakistan* (London: Hurst & Columbia University Press, 2009).

86. "The Muslim countries," he declared, "are now so placed as to be able to play a most constructive and rewarding role for co-operation among themselves and with the other countries of the Third World." See Bhutto's keynote address to the second Islamic Summit Conference, "The Role of the Muslim States," in *The Third World,* 86.

87. Ibid., 85.

88. Ibid., 88.

89. Zulfikar Ali Bhutto, *If I Am Assassinated* (New Delhi: Vikas Publishing House, 1979), 138. See also Steven Weissman and Herbert Krosney, *The Islamic Bomb* (New Delhi: Vision Books, 1983); originally published as *The Islamic Bomb: The Nuclear Threat to Israel and the Middle East* (New York: Times Books, 1981), 29. Page reference is to the 1983 edition.

90. The two articles, "The Imperative of Unity," written in September 1976, and "Bilateralism," written in October 1976, appeared in a compilation published in 1977 and subsequently republished in 1980 with an introduction by Hugh Trevor-Roper. See Zulfikar Ali Bhutto, *The Third World,* 17–59.

91. See Bhutto, "The Imperative of Unity," 17–28.

92. Ibid., 19.

93. Ibid., 25.

94. See Bhutto, "Bilateralism," 31–59.

95. Ibid., 36.

96. Ibid., 37.

97. Ibid.

98. Ibid., 40.

99. Ibid.

100. Ibid., 41–50.

101. For a classic statement of this argument, see S. J. Burki, *Pakistan under Bhutto, 1971–1977.*

102. See K. B. Sayeed, *Politics in Pakistan: The Nature and Direction of Change* (New York: Praeger, 1980).

103. For a discussion of these and related issues concerning the 1977 elections, see Martin B. Weinbaum, "The March 1977 Elections in Pakistan: Where Everyone Lost," *Asian Survey* 17, no. 7 (July 1977): 599–618.

104. Wolpert, *Zulfi Bhutto,* 283.

105. Roedad Khan, *A Dream Gone Sour* (Karachi: Oxford University Press, 1997), 70.

106. See Wolpert, *Zulfi Bhutto,* 327. Khan's recollections have gained credence from the fact that at the time, as the senior administrative officer in the Interior Ministry, he had been responsible for processing mercy petitions urging Zia to commute Bhutto's death sentence.

ACKNOWLEDGMENTS

Makers of Modern Asia has its origins in a conference made possible by that generous patron of historical scholarship, Emmanuel (Manny) Roman. It was held in May 2012 and hosted by the IDEAS unit of the London School of Economics and Political Science, where I was then holding the Philippe Roman Chair in History and International Affairs.

The idea for the conference—and the book—arose out of a conversation with Professor Odd Arne Westad. I am thankful to Arne for suggesting names of scholars who could write on subjects beyond my own areas of research and knowledge. The essay writers—most of whom I did not know before—responded promptly to my invitation, producing fully formed drafts for the conference and then revising them for publication.

I was myself unable to attend the conference because of injuries suffered in a road accident in India. The meeting went ahead regardless. I am grateful to the staff of LSE IDEAS, and particularly to Emilia Knight and Tiha Franulovic, for helping to put the meeting together. I also owe a great debt to my research officer, Dr. Akhila Yechury, who, in my enforced absence, took up the intellectual as well as administrative responsibility for guiding the proceedings.

Finally, I must thank the staff of Harvard University Press for seeing this book through publication. My editors, Sharmila Sen and Heather Hughes, have, once more, been models of professional excellence and personal courtesy.

NOTES ON CONTRIBUTORS

MICHAEL D. BARR (Lee Kuan Yew) is a Senior Lecturer in International Relations in the School of International Studies, Flinders University, Australia, and the Editor in Chief of *Asian Studies Review*. His books include *Lee Kuan Yew: The Beliefs behind the Man* (Curzon, 2000; New Asian Library, 2009), *Paths Not Taken: Political Pluralism in Post-War Singapore* (edited with Carl Trocki, National University of Singapore Press, 2008), and, most recently, *The Ruling Elite of Singapore: Networks of Power and Influence* (I. B. Tauris, 2014).

CHEN JIAN (Zhou Enlai) is Michael J. Zak Professor of History for US-China Relations at Cornell University. He joins New York University/NYU-Shanghai as a Distinguished Global Network Professor of History in 2014. He held the Philippe Roman Chair of History and International Relations at the London School of Economics and Political Science in 2008–2009. His books include *China's Road to the Korean War* (Columbia University Press, 1994) and *Mao's China and the Cold War* (University of North Carolina Press, 2001). He is now writing a biography of Zhou Enlai.

RAMACHANDRA GUHA (Gandhi, Nehru) is a historian and biographer based in Bangalore. He has taught at the University of Oslo, Yale University, and Stanford University, as well as at the Indian Institute of Science. In 2011–2012 he held the Philippe Roman Chair of History and International Relations at the London School of Economics and Political Science. His books include *The Unquiet Woods* (University of California Press, 1989), *A Corner of a Foreign Field* (Picador, 2002), *India after Gandhi* (Macmillan/Ecco Press, 2007), and, most recently, *Gandhi before India* (Knopf, 2014).

RANA MITTER (Mao Zedong) is Director of the University China Centre at the University of Oxford, where he is Professor of the History and Politics of Modern China. He is also a regular presenter for BBC Radio 3's "Night Waves" arts and culture program. His most recent book is *China's War with Japan, 1937–45: The Struggle for Survival* (Penguin, 2013; published in the United States as *Forgotten Ally*), which was named a Book of the Year in the *Financial Times* and the *Economist*.

SOPHIE QUINN-JUDGE (Ho Chi Minh) is an Associate Professor of History and Associate Director of the Center for Vietnamese Philosophy, Culture, and Society at Temple University in Philadelphia. She is the author of *Ho Chi Minh: The Missing Years* (University of California Press, 2003) and co-editor of *The Third Indochina War* (Routledge, 2006). She is currently working on a manuscript about Vietnamese efforts at reconciliation during the Vietnam War. She is a member of the editorial team of the *Cambridge History of Communism*.

SRINATH RAGHAVAN (Indira Gandhi) is Senior Fellow at the Centre for Policy Research, New Delhi, and Senior Research Fellow at King's India Institute, King's College London. He is the author of *War and Peace in Modern India: A Strategic History of the Nehru Years* (Palgrave Macmillan and Permanent Black, 2010) and *1971: A Global History of the Creation of Bangladesh* (Harvard University Press and Permanent Black, 2013). He is now writing a history of India in the long 1970s.

JAMES R. RUSH (Sukarno) is Associate Professor of History at Arizona State University. He is the author of *Opium to Java: Revenue Farming and Chinese Enterprise in Colonial Indonesia, 1860–1910* (Cornell University Press, 1990). He is now working on a book on Islam in modern Indonesia. As a public historian, Rush led the biography project of the Ramon Magsaysay Award Foundation (Philippines) from 1987 to 2008, conducting oral-history interviews with over one hundred Magsaysay Awardees and editing six volumes of biographical essays.

FARZANA SHAIKH (Bhutto) is an Associate Fellow of the Royal Institute of International Affairs in London, where she coordinates the Pakistan Study Group. She has held university lectureships in the United Kingdom, the United States, and Europe, and was named a Visitor at the Institute for Advanced Study in Princeton. Most recently she was elected to a Fellowship at the Paris Institute for Advanced Study. Her books include *Community and Consensus in Islam: Muslim Representation in Colonial India, 1860–1947* (Cambridge University Press, 1989) and *Making Sense of Pakistan* (Hurst, 2009). Her new book project explores the politics of Sufism in Pakistan.

JAY TAYLOR (Chiang Kai-shek) served thirty-seven years in the US Foreign Service, mostly on Chinese affairs in Taiwan, Hong Kong, and China, as well at the

State Department and the National Security Council. He is the author of five books. The latest, *The Generalissimo: Chiang Kai-shek and the Struggle for Modern China* (Harvard University Press, 2009), won the 2010 Gelber Prize. Currently, he is Associate in Research at the Fairbank Center for Chinese Studies at Harvard University.

ODD ARNE WESTAD (Deng Xiaoping) is Professor of International History at the London School of Economics and Political Science and Director of LSE IDEAS. His book *The Global Cold War* (Cambridge University Press, 2005) won the Bancroft Prize. His most recent book is *Restless Empire: China and the World Since 1750* (Basic Books, 2012), which won the Asia Society book award. He is co-editor of the journal *Cold War History* and of the three-volume *Cambridge History of the Cold War*.

CREDITS

Chapter 1, "Gandhi, India, and the World" © 2014 Ramachandra Guha

Chapter 2, "Chiang Kai-shek and Chinese Modernization" © 2014 Jay Taylor

Chapter 3, "Ho Chi Minh: Nationalist Icon" © 2014 Sophie Quinn-Judge

Chapter 4, "Mao Zedong and Charismatic Maoism" © 2014 Rana Mitter

Chapter 5, "Jawaharlal Nehru: A Romantic in Politics"
    © 2014 Ramachandra Guha

Chapter 6, "Zhou Enlai and China's 'Prolonged Rise' " © 2014 Chen Jian

Chapter 7, "Sukarno: Anticipating an Asian Century" © 2014 James R. Rush

Chapter 8, "Deng Xiaoping and the China He Made" © 2014 Odd Arne Westad

Chapter 9, "Indira Gandhi: India and the World in Transition"
    © 2014 Srinath Raghavan

Chapter 10, "Singapore's Lee Kuan Yew: Traveling Light, Traveling Fast"
    © 2014 Michael D. Barr

Chapter 11, "Zulfikar Ali Bhutto: In Pursuit of an Asian Pakistan"
    © 2014 Farzana Shaikh

INDEX

India (continued)
222, 232, 237–238, 279–281,
290–291; Green Revolution, 229,
230–232, 239; US, relations with,
230–231, 237–238, 286; Soviet
Union, relations with, 237–240;
security environment in, 241–242;
Bhutto's views on, 268. *See also*
Gandhi, Indira; Gandhi, Mohandas;
Nehru, Jawaharlal
Indian-Chinese partnership in
Transvaal, 38–39
Indian National Congress, 22, 25–26,
120, 132
Indies, 174–177. *See also* Indonesia
Indies Association (Indonesian
Association), 178
Indies Council (Volksraad, People's
Council), 177, 184
Indies Party, 177
Indies Social-Democratic Association
(ISDV), 176–177
Indira Hatao (Remove Indira), 224
Indochina Federation, 74
Indochinese Communist Party (ICP),
69–70, 72–73, 76–77, 79, 81, 84–87
Indonesia: colonial control of, 3;
nationalist consolidation, 6;
postcolonial political systems, 7;
national identity, 177–178,
186–188; defense force, Japan's
contribution to, 184; independence,
struggle for, 184–186; army's
political role, 187, 190, 191;
political parties, multiplicity of,
187; Muslims in, 190–191,
193–194; culture wars, 194–197;
coup attempts, 196–197; Gestapu
(coup), 196–197. *See also* Sukarno
"Indonesia Accuses" (Sukarno),
181–182

Indonesian Association (Indies
Association), 178
Indonesian menial laborers
(romusha), 328n87
Indonesian Nationalist Party (PNI),
180–181, 182, 187–188, 192, 193
Indonesian Party (Partindo), 183
Indo-Soviet Treaty of Friendship, 296
Industrialism, Gandhi on, 36–37
Inggit (Sukarno's wife), 183
Institute of Marxism-Leninism
(Workers' Party of Vietnam), 90
Intermediate Zone thesis, 154, 162
International alliances, Bhutto on,
277–278
International Fellowship of Religions,
36
International Monetary Fund (IMF),
230, 233
Iraq, 279
Irwin, Lord (Edward Frederick
Lindley Wood, Viceroy of India), 26
ISDV (Indies Social-Democratic
Association), 176–177
Islam: Gandhi's approach to, 24,
126–127; in India, 29, 30, 126–127;
women's position in, 128;
anticolonialism and, 179; Sukarno
on, 179–180; in Indonesia, 190–191,
196; Bhutto on, 271–272, 286, 289,
293–295; Hinduism, relationship
to, 282. *See also* Pakistan
Islamic League (Sarekat Islam, SI),
176, 177, 180
Islamic socialism, 299
Ispani, Nusrat (later Nusrat Bhutto),
347n21
Italy, 106

Jackson, R. M., 247
Jallianwala Bagh massacre, 24

Pakistan People's Party (PPP), 283–286, 288–289, 292, 297–298

Pan-Asianism, 134–135

Panca Sila (five principles of Indonesian national identity), 184, 187, 190, 197

Panch Shila agreement (between India and China), 277

Pan-Islamism, 271, 273, 279, 293–294

Pant, G. B., 220

PAP (People's Action Party, Singapore), 192, 248–251

Paris Peace Conference, 68

Park Chung Hee, 12–13

Partindo (Indonesian Party), 183

Partition of India, 32–33, 126

Party and Government Work Evaluation Commission (China), 53

Party Organization Commission (Vietnam), 90

Passive resistance. *See* Nonviolence

Patel, Vallabhbhai, 124–125

Patriarchy, 9. *See also* Gender equality; Women

Pedoman Masyarakat (People's Compass, weekly newspaper), 184

Peking Review, 106–107

Pendidikan Nasional Indonesia (PNI, Indonesian National Education), 183

Peng Dehuai, 159

The People (Nhan Dan, party newspaper), 87, 89

People's Action Party (PAP, Singapore), 192, 248–251

People's Communes (China), 211

People's Council (Volksraad, Indies Council), 177, 184

People's Daily (newspaper), 112, 113

People's Liberation Army (PLA), 55, 56–57

People's Republic of Bangladesh, 224, 238, 239, 290–291, 294

People's Republic of China (PRC): *danwei* (work unit) system, 52; Western study of, 103; international isolation, 109, 165; Nehru's interest in, 135; India, relations with, 137–138, 160–161, 238–239, 286; Soviet Union, relations with, 138, 160; establishment of, 155; foreign policy of, 155; Africa, influence in, 163; Cultural Revolution's impact on, 164; US, relations with, 165–166, 168, 210–211, 240; moral crisis of, 171; Sukarno in, 190; Deng and modernization of, 203–204, 206–209, 211; political reform, lack of, 213–214; Pakistan, relations with, 239, 287–288, 299; rise of, Lee's recognition of, 260–261; Singapore as model for, 262; Taiwan, relations with, 264; UN membership, 277. *See also* Chiang Kai-shek; Cultural Revolution; Deng Xiaoping; Great Leap Forward; Mao Zedong; Zhou Enlai; *entries beginning "Chinese"*

Pham Ngoc Thach, 73, 80, 81

Pham Van Dong, 71, 73, 74

Phan Anh, 84

Phan Boi (Hoang Huu Nam), 73, 76, 79–80

Phan Boi Chau, 67

Phan Chau Trinh, 67, 68

Phan Ke Toai, 84

Phan Van Truong, 67, 68

Phibun Songkhram, 81

Pigou, A. C., 131

Ping Pong diplomacy, 166

PKI (Communist Party of Indonesia), 178, 180, 185, 188, 191–194, 196–197

RAMACHANDRA GUHA is a leading historian of modern India, living in Bangalore. His books include *Gandhi Before India* and *India After Gandhi*.